HEADING FOR
THE ABYSS

Lichnowsky

HEADING FOR
THE ABYSS

Reminiscences

BY

PRINCE LICHNOWSKY

NEW YORK
PAYSON & CLARKE LTD.
1928

Translated into English

BY

PROFESSOR SEFTON DELMER

FORMERLY ENGLISH LECTURER AT THE UNIVERSITY OF BERLIN

PRINTED IN GREAT BRITAIN BY ROBERT MACLEHOSE AND CO. LTD.
THE UNIVERSITY PRESS, GLASGOW.

PREFATORY NOTE BY THE TRANSLATOR

> And Kung said : ' Wang ruled with moderation ;
>   In his day the State was well kept ;
> And even I can remember
> A day when the historians left blanks in their writings,
> I mean for the things they did not know ;
> But that time seems to be passing.'
>
> And Kung said, ' Without character you will be unable
>   to play on that instrument
> Or to execute the music fit for the Odes.'
>
> ' The blossoms of the apricot blow from the east to the
>   west ;
> I have tried to keep them from falling.'
>
> (From Ezra Pound's *Thirteenth Canto*.)

THE German edition of Prince Lichnowsky's work was published at Leipzig in November 1927, under the title *Auf dem Wege zum Abgrund*. Repeating as it did the strictures written by its author years before on the methods and policy of the military bureaucracy, the book aroused a storm of bitterly hostile criticism throughout the length and breadth of Germany. In the *Kölnische Zeitung* (11th Dec., 1927) and in the *Archiv für Politik und Geschichte* (Heft i, 1928) Prince Lichnowsky was denounced by Dr. Thimme, and elsewhere by other official protagonists of the old regime, as the ' Ambassador who had *during the war* turned King's evidence against his own country.' In order to give the book the *coup de grâce*, Dr. Thimme even had the hardihood to hint that Lichnowsky had himself had a hand in the publication in Switzerland in January 1918 of the notorious document known as *My Mission to London* (here given on page 48 *et seqq.*), a document which had been immediately picked up by the Entente and had become in their hands a flaming sword of propaganda. This cruel charge, published without a tittle of evidence in its favour, went uncontradicted in the German Press till Emil Ludwig, just back from America, wrote to the Swiss historian and publicist, Prof. Otto Nippold (who had edited the pamphlet in question) and obtained from him a positive declaration that Dr. Thimme's insinuation was baseless (cf. *Vossische Zeitung*, 28th March, 1928).

Whatever be the merits and demerits of the present work as a criticism of German policy, one cannot help hoping that the better soul of Germany will someday come to perceive that the author, whether he had been used as a decoy duck or not by those who despatched him to England on such an important mission, had when he returned a perfect right to defend himself against the calumnies and contempt of those who blamed him for misleading them with regard to England's attitude. Although originally prompted no doubt by righteous indignation and by a desire to parry the taunts and sophistries of the militarists, Prince Lichnowsky wrote his *apologia* in a spirit of European charity rather than in one of recrimination. It cannot be called heroic, for it lacks downrightness. Its saving virtue is its sincerity. At any rate the world cannot afford to allow such an intensely human document to be snuffed out by the pedants and pundits of Potsdam.

When Messrs. Constable and Co. wrote asking me if I would undertake the translating of the Prince's Memoirs into English I at once assented ; and I did so the more readily as I had for years past shared the author's hope that Germany herself would one day come to contemplate in a more enlightened spirit the motives that forced England to take up arms against her in 1914.

A good deal of unnecessary pother has been made in Germany over the fact that Prince Lichnowsky, between 1914 and 1917, thought it necessary to emend and retouch two of the principal documents here printed : *England before the War* (pp. 4-16) and *My Mission to London* (p. 48 *et seqq.*). Dr. Thimme, who thinks that each of these manuscripts should have been left exactly in the primal form in which the author dictated it to his typist, seems to be far more horrified at Lichnowsky's revision of these texts than at the Great War itself. To forestall further bickering on the matter of the alterations, I have in the present edition reinserted the deleted words in *My Mission to London*, and have indicated the insertions by means of square brackets. In the case of *England before the War*, the emendations and omissions are more numerous. The principal alterations will be found translated on page 16.

I have throughout the book reproduced English documents whenever possible in their original form. Where official English translations of German documents and dispatches were available I have, for the sake of uniformity, though not slavishly where deviation seemed advisable, followed in the footsteps of my predecessors. For the sake of completeness various dispatches which were, in order to save space, omitted from the German edition, have been added to the present edition, the headlines of such additional dispatches being enclosed in square brackets.

With the Author's consent the marginal notes inserted by the

Kaiser have everywhere been added in the dispatches of July 1914. Some few alterations have also been made in the order in which the subject matter is presented. The Aphorisms, for instance, have been transferred to a later part of the book, and the important note with which they were prefaced in the German original has in the English edition been placed in front of the dispatches.

Prince Lichnowsky did not live to see his book appear in English. On 27th February, 1928, worn out with the storm of personal abuse that his work had aroused among his fellow-countrymen, he died. He will always be numbered in history with those tragic figures who ' with the best intentions have incurred the worst.'   He was the last of Central Europe's *grands seigneurs*, and in the part he played in the tragedy of European civilization will always be remembered as ' a very noble gentleman.'   But it needed a greater than a *grand seigneur* to accomplish the Herculean task to which he set his hand ; he fled, leaving the plough in the unfinished furrow.

F. S. D.

CONTENTS

ILLUSTRATIONS

AN INTRODUCTORY LETTER FROM PRINCE LICHNOWSKY

GENTLEMEN,

It affords me especial satisfaction to learn that your firm has undertaken the publication of an English edition of my book *Auf dem Wege zum Abgrund* which has just been published in Germany. I should rejoice if the book were to find understanding in England and if it served in some measure once more to bring the two nations closer together. My aim in publishing it has been to investigate the deeper causes of the catastrophe, and to do this if possible without touching on the so-called war-guilt question and without attributing the whole burden of responsibility to this or that individual in Germany or elsewhere.

I have attempted to show that it was mainly the fatal system of groups and alliances inaugurated by Bismarck that led to the world war, and that the Great Powers were thereby drawn into conflicts which were quite alien to their real interests.

It is one of the tragic ironies of the world's history that the Anglo-German understanding which before the war, thanks to the sympathetic attitude of Sir Edward Grey, was on the point of becoming an accomplished fact, should at the last moment have been wrecked on the Serbian question.

I sincerely hope that the English translation of my book may shed light on the historical origins of the catastrophe and that it may, by laying bare the errors of the past, serve to foster a spirit of reconciliation and *rapprochement*, while at the same time contributing to the consolidation of the peace of Europe.

The policy of alliances, supported by the insane race for armaments, could not fail to lead to war. One may hope that the nations will from this learn a lesson for the future. For the present it must be confessed that there are but faint signs that they have begun to do so.

If the race for armaments continues and the group system survives, we shall assuredly drift into another war, and all the blood that has been shed will have been shed in vain.

I am, Gentlemen,

Yours faithfully,

LICHNOWSKY.

KUCHELNA,
9th December, 1927.

At Prince Lichnowsky's wish all sums accruing to him from the publication of this book in Germany and abroad are to be placed at the disposal of the Homes for German Soldiers Blinded in the War.

FOREWORD

THE publication of the German Foreign Office Records for the period 1871-1914 [1] makes it possible for the historian to form an independent opinion of the foreign policy of the Hohenzollerns.

The student of this collection of documents will find that the Iron Chancellor had in 1870-1871 already reached and passed his zenith. After that date we witness not without dismay a marked slackening in his statesmanship. We get the impression that the ' sleepless nights ' and neuralgia he so frequently complains of had seriously affected his mental powers. One reads with a feeling akin to horror such documents as Nos. 455 and 461 in *Die Grosse Politik*, written by Bismarck to justify Germany's disastrous alliance with Austria. Had their author been less famous, we should dismiss his crude explanations as the whims and vapourings of a fantastic sophist. At the very time when our diplomatic representatives at St. Petersburg and Paris are at one in reporting the unqualified wish of both these Powers to live at peace with us and merely refer to fear mingled with distrust and a sense of grievance, the First Chancellor of the Reich is at pains to conjure up imaginary dangers that existed only in his own brain, his sole object being to make the alliance with Austria seem plausible in the eyes of the old Emperor. He invents another Coalition à la Kaunitz, although not the faintest sign of such a scheme was to be detected, either in Russia, in France or in Austria. Reminiscences of the old German Confederation were hauled forth from the political lumber-room and a plan was broached for the safeguarding of the line between Cracow and Lake Constance, as if the population of this region were not overwhelmingly German by race and far more likely to want to join up with Germany than to attack her.

---

[1] The work referred to, *Die grosse Politik der Europäischen Kabinette* 1871-1914, contains in forty large octavo volumes a collection of the Diplomatic Documents of the Foreign Office. Published at Berlin, 1922-24. The student may also consult the valuable Kautsky Documents on ' The Outbreak of the World War,' published in German under the title *Die deutschen Dokumente zum Kriegsausbruch*, 4 volumes (Berlin 1919) and in an English translation by the Carnegie Endowment, in one volume, 608 pp. New York, 1924. (Translator's note.)

When in April 1875 Prince Hohenlohe, our Ambassador at Paris, reported (GP 169) that the then Minister for Foreign Affairs, Duc Decazes, had proposed to get rid of the mutual distrust by mutual disarmament, and that both the Duke and President MacMahon were filled with a sincere love of peace, and that France was unprepared for any immediate war—a view which was confirmed by the German military attaché, Herr von Bülow—he was promptly corrected and informed that ' France's chief aim and object was to prepare her army for an early assault on Germany.'

Prince Hohenlohe's successor at Paris, Count Münster, in a report addressed direct to the Emperor (GP 1240), expressed the opinion that the mood throughout the country was decidedly in favour of peace. The *revanche* idea, Count Münster wrote, was losing ground, the general feeling throughout France being one of anxiety and even of terror, lest there should be a new war. ' In short,' he concluded, ' as long as the French are in their present mood, I cannot believe that we have any reason to apprehend war from this quarter.' In reply to this he received a tart note in which he was informed that in the face of such views the Imperial Government could hardly come forward in the Reichstag in support of the new Army Bill. ' By addressing to His Majesty in person such a detailed and emphatic exposition of your convictions concerning the pacific intentions of France and the French Government, you are running directly counter to a policy to which the German Federal Governments, by bringing in the new Army Bill, have officially and publicly professed their adherence.' Count Münster was informed that should his report leak out, the Government would be compelled to explain that His Imperial Majesty's ambassador at Paris was the victim of a misapprehension. In accordance with the wish of the Dictator, the report to the Emperor was consequently withdrawn and neither the monarch nor the Reichstag was permitted to learn the truth. In order to justify new military grants, perils were proclaimed that never existed, and the taxpayer, both then and later, was deliberately misled by means of false statements. The same thing happened in 1914.

Now that the archives have been opened, the figure of the old Emperor stands out in all its greatness. What deep insight and touching modesty ! What noble simplicity and true wisdom ! Invariably he hits the nail on the head. He alone sees straight. He alone protests against the insane alliance with Austria that was ultimately to lead Germany to the abyss. His notes reveal a

HERR VON HOLSTEIN

wonderful clearness and directness of political judgment, and one
watches with deep emotion the tragic mental struggle revealed in
these records and the ruthless violation of the old monarch's deepest
convictions. Unfortunately he in the end yielded to the disgraceful
threat put forward by a Ministry which was but a willing tool in the
hands of the Dictator and which declared that it would resign unless
the alliance were granted. Had the Monarch but stood his ground at
that crisis and had he but let the Great Man go, the most terrible
catastrophe in the world's history would have become impossible,
and Germany to-day would be the first nation on the Continent.

The Epigones, led by Herr von Holstein, concentrated their efforts
at the beginning of the new era on trying to prevent the return of the
Master by adopting a policy that was the very contrary of his. This
tendency led first of all to the non-renewal of the Re-insurance
Treaty with Russia. Bismarck's very imperfect knowledge of
Austrian conditions was on a par with his ignorance of the Roman
Church. He even felt anxiety lest Austria should revert to the
policy of the *status quo ante* 1866,—a quite unthinkable contingency
that neither the Austrian Germans nor the Austrian Slavs for a
moment contemplated. His habit of underrating national movements and their importance in Balkan politics—his whole attitude
as a *Conservative and dynastic politician,* which led him to overestimate the imperial power of the Habsburgs,—his quite unfounded
fear of Coalitions, and, from 1875 on, his hatred of Prince
Gortschakoff,—these were among the considerations that induced
the Dictator to enter into alliance with the effete old firm known as
Austria. Nowhere but in Berlin, not even in Vienna, was this
dynastic and medieval congeries of nationalities taken seriously.
The Master's mistakes dominated the whole age of the Epigones, as
these Post-Bismarckian statesmen are called, and the Master's
errors were developed into a system that finally led the country to
catastrophe.

The Official Records now published reveal the despair into which
M. de Giers, the Russian Minister of Foreign Affairs, was plunged
when he heard of Germany's refusal to renew the Re-insurance
Treaty. For this treaty had given the Russian Empire security on
its western frontier. In the subsequent documents we read too that
M. de Giers repeatedly expressed his regret that there should be no
kind of *written agreement* between the two Empires. It was this
regret, coupled with the noisy renewal of the ill-starred Triple

Alliance, that in 1892 called into being the Franco-Russian treaty. Article 6 of this treaty provided that ' La présente convention aura la même durée que la Triple Alliance,' a sentence that speaks volumes.

The Petty Princes, whose policy was in reality more often than not directed by men whose mental state is best described as pathological, looked upon the Triple Alliance as the very keystone of our foreign policy. Outside Germany, this Alliance was either sneered at or regarded with apprehension as a permanent menace to the peace of Europe. We, however, insisted on regarding it as the very quintessence of wisdom. As a matter of fact, it was but folly made sacrosanct by its association with a great name.

This policy subsequently led to an ever-increasing tension between Germany and Russia, a country with whose interests our own need nowhere have come into collision, had we but consented to forgo our senseless interference in Balkan questions. It was, moreover, to Russia's goodwill, as Wilhelm I. acknowledged in his well-known Versailles telegram to Alexander II., that we mainly owed our successes and the foundation of the German Empire. As a Slav-Orthodox theocracy Russia was naturally opposed to Austria-Hungary and Turkey, for she regarded the achievement of unity and independence for her Balkan brethren as her special ecclesiastical and national mission. This was the movement that we dubbed the ' Pan-Slav danger ' or ' Russia's greed for power ' !

Even in the Dictator's time we had already been pursuing an anti-Russian Balkan policy. At the end of the 'eighties, when I was secretary to our Embassy at Constantinople, and later on when I was at Bucharest, we persisted in regarding our great eastern neighbour as an adversary whose ' intrigues ' it was our duty to thwart. Austria-Hungary and Turkey were our ' friends,' a policy which struck at the very roots of Russia's Caesaro-Papism.

The maintenance of the *status quo* in the Orient and semi-Orient, that is to say in the Balkans and in Austria-Hungary, served later on as a convenient excuse for political helplessness and embarrassment. The estrangement from Russia, which began in 1875 with Bismarck's outburst of wrath against Gortschakoff, was without doubt the primary cause of our decline. The Jugoslav, Greek and Bulgarian national movements in favour of unity stood under the protection of Russia. It was in the long run just as hopeless to try to stamp out such movements as it had proved in years gone by to suppress a similar evolution in Italy. But the Post-Bismarckian Epigones looked upon the Austro-Magyar and Ottoman Empires, the two political invalids of Europe, as the mainstays of their system. Not content with this, they let no opportunity pass of scaring Russia and of bullying England and France, and occasionally Japan and the United States into the bargain, if they got a chance. We began by driving Russia into the arms of France, and then completed the business by driving her into the arms of England.

Germany, although by far the strongest Power on the Continent, insisted on keeping the world in a constant state of nervousness with her everlasting new grants for Army and Navy, with provocative speeches about the 'mailed fist' and 'shining armour,' and with swashbuckling rodomontades and fanfaronnades of all descriptions. To crown all, she refused to listen to any proposals made at the Peace Conferences for the limitation of armaments. One crisis followed another, each leaving our neighbours no choice but to submit to humiliation or to fight. Abroad, these everlasting crises created the impression that a new appeal to arms would be by no means unwelcome to our rulers. We thus induced the other Powers to forgo their old differences, and forced them to come to terms with one another in order to safeguard themselves against the 'German Peril.' This process led silly people to believe that we were being 'hemmed in' and 'encircled.'

The *entente* was the direct result of the Morocco crisis which had been staged by Herr von Holstein. The crisis had arisen despite M. Delcassé's efforts to come to an understanding with us. In a two hours' talk we one day had after dinner at the German Embassy at Paris in July 1904, M. Delcassé, who greatly overestimated my political influence, declared himself, to the unbounded rage of Herr von Holstein, ready to negotiate with Germany concerning Morocco. But Herr von Holstein was at that juncture just as little desirous of coming to an understanding with France as was his successor ten years later of coming to an agreement with England.

Herr von Holstein, who by his intimates was considered to be not quite normal, was undoubtedly a man of intellect and knowledge. He was at the same time a master of intrigue. He wielded a fluent pen and knew the archives inside out. The Great Man, whose secretary he had been at St. Petersburg, and who had said of him that 'he saw things that had no existence,' both used and abused his talents. Holstein was afterwards one of the first to betray the master, just as he had in earlier days [1] betrayed Count Arnim, his chief at Paris. He knew not only how to impress his superiors but how to intimidate and even completely dominate them. Politics were for him a game—a game with enormous stakes. That politics also meant for him gambling for his own private ends, I should never have believed.[2]

His chief aim was personal power and influence. Both of these he possessed during his life and both he continued to possess even after his death. ' The living are ruled by the dead,' says Nietzsche. After the fall of the Great Man, it was von Holstein who guided our foreign policy with an ascendancy that knew practically no limits. Whenever he failed to get his way, he would threaten to resign, whereupon they would all, in their dread of public revelations, crumple up and sink on their knees in dismay. As a rule, he allowed himself to be placated by beseechings and implorings. He remained in office, and the mismanagement of foreign affairs remained with him. The policy which Holstein pursued was capricious and lacked any big objective. It was fantastic and whimsical and full of contradictions. Hardly had he issued an order than he would again countermand it. This was especially likely to happen when the other side accepted his proposal, a thing that inevitably filled him with distrust. He quite lost touch with realities and lived in a world of illusions. He even went so far as to give his protégés instructions as to what should be the tenor of their reports. If one of our representatives abroad reported things this fantast and misanthrope did not wish to read, he henceforth had to reckon with Holstein as his enemy and to expect a reprimand or a removal to some less desirable post. As a rule Holstein protected only mediocrities or diplomats who were content to be as putty in his hands. Officials of ability or character he dreaded. It thus very often came about that men who were mere nonentities attained to most important posts. He was, in short, a national misfortune and the real begetter of the world war.

---

[1] When he gave evidence for the prosecution in the famous Arnim trial. (Tr.)

[2] This remark refers to the startling revelations made by the *Berliner Tageblatt* in its issue No. 593 of 16th December, 1925. This paper had come into possession of several hundred private letters written by Holstein to his financial agents between 1875 and 1897. The extracts published from this correspondence proved that Holstein, who for nearly a quarter of a century had had such a decisive voice in shaping Germany's foreign policy, was as corrupt as he was unscrupulous, and that throughout the period in question he had not only been a heavy speculator on the Bourse but that he had been in the habit of using official information obtained through his connection with the German Foreign Office for the purposes of his clandestine transactions in international stocks. The letters showed, too, that he had on occasion even tried to manipulate German foreign policy for egoistic financial ends. (Tr.)

Herr von Kiderlen, a disciple and intimate friend of Holstein's, a few years after the death of the latter, took charge of the German Foreign Office. This official was underhand, artful, sly and crafty, not without commonsense and not without humour, but unmannerly, untidy, spiteful, malevolent and malicious. By the time he came to hold office, alcohol and a rakish bachelor life had already sapped his powers. In spite of this, however, he would never have committed the astounding blunder of the year 1914 ; he was far too astute for that, although he, too, failed to realise how necessary it was for us to refrain from all meddling in Balkan affairs.

I have never on any occasion maintained that our so-called statesmen in July 1914 wanted the world war, so far as they had any clear idea of what they actually did want. I have tried to show that the world war was the ultimate consequence of an entirely mistaken policy and that if you stumble from one crisis into another, the moment is bound to come when things will go wrong, whether you want it or not. In my Memorandum[1] which, to my deep regret, was divulged during the war and which though much discussed since, has, as I have often enough perceived, been more condemned than read, I have reproached our ' statesmen ' of that time not with their will for war but with their hasty decisions, their infatuation and their incompetence. In my petition to the Prussian Upper Chamber in 1918, I showed that the statements contained in the official German White Book of 3rd August, 1914, were far more damaging for Germany's cause than was my Memorandum. For the White Book in the following passage admits the *dolus eventualis* [2] which I had not included among my assumptions :

' Under these circumstances, Austria was forced to the conclusion that it would be compatible neither with her dignity nor with the safety of her Empire for her to look on any longer inactive at the doings on the other side of the frontier. The Austrian Government informed us of this view and asked for our opinion. We were able to inform our ally of our cordial concurrence with her estimate of the situation and to assure her that any military action she

---

[1] See p. 48 n., ' My Mission to London.' (Tr.)

[2] *Dolus*, in German law, means the deliberate intent to commit a deed despite the fact that the doer recognises that the deed in question involves a criminal action. According to both the Penal and Civil codes it is indifferent whether the man who commits a crime merely regards the criminal consequences of his action as a contingent possibility (*dolus eventualis*) or whether he has imagined various consequences as possible of which he only desired one (*dolus alternativus*). (Translator's note.)

might deem necessary in order to put an end to the Serbian movement directed against the integrity of the Monarchy would be endorsed by us. In giving this assurance, we were well aware of the fact that any military procedure on the part of Austria-Hungary against Serbia might bring Russia into the field and thus in accordance with our treaty obligations involve us in a war. Recognising, however, that Austria-Hungary's vital interests were at stake, we could neither advise our ally to leniency incompatible with her dignity nor could we deny her our support when the grave moment arrived.'

And then the war-guilt question !

Who was to blame for the war of 1870 and who for the wars of 1856 and 1863 ? Does anyone suppose that a man like Bismarck would have let himself be taken by surprise or that he would have waged war had he not wanted to do so ? Who, it may be asked, was to blame for the three Silesian wars or for the Thirty Years' War, or for the Trojan War ? Was it really the fair Helen's face that ' fired the topless towers of Ilium ' ? There are only two kinds of wars— foolish wars that are a crime, and wars that have a definite end and aim that cannot be achieved by other means. Can a nation's policy be judged from the standpoint of a penal code ? Such a code protects the individual from violation of his rights, but who is there to protect that collective association of individuals known as a nation or a state ? And who is to liberate a nation, unless it be the nation itself, with or without the help of others ? A war that is willed and waged for some definite end need by no means be a crime, but to cause a war without having willed it, is an offence unpardonable. No worse accusation can possibly be brought against a statesman.

We just blundered into the world war by mistake !

My contention is that the methods of the age of the Epigones were bound, sooner or later, to lead to the Great Catastrophe, and nothing I have found in the works published since the war, or in the Official Documents now thrown open to the world by our Foreign Office, has shaken my conviction or robbed the arguments brought forward by me of their cogency.

The Official Records now published are, by their sheer voluminousness, rendered inaccessible to all but a few. I have therefore resolved to publish a special edition of the weightiest of my London dispatches, written between 1912 and 1914, and have appended to them a number of other correlated documents. In taking this course, I have not been actuated by any desire for personal justification. Events themselves have shown only too completely that I was right. Unluckily, among our diplomats mine was the only voice raised in protest to predict what has since come to pass. I am anxious that the reasons that led England to enter the war may be made evident through my dispatches.

In these messages I repeatedly pointed out that the British Government, and especially Sir Edward Grey, desired to meet us halfway and to arrive at an understanding with us ; in other words, that the British wanted to settle amicably the points at issue between us and find for both parties a satisfactory solution which would at the same time guarantee the maintenance of peace in Europe. I argued that in the case of another Franco-German war no British Government would ever again, as happened in 1870, adopt towards us an attitude of benevolent neutrality. Whether Alsace-Lorraine belonged to us or to the French was a matter of indifference to Great Britain. This being the case the British would never have supported a firebrand policy à la Boulanger. A new defeat of the French together with the overthrow of Russia would, however, have made us masters of the Continent, a contingency that Britain could not possibly brook. It is therefore a mistake to say that it was our refusal to listen to the suggestions put forward in the 'nineties by Chamberlain to the effect that we should form an Anglo-German alliance against Russia that was to blame for the political situation in which we found ourselves in 1914. *With or without an alliance, with or without the Fleet,*—and the Fleet, it must be remembered, formed only a part of the mighty and senseless armaments that alarmed our neighbours, and induced them to form a ring around us, —*with or without the unpardonable breach of Belgian neutrality, England would never have permitted a second Sedan.*

This is borne out by the recently published letters and diaries of Queen Victoria, dating from the 'seventies, a time when there was no talk either of Belgian neutrality or of the menace of a German Fleet. The Queen, disturbed by the attitude of Prince Bismarck, a man she distrusted as much as did the Russians, turns to her daughter, turns to Wilhelm I. and even to Alexander II., and writes letter after letter, in order to warn Germany. These letters, it goes without saying, were written at the instigation of her Ministers.

Inability to understand this important question shown by our Foreign Office was evident enough in the opinion they expressed that the mere existence of a German fleet would suffice to prevent the British from coming to the aid of the French, the weaker side.

From Sir Edward Grey we could have got almost anything we desired. In every direction he was ready to meet us. There was only one point on which he could not budge. When we attacked France, and then proceeded to clinch this action by violating the neutrality of Belgium, it became impossible for him to keep England out of the war.

That was the tragedy of my mission ! I had succeeded, thanks to the sincere wish of Sir Edward Grey and to the support of Sir W. Tyrrell, in arriving at an understanding with Great Britain and in improving our relations to such an extent that we could count upon her co-operation in all questions except those that involved the danger of a war.

Among the subjects dealt with in my dispatches will be found (1) the London Ambassadors' Conference, where that Austro-Italian homunculus, the Kingdom of Wied, was called into being ; (2) the Bagdad Railway, a question in which Sir Edward Grey showed such willingness to meet our wishes that he conceded to Germany the port of Basra as a terminal for the line ; (3) the Colonial Treaty by which we acquired wide spheres of interest in the Portuguese colonies. In concluding this agreement, which was of vital importance for Germany, I enjoyed the zealous and sympathetic support of Dr. Rosen, our Minister at Lisbon, support which was the more notable, as it was in marked contrast to the policy of obstruction pursued by our Foreign Office ; (4) finally my dispatches, containing an exposition of our relations with England and my urgent warning against the foreign policy that eventually led to the great collapse. I leave the reader himself to judge on which side lay delusion and on which a sane appreciation of the situation.

Among the grave mistakes committed by the Great Man during his period of dictatorship (1870-1890) may be instanced the campaign against the Roman Curia, the repulsive Arnim trial and the pitched battle against democracy and Social Democracy. His chief error, however, was the attitude he took up towards Prince Gortschakoff at the Berlin Congress. This the Czar's Government never forgave us. Finally there was the disastrous alliance with Austria, an alliance whose spearhead was pointed against Russia, and which was in a certain sense a return to the traditions of the Holy Roman Empire.

The debit account of the Dictator's mistakes is nevertheless balanced to a certain extent by one great deed that must be placed on the credit side, the so-called ' Re-insurance Treaty ' with Russia.

In his great period the Iron Chancellor went with Russia and against Austria.   In the period of his decline, he went with Austria and against Russia.

Bismarck's successors, on the other hand, intoxicated by our greatness and power, stumbled from one blunder to another. I shall confine myself to an enumeration of only their most momentous errors : The failure to renew the treaty with Russia (1890) ; the noisy renewal of the disastrous Triple Alliance (1892) ; the Triple Alliance in the Far East (1895) in which we played the rôle of a circus clown and alienated Japan ; the Krueger telegram (1896) ; the senseless occupation of Tsingtau which started the China question (1897) ; the grotesque ' Welt-Marschall ' (Waldersee) expedition (1900) ; the snubbing of Chamberlain (1901) ; the insane naval policy which, although it was not the cause of the war, nevertheless made England restless and helped to throw her into the arms of France ; the still insaner Morocco crisis, which, in flat contradiction of the doctrines of the Master, denied the French the possibility of finding compensation on African soil for Alsace-Lorraine, and for which a moment was chosen when the anti-militarists and pacifists had got the upper hand in France ; the voyage of our Argonauts to Tangier, an expedition against which Wilhelm II. struggled vehemently before yielding to the orders of Herr von Holstein, whose object was to provoke both the French and the British.

But the worst was yet to come,—the Bosnian crisis, the real prelude to the world war. For since Algeciras we had fallen into a state of dependence on Vienna, feeling apparently that we must return the services that had been rendered us by our ' brilliant second.'

Steadily we marched forward along the road to the abyss. Our foolish military mission to Constantinople, apparently undertaken merely to annoy the Russians ; the Agadir escapade, which brought us a snub from England ; the breakdown of the Haldane mission, because we were dissatisfied with the formula proposed by Sir Edward Grey and demanded from England a declaration of neutrality, a demand to which she could never assent, since it would have been tantamount to deserting France ; our Austrophile and anti-Serbian attitude during the wars fought by the Balkan peoples in the cause of national unity and independence ; the founding of the principality of Albania, by which we blocked Serbia's access to the sea ; and finally, as the keystone to this arch of errors, the punishment of the ' assassins of the Princes ' for the sake of the ' vital interests ' of an ally who to-day has completely disappeared. Then followed in rapid succession our refusal to accept the British offer of mediation, the ignoring of the Russian proposal to submit the quarrel to the Hague Court of Arbitration, the suicidal declaration of war on Russia, the invasion of Belgium, the restoration of Poland, and—to crown all—unrestricted submarine warfare.

It was as though Germany in 1859 had plunged into a world war in order to frustrate Italian unity and to defend the German Confederation on the Mincio, as certain politicians of that time would fain have had us do.

I ask any normal person whose head is not clouded with a belief in the doctrine of authority and befogged with phrases, legends and traditions, what actual interest the German people had in the Serbian question or in Bulgarian or Rumanian grievances, or what we wanted at the Dardanelles ? Germany surely was as little interested in these questions as she was in the affairs of Spain or Portugal or in a mission to the Pillars of Hercules.

Why had we to put our finger into every pie and, even at the risk of war, meddle in matters which were no concern of ours ? I am well aware that these statements will again lay me open to attack, and I am fully prepared to be reproached with having injured the German cause by publishing such comments. Can anyone do harm to our cause by submitting to closest scrutiny and unsparing criticism the events that led up to the great disaster ? There need be neither whitewash nor sophistry. Neither the politicasters, civilian and military, nor other simpletons and dabblers in erroneous patriotism will ever succeed in convincing a single soul or in winning back a single village that we have had to surrender, or in modifying a single paragraph of the Treaty of Versailles.

What is past belongs to history, and the study of history entails an investigation of the truth and the ascertaining of connections between cause and effect.

Our cause has been injured by those who, contrary to my repeated warnings, insisted on pursuing a line of policy which, albeit against their will, inevitably led to war and to the collapse of the Fatherland.

A treaty with Russia to guard us against the danger of a war on two fronts and we should have needed neither alliances nor armaments.

MY APPOINTMENT TO LONDON

MY appointment to the post of ambassador at London marked the culminating point of my official career. What made them hit on me ? Why was I in 1912 suddenly and unexpectedly chosen for such an important diplomatic post,—plucked from the retirement of country life, although in my diplomatic career I had never got beyond the rank of Minister ? I had retired in 1904—having long since abandoned all hope of being employed on any diplomatic task that did not consist merely of dinner-parties and receptions. My inadequacy as a diplomat was obvious, at least in Herr von Holstein's opinion. He described me as a muddlehead. Probably because I could not follow his labyrinthine ideas. He also considered me to be far too independent in my views. And people of independent views are dangerous, for they disturb the pleasant atmosphere. The only ambassadors who are to be tolerated are those whose dispatches contain just what one wants to find in them. This standpoint was, of course, perfectly justifiable, as long as politics were merely regarded as a kind of sport. There was no control of any kind ; the ' plebs, pecus, vulgus ' swallowed everything you liked to lay before them in word and script. ' Encirclement,' ' Germany surrounded by a host of foes,' and similar terrifying phrases were coined by ignorant bureaucrats and soldiers, in order to frighten the taxpayer into granting the necessary sums. There was no end to the new armaments asked for. And these cost money. No one is willing to put his hand in his pocket unless either love or fear induces him to do so. In short, we set up the hypothesis that we were ' ringed round by enemies,' while all the time it was the others who were in fear of us.

The real reason why the choice fell on me for the London post I am unable to tell you. It certainly cannot have been because of my abilities, since of these the Foreign Office did not avail itself. Was it perhaps on account of my incompetence ? Hardly, for had that been the case they would have thought of me sooner. His Majesty had, it is true, always been most gracious to me, but I was never one of his intimate friends. Besides, anyone to whom he showed favour was generally cold-shouldered by the Foreign Office.

Count Metternich had been given a hint to go, and they were looking for his successor. The heads of the Foreign Office, whose activities, apart from fantastic political scheming, lay chiefly in finding pleasant posts for their nominees, had fixed on one of their colleagues. But the man in question, besides lacking the necessary qualities—a matter of no great importance—turned out to be too young. He nevertheless continued to regard the London post, where he had not, as an assistant, left behind too favourable an impression, as his by right of reversion. Some elderly gentleman had therefore to be found, if possible with one foot in the grave, who would mark time in London until the young official in question had arrived at the necessary years of maturity. At first they hit on Herr von Eisendecker. He was old. That was the main consideration. He had also won laurels on board the Emperor's yacht at Cowes, a highly estimable achievement. He was also friends with a host of Bible Societies in England, another point in his favour. For the rest, he was a most honourable man and a friend of the Grand Duchess Luise.[1] He had the good sense, however, to decline the appointment; so they had to look about them for another 'greybeard.' They did not hit upon me, for at that time I was not ancient enough. The chief qualification required in the candidate was that he should be so old that the post would become vacant within a short period. Baron Marschall was the oldest ambassador; why not trot him out? Unfortunately he died earlier than the programme stipulated. Great embarrassment! The candidate-elect seemed still too young. The Wise Men put their heads together. They found they had run out of greybeards and had no really senile candidates in stock. What was to be done?

Herr von Bethmann-Hollweg, whose brilliant career had aroused no little amazement among his friends, was a most amiable guest and companion. It is said, too, that he played the piano rather well. The idea occurred to him to come and see me on my Silesian estate on his way back from Buchlau [2] where he had been to get instructions. We motored into the Silesian mountains and he found that I was not

---

[1] Of Baden, daughter of Emperor Wilhelm I. (Tr.)

[2] Count Berchtold's seat in Moravia. (Tr.)

HERR VON KIDERLEN-WÄCHTER

as black as I had been painted.   In short, he hit on the extraordinary
idea of summoning me from my rural retirement, much to the disgust
of Herr von Kiderlen, who would fain have had none but his own
set.[1]   I, unfortunately, had not the honour to belong to it, having no
particular taste for scabrous stories or for uncouth jests and carous-
ings.   Well, I was appointed.   Shall I go on with the story ?
History will do that for me.   Everything would, perhaps, have gone
as desired had I had no success in London, and had our relations with
England not begun visibly to improve.   That was an unpardonable
sin.   One man wanted my post, another thought that I wanted his.
Finally, too, they even came to believe in what they called the
' Localization of the conflict,' merely because I held an opposite view.

[1] Out of loyalty to Wilhelm II., Prince Lichnowsky here omits to relate that
the Chancellor brought with him a letter from the Kaiser appointing him to the
London post.   This letter, which Lichnowsky in his pique could not refrain
from showing to a friend in 1920, (cf. *Die Weltbühne*, xxiv. p. 430), was anything
but a formal official document.   Carelessly scrawled in lead pencil, discon-
nected in its composition, arrogant in tone, and full of childish expressions of
hate for England, it was characteristic of the mood that was to lead its writer
and Germany to disaster.   (Translator's Note.)

ENGLAND BEFORE THE WAR [1]

On the way back from Kiel, where I had heard the news of the assassination of the Archduke Ferdinand, I reported to the Chancellor in the last days of June, and at the Foreign Office. I explained to Herr von Bethmann-Hollweg that I thought the foreign situation, as far as we were concerned, very satisfactory, especially as our relations with England now manifested a warmth and cordiality that had hitherto been conspicuously absent.

I told him that England attached the greatest importance to the maintenance of peace, and this partly for economic reasons, seeing that any war between the Great Powers of Europe must inevitably cause England grave financial losses. I further explained that England desired the maintenance of the balance of power among the European groups. Any shifting in the relations of the Great Powers would, in the opinion of the English, disturb the present group equilibrium. Nor did England's policy by any means aim at crushing Germany. Indeed, a powerful Germany helped, England thought, to make France and Russia amenable to British wishes. Otherwise the pressure exerted by Germany on France and Russia would cease. On the other hand, English policy, no matter whether directed by Sir Edward Grey or by any other statesman, would never permit Germany to destroy or even to weaken France. The maintenance of France at her present strength as a counterpoise to Germany, and especially England's anxiety lest Germany should, by bringing Western Europe into a relation of dependence, extend her power to the coasts of England, formed the very foundation stone of Great Britain's foreign policy.

We ought clearly to understand, I said, that a war with France would mean a simultaneous war with England, for Great Britain

[1] The original text of this document was dictated by Prince Lichnowsky on Aug. 19, 1914, to an official of the German F.O. The wording was afterwards, apparently in the summer of 1916, altered in parts. The author wished, as he says, to tone down certain statements which might have put too severe a strain on the patience of the private friends to whom he intended to show the MS. (Tr.)

would, under all circumstances, hold a protecting hand over France. Given a war between Germany and France, England's entry into such a conflict would be only a question of time.

While in London, I had repeatedly sent in reports to this effect. In the first few weeks of my official activities in London, when the First Balkan War broke out, Lord Haldane came to see me and gave me clearly to understand, probably at the wish of his friend Sir Edward Grey, that as the maintenance of France was of vital importance to England, England could not stand aside should the Balkan War lead to a European war. Repeated hints to this effect from Sir Edward Grey in the course of my period of office at London strengthened my conviction on this point. The Ambassadors' Conference in London, which had met at the suggestion of Sir Edward Grey, was really due to this statesman's wish to create a kind of clearing-house where any points of difference that might arise between the European groups might be toned down and amicably settled. The creation of the principality of Albania at the instigation of Austria and Italy was strongly opposed by M. Cambon. Sir Edward Grey, however, used his influence on the side of the Powers of the Triple Alliance, and it was owing to Sir Edward's co-operation that the boundaries of this principality were fixed on lines that were essentially in accordance with our wishes.

In the question of North Epirus, Italy retained the upper hand against France, and Austria against Russia in the matter of Scutari and the Serbian harbour on the Adriatic. The first Balkan Peace, which was concluded in London, accorded, too, in the main with the wishes of Austria. Bulgaria's megalomania, fostered by Austria under the Daneff Ministry, led, however, to the Second Balkan War, in which Bulgaria, on whom Austria had placed her hopes, was defeated, and this finally led to the Peace of Bucharest, which was concluded amidst loud protests from Austria.

I also took the liberty to lay before the Chancellor my views as to the position in France. These views were based upon what I had observed in London. I had gathered that although the *revanche* idea still existed in France, this idea possessed theoretical rather than practical importance, firstly, because the French dreaded a war with us, and secondly, because the Radical Government then in power in France was pacifist in character. The London statesmen on their return from Paris at the time of the King's visit had got this impression and had passed it on to me.

As far as Russia was concerned, Sir Edward Grey had repeatedly told me that since the settlement of the Liman von Sanders affair there had in his opinion been no reason for any disquieting conclusions with regard to Russia's policy. Both the Czar and M. Sazonov desired peace. I gained the same impression from my conversation with Count Benckendorff, the Russian Ambassador in London, who, it is true, seemed greatly to regret that Berlin and Petrograd were not in closer touch.

The Chancellor replied that he could not share my optimistic views. The Russian armaments, concerning which the General Staff had sent him a full report, were assuming proportions that could not but cause uneasiness in Germany. An increase of 900,000 men was being provided for, and in addition to this the Russians were building railways to our frontiers. Finally, he said he would tell me in confidence that, according to secret and reliable reports he had received, a Naval Agreement between Russia and England was being drawn up. This agreement provided that in case of war English freight steamers were to transport Russian troops to the coast of Pomerania.

To this I replied that I had been hearing tales of Russia's threatening armaments for some thirty years past and that the same old story had always been current to the effect that Russia would be ready by a given time and would then proceed to crush us. I pointed out that each time the predicted year had come round, Russia was just as unready as the time before. Even in Bismarck's day the General Staff, and especially Count Waldersee, had done their utmost to get Germany to declare what they called a prophylactic war, but Prince Bismarck had always been opposed to this idea, and experience had shown that he was right. I promised Herr von Bethmann, however, that when I got back to London, I would not fail to warn the English confidentially that such agreements, in substance if not perhaps in form, were at variance with the repeated solemn assurances that English Ministers had given us to the effect that England had entered into no secret commitments with foreign Powers. The Chancellor authorised me to give Sir Edward Grey to understand that it would be difficult for him successfully to resist the demands of certain circles that were agitating for increased naval armaments, should such reports get about and find credence. Such a secret understanding would also serve as a dangerous encouragement to the Russo-French war party, a party which Sir Edward Grey himself opposed.

(The Anglo-French naval pact as well as other agreements of a defensive nature which had arisen out of the Morocco crisis, although for a long time known to the German Foreign Office through the reports of their secret agents, had not been communicated to the German Embassy in London.) Sir Edward Grey, who in Paris had held aloof from the French suggestions of a formal alliance, had finally and, it is to be assumed, principally at the instigation of M. Isvolsky, found himself compelled to make a further concession to his friends of the Entente. As to the practical value of such a plan, I did not permit myself an opinion. But it seemed hardly likely that should war actually threaten, British merchant ships would be able to pass the Sound unhindered, in order to take on board large bodies of troops at some point or other on the Baltic coast and transport them under the eyes of our Fleet to Pomerania. The improvement noticeable of late in Anglo-German relations, as I could remark from certain confidential utterances, had caused some uneasiness, especially in Paris. Supported by M. Isvolsky, the French kept pressing in London for some tangible proofs of the genuineness of the British feeling towards the Entente and were asking for a downright alliance. How greatly M. Cambon, the French Ambassador in London, had begun to doubt the reliability of England's friendship becomes evident from a few words he let fall towards the end of my stay in London, to a lady with whom we were both acquainted. ' Les Anglais interviendront,' said M. Cambon, ' mais ils le feront quand ce sera trop tard.' M. Cambon was much perturbed, too, about the impending conclusion of the Bagdad agreement and the Colonial Treaty, seeing, as he did, in these agreements the basis of an Anglo-German *rapprochement*. A high official at the British Foreign Office told me that M. Cambon had left no stone unturned in his efforts to wreck the Colonial Treaty, and had bitterly complained that England had sacrificed to Germany the islands of San Thomé and Principe. As these islands lay to the north of the equator the French considered that according to the terms of the existing agreement they fell within the French sphere of interest. M. Cambon also received instructions from Paris to show himself in public more frequently than he had been doing, and was also advised to deliver speeches from time to time, in order to counteract the effect of my propaganda.

After my arrival in London on 6th July, 1914, I lost no time in visiting Sir Edward Grey and laid the following three points before him. I told him, first, that Russia's attitude and the knowledge that

Russia was increasing her armaments had aroused in Germany a
feeling of uneasiness.   The Minister replied that since the Liman
affair nothing had happened so far as he knew that could give rise to
any anxiety with regard to Russo-German relations.   I then said to
him that he must permit me to make a more private and friendly
remark.   It was not for me, I said, to ask him indiscreet questions,
but as he had repeatedly declared that there were no secret agreements between England and a foreign Power, I felt it would be in the
interest of our mutual good relations to point out that the rumours
that had got abroad of late concerning Anglo-Russian naval agreements had created a painful impression in Germany.   In any case,
I thought it would be wiser to postpone such agreements for the
present, as it would otherwise be difficult for my government any
longer to oppose certain exaggerated demands for new armaments.
The Minister replied that there were in existence no secret treaties
which in any way bound the government, but that he would come
back to this matter in a few days' time.

In the third place, I told the Minister that although I had no
instructions to do so, I nevertheless thought it my duty to draw his
attention to the fact that Austro-Serbian relations were beginning to
take a rather critical turn.   The assassination of the Archduke, with
the connivance of official Serbia, had at last led Vienna to resolve to
take up an energetic attitude towards these Serbian acts of defiance
and to demand satisfaction and pledges for the future.

I did not know, I said, what line of action Austria meant to adopt,
but I could well imagine that it might give rise to a state of tension
and prove a danger to the peace of Europe.   It was therefore
necessary that Sir Edward Grey should, even at this early stage, get
into touch with Petrograd in order to advise coolness and calmness,
so that the Russians might realize that Austria, as the aggrieved party,
had a right to satisfaction.   The Minister was visibly affected by my
statements and seemed in the main to agree with what I said.

A few days later Sir Edward Grey sent for me and told me that he
would not deny that ' conversations ' of a technical nature had taken
place between the British and Russian naval authorities, as had also
repeatedly been the case between Great Britain and France during the
Morocco crisis.   These conversations had, he said, no aggressive
character and consequently there was in them nothing in the nature
of a menace to Germany.   For the rest, however, he did not
wish to mislead me and wished therefore to point out to me

that British relations with the Entente Powers were of a very intimate nature.

When, a few days later, I visited Lord Beauchamp, the Minister of Public Works, at his country-house, he told me that Sir Edward Grey had made my communication the subject of a speech in the Cabinet and that the Cabinet had been no little dismayed at the possibility of another acute crisis in European affairs.

In the period that followed, I found both among members of the Cabinet and in the London press full understanding for the Austrian standpoint. Austria's attitude was placed before the public more and more clearly in the reports sent from Vienna and Budapest and was elucidated by explanations supplied by Count Mensdorff, the Austro-Hungarian Ambassador in London. It was not till Count Tisza delivered his bellicose speech that public opinion in London began to become uneasy. Journals like *The Times* and *The Morning Post* were the first to show a change of front, scenting in the intentions of Austria something more than a desire to exact a righteous penalty for the crime of Serajevo. Both papers warned Austria not to try to exploit the incident for political ends. During this time it was my constant endeavour to convince Sir Edward Grey and his private secretary, Sir William Tyrrell, of the necessity of taking energetic measures against the Serbian disturbers of the peace. I urged that the Minister should use his influence in Petrograd to prevent Russia's identifying herself with the 'Serbian assassins,' and that he should get Russia to recognise the justification of the Austrian standpoint.

Sir Edward Grey at first took a calm view of the situation, and repeatedly promised me that he would use his influence in Petrograd in the sense I had suggested. He assured me then, as he did later on, that he had no desire to interfere in the affair, as long as the dispute remained confined to Austria and Serbia.

It lay in Britain's interests, too, to 'localize' the conflict. But if this 'localization' failed of achievement, said Sir Edward, and if the Serbian question developed into a dispute between Austria and Russia, then the moment would have come when the Powers that were not direct participants would be bound to mediate.

(As I had not the slightest belief in the possibility of 'localizing' the quarrel, I during this time repeatedly warned Berlin against any dangerous or adventurous policy and counselled moderation. Herr von Jagow assured me in reply that the more firmly we backed up Austria, the sooner would Russia give way.)

The publication of the ultimatum despatched by Austria to Serbia aroused marked uneasiness in London. Nor did the Austro-Hungarian Embassy make any secret of the fact that the ultimatum had been deliberately couched in terms which were calculated to provoke a refusal. At the British Foreign Office I was informed that the demands contained in the ultimatum amounted to an infringement of Serbia's sovereign rights. The demands were considered exaggerated and even monstrous, and, though to some extent this might be attributed to their clumsy wording, I had to listen to some very unflattering criticisms of the Viennese statesmen and their statesmanship. On the whole, however, London still took a calm and not unhopeful view of the possibility of maintaining peace in Europe. I pressed energetically for the unconditional acceptance of the ultimatum. I urged that ' Austria's bark was worse than its bite,' and that when the Austrian demands came to be carried into execution, there would doubtless be an opportunity of sparing Serbia's *amour propre*.

When Serbia's answer became known, Sir Edward Grey went through the various points with me. He told me that the far-reaching concessions made by Serbia in her reply were due to the pressure which London and Petrograd had brought to bear on Belgrade. There remained, strictly speaking, he said, only one demand of Austria's that the Government of Belgrade had not accepted in its entirety. That Austria should under these circumstances have broken off diplomatic relations did not, he said, cast a very favourable light either on her goodwill or her desire for peace. Austria's declaration of war, which immediately followed, created a thoroughly unfavourable impression in London. From day to day the opinion grew stronger and stronger that Vienna had made up its mind that there was either to be war or that Russia was to be humiliated without war and her influence in the Near East destroyed.

Undeterred by these portents, Sir Edward Grey continued to try to think out ways and means of averting the threatening storm. He now clearly saw that unless the other Powers succeeded in bringing about a compromise that would be acceptable to both Russia and Austria, it was hopeless to think of localizing the conflict. He showed me telegrams from Sir Maurice de Bunsen in which Count Berchtold had turned down all suggestions that he should discuss his demands with Russia. As Sir Edward Grey now no longer believed in the possibility of a direct understanding being arrived at between

Vienna and Petrograd, the only way out of the impasse was for Great Britain and Germany to work together. Sir Edward sent a message to me through Sir W. Tyrrell, telling me that if by our common efforts we could but avert the present severe crisis and save the peace of Europe, he felt that Anglo-German relations would be put on a sure foundation for many a year to come. Unfortunately, up to the end of July I was not in a position to offer him anything whatever that might have been interpreted as a wish to meet him halfway in reciprocation of this suggestion or as evidence of any sincere wish on our part to maintain peace. In spite of the fact that I had incessantly pointed out to Berlin the threatening danger of a world war, I could get nothing to offer the Minister beyond an assurance that we wished to localize the conflict and that we considered Austria's action justified.

When at the end of July, in accordance with my instructions, I had to put Austria's standpoint before Sir Edward Grey, unaccompanied by any proposal for mediation, and had to explain to him that Serbia must first be subjugated, then occupied by Austrian troops, and not evacuated till after the fulfilment of the Austrian demands (whose extent was left undefined), Austria at the same time giving assurances that it was not her intention to seek any extension of territory, the British Minister declared to me that it was quite possible to humiliate a state and reduce it to a condition of vassalage without interfering with its boundaries. Austria's attitude, he said, could not fail to arouse the suspicion that a humiliation of Russia was intended.

I did not fail to draw the attention of Berlin to the fact that the cool reserve with which we met all Sir Edward Grey's attempts to get us to join with him in building a bridge of understanding was producing in London a growing feeling of depression, as people were beginning seriously to doubt our good intentions. When I begged Sir Edward Grey to use his influence in Petrograd to urge moderation, he replied that he was not aware that any corresponding pressure was being brought to bear in Vienna. On the contrary, he said, Sir Maurice de Bunsen had reported to London that Herr von Tschirschky, the German Ambassador at Vienna, was untiring in his efforts to incite Austria to go to war, and was trying to stiffen the backs of the Austrian statesmen. Count Mensdorff and his staff in London, too, related that in response to an enquiry in Berlin, Austria had been exhorted to take up a firm and energetic line of action.

In spite of all my assurances to the contrary, the belief continued to gain ground in London that Germany was not at all averse to war. I was told straight out that if Germany only showed a little energy it would be quite possible for her to get Austria to take up a more conciliatory attitude towards Russia.

Sir Edward Grey's growing doubts as to the sincerity of our professions of peace finally caused him, after he had already given me several broad hints, to give me on July 29 the well-known warning, couched in very friendly terms, to the effect that England, in the case of a European war, would not be able to hold aloof for very long.

I answered, as the British Blue Book shows, that my reports to Berlin had repeatedly dwelt on that point. Sir Edward Grey was indefatigable in his search for some way of escape from the peril that threatened Europe. When I announced to him that direct negotiations had again been taken up between Petrograd and Vienna, he heaved a sigh of relief. ' If that is possible, all the better,' he said. His further proposal that the interpretation of those points of the ultimatum which were still in dispute should be left to a conference of the ambassadors of the four non-participant Great Powers with the object of finding a basis for some agreement, appeared to me an opportune means of avoiding the threatening catastrophe. I warmly endorsed the suggestion in my report to Berlin, and pointed out that a world war ' in which we had everything to lose and nothing to gain,' would otherwise be unavoidable. (Had my advice been followed and the British proposals accepted, the world would have been spared the greatest catastrophe in history. The proposal for the mediation of the Great Powers contained nothing that was inconsistent with the dignity of Austria-Hungary and would have assured Germany a brilliant diplomatic success.) Sir Edward Grey's last proposal, which he sent to the British Ambassador at Petrograd in a dispatch he discussed with me as he wrote it, would also, I think, have formed a suitable basis for an understanding. Starting from the assumption that Austria had already occupied Serbian territory, the British Minister proposed that both Austria and Russia should immediately cease their warlike operations, and that on the basis of the pledges Austria already had in hand there should be a discussion which, through the mediation of the Powers not directly concerned, should settle the interpretation of the points in the Austrian demands still under dispute.

When I received the news of the Russian mobilization and was instructed to inform the British Government of the fact, and to add that our attempts at mediation, undertaken at the desire of the Czar, had been paralysed by this action on the part of Russia, I sent the message to Sir William Tyrrell, by our Secretary of Legation, Herr von Schubert. It was late in the evening and I did not know where Sir Edward Grey was to be found. In London this was the first they had heard of the Russian mobilization. Sir William Tyrrell hastened with the news to Mr. Asquith, who immediately went to the King, wakening him to give him the news. At 2 a.m. I was called to the telephone and Mr. Asquith's private secretary informed me that the King had at once telegraphed to the Czar appealing to him to stop the mobilization. Our ultimatum, and the declaration of war on Russia which followed, filled London with dismay. It was difficult to explain to Englishmen, with their somewhat vague ideas of military necessities, why Germany could not, as Russia had done, confine herself merely to a mobilization of her troops. The English interpreted the German declaration of war on Russia as conclusive evidence of the victory of the military party in Berlin.

When people say that Sir Edward Grey wanted the war, or that he could at least have stopped it if he had sincerely and earnestly desired to do so, I cannot help thinking of a man who in order to score off his next-door neighbour, wantonly sets fire to his own house. Anyone who actually saw the collapse of London's business life just before the actual outbreak of the war, and witnessed the suspension of the Banking Act, the proclamation of the moratorium and the closing of the Stock Exchange, could no longer be sceptical as to the sincerity of England's desire to maintain peace in Europe, nor fail to understand why an English Minister would strain every nerve to prevent war. We must not forget that only a small part of England's wealth lies in her agricultural resources, whereas in the case of countries like Germany, as long as the enemy is not actually inside the borders, no material damage is done to agrarian interests. England's wealth is based on her international trade, on her widespread system of credits, on fictive values, the assessment of which depends upon undisturbed human labour in all parts of the world. People knew that a great Continental war would be bound to play havoc with all the commercial hypotheses on which the estimates of British wealth were based and this knowledge brought ruin in its train, so that persons in England who only a few days before had been millionaires, suddenly found themselves doubtful as to whether they any longer possessed a penny.

Sir Edward Grey saw in the outbreak of the war nothing short of the collapse of his foreign policy. Up to the very last moment he was in council with Sir William Tyrrell, pondering whether some method could not be found of warding off the disaster. Even as late as the morning of August 1, after Germany had already declared war against Russia, he got Sir William Tyrrell to tell me that he hoped that he would be able that afternoon to lay before me a proposal which would enable both Germany and England to remain out of the conflict. In reply to my question as to the nature of the proposal, Sir William answered with another question, and asked me whether Germany, if France did not attack her, would also remain neutral ; this I took to mean that Germany should in that case not attack France. He had, however, meant that Germany should in that event remain quite neutral. (He hastened to Sir Edward Grey, who then put the same question to me by telephone, speaking from the room where the Cabinet was at that moment assembled.) Shortly afterwards I got Sir William Tyrrell to correct the error.

When I visited Sir Edward Grey that afternoon, he spoke to me, as he had often done before, about the question of Belgian neutrality, the preservation of which was a matter to which he and the Cabinet, he said, attached the greatest importance. At the same time he expressed his regret at the answer given by Herr von Jagow with regard to this matter, an answer which was the very opposite of the assurances given by the French. He tentatively raised the question, too, whether it would not be possible for Germany and France to confront each other in arms without attacking each other. In answer to my question whether he could undertake any guarantee for the behaviour of the French in such a contingency, he could give me no satisfactory answer. I saw that he himself was convinced of the impossibility of keeping two fully equipped armies facing each other inactive for months at a time.

When I asked him whether England would remain neutral if Germany refrained from infringing Belgian neutrality, he was unable to give me any definite answer. He repeatedly came back to this matter of Belgian neutrality and, just as did Mr. Asquith shortly afterwards, pointed out that Great Britain regarded the demand for the neutrality of Belgium and the protection of the northern coast of France as absolutely essential.

In the meantime our troops had marched into Luxemburg, an action which I argued was justified by the fact that the railway lines in that state were the property of the Prussian State. The infringement of the neutrality of Luxemburg had already sufficed to create a painful impression in London and to bring about a revulsion in the hitherto favourable feeling towards us. When it was followed by the news of the breach of Belgian neutrality, this proved the last straw. In a state of great excitement Sir Edward Grey declared to me in answer to my representations to him on the subject, ' It is not a question of territorial integrity. It is a question of neutrality.' He declined to discuss the matter any further with me. On the 1st and 2nd of August, the decisive meetings of the Cabinet took place. The hitherto peaceful mood had given place to one that was the very reverse. On Sunday, the 2nd of August, Sir Edward Grey for the first time gave M. Cambon a promise that he would under certain circumstances stand by France. On Monday, the 3rd of August, Sir Edward Grey delivered his famous speech in favour of war, and on the 4th of August came Great Britain's declaration of war.

Early on the Sunday, before the Cabinet's last decisive session, I had been to Mr. Asquith to try and win him over to take a neutral attitude. The Prime Minister was deeply moved and spoke of a war with Germany as ' quite unthinkable.' ' It would be very unpopular in this country,' he said. He did not, however, give me any definite assurances.

That England would have remained neutral had we refrained from infringing Belgian neutrality is hardly likely. I think, however, that, in view of the strong sympathy for Germany there was in England at that time, I should have succeeded in restraining the government from intervening, at least for a while. Perhaps the British Cabinet might even have held its hand until the decisive battle had been fought. One adversary we certainly had at the Foreign Office in the person of Sir Arthur Nicolson. From the very beginning Nicolson was in favour of England's taking a hand in the war and had contrived to influence Sir Edward Grey in this direction. In the Cabinet Winston Churchill is said to have been strongly opposed to Great Britain's remaining neutral.

After the declaration of war and before my departure, I went to Sir Edward Grey's house, at his special wish, to say goodbye. On this occasion the Minister gave me to understand that England hoped that the war might be over as quickly as possible and said that he would always be ready to mediate in the event of our not achieving the successes we hoped for.

' We don't want to crush Germany,' were his words.

My dispatches and the tenor of my repeated urgent warnings shield me from the reproach that I had not foreseen and predicted the development of events. Although it was the Russian mobilization that had from a military point of view precipitated the war, it was all along clear, and I never made any secret of my conviction of the fact, that Russia would not a second time, as she did in the case of Bosnia, climb down at the threat of Germany's ' gleaming armour,' and look on with folded arms while the Serbian army was butchered by Austria. From the political standpoint, therefore, it was Austria's assault on Serbia that precipitated the world war. Everything else had to follow as a matter of course, unless Russia, which, as everybody knows, has repeatedly waged war for the liberation of its Slav brethren of the Orthodox Church, had been willing to renounce once and for all its theocratic leadership and forfeit for ever its influence in the Balkans.

Passages omitted in the revised text are here given in square brackets. The passages inserted in the later text but not occurring in the first text have been indicated by the use of round brackets in the text itself.

Omitted p. 7, line 4 from bottom, after " propaganda."

[On my return from Silesia on July 5, I had a conversation with the Under-Secretary of State (Herr Zimmermann) shortly before my train left. He told me that a letter had just arrived from the Emperor of Austria to the effect that Vienna now intended to put an end to the intolerable state of things on the Serbian frontier by energetic action. The Under-Secretary seemed to think that if war was now after all inevitable for us in consequence of the unfriendly attitude of Russia, it would perhaps be better to have it now rather than later. I did not fail to express serious scruples as to the wisdom of this view and pointed out that warlike action on the part of Austria against Serbia would undoubtedly bring the world-war in its train.]

Omitted p. 11, last line, after " line of action."

[and that both His Majesty the Emperor and the Imperial Chancellor had declared that it did not matter if a war with Russia should result.]

p. 12, line 13 from top, after " on that point."

[When on another occasion I drew Sir Edward Grey's attention to the advantages which the neutrality of England would bring him and pointed out that he would then be in a position to throw his word with much more weight into the scale, he replied that his position would be stronger if he took part in the war, as he would then be able to withdraw at any time. England's intention was, he said, not to crush Germany but only to protect France.]

DELUSIONS

(Notes made in January 1915)

I

IN a famous chapter of his *Reflections*, Prince Bismarck, commenting on the Triple Alliance, observes that it is no part of the function of the German Empire to call upon its subjects to shed their blood and spend their substance in order to help its neighbours to a realisation of their wishes. The maintenance of the Austro-Hungarian monarchy as a strong and independent Great Power he regards as necessary for the balance of power in Europe, a necessity to which Germany might with a good conscience sacrifice the cause of peace, should need arise. But Vienna should refrain, he says, from deducing from its alliance with Germany any claims that went beyond this degree of insurance, claims beyond the scope and intention of the treaty. The first Chancellor had, it is clear, conceived the treaty with Austria in an exclusively defensive sense, first as a safeguard against an attack on two fronts and in the second place to secure Austria against the danger of attack from Russia. The text of the treaty confirms this interpretation of its object, and there is nothing in it that implies that Germany ought to feel herself bound to support her ally in a policy that goes beyond the framework of the treaty in pursuit of warlike and adventurous aims.

Prince Bismarck has elsewhere specially warned German statesmen against allowing any irreparable breach to arise between Berlin and Petrograd, if for no other reason than at least to prevent the growth in Vienna of claims that the Austrians might think they could make on the services of their German ally, either in the form of extensions of the *casus foederis* (which according to the published text provides only for the repulse of a Russian attack on Austria) or in the attempt to substitute for the said *casus foederis* an arrangement which would make Germany the protagonist of Austro-Hungarian interests in the Balkans and the Near East.

The first Chancellor was well aware that if we unconditionally championed Austria-Hungary's special interests in the Balkans, our action would probably lead to an irreparable breach with Russia. It is well known, too, that the disappointments which Russia thought she had experienced at our hands at the Balkan Congress led Czar Alexander II. to send his highly esteemed uncle a letter containing certain veiled threats and that Kaiser Wilhelm thereupon deemed it advisable to offer his nephew an opportunity for a discussion and reconciliation, the meeting taking place at Alexandrovo. At a later period, Germany's relations with Russia repeatedly passed through acute stages ; but although military men urged a preventive war on the ground that in a few years Russia would have completed her preparations, Bismarck never felt himself called upon to adopt such a course. On the contrary, he once declared that should he ever demand money for such a purpose, he hoped the Reichstag would refuse to vote him the necessary grants.

Our geographical position made it seem advisable to Bismarck to keep tacking between Austria-Hungary and Russia. In other words, he promised to protect the one while avoiding any breach with the other, a policy that was the more possible as there was *no real conflict of interests between Germany and Russia.* On the contrary, the two countries had many interests in common. They were, moreover, linked together by their common loyalty to the monarchical principle. Nor should it ever be forgotten that Russia had no interest whatever in helping the French to secure their *revanche*, as the possession of Alsace-Lorraine and the destruction of Germany would inevitably annihilate the premises on which were based France's subservience and generosity towards Russia. As Russian statesmen could hardly afford to destroy the *revanche* idea of the French, Russia could not but regard with repugnance anything that tended towards the disintegration and obliteration of this French ideal. This was one of the reasons why Russia did not wish to wage war against us. Just as little, on the other hand, could she consent to let France be destroyed, unless she wished to have afterwards to confront us single-handed and to be dependent upon us.

The assumptions on which the alliance with Austria was based afterwards underwent a not inconsiderable modification ; the probability of Germany's having to face a war on two fronts had in course of time become smaller and smaller, owing partly to the decrease

of the birth rate in France and partly to the diversion of Russia's
attention to her interests in Asia. The policy of Prince Gortshakoff,
a statesman who aimed at assuring for Russia a preponderant
position in the European comity of nations in the sense previously
advocated by Nicholas I., had been replaced by a policy of Russian
imperialism directed against Japan and England. It was not
Germany but Austria that was threatened by Russia, Petrograd
regarding the Dual Monarchy as hostile to the free development of
the Serbians.

The most delicate point in Russia's European policy was at that
time, and still is, the European Orient. The world of Slav Orthodoxy
had grown accustomed to regard the Czar as its Protector and
Supreme Head, not only in political and intellectual but also to some
extent in ecclesiastical affairs. This mission, generally known as the
Protectorship of Orthodoxy, ' has become indissolubly associated
with the crown of the Autocrat of all the Russias,' says Prince
Trubetzkoi in his book, *Russia as a Great Power*. Nor should we
forget that, in contrast to the rationalist constitutions of the
Western Powers, there clings to such semi-Oriental states as Russia
a marked theocratic character. The position of the Czar in the eyes
of his own people rests to some extent on the mystic nimbus which
surrounds the Russian crown by virtue of its function as the Protector
of orthodoxy and Slavdom, and it is clear that the Czar could not
renounce this mission without forfeiting much of his prestige and,
perhaps, even endangering his throne. In addition to this fact, there
are the bonds of a common creed and kindred blood and a tradition
which has its roots in the history of Russia—a country whose culture
dates back to Byzantium—to the effect that the Russian Czar is the
lineal successor of the East Roman Emperors. The Byzantine
double eagle still stands in the Russian coat of arms, and the many
wars that Russia has waged for the liberation of her orthodox
brethren lead us to conclude that Russia would refuse to sacrifice the
Serbs, even though we brand them, one and all, as ' assassins of
princes.'

In 1908, during the Bosnian annexation crisis, we only just managed
with the greatest difficulty to steer clear of war, mainly because Russia
had been weakened in the war with Japan. Our experience on that
occasion ought to have made us doubly cautious, if we were really
opposed to going to war. In 1908 it was not Serbia herself that was
at stake, but a province that Russia had conceded to the Austrians

in the Treaty of Reichstadt and which, as a matter of fact, had been in the possession of Austria since 1876. Nevertheless, the final incorporation of this province was regarded in Petrograd as a humiliation for Russia and aroused much indignation. The resentment Russia felt against us and Austria-Hungary never altogether died out. It led to increased armaments, and the new military grants made necessary by the new battalions were coupled with a frank statement that Russia would not a second time give way to the ' shining armour.' It cannot be said that Russian statesmen ever for a moment left us in doubt as to their attitude. They regarded the attack on Serbia as a *casus belli*, a ' question of life and death,' as M. Sazonov put it, and they were the better able to adopt this attitude as after their reconciliation with Japan, their treaty of 1907 with England concerning Asiatic questions had relieved them of all anxiety as to Russian policy in the Far East. The Austro-Hungarian attack on Serbia, undertaken as it was with Germany's support, could not but be interpreted in Russia as a challenge and be given a fitting answer, as otherwise the Czardom, which rests not on the support of democrats and Jews but on that of the ' genuine Russians,' *i.e.*, on the Nationalist-orthodox parties, would have found the ground slipping from beneath its feet. It was therefore incomprehensible from the very beginning that German statesmen should seriously believe in the ' localization of the conflict ' they talked about.

To this argument my opponents retort that the attack on Serbia was an attempt to inflict a righteous punishment for the murder of the Archduke.

But the murder at Serajevo was only one of the many occurrences that characterised the tension that had been in existence for years between Austria-Hungary and Serbia. From national as well as economic reasons this tension grew more and more marked as time went on. The only question, then, is whether an appeal to arms was really necessary for the maintenance of our ' ally's ' position, and whether any German interest was sufficiently affected to warrant our waging a world war.

The ' Greater Serbia ' movement—which was the immediate cause of the crime and to which Austria intended to administer the *coup de grâce*—is rooted in national affinities that bind together the inhabitants of Serbia, Montenegro, Bosnia and, if one overlooks the difference of creed, Croatia and Dalmatia as well. The more advanced a people's civilization and culture, the stronger becomes their national feeling and the more pronounced their need of a co-ordinated state life, of a common organization and development. Such a movement cannot be killed by mere violence. And if for political reasons the sole radical solution, viz., the organization of a common state, seems out of the question, statesmen must nevertheless continue to reckon with such a movement. The Hapsburg monarchy, a conglomeration of states resting altogether upon a dynastic and historical basis, has to reckon with such nationalist currents in other parts of its dominions. Movements which go in Italy by the name of *irredenta* are to be found among the Italians of Trieste and the Trentino, among the Rumanians in Transylvania, among the Galician Ruthenians, who are constantly ogling in the direction of Russia, and even among the Pan-Germans of the Sudetic and Alpine lands. The Magyars and the Czechs alone have no such centrifugal tendencies, because they are all included within the Monarchy. In this heterogeneity is to be found the germ of decay and weakness, a warning against any policy of main force, for the fragile structure of the Dual Monarchy is not equal to the strain such a policy involves. The stability of a state depends upon the power of a unifying idea and upon the ethical strength immanent in this idea. But in Austria-Hungary there is neither a common ideal nor a common language. Bismarck had this fact in mind when he wrote that he had an almost superstitious dread of interweaving German interests too intimately with the destiny of Austria, an idea, by the way, that Napoleon III. had also expressed in somewhat similar words.

A campaign against Serbia, even if successful, would not have put an end to the Greater Serbia movement, but would at most have only checked it for a time. The amalgamation of the Serbo-Croats into one people and the extension of Serbia to the sea were movements that in the long run it was just as impossible to frustrate as the movement towards Italian unity. To delay such movements by skilful manoeuvring was all that could be hoped. Austria proper, that is to say, the part of it that formerly belonged to the German Bund, the Sudetic and Alpine lands, would have kept their full integrity, as would also the Magyar region, and both would have had to seek contact with us, even had they not had the trying Jugo-Slav connection to put up with ; the national tendencies of our common Germanic blood and the clash of interests with the Magyars and Slavs both point to such a union.

Even had the Serbo-Croats broken away from Austria, Germany could still reckon on the German-Austrians and Magyars being drawn towards her. At any rate, German interests by no means demanded the extermination of the Serbs. The Serbian affair was, on the contrary, one that concerned only the private interests of Austria-Hungary and the localisation of the conflict was certainly justifiable in so far as it did not concern us in the least. Whatever way out of the difficulty the Vienna statesmen liked to find, they had not the faintest right to undertake a war counting on our assistance. The annihilating defeat which Austria has since suffered at the hands of the Serbs is a dreadful judgment on their insane policy. San Giuliano rightly characterized this policy as adventurous, dangerous and aggressive, and as lying outside the terms of the Triple Alliance. To-day this policy is universally condemned in Austria itself. San Giuliano declined to associate himself with it at a time when Franz Ferdinand was still alive—clear proof that political and not ethical reasons were responsible for the attitude adopted by Vienna. Which, I ask, was more important for Germany, the suppression—provided all went well—of the Greater Serbian movement in Bosnia or the avoidance of a world war in which Anglo-German relations, which had just been improved and consolidated, must inevitably be ruined ?

Had not Italian unity been achieved by much the same violent means as those employed in Serbia ? Is it not exactly the same thing that is now happening among the South Slavs as happened in 1848, 1859 and 1866 in Italy ? There, too, the Austrians in the Lombardo-Venetian provinces tried with fire, sword and gallows and the notorious ' Bankrl '[1] to gag the national movement. Did not the Conservatives in Prussia try to get their government to espouse the cause of Austrian imperial rule on the Mincio, in order thus to throttle what they called the ' revolution ' ? In their fight for liberty, the Italians, like the Serbs, used bombs and daggers to obtain their political aims, not scrupling to abolish the Divine Right both of kings and of the Holy Father. Did a consideration of such facts induce us to decline any alliance with Italy or did we, because an Italian named Orsini hurled a bomb at Napoleon, think ourselves bound to declare war on Italy ? Is not the unity of modern Italy based on actions just as revolutionary as were the tendencies of the

---

[1] A wooden bench to which ' rebels ' and ' traitors ' were bound face downwards before being flogged. (Tr.)

Greater Serbian movement against Austria ? Are there ever in politics absolutely stable conditions which ought to last forever and which cannot be changed according to the changing needs of nations ? Nor are treaties everlasting, being concluded only for definite purposes and for definite periods—*rebus sic stantibus*, to use Bismarck's phrase. Let the reader who is in doubt about such principles consult Bismarck's famous letter to General von Gerlach. In this document the Great Chancellor discusses not only the theory of hereditary right but also speaks of the necessity of negotiating agreements with movements, dynasties and states branded as revolutionary, should the interests of the state demand it.

What on earth made the German people plunge into a world war to fight against the South Slavs' movement for national unity ? The Austrians could perhaps for a time have checked the Jugo-Slavs' enthusiasm for their cause. Crush it or stamp it out they could not.

What business had Germany to avenge the murder of an Austrian Archduke ? Even if ten Archdukes had been murdered and King Peter got rid of into the bargain, together with his offspring, it would have been no concern of ours. If the Austrians chose to send their Heir Apparent into Bosnia to run the gauntlet of assassins in ' streets lined with bomb-throwers,' it was no affair of ours to take part in the so-called reprisals. The fact is that Germany, instead of pursuing *Realpolitik*, here embarked on a will-o'-the wisp policy of sentimentality. ' In a policy of sentimentality there is no such thing as reciprocity,' says Bismarck in one of his letters to Gerlach. ' Sentimentality in politics is a purely Prussian peculiarity ; every other country takes its country's interests as the sole standard of its actions, no matter how it may drape these actions in legal or sentimental motives. Other countries accept our fine sentiments, exploit them to their hearts' content and then build on the hope that these sentiments will not permit us to escape from the meshes they have cast around us. Nor do they even thank us afterwards for our trouble, but only regard us as a sort of useful dupe.'

Was Count Aerenthal grateful to us for the service we rendered him at the time of the annexation crisis. Later on, his one idea was to withdraw from our guardianship and stand on his own feet. He caused reports to be spread to the effect that the tension that at that time had arisen between Russia and Austria had been solely a reaction resulting from the conflict of Anglo-German interests. To-day the

Austrians are already saying that Germany used Austria as a cat's-paw, and drove the Dual Monarchy into the war because she herself wanted it. Feeling against Germany is growing in Austria from day to day ; the Austrians are saying that they are being forced to shed their blood in a war waged for German interests, and Austrian diplomatists are trying to create the impression abroad that Austria was in July 1914 inclined to come to an understanding, but that Germany had pressed for war.

A further cause of the tension that came about between Austria-Hungary and Serbia lay in economic questions. For years before the war the Serbs, mainly an agrarian nation, had been plagued with all sorts of frontier chicanery. Under the influence of the all-powerful Magyar agrarians, the Hungarian government tried to prevent the import of Serbian products. Serbian cattle, for instance, would be left at Semlin on the border for days without water, and a specially high tariff was devised to prevent the import of Serbian grain. For this reason Serbia longed for a harbour of her own and after the Balkan war tried to obtain some such outlet on the Adriatic. During the Ambassadors' Conference in London, Austria tried to thwart Serbia's wishes wherever possible, Germany invariably giving Austria her unconditional support in such affairs. My one and only task at the Conference was to back up Austria's wishes. In the case of Italy's demands we were far more reserved, out of considerations based on our dynastic sympathies for Greece. As a matter of fact, Austria and not Germany was the leading power of the Triple Alliance at the Conference in question.

The principality of Albania, a state which, as M. Paul Cambon foresaw, was destined to be but short-lived, was called into being against the wishes of Russia and France. Both these nations would have preferred to see Albania divided up between Serbia and Greece. The Serbs were denied access to the Adriatic and Montenegro was again, though not without difficulty, got out of Scutari. Each of these questions in turn threatened to cause a European conflagration, unless Russia gave way. Count Mensdorff was supported in London by Baron Giesl, a well-known enemy of the Serbs, who was afterwards Austria's Minister at Belgrade. Count Mensdorff repeatedly gave it to be understood that his government was prepared, in case of a refusal, to take up arms, naturally with Germany's most obedient support.

During my ambassadorship I repeatedly warned our government

against any such far-reaching subservience to Austria. The Kaiser at first shared my opinion that it would be better to split up Albania between Serbia and Greece, but the German Foreign Office, as usual, gave its decision unconditionally in the sense desired by Austria. The Ballplatz had only one end in view. It was determined, if it could, to manacle both Serbia and Montenegro.

In all these questions, Russia, the natural protector of Serbia, yielded to the pressure we brought to bear. It was, however, the attitude of Sir Edward Grey that was the decisive factor. In order to preserve peace, the British Minister came forward as a mediator and was untiring in his efforts to induce his Russian friends to give way.

It is not difficult to imagine that Germany's attitude at the London Conference, the chief result of which was the creation of the principality of Albania under Austro-Italian protection, was hardly calculated to arouse any very strong feeling of gratitude in the Russian capital.

The diplomat is not a spy any more than is the military or naval attaché. Any attempt to get hold of the secrets of the government to which he is accredited by illicit means, such as bribery and the like, would be dangerous if not fatal. He would be delivering himself into the hands of doubtful persons and would run the risk of being exposed and made impossible. First and foremost it is necessary for him to gain the confidence of the leading people of the country to which he is accredited. He should, if possible, be friends with the monarch and his chief ministers and should be in touch with leading circles, not only at the Court but also in commercial life, in countries where these circles play a prominent part. If he does this, he can gain influence and will be able to act as a mediator. If he has the gift of arousing personal sympathies, he can also win people's goodwill for the country he represents. Above all, he must be a man of keen discrimination ; he must be a judge both of men and affairs and be able to utilise both for his own ends. With these qualifications he will be able to serve his government and give it right counsel, always provided, of course, that his government is willing to listen to him and does not place obstacles in his path. It is not the ambassador, however, but the government that decides the policy to be adopted. It is the government that is responsible for the course things take. It is only when an ambassador's reports are based on false assumptions that he can be held to bear a measure of responsibility. If his warnings and counsels are disregarded and if he is given no support, he deserves no reproach if the policy pursued proves disastrous. It is not that our diplomats are, as a rule, inferior to those of other countries ; it is the method pursued by our statesmen that is wrong. Instead of having a clear programme that takes into account the power and the interests and feelings of our neighbours and fellow-men, and that does not overlook the impression that our attitude is likely to make upon them, we have been apt to attach too much importance to displays of strength and to mere outward successes that flattered our vanity. We have tried by dint of threats, sometimes by means of a dig in the ribs and sometimes by a flourish of trumpets, to intimidate and impress. These diplomatic methods created an atmosphere of uneasiness and this uneasiness, in its turn, found expression in utterances that were interpreted by us as the outcome of hostile intentions.

'Loyalty to our allies' and 'comradeship in arms' are undoubtedly valuable stock phrases, but they in no wise exhaust the requirements of a practical policy. Such stock expressions are all very well for use at Kaiser's birthday banquets or at the anniversary celebrations of Veterans' Associations, but they by no means suffice for the political orientation of a country like Germany. During the London Conference I strongly urged that greater consideration should be shown for the feelings of Russia and that we should refrain from identifying ourselves unconditionally with Austria's anti-Serbian policy. I argued that if the Vienna Cabinet felt sure enough of our unquestioning support, this policy would sooner or later lead to a collision with Russia and to a catastrophe. This was inevitable seeing that Russia, rightly or wrongly, would not renounce her rôle as protector of her Serbian brethren. Russian statesmen had never for a moment left us in doubt on this point. In politics, as in life, as M. Paul Cambon once said to me, it is essential that one be able to look at things from the standpoint of the other side.

The policy pursued by us last summer when we put 5,000,000 German soldiers at the disposal of the old Emperor Franz Joseph to avenge the murder of a member of his family reminds one of the wars of bygone ages when feuds between princely families over some personal difference devastated whole realms ; it smacks of the wars of the Crusaders, which were undertaken to liberate the tomb of our Lord from the Infidel, or of the Trojan War, that was waged to avenge the wounded honour of King Menelaus. But neither the murder at Serajevo nor the subjugation of Serbia by Austria concerned German interests one jot, and the attitude adopted by us was the last disastrous consequence of a mistaken notion of our treaty obligations towards Austria, and the pursuit of a policy which in this form entailed many more hazards than advantages.

I was always in favour of protecting Austria, but was equally emphatic concerning our duty of maintaining an attitude of reserve in the Serbian question. The latter I looked upon as being Vienna's private affair. We should not have left any doubt, either in Vienna or in Petrograd, on this point, if we meant to avoid a world war and to safeguard peace.

Far better to have had no alliance at all than one that brought in its train more peril than profit.

The idea of taking military action against Serbia was, moreover, by no means new. It was a topic that had often been discussed in Vienna and seems to have assumed a more definite form in the period following the Peace of Bucharest, a Peace which was concluded under protest from Austria. By the terms of this Peace, Serbia's frontiers had been extended at the cost of Bulgaria, whose leading statesman, M. Daneff, had unfortunately allowed himself to be duped by the flattery of the Austrian and Hungarian statesmen into waging a second Balkan war, a war which ended in the defeat of Bulgaria and the estrangement of Rumania from Austria. The question now was to find a remedy for the pessimism prevailing in Austria and for her stagnating commerce. How could the prestige of the Dual Monarchy be refurbished and the reproaches directed against Count Berchtold's policy be robbed of their sting ? In finding an answer to this question the Austrian statesmen happened to overlook the fact that a policy of recoupment in Serbia must needs lead to a conflict with Russia and end in the disintegration of the Dual Monarchy. The numerous cases of high treason at the beginning of the war and even the open desertion of whole units to the enemy show how little the hearts of the Austrian Slavs were in this war. In Galicia and Bosnia the gallows-tree was called upon to play its gruesome part as an enforcer of patriotism, and in Prague nobody showed the slightest shame at openly espousing the cause of Russia.

The Austrians overlooked the fact that their monarchy possessed neither of the factors essential for a policy of main force, for Austria lacked both homogeneity of construction and a common ideal, two things that a nation must possess if it is to accomplish extraordinary achievements. An army made up of Magyars, Czechs, Poles, Ruthenians, Rumanians, Croats and Serbs, was without the ethical force that inspired other nations fighting for a national idea. When two state organisms clash, the stronger and more stable of the two must triumph over the weaker. The Austro-Hungarian army, which is only held together by dynastic bonds of allegiance to a common ruler, can therefore not stand up against the assault of a really united nation. The Austrian defeats that have taken place of late are ascribable in part, it is true, to the inferiority of their leaders as well as of their troops. But they are due, too, in no small measure to the law of development, a law that has always prevailed in the history of the world. The rule of the Austrian black and yellow flag had perforce to give way before a nation inspired with a national ideal. Just as the Austrians, despite their military successes, were obliged to withdraw from Italy, and just as Austria, despite all her measures of violence, had to give up Hungary and proved unable to keep the leadership in the German question, so the Jugo-Slavs will in their turn, despite the help Germany is now lending Austria, continue to push forward in their own independent national development. ' In its methods of revision,' says Bismarck, ' history observes a logic that is more exact than any Prussian Auditing Office ! '

Germany's policy reminds one of Czar Nicholas who gave way to romantic dreams of legitimacy and allowed his armies in 1848 to be used for the suppression of the Hungarian rebellion. It is notorious that Austria never felt grateful to him for his services !

The terms in which the ultimatum was couched left no doubt that the Vienna Cabinet wanted Serbia not to accept but to reject its demands. The Austrian diplomats were actually afraid lest Serbia might accept their terms. Baron Giesl, the Austrian Minister at Belgrade, had already packed his trunks and was ready to leave for Vienna when the Serbian answer arrived. Without stopping to examine the document, he straightway declared that it was unsatisfactory, although it accepted almost everything that Austria had demanded, and made a reservation only on one point, viz.,—the demand that Austro-Hungarian officials should take part in the criminal investigations on Serbian soil. If there had been a real desire for peace on the part of Austria, it would have been an easy matter for her to have made the Serbian reply a basis for further negotiations. But there was no such desire. Both in Vienna and in Berlin the men who were pulling the strings *wanted war with Serbia*. The movements of Russian troops and a remark made by M. Sazonov at Constanza, ' We shall only go to war if Austria attacks Serbia,' show that St. Petersburg already suspected Vienna's intentions. As a matter of fact the policy adopted by Austria in Serbia had for some time past been the cause of a growing feeling of hostility in St. Petersburg, not only towards Vienna, but also, indirectly, towards Berlin.

II.

Public opinion in Germany is much exercised to discover the reasons that induced Great Britain to take part in the war. People ask whether Great Britain was not the real instigator of the war. They wonder whether England brought about the war in order to crush Germany, or whether, seeing that she could have prevented it, she did not merely let it come about, with the same end in view.

When in November 1912 I entered upon my duties as Ambassador at London, Sir Edward Grey and M. Cambon were still exchanging views as to how England and France could collaborate for mutual protection in case of an attack or in case war should threaten. The correspondence that then took place between these two statesmen has since been published. The agreements which had from time to time been arranged between the military and naval staffs of the two countries, although without binding force, served as the basis of the new understanding. This was not an alliance, but an agreement of a defensive nature ; it was only in the event of an attack that it would become actual ; no definite pledges were given on either side. Our anti-English attitude during the Boer War,—the lively sympathies of the German people for colonists of a kindred race settled in far-away South Africa,—Count Bülow's notorious speech, coupled with his attitude towards Mr. Chamberlain, whose attempts at bringing about a *rapprochement* had met with such a chilly reception, and especially Germany's new naval policy,—all these things had led to a feeling of hostility in England ; and this feeling was certainly growing. In addition to all this came the personal likes and dislikes of King Edward, who made no secret of his fondness for everything French. This was the soil on which the wish for a *rapprochement* with France sprang up. France, too, at that time felt herself threatened by Germany. Thus came about the Morocco-Egypt agreement, an agreement that later on was destined to form the basis of the Triple Entente. Throughout the Morocco affair our attitude wavered between approval and threats. No one could tell what we were aiming at, whether it was war we wanted or whether our object was to extend our colonial power on the basis of a peaceful agreement. The attitude adopted by us in 1905 and 1911 towards France had no doubt led to a strengthening of the *rapprochement* between the two Powers. It now helped to foster the ill-feeling that was growing up against us in England as the result of our naval policy. England, in the interests of the balance of power in Europe and of her own independence, and moved by a desire to protect her own coasts, could not tolerate any further extension of the German sphere of influence in Western Europe. The maintenance of France as an independent country with undiminished power was of vital interest to Great Britain. English statesmen more and more clearly recognised that a repetition of the events of 1870 was incompatible with British interests, but did not allow themselves to be led into making agreements that were anything more than technical in their nature. It was clearly stipulated that these agreements were only to come into force in the event of a German attack on France, an attack of which, as I constantly pointed out in my London dispatches, both French and English lived in constant dread. That this *rapprochement* and the agreements referred to were anything more than an attempt on the part of France and England to make themselves secure against the vast armaments of Germany, or that these agreements were intended for aggressive purposes has never been shown by anything that has yet been published. Nor was it in the interests of Great Britain to free the French from the German nightmare, seeing that it was this danger from her eastern neighbour that kept France so subservient to England. Just as little, however, can British foreign policy get on without the pressure that we exercise on Russia, as Russia would otherwise obtain a free hand in Asia, with inconvenient consequences for England. These simple considerations suffice to show how unlikely it was that bellicose aims could be included in the British programme.

Mr. Lloyd George's well-known speech made in the summer of 1911 was delivered merely to warn us that statesmen in London were feeling disturbed by our failure to send any explanation as to why we had sent the *Panther* to Agadir, and were beginning to believe that Germany intended war.

When I got to London in November 1912, the First Balkan War had just ended with the victory of the allied states over Turkey, and the partition of the Turkish inheritance had again summoned up the spectre of a European war.

Shortly after my arrival Lord Haldane, a close friend of Sir Edward Grey's, called on me. He assured me that England wanted peace and friendship with Germany and that he hoped that with my help it would be possible to strengthen the relations between the two countries and remove all misunderstandings. He would, however, he said, at once draw my attention to one important point : England could never permit the destruction or the weakening of France. This was a vital question for Great Britain. She must hold a protecting hand over France just as Germany did over Austria. As Great Britain might through France be drawn into a European war, the basis of any understanding between Great Britain and Germany must necessarily be a perfectly unambiguous policy of peace. England, said Lord Haldane in conclusion, wished just as little to attack Germany as to encourage any *revanche* idea among the French.

During my stay in London, many people in high places expressed similar views in conversation with me. Both in my dispatches and by word of mouth I repeatedly drew attention to this important point, and time after time emphasised the fact that Germany would have to reckon with Great Britain as an opponent should France be attacked.

There could be no possible doubt as to what England's attitude would be and it was therefore quite incomprehensible to me how the German Chancellor, in spite of Sir Edward Grey's repeated warnings and my own written and oral reports, could be so taken by surprise by the British declaration of war.

My view that the leading principle of British foreign policy was in the first place to maintain peace and in the second place resolutely to protect France, was shared by my two colleagues of the Triple Alliance.

Prompted by the wish to maintain peace, Sir Edward Grey soon after my arrival suggested the London Conference of Ambassadors. This exchange of views had only one object, viz. to prevent the outbreak of a European war into which England feared she might be drawn. If the British Minister for Foreign Affairs had wanted war, these tedious negotiations would have been quite superfluous. While the negotiations were going on there was no lack of opportunity to set the match to the pile, and it was chiefly due to Sir Edward Grey's activity as a mediator that a collision was at that time prevented, and this despite the fact that Germany invariably identified herself with the claims put forward by the Ballplatz.

Anglo-German co-operation during this conference formed the basis for the understanding aimed at by Sir Edward Grey, an understanding which I afterwards did my utmost to further. The British Government thus learned to trust our will for peace, and gradually came to take a more friendly view of our intentions. In other questions, too, the English were ready to meet Germany half-way. Simultaneously negotiations were being carried on between Germany and England for the settlement of our respective spheres of interest in Asia Minor, including the Bagdad Railway question, etc. Here, too, I found England ready to show us every consideration possible, and in the contract that was already drawn up ready for signature when the war broke out we got far more than the founders of the railway had ever dared to dream of. I succeeded, for example, in securing Basra as the terminus, after we had already given up all hope of such a thing.

A new treaty dealing with colonial questions in Africa was also agreed upon between us. It was already drawn up and was, at the wish of the British Government, to have been signed at the beginning of 1915, and published immediately. Owing to scruples felt by the German Government with regard to the publication, a proviso upon which the English laid particular stress, and one to which we objected on formal grounds, the treaty threatened to fall through. In this Colonial Treaty our Foreign Office found itself opposed by France. M. Paul Cambon left no stone unturned to put difficulties in the way of the new agreement, as he regarded it as an encroachment upon French interests.

Not only at Court and in official circles but also in society and in commercial circles, which in England have great influence, I everywhere found during my stay in England the most cordial friendliness and a sincere wish to come into closer relations with us. Everywhere and in ever-growing measure, I met with the warmest sympathy, and I finally succeeded in achieving a marked improvement in the mood towards Germany.

I was received as a guest of honour by great commercial cities ; at public dinners at which I presided thousands of pounds were subscribed by the British people present for various German charities, such as a Home for German Seamen and a German Hospital ; Oxford conferred upon me the degree of D.C.L., *honoris causa*, a compliment paid to none of my colleagues, with the exception of M. Cambon, the doyen of the Diplomatic Corps ; and, in every city and in all circles, I was received with the utmost courtesy and consideration. All this, I am told by wiseacres, was mere eyewash, a part of the myriad-headed conspiracy to deceive and mislead Germany.

The honorary degree of D.C.L. was conferred upon me at Oxford on the 3rd of June, 1914. The *Berliner Tageblatt* describes the ceremony as follows :

" Prince Lichnowsky to-day received the degree of D.C.L. *honoris causa* from the University of Oxford.   At the conferring of the degree, despite the *milieu* of venerable tradition, there was a typically English absence of formality.   The ceremony took only a few minutes and was held in a moderately filled hall, the doors of which were left open. The heads of the various colleges wore red or black gowns, as is usual in Germany, too, on such occasions.   In a great chair sat the Vice-Chancellor of the University, murmuring almost inaudibly Latin words pronounced like English.   The German Ambassador, wearing a red gown, was then led in by the Public Orator of the University.   The Public Orator delivered a long speech in Latin, praising the Prince's services to letters and emphasising the fact, amid the applause of those present, that the honour done to Prince Lichnowsky was a token of English admiration for German scholar-ship and for the German nation.   It sounded very fine to hear this Englishman's voice ring through this ancient hall of Oxford as he cried, ' Totam Germaniam animo salutamus.'   For a moment one had the feeling that an ambassador could really form a link between two nations.   We give the text [1] of the speech delivered by Prince Lichnowsky at the dinner given in his honour last evening at Oxford by the German Literary Society and the Anglo-German Club:

Ladies and Gentlemen,—I fully appreciate the honour which has

[1] Professor Fiedler of Oxford has been good enough to place his copy of Prince Lichnowsky's speech at the publishers' disposal, together with a trans-lation made in Oxford at the time, thus making possible an authentic and somewhat fuller version than that contained in the *Tageblatt*. (Tr.)

been conferred on me by the ancient and venerable University of Oxford in making me one of its Honorary Doctors, and I should like to take this opportunity of conveying to the authorities of the University an expression of my profound gratitude. At this morning's impressive ceremony, the red gown, the outward sign of my new dignity, was placed upon my shoulders in the historical surroundings of a hall whose walls bear witness to the fruitful educational activities of many centuries ; the impressive picture presented by the presence of so many representatives of the highest learning will remain for ever in my memory and remind me that a personal tie has been formed between the University of Oxford and myself and that from to-day I can count myself one of yourselves, and a member of the great community of British learning.

I am aware, gentlemen, that this distinction has not been conferred upon me on account of my attainments in the field of knowledge. It is probable, gentlemen, that I am not far wrong in the assumption that the great honour of making me a D.C.L. has been bestowed upon me with the purpose of encouraging the efforts I have made to become more closely acquainted with English life and English thought, and also to express approval of the political line I have followed. But above all, I believe it has been desired to mark the community of ideas which this celebrated University has maintained with German thought for centuries past by fostering and furthering German intellectual life. It is this ancient and constantly renewed intellectual connection that has given rise to the wish to confer upon the political representative of the German Empire in England an honour rarely, and only in exceptional cases, bestowed upon foreign diplomatic representatives. I can truly say that when the news reached me that from this time forward I should have the right to call myself an Hon. Doctor of the University of Oxford, the pleasure and the pride I felt were only exceeded by one other feeling and that was satisfaction at this real proof of your warm sympathy with German culture and with my German Fatherland. Professor Fiedler in his pregnant speech referred to the fact that the Emperor William is an Hon. D.C.L., and that exactly one hundred years ago His Majesty's great-grandfather was also made an Hon. Doctor at your University. The latter stayed here with his two sons, one of whom became King Frederick IV. and the other the Emperor Wilhelm I. Great events have happened during these hundred years. The balance of power has shifted and as a result the

PRINCE LICHNOWSKY (1912)

grouping of the Powers has also been changed. But the goal towards which the British and the German peoples were striving in those stormy times after years of fighting is still their aim to-day in the unclouded atmosphere of civic progress. Their ideal has remained the same. Then, as now, our Monarchs joined hands to maintain peace and to protect civic industry. Then, as now, both British and German policies were in agreement in the endeavour to secure for their peoples the blessings of undisturbed intellectual and economic development.

In those days Goethe still lived ; Schiller had been dead only a few years. A period of intellectual development and literary growth had preceded the period of political progress and the mighty awakening of Germany to the consciousness of her nationality. Our great poets had contributed towards arousing a sense of the ideals of mankind in the German people. By their immortal works they had greatly enhanced the intrinsic value of German culture and thus helped to found the proud sense of nationality. After a period of national listlessness they had laid the foundations for the great awakening which followed. It has often been debated whether there is any connection between the literary and political growth of a nation. I think I may say that they are necessarily parallel influences dependent one on the other (a view also shared by Treitschke), and that it is the feeling for the ideal instilled by the Universities, by the men of learning and the great poets, which makes a nation capable of aiming at national ideals, of having faith in itself and carrying out great political aims. Thus we see that the growth of intellectual power frequently precedes political action, and if, according to Friedrich Nietzsche, human culture depends on the dominance of ideas, the fostering of these ideas which crystallise into ideals, rests with the Universities. That is why political movements which pay homage to the national ideals are so often set in motion and carried out by the enthusiastic youth of the Universities. But the national conception which forms the intermediary stage between individuality and humanity reposes mainly on the community of the leading ideals which have received their character from our poets and historians and become embodied in our great monarchs, statesmen and generals, and in the foremost representatives of learning and the Arts.

If they are not to die, these ideals must be renewed and revived, remodelled and developed according to modern requirements ; for, as Nietzsche puts it, the living are not to be ruled by the dead. According to Helmholz it is the pure love of truth that leads to the greatest victories. By this we penetrate into the realm of the unknown.

This high task is undertaken by both the British and the German Universities, and it would therefore be idle to discuss which of their respective methods of teaching is to be preferred. I like to think that the one very happily completes the other, and that in this case, too, he only would err who pretends that he alone is the possessor of the genuine ring. The more German learning and literature are studied in Britain and British learning and literature in Germany, the more will the intellectual possessions and values of both nations become their common property. The two nations will thus be drawn nearer to one another in their inner lives. The foundation of a mutual appreciation based on the possession of the same ideals and a community of culture and ethics will be widened, and in this way the Universities will also help forward political aims.

I cannot sufficiently express the pleasure it gives me to see numbers of my youthful fellow-countrymen gathered here this evening whose mission it will some day be to help the German people to an understanding of British feeling and British customs and to spread among us a knowledge of the ideals which give to British culture its distinctive character and which thus govern the soul of the British nation. No one has depicted in more eloquent words than Matthew Arnold the magic of Oxford and the impetus given by Oxford to our aspirations towards higher aims.

" Steeped in sentiment as she lies, spreading her gardens to the moonlight, and whispering from her towers the last enchantments to the Middle Age, who will deny that Oxford, by her ineffable charm, keeps ever calling us nearer to the true goal of all of us, to the ideal, to perfection,—to beauty, in a word, which is only truth seen from another side ?—nearer, perhaps, than all the learning of Tübingen."

Nevertheless it was Matthew Arnold who in his well-known verses on Goethe showed a complete understanding of German intellectual life, and no one more than he led the way here in Oxford to an appreciation of German research and the German spirit. Hardly any other English poet has fostered and spread the love of German literature here in Oxford more than Matthew Arnold has done.

I am also especially pleased to know that a large number of German students meet in Oxford every year to worship at the shrine of British learning. Nor must I forget British sport, which finds so many followers in our midst and which conduces greatly to the moral and physical strengthening of the nation.   It may be said that the people who cultivate sports govern the world and will do so more and more.   I regret sincerely that I had not the privilege of studying here myself, but I hope to make up for it by letting my sons keep some terms.   I need not dwell on the merits of English Universities, they are known to us all.   They tend to the development of a strong personality and the formation of men of independence and character who are well fitted to be pioneers and to carry West European culture to the furthermost regions of the earth.

It is through British university life that the word " Gentleman " has gained the superlative meaning which enables it to be accepted by all nations as a standard of culture, so that one may say that the gentleman has conquered the entire civilised world.   To-day the term gentleman represents the generally accepted standard of social worth, by which all people are measured.   The standpoint of a gentleman has become part of the ethics of modern life, it is the " virtus " of to-day ; to use a German student's expression, the social manners of a gentleman represent the international " comment."

If I am rightly informed, Cecil Rhodes held this view when he became a leader of British Imperialism.   Rhodes also recognised the compatibility of British and German political needs, he recognised that there was a place in the sun for both, and he was further con- vinced of the near relationship of British and German culture, I may say of their mutual completion.   He thought that the Teutonic race on the foundation of Latin culture was fitted as was no other race to fulfil the mission of Western European civilisation.   He expressed this idea when he founded the scholarships to which we owe the presence here of many young Germans.   Cecil Rhodes, it is true, was above everything an Englishman, but his political and philosophical views were not hidebound by national prejudice or narrow political egoism ; nor did he belong to those idealogues who with mistaken humanitarianism and philanthropy would give to all races of man- kind the same political rights to assert themselves according to their own laws and desires.   He was of opinion that in the case of the whole of mankind the law held good that the fittest will survive.   He believed that mankind develops according to law and not according to discretion.

I am of opinion, gentlemen, that the roots of political ethics are to be found in the recognition of this law, in the extension and the

dominance of the most powerful and superior races, whose success
must simultaneously benefit and improve the whole of mankind.
Cecil Rhodes was of opinion that the whole of humanity would be
best served if the Teutonic peoples were brought nearer together and
would join hands for the purpose of spreading their civilisation to
distant regions.

In the presence of so many distinguished representatives of literature and learning I need not explain how deeply rooted among us in
Germany is the admiration we feel for the great names of British
poetry.   I will merely remind you that only a few weeks ago the
German Shakespeare Society celebrated its fiftieth anniversary.
This society is not only the first German society of its kind to have
been formed, for it has been followed by the Goethe, Dante, and
other similar societies, but it is also the only one which has been
successful in devoting itself solely to the study of a foreign poet.

The causes which have made it possible for a foreign poet to exercise so potent an attraction are manifold.   Primarily they lie in the
fact that in our feelings this greatest of British poets has already
almost become a German, and that the works of no other foreigner
have penetrated so deeply into the soul of the German people.
Heine says : " The only thing the Germans cannot forgive in Shakespeare is that he did not choose to be born in Germany."   This great
poet has special political attractions for us because of his outspoken
patriotism and national public feeling.   Besides this it has been in
his favour that England has always been regarded as the land of
political liberty and that here originated those constitutional rights
and that here was laid the foundation of those civic rights which
have spread victoriously throughout the whole of Europe.   Hence
it is that for us Shakespeare has become a political poet whom
we claim as our own together with Goethe and Schiller.

I fear, gentlemen, I have already taken up too much of your time,
and that I have exceeded the limits of an after-dinner speech.   I
wanted so much to tell you how I feel I ought to interpret my newly
acquired connection with this celebrated seat of learning and to say
that I shall look upon it as my duty in future to further and develop
as much as possible the relations between the University of Oxford
and the country which I have the honour to represent.   I rejoice to
find that the advanced study of the German language here is especially helpful to our aims, and this evening I have again noticed with
satisfaction how much our mother tongue is in evidence in this

University. The days are past when the Briton learnt no foreign language, and it is no longer a mark of the unadulterated Englishman that he should understand no foreign idiom. It is not very long ago that Prince Bismarck was said to have expressed the opinion that he distrusted every Englishman who spoke foreign languages ; he did not look upon him as a genuine Britisher, but as a colourless international type—to be regarded with suspicion. My experience has shown me that the present-day Englishman speaks German as well as we speak English, with this difference only, that the English are less venturesome than we in the region of foreign tongues. Many years ago Prince Bismarck in a letter to General von Gerlach complained that every Berliner felt proud when a real English jockey gave him the opportunity of torturing the Queen's English.

Finally, gentlemen, let me thank you once more for the great honour you have done me and for the very pleasant evening which I have been allowed to spend in your midst. I have to-night felt almost as though I were at Heidelberg or Göttingen. I beg you will drink with me to the health of the celebrated old University of Oxford as well as to that of the two Societies whose guests we are and to their continued successful work in helping forward British-German intellectual brotherhood."

Everyone who knows anything about life and conditions in England is aware of the important rôle played by public dinners and by the inevitable after-dinner speeches that accompany them. It is the only way a diplomat can get into touch with those City and commercial circles with whom social life does not ordinarily bring him into contact. If one is a guest of honour, one cannot remain silent when called upon to respond to the words of greeting and welcome addressed to one. On these occasions I as far as possible avoided touching on political topics, always laying chief stress on the commercial relations between our two countries, and the important interests Great Britain and Germany had in common. Such speeches contributed in no small degree towards creating good-feeling towards the country I represented, and my French colleague received instructions from his government to counteract what they called my ' propaganda ' by appearing more frequently at public functions.

In general it is agrarian countries and countries that have not yet found a national basis that are most inclined to be bellicose. Satiated nations with a widespread network of commercial relations always have more to lose than to gain by a war. It is inconceivable that a nation like the British, which has such a high standard of living, should wish to be disturbed both in its material interests and in its accustomed pleasures by the privations inseparable from war.

What had Great Britain to gain from a war with Germany ? Why should she want to destroy German trade, British trade being largely dependent upon trade with Germany ? In the year 1913, for example, the value of the goods imported into Great Britain from Germany was £80,500,000, while British exports to Germany amounted to £59,500,000. Among all the countries we dealt with, Great Britain's trade with us tops the list ; if one excludes the United States and the British colonies, Anglo-German trade represents the most important exchange of goods in the whole circle of British commerce. Apart from this, the British market is largely dependent on such German products as sugar, chemicals, silk goods, etc. A European war could not but have a disastrous effect on British prosperity, based as this prosperity was on international commercial values and not on agrarian or home products. This would be the case even in a war in which England did not directly participate. As for England's wanting to destroy our fleet, both British naval experts and statesmen, even before the war, were well aware that that would be no such easy task. They had become reconciled to the idea of a German fleet. They did not mind as long as our building programme did not exceed that laid down in the Navy Bill placed before the Reichstag in the Budget. The German fleet was certainly inconvenient to the British, but as long as we did not bring in any supplementary estimates, they did not let it worry them. British superiority was secure ; proposals like that for a naval holiday were allowed to drop without causing ill-feeling. I never discussed the fleet officially. I purposely avoided doing so, thus letting it be known that I regarded the naval estimates as a purely internal affair of Germany's. The British were willing to refrain from interfering with our colonial development, if for no other reason than because the colonies distracted our attention from the North Sea. This was shown, too, by their readiness to meet our wishes in the matter of the Portuguese colonies. England had the best colonies and needed no war with us to acquire new ones. Had she wanted to extend her colonial interests, the Portuguese protectorate would have afforded her an opportunity of doing so.

The outbreak of the war was in short an unspeakable catastrophe for Great Britain, even could she have been sure of crippling us.

It would have been downright madness from the British standpoint to bring about such a war.

England was ready to come to a full understanding with us and to enter into closer relations with us, always provided that her other friendships did not suffer in consequence, and on the understanding that Germany would pursue an unambiguous policy of peace. But we quitted this path when we induced Count Berchtold to strike at Serbia. Such a policy was bound, even though this was not our intention, to lead to a world war and to the collapse of all my efforts to bring about an understanding. For it was not to be expected, from reasons already explained, that the conflict could be localized.

' But if Sir Edward Grey had really wished to prevent war,' say my critics, ' Russia would have kept quiet.' Even if the British Foreign Minister had explicitly declared in Petrograd that England would not join in, Russia would nevertheless have moved. Things being as they were, she had no choice. Is it likely that a Great Power like Russia could allow another Power to prescribe a course of action in questions which she herself regarded as of vital importance ?

In a matter in which she regarded herself as bound by obligations and in which the very existence of the nation was at stake, Germany had up to the end of July declined to bring the faintest pressure to bear on her Austrian ally. And yet we expect of Sir Edward Grey that he should speak in a tone of authority to a friendly state towards which he was bound by no obligation ! Germany demanded of him that he should identify himself with the Austrian standpoint just as completely as she herself had done, that he should come forward as an advocate of Austria's interests in the Balkans and that he should give his blessing to a policy which Marquis di San Giuliano had rejected after branding it as ' adventurous and aggressive.' Germany expected Sir Edward Grey to be more friendly towards the Triple Alliance than was San Giuliano himself and that the British statesman should take sides with Austria against Russia.

I have never led anyone to suppose that Sir Edward would adopt such a course ; I am prepared, however, to maintain that he left no stone unturned in his efforts to ensure peace. Even after the publication of the ultimatum he laid before us proposals for mediation. These we turned down. He begged us to put forward some proposal of our own, but we did not do so. In reply to the urgent entreaties I addressed to my government, asking them to bring about a compromise, as otherwise the world war was inevitable, I received the curt reply that Germany must decline to meddle in the Serbian quarrel, this quarrel being ' purely the affair of our ally.' We were ready on the other hand, I was told, to mediate between Vienna and Petrograd. This would have meant a mediation that excluded the object in dispute. In other words, instead of mediation,—which must necessarily be two-sided,—we proposed a one-sided pressure. This pressure was to be brought to bear on Petrograd and not on Vienna.

We imagined that by taking up a stand-to-attention, drill-book attitude we could win a diplomatic success and thus rejuvenate Austria-Hungary. That was our fatal and terrible mistake.

Sir Edward Grey's formula ran, ' So long as the dispute remains confined to Austria and Serbia, I will not intervene, but should it develop into a quarrel between Austria and Russia, the time will have come for the Powers who are not directly concerned to mediate.'

Sir Edward Grey repeatedly said to me, ' If war breaks out it will be the greatest catastrophe the world has ever seen.' A statesman who is bent on war does not use such words. To Sir Edward Grey war meant the collapse of his whole foreign policy. Even as late as 29th July, when through me he warned the German Government in the well-known words, he declared to M. Cambon that France should not deduce from his statement that England would support her under all circumstances. As late as July 31 the correspondence between King George and Poincaré took place in which the King declined to make any binding statement in France's favour. Once the ultimatum had been issued, it was clear that the British Fleet could not be dispersed. The ships had already been assembled before the publication of the ultimatum and had to be held in readiness. For all Europe knew what the ultimatum meant. Sir Edward Grey told Count Mensdorff that he would not have specially assembled the ships, but now that they were together he did not intend to disperse them.

Our policy reminds me of the story of King Canute who had his throne brought down to the water's edge and forbade the tide to wet his feet. It was not his fault that his feet got wet, but that of the disobedient waves. They ought to have stopped when he told them.

M. Sazonov, it is true, could reckon on England's supporting him, as the Belgian attaché reported. For the Russian statesman knew for certain that in spite of all Sir Edward Grey's evasive answers, England could not remain neutral if France came in. ' Sooner or later you will be drawn in if war breaks out,' observed M. Sazonov to the British Ambassador on 24th July.

Sir Edward Grey has said, ' Some people think that I could have prevented the war if I had from the very outset declared that I would not join in. Others tell me that I could have prevented it if I had said straight out, " I intend to come in." In the first case, Russia would, they maintain, have given way, and in the second case, Germany. Both assumptions are wrong.' The world-war could only have been prevented by forcing Count Berchtold to renounce the idea of a war with Serbia or by Germany's declaring that the question at issue between Austria and Serbia lay outside the terms of the Triple Alliance. To begin with, Austrian troops were to occupy Serbia, in other words, according to the usage that prevails in that part of the world, Serbian territory was to be harried and laid waste. Parts of Serbia were to be presented to her neighbours and, as a generous concession, Austria-Hungary would refrain from making any territorial acquisitions for herself. That is what Berlin called a ' colossal act of grace.' And while this operation was taking place, Russia, who all along had emphasised her community of blood and creed with the threatened provinces, was to remain an idle spectator. Could anyone seriously suppose that public opinion in Russia, which had forced Alexander II. into a war against Turkey for the liberation of the Slav brethren of the Orthodox Church, would for a moment tolerate such a thing, even if Sir Edward Grey in the tone of a commander-in-chief of the Triple Entente had demanded it ? Consider for a moment what had happened. On 23rd July Austria's ultimatum to Serbia was published, clearly revealing that it was drafted with a view to rejection—in other words, with a view to war. Russia immediately and unambiguously declared that she could not permit the annihilation of Serbia. The promise that there would be no annexation of Serbian territory was not sufficient. The Serbian answer had accepted nearly every demand, Serbia asking only to be allowed to negotiate with regard to the two points still in dispute. Whereupon Austria declares war. Germany supports the Austrian standpoint, declines any intervention, declines Sir Edward Grey's offers of mediation. The proposal made by the Czar to hand the matter over to the Hague Tribunal is left disregarded.

Even supposing that Sir Edward Grey had succeeded in keeping Russia passive, what advantage could we have promised ourselves from it ? Could we have hoped for an improvement in our relations with Russia when it was owing to our subservient support of Austria that these relations had become so bad and when we were ready at all times to grant our support to our ally in her anti-Serbian policy ? Seeing that the Entente was based upon a common hostility to Germany, owing to anxiety at the strength of Germany's position, was not such an increase of tension bound to establish on a still firmer basis the Triple Entente, the cordiality of which we already lamented ?

The Triple Entente, which had originated in the antagonisms between Germany and France, Germany and Great Britain and between Russia and Austria, could only be loosened by improving our relations with England and with Russia and by putting a stop to the sabre-rattling with which we kept on alarming the French just when they were beginning to regard the *revanche* idea as nothing more than a beautiful dream and were settling down to enjoy prosperity and repose.

There was no hope of our being able to break up the Entente by violent methods. The only thing to do was ' to bring the two groups into closer touch,' as Sir Edward Grey himself would fain have done. A *rapprochement* with England had already been reached, and we could have had a similar *rapprochement* with Russia had we but been willing unambiguously to renounce our policy of lending support to Austria's projects in the Balkans. An agreement with Russia couched in some such terms as the following would have completely assured the peace of Europe. ' La Russie s'engage à ne pas attaquer ni l'Allemagne ni l'Autriche et à ne pas appuyer une attaque de la France ou de l'Angleterre dirigée contre l'Allemagne. L'Allemagne s'engage à ne pas attaquer ni la Russie ni la France et à ne pas appuyer une attaque de l'Autriche dirigée contre la Serbie ou le Monténégro.' Not Vienna and Paris but London and Petrograd are the two pivots of our foreign policy. It is London and Petrograd that we must always consider, the other two are minor gods and will fall in line of themselves. London had been carefully nursed and there had been a marked improvement in our relations. Petrograd, out of consideration for Vienna, was treated with an entire lack of understanding. Nor did we take the trouble to send the right men there. Nothing at all was done to cultivate good relations with this important capital.

The result of the war will be that Austria will break up and no longer have any say in Balkan affairs. At such a price we could have secured peace in Europe and have put our relations with Russia on a durable basis.

Is it for a moment to be supposed that the war will split up the Entente ? Even should we come out of the struggle victorious, the Entente will in the long run grow stronger than ever and will develop into a Quadruple Entente. On two occasions in July, as a result of confidential hints let drop by Sir Edward Grey and my Italian colleague in London, I was able to warn my government not to reckon on Italy's support. In reply I was told that Italy had given the ' friendliest possible assurances ' with regard to the Triple Alliance. How imperiously British interests demanded the intervention of England is shown by the attitude of the Opposition. Bonar Law, in his letter of 2nd August, said that he and Lord Lansdowne, and the Unionist leaders without exception, were of opinion that it would be disastrous for the future of the Empire for England not to support France and Russia at such a juncture. This letter certainly influenced the Cabinet that day in coming to their final decision. In this letter there was no mention whatever of Belgium, but only of the two Entente powers.

In any case, the Liberal Cabinet was much more friendly in its attitude to Germany than a Conservative Cabinet would have been. Among the Unionists, sympathy with the French was much more pronounced. They occasionally complained that Sir Edward Grey's policy might tend to alienate France.

Belgium, although it precipitated the decision, was not the real cause of the British intervention. Our invasion of Belgium, although it did not actually cause the crisis, rendered it more acute. Even without our invasion of Belgium, England would have intervened, though perhaps not immediately.

History teaches that whenever the Netherlands were occupied England invariably took up arms, and as a matter of fact, against France. This was the case both in the War of the Spanish Succession and in 1793 against the Revolutionary Armies. The documents that have hitherto been published merely bear witness to the existence of defensive agreements come to with the object of protecting Belgium. Since 1906 it has been no secret that we intended, in case of a war with France, to violate Belgian neutrality.

To anyone familiar with even the elements of English history, it must have been clear that war with Great Britain became inevitable the moment our armies crossed the Belgian frontier.

What is now to be the upshot ? How is an honourable peace to be achieved, a peace that shall make it possible for us again to get into touch with our opponents and resume relations with them ? A nation can no more live in isolation than can a human being. Intercourse with others is an indispensable condition of existence. Even the great spirits of the Middle Ages shrank from the penalty of the ban and from expulsion from the community. The longer the war lasts, and the bitterer men grow, the more difficult will it be to conclude a peace that will be in keeping with the sacrifices made, and the greater will be the danger of an economic collapse. Austria's powers of resistance, too, will give out sooner than ours.

Belgium will be one of the most difficult questions to deal with. One of England's primary conditions will be that we shall restore Belgium and make adequate compensation to her. We have no use for Belgium, from either a geographical or an ethnographical stand-point.

We have never been able completely to digest Alsace-Lorraine or Posen and West Prussia. By breaking our treaty obligations with Belgium and by violating the neutrality of a little country, a slur has been cast on Germany's good name in the eyes of the whole civilised world. All attempts to justify this action by the publication of documents are doomed to failure, since nothing that we can publish can prove that the agreements come to with Belgium were aggressive in character.

I regard as a great mistake the anti-English agitation that is at present being carried on with such zeal. It can only make the conclusion of peace more difficult and lead to expectations that will end in disappointment and bitterness. Later on we shall have to find some way of getting along with England. Down her we certainly cannot.

Does anyone seriously believe that India is going to secede or that South Africa, where the Boers have already given in, will declare its independence, or that the Turks will be able to seize Egypt ? In the latter country it is only the Arab element, the intellectuals of Cairo, that can be regarded as anti-English, not the broad masses of the agricultural population. For these classes appreciate the benefits of British rule which within a few decades has worked wonders in the improvement of the country.

Millions of fighting men are being sacrificed ; the German nation has been plunged into a struggle for its very existence, and European civilisation has been thrown back by centuries—and all this merely in order that there might prevail in Bosnia for a time a ' churchyard peace ' like that that came upon Hungary after 1848 !

We have forfeited an international position that apart from a flaw or two in the East was nothing short of brilliant, and have got our-selves into a hopeless muddle the end of which no man can see.

My dispatches protect me from the reproach that I did not foresee and predict that which has since come about. From the very outset, even before the ultimatum was sent to Serbia, I warned our Govern-ment, and after the ultimatum came out, I over and over again urged the necessity of coming to an understanding.[1]

Bernard Shaw has expressed the opinion that if Russia and France had attacked us without good reason and had forced us into a corner, we could have reckoned on England's coming to our aid. I quite share this view. England is now fighting against us, as in former centuries she fought against Louis XIV. and Napoleon I., not in order to crush us but to prevent one single nation getting the upper hand in Europe. For England's position as a world power, with a population of only forty-six million in the British Isles, is essentially dependent upon the continuance of the balance of power in Europe.

[1] There is nothing either in this or the preceding chapters to show that Lichnowsky had any definite knowledge of the secret extension of the *casus foederis* as agreed upon by Germany and Auatria in 1909. The new treaty verbally arranged in the first place by Field-Marshall von Moltke and Field-Marshall Conrad von Hoetzendorff and afterwards confirmed by the rulers of the two states was not communicated to Italy, the third partner in the Triple Alliance. As set forth by Conrad von Hoetzendorff in his recently published memoirs (*Aus Meiner Dienstzeit*, vol. i. pp. 631 *et seqq.*), Germany under the new arrangement pledged herself to support Austria-Hungary in an aggressive policy against Serbia. At the same time Germany promised full military co-operation should this policy lead to intervention on the part of Russia. (Translator's note.)

MY MISSION TO LONDON [1]

1912-1914 (written in August 1916). [2]

MY APPOINTMENT

IN September 1912, Baron Marschall died. He had been at his post in London only for a few months. His appointment, which no doubt was principally due to his age and to the desire of a junior official to go to London, was but one of the many mistakes that characterized our foreign policy.

In spite of his striking personality and great reputation, he was already too old and too tired to adjust himself to the Anglo-Saxon world, a world completely alien to him ; [he was an official and a lawyer rather than a diplomat and statesman. From the very outset he was at great pains to convince the English of the harmlessness of our fleet, and naturally this only produced the contrary effect].

Hardly a month had elapsed when, much to my surprise, I was offered the post. After several years' work on the Appointments Board at the Foreign Office, I had retired to my estates in Silesia, there being no suitable post available for me. I passed my time between flax and turnips, among horses and meadows, read extensively and occasionally published political essays.

Thus I had spent eight years, thirteen altogether having passed since I had left the Embassy at Vienna with the rank of Minister. That had been my last real sphere of political activity, as in those days such activity was impossible unless one was prepared to help a half-crazy chief [3] in drafting his crotchety orders with their crabbed instructions.

I do not know who was responsible for my being appointed to

[1] Owing to a most regrettable indiscretion this memorandum was published in Switzerland during the war. In Germany its theses aroused violent contradiction and this in spite of the fact that I nowhere in it maintained that we *willed* the war but only that we stumbled into it. (Author's note.)

[2] The passages enclosed in square brackets do not appear in the German edition published in Berlin in 1919 or in *Auf dem Wege zum Abgrund* (1927). With the author's assent they have been re-inserted in the present volume. The document here given thus corresponds with the translation issued in pamphlet form by Cassell and Co. in London in 1918. (Translator's note.)

[3] This refers to Herr von Holstein. Cf. p. xx n. (Tr.)

London. It was certainly not due to H.M. alone—I was not one of
the Monarch's intimates, though he was at all times gracious to me.
I knew by experience, moreover, that his nominees generally met with
successful opposition.   Herr von Kiderlen had really wanted to send
Herr von Stumm to London ! He immediately manifested unmistakable ill-will towards me, and endeavoured to intimidate me by his
incivility.   Herr von Bethmann-Hollweg was at that time kindly
disposed towards me, and had paid me a visit at Grätz only a short
time before.   I am therefore inclined to think that they all agreed
on me mainly because there was no other candidate available at the
moment.   But for Baron Marschall's unexpected death, I should no
more have been called out of retirement then than at any other time
during all those previous years.

Morocco Policy

It was certainly the right moment for a new effort to establish
better relations with England.   Our enigmatic Morocco policy had
repeatedly shaken confidence in our pacific intentions and, at the very
least, had given rise to the suspicion that we did not quite know
what we wanted, or that it was our object to keep Europe in a
constant state of alarm and now and again to humiliate France.   An
Austrian colleague, who had been in Paris for a long time, once said to
me : ' Whenever the French begin to forget about *revanche*, you
always remind them of it with a jack-boot.'

After we had repulsed M. Delcassé's efforts to arrive at an understanding with us about Morocco, and prior to that had formally
declared that we had no political interests there—an attitude which,
by the way, was quite in keeping with the traditions of the Bismarckian policy—we suddenly discovered a second Krueger in Abdul Aziz.
We assured this latter potentate, as we had assured the Boers, of the
protection of the mighty German Empire, with the same display and
with the same result ; both demonstrations ended in our having to
retreat, as was bound to be the case, if we had not made up our
minds then and there to embark on a world-war.   The congress at
Algeçiras, at which we had cut such a sorry figure, did not improve
matters ; still less did the fall of M. Delcassé.

Our attitude promoted the Russo-Japanese *rapprochement* and later
on brought the English and Japanese together.   In face of ' the
German Peril ' all other differences faded into the background.   The
possibility of a new Franco-German war had become apparent, and

it was out of the question that such a war could, as in 1870, leave Russia and England unaffected.

The worthlessness of the Triple Alliance had been shown at Algeçiras, while that of the agreements arrived at there was demonstrated shortly afterwards by the collapse of the Sultanate—a development that naturally could not be prevented. Among the German people, however, the belief gained ground that our foreign policy was feeble and was giving way before the 'Encirclement'—that our dashing gestures were succeeded by pusillanimous surrender.

It is to the credit of Herr von Kiderlen, who is mostly overrated as a statesman, that he wound up our Moroccan inheritance and did the best he could with facts that could no longer be altered. Whether, indeed, it was necessary to alarm the world by the Agadir incident I will leave others to say. The *coup* was jubilantly acclaimed in Germany, but it had caused the more disquiet in England, whose Government was kept waiting for three weeks for an explanation of our intentions. Lloyd George's speech, which was meant as a warning to us, was the consequence. Before Delcassé's fall, and before Algeçiras, we might have had a harbour and territory on the West Coast of Africa. After these events such concessions were impossible.

Sir Edward Grey's Programme

When I came to London in November 1912 the excitement over Morocco had subsided, as an agreement with France had been reached in Berlin. Lord Haldane's mission had failed, it is true, as we had required the assurance of neutrality, instead of being content with a treaty securing us against British attacks and attacks with British support. Yet Sir Edward Grey had not relinquished the idea of arriving at an agreement with us, and in the first place tried to do this in colonial and economic questions. Conversations were in progress with the capable and businesslike Counsellor of Embassy Herr von Kühlmann concerning the renewal of the Portuguese colonial agreement and concerning Mesopotamia (Baghdad Railway), the unavowed object of which was to divide both the Portuguese colonies and Asia Minor into zones of influence.

The British statesman, after having settled all outstanding points of difference with France and Russia, wished to make similar agreements with us. It was not his object to isolate us, but to the best of his power to make us partners in the existing association. Just as he had succeeded in removing Anglo-French and Anglo-Russian differences, so, too, he wished if possible to eliminate Anglo-German differences, and by a network of treaties—which would no doubt in the end have led to an agreement on the thorny question of naval armaments—to ensure the peace of the world, after our previous policy had led to an association—the Entente—which represented a mutual insurance against the risk of war.

Such was Sir E. Grey's plan. In his own words : Without interfering with England's existing friendship with France and Russia, a friendship which has no aggressive aims and does not entail any binding obligations on England, he wished to arrive at a friendly *rapprochement* and understanding with Germany, in order ' to bring the two groups nearer.'

England, like Germany, was at that time divided into two camps on this question. The optimists, on the one hand, believed in the possibility of an understanding ; the pessimists, on the other, thought that sooner or later war was inevitable.

Among the optimists were to be found such men as Mr. Asquith, Sir Edward Grey, Lord Haldane and most of the Ministers in the Radical Cabinet, and their views were shared by such leading Liberal papers as the *Westminster Gazette*, the *Manchester Guardian* and the *Daily Chronicle*. The pessimists were mainly Conservative politicians like Mr. Balfour, who repeatedly made this clear to me ; also leading Army men, like Lord Roberts, who pointed out the necessity of universal military service (' The Writing on the Wall ') ; further, the Northcliffe Press and the eminent English journalist, Mr. Garvin, of *The Observer*. During my period of office, however, they abstained from all attacks, and maintained both personally and politically a friendly attitude. But our naval policy and our attitude in 1905, 1908 and 1911 had aroused in them the conviction that it would nevertheless some day come to war. Just as is the case in Germany, the optimists are now being accused of short-sightedness and simplicity while the pessimists are looked on as the true prophets.

THE ALBANIAN QUESTION

The first Balkan War had led to the collapse of Turkey and thus to a defeat of our policy, which had been identified with Turkey for a number of years. Since Turkey in Europe could no longer be saved, there were two ways in which we could deal with the inheritance left by her ; either we could declare our complete disinterestedness with

regard to the frontier delimitations and leave the Balkan Powers to
settle them, or we could support our ' Allies ' and carry on a Triple
Alliance policy in the Near East, thus giving up the rôle of mediator.

From the very beginning I advocated the former course, but the
Foreign Office emphatically favoured the latter.

The vital point was the Albanian question. Our Allies desired the
establishment of an independent Albanian state, the Austrians not
wishing that the Serbs should obtain access to the Adriatic, while the
Italians did not want the Greeks to get to Valona or even to the
north of Corfu. As opposed to this, Russia, as is known, was backing
Serbia's wishes and France those of Greece.

My advice was to treat the whole question as outside the scope of
the Alliance, and to support neither the Austrian nor the Italian claims.
Without our aid it would have been impossible to set up an independent Albania, which, as anyone could foresee, had no prospect of
surviving ; Serbia would have reached the sea-coast, and the present
world-war would have been avoided. France and Italy would have
quarrelled over Greece, and unless the Italians had been willing to fight
France unaided they would have been compelled to acquiesce in
Greece's expansion to the north of Durazzo. The greater part of
Albania is Hellenic. The towns in the south are entirely so ; and
during the Conference of Ambassadors delegations from the principal
towns arrived in London to advocate their annexation to Greece.
Even in present-day Greece there are Albanian elements, and the so-
called Greek national dress is of Albanian origin. The inclusion of the
Albanians, who are principally Orthodox and Moslem, in the body
of the Greek state was therefore the best and most natural solution.
For dynastic reasons H M. was also in favour of this solution. When
I supported this view in a letter to the monarch, I received agitated
reproaches from the Chancellor. He said that I had the reputation
of being ' an opponent of Austria's ' and that I was to abstain from
such interference and from direct correspondence.

The Near East and the Policy of the Triple Alliance

We ought to have made up our mind to break with the fatal tradition of pursuing a Triple Alliance policy in the Near East, and have
recognised the mistake identifying ourselves in the south with the
Turks and in the north with the Austro-Magyars. For the continuance of this policy, upon which we had entered at the Berlin
Congress and which we had actively pursued ever since, was bound

to lead in time to a conflict with Russia and to the world-war, more especially if the requisite diplomatic skill were lacking in high places. Instead of coming to terms with Russia on a basis of the independence of the Sultan, whom even Petrograd did not wish to remove from Constantinople, and of confining ourselves to our economic interests in the Near East and to the partitioning of Asia Minor into spheres of influence while at the same time renouncing any intention of political or military interference, it was our political ambition to hold a dominating position on the Bosporus. In Russia they began to think that the road to Constantinople and the Mediterranean lay *via* Berlin. Instead of supporting the vigorous development of the Balkan states —which, after their liberation proved anything but pro-Russian, and with which our experiences were very satisfactory—we took sides with the Turkish and Magyar oppressors.

The fatal mistake of our Triple Alliance and Near East policy was to force Russia, by nature our friend and an excellent neighbour, into the arms of France and England and away from its policy of Asiatic expansion. This was quite plain, as a Franco-Russian attack, which was the *sole* hypothesis that justified a Triple Alliance policy, could then have been left out of our calculations.

The value of the Italian alliance needs no further reference. Italy will want our money and our tourists even after the war, with or without an alliance. That Italy would fail us in case of war was patent from the start. In short the alliance was *worthless*. Austria needs our protection in war as in peace, and has no other support. Her dependence on us is based on political, national and economic considerations, and is the more pronounced the more intimate our relations with Russia. The Bosnian crisis taught us this. Since the days of Count Beust no Vienna Minister has adopted such a self-confident attitude towards us as did Count Aerenthal during the later years of his life. If German policy is conducted on right lines, cultivating good relations with Russia, Austria-Hungary is our vassal and dependent on us, even without an alliance or recompense ; if it is wrongly conducted, then it is we who are dependent on Austria. Hence there was no reason for the alliance.

I knew Austria too well not to be aware that a return to the policy of Prince Felix Schwarzenberg or Count Moritz Esterhazy was inconceivable there. The Slavs there have no particular affection for us and have no desire to return into a German Empire, even with a Habsburg-Lorraine emperor at its head. They are striving for a federation in Austria on national lines, a state of things that would have even less chance of being realised within the German Empire than under the Double Eagle. The Germans of Austria, however, acknowledge Berlin as the centre of German might and culture, and are well aware that Austria can never again be the leading Power. They wish for as intimate a connection with the German Empire as possible, not for an anti-German policy.

Since the 'seventies the position has fundamentally changed in Austria as in Bavaria. As in the latter a return to Great German particularism and old Bavarian policy is not to be feared, so with the former a resuscitation of the policy of Prince Kaunitz and Schwarzenberg was not to be expected. By a federation with Austria, however, a state which resembles a big Belgium, since only half its population, even without Galicia and Dalmatia, is of Germanic stock, our interests would suffer as much if we subordinated our policy to the views of Vienna or Budapest—thus espousing Austria's quarrels as our own (' d'épouser les querelles d'Autriche ').

Hence we were not obliged to take any notice of the desires of our ally ; they were not only unnecessary but also dangerous, as they would lead to a conflict with Russia if we looked at Balkan questions through Austrian spectacles.

The development of the alliance, from a union formed on a single hypothesis for a single specific purpose, into a general and unlimited association, a pooling of interests in all spheres, was the best way of producing that which diplomacy was designed to prevent—war. Such an ' alliance policy ' was also calculated to alienate from us the sympathies of the strong, young, rising communities in the Balkans, who were prepared to turn to us and open their markets to us.

The difference between the power of a Ruling House and a National State, between dynastic and democratic ideas of government, had to be decided, and as usual we decided on the wrong side.

King Carol told one of our representatives that he had entered into the alliance with us on the assumption that we retained the leadership ; but if the lead passed to Austria, it would alter the foundations of the relationship, and under such circumstances he would not be able to go on with it.

Things were similar in Serbia, where, contrary to our own economic interests, we were supporting the Austrian policy of strangulation.

Every time we consistently backed the wrong horse, whose breakdown could have been foreseen : Krueger, Abdul Aziz, Abdul Hamid,

Wilhelm of Wied, ending—the most fatal of all mistakes—with the great plunge on the Berchtold stable.

The Conference of Ambassadors

Shortly after my arrival in London, at the end of 1912, Sir Edward Grey proposed an informal conference to prevent the Balkan War from developing into a European one. When the war broke out we had unfortunately refused to agree to the French proposal of a declaration of disinterestedness. The British statesman from the very beginning took up the position that England had no interest in Albania, and that she had no intention of going to war over this question. He merely wished to mediate between the two groups as an ' honest broker' and smooth over difficulties. He therefore by no means took sides with the Entente, and during the eight months or so of the negotiations, his goodwill and his authoritative influence contributed in no small degree to the attainment of an agreement. We, instead of adopting an attitude similar to the English one, invariably took up the position prescribed for us by Vienna. Count Mensdorff was the leader of the Triple Alliance in London ; I was his ' second.' It was my duty to support his proposals. That clever and experienced man, Count Szögenyi, was conducting affairs in Berlin. His refrain was ' Then the *casus foederis* will arise,' and when I once ventured to doubt the correctness of this conclusion I was severely reprimanded for ' Austrophobia.' [It was also said that I had an ' hereditary weakness,' [1] the allusion being to my father.]

On all questions we took sides with Austria and Italy—about Albania, a Serbian port on the Adriatic, Scutari, and also about the delimitation of the frontiers of Albania—while Sir Edward Grey hardly ever supported the French or Russian claims. He mostly supported our group in order not to give a pretext like the one that a dead Archduke was to furnish later on. Thus with his assistance it was possible to coax King Nikita out of Scutari again. Otherwise this question would already have led to a world-war, as we should certainly not have ventured to induce ' our ally ' to give way.

Sir Edward Grey conducted the negotiations with circumspection, calm and tact. When a question threatened to become involved, he sketched a formula for agreement which was always to the point and

---

[1] Prince Lichnowsky's father had had to leave Vienna owing to the disfavour into which he fell after he had killed in a duel a Hungarian nobleman who had challenged him. He settled in Potsdam, where he became a General in the Hussars. (Translator's note.)

was always accepted.   His personality inspired confidence in all the participants.

As a matter of fact we had again successfully emerged from one of those trials of strength which characterise our policy.   Russia had been obliged to give way to us on all points, seeing that she was never in a position to procure success for the Serbian aims.   Albania was set up as a vassal state of Austria, and Serbia was pressed back from the sea.   Hence this conference resulted in a fresh humiliation for Russian self-esteem.   As in 1878 and in 1908, we had again opposed the Russian plans although no *German* interests were involved. Bismarck was clever enough to mitigate the mistake of the Congress by the secret treaty and by his attitude in the Battenberg question ; but we continued to pursue in London the dangerous path upon which we had once more entered in the Bosnian question, nor did we leave it while there was yet time, even when we saw it leading to the abyss.

The ill-humour which prevailed in Russia at that time was shown during the conference by attacks in the Russian press against my Russian colleague and against Russian diplomacy.   The dissatisfied circles made capital out of his German descent and his Roman Catholicism, his reputation as a friend of Germany and the accident that he was related both to Count Mensdorff and to me.   Although not, perhaps, a very eminent personality, Count Benckendorff is endowed with a number of qualifications that distinguish a good diplomat—tact, polished manners, experience, courtesy, and a natural eye for men and affairs.   He was always at pains to avoid a brusque attitude, and was supported in this by England and France.

Later on I once remarked to him : ' I presume that Russian feeling is very anti-German.'   He replied : ' There are also very strong and influential pro-German circles, but in general people are extremely anti-Austrian.'

It is hardly necessary to add that our ' Austrophilie à outrance,' our friendship for Austria through thick and thin, was hardly calculated to loosen the Entente and to divert Russia's attention to her Asiatic interests !

The Balkan Conference

At the same time the Balkan Conference was sitting in London and I had occasion to come into contact with the leaders of the Balkan

States.   M. Venizelos was probably the most distinguished personality there.   At that time he was anything rather than anti-German,
and visited me several times ; he was especially fond of wearing the
ribbon of the Order of the Red Eagle—he even wore it at the French
Embassy.   His prepossessing charm and ways of a man of the world
made him very popular.   Next to him M. Daneff, at that time
Bulgarian Premier and confidant of Count Berchtold, played a great
part.   He gave the impression of a subtle and energetic man, and it
is probably only due to the influence of his Vienna and Budapest
friends, of whose homage he often made fun, that he was induced to
commit the folly of entering upon the second Balkan War and of
refusing Russian arbitration.

M. Take Jonescu was also frequently in London and visited me
regularly at this time.   I knew him from the time when I was
Secretary at Bucharest.   He was also one of Herr von Kiderlen's
friends.   In London he was endeavouring to obtain concessions
for Rumania from M. Daneff by means of negotiations, in which
he was assisted by the very able Rumanian Minister, M. Misu.   It
is known that Bulgarian opposition brought about the failure of
these negotiations.   Count Berchtold was entirely on Bulgaria's
side, and we, of course, with him ; otherwise by putting pressure
on M. Daneff we might have secured the desired satisfaction for
Rumania and placed her under an obligation to us ; she was finally
estranged from the Central Powers by Austria's attitude during and
after the second Balkan War.

THE SECOND BALKAN WAR

The defeat of Bulgaria in the second Balkan War and the victory
of Serbia, with the Rumanian invasion, naturally constituted a
humiliation for Austria.   The plan to rectify this by an expedition
against Serbia seems to have been evolved in Vienna soon after.
The Italian revelations prove this, and it may be assumed that
Marquis di San Giuliano, who very aptly described the plan as a
pericolosissima avventura, saved us from being involved in a world
war as early as the summer of 1913.

Owing to the intimacy of Russo-Italian relations, the Vienna plan
was doubtless known in Petrograd.   In any case, M. Sazonov
openly declared at Constanza, as M. Take Jonescu told me, that an
Austrian attack on Serbia would be regarded as a *casus belli* by
Russia.

When one of my staff returned from leave in Vienna in the spring of 1914, he said that Herr von Tschirschky had declared that there would soon be war. As I, however, was always left in ignorance about important events, I considered this pessimism to be unfounded.

As a matter of fact it would appear that, ever since the Peace of Bucharest, Vienna had been bent on securing a revision of the treaty by her own effort and was apparently only waiting for a favourable pretext. Vienna statesmen could, of course, depend on our support. They were aware of that, as they had been repeatedly accused by us of lack of firmness. In fact, Berlin was pressing for a ' rehabilitation of Austria.'

Liman von Sanders

When I returned to London in December 1913 from a lengthy leave, the Liman von Sanders question had led to a fresh crisis in our relations with Russia. Sir Edward Grey, not without concern, pointed out to me the excitement there was in Petrograd over it. ' I have never seen them so excited,' he said.

I received instructions from Berlin to request the Minister to exert a restraining influence in Petrograd, and to assist us in settling the dispute. Sir Edward gladly did this, and his intervention contributed in no small degree to smooth the matter over. My good relations with Sir Edward and his great influence in Petrograd were repeatedly made use of in similar fashion when we wished to attain anything there, [as our representative proved quite useless for such a purpose].

During the fateful days of July 1914 Sir Edward said to me, ' When you want to obtain anything in Petrograd you always apply to me, but if I appeal to you for your influence in Vienna you fail me.'

The Colonial Treaty

The good and confidential relations which I had succeeded in establishing, not only with society and the most influential people, like Sir Edward Grey and Mr. Asquith, but also with the great public at public dinners, produced a marked improvement in the relations of the two countries. Sir Edward honestly tried to confirm this *rapprochement*, and his intentions were most apparent on two questions—the Colonial Treaty and the Baghdad Railway Treaty.

In 1898 Count Hatzfeld and Mr. Balfour had signed a secret agreement dividing the Portuguese colonies into economic spheres of influence between us and England. As the Government of Portugal had neither the power nor the means to open up her extended possessions or to administer them properly, she had some time before thought of selling them in order to put her finances on a sounder basis. An agreement had been come to between us and England defining the interests of both parties. This agreement was of the greater value seeing that Portugal, as was generally known, was entirely dependent on England.

Nominally this agreement was to safeguard the integrity and independence of the Portuguese State, and merely declared the intention of being of financial and economic assistance to the Portuguese. So far as its actual text went, it therefore did not contravene the ancient Anglo-Portuguese Alliance of the fifteenth century, which was last renewed under Charles II. and gave a reciprocal territorial guarantee.

In spite of this, owing to the endeavours of Marquis de Soveral, who was presumably aware of the Anglo-German agreement, a new treaty—the so-called Treaty of Windsor—was concluded between England and Portugal in 1899, confirming the old agreements, which had always remained in force.

The object of the negotiations between us and England, which had commenced before my arrival, was to amend and improve our agreement of 1898, as it had proved unsatisfactory on several points as regards geographical delimitation. Thanks to the accommodating attitude of the British Government[1] I succeeded in making the new agreement fully accord with our wishes and interests. The whole of Angola up to the twentieth degree of longitude was assigned to us, so that we stretched up to the Congo Free State from the south ; we also acquired the valuable islands of San Thomé and Principe, which are north of the equator and therefore really in the French sphere of influence, a fact which caused my French colleague to enter strong but unavailing protests.

Further, we obtained the northern part of Mozambique ; the Licango formed the border.

The British Government showed the greatest consideration for our interests and wishes. Sir Edward Grey intended to demonstrate his goodwill towards us, but he also wished to assist our colonial development as a whole, as England hoped to divert the German development of strength from the North Sea and Western Europe to the

[1] Cf. the dispatches on this question and draft treaty, pp. 270-318. (Tr.)

Ocean and to Africa. ' We don't want to grudge Germany her colonial development,' a leading member of the Cabinet said to me.

The British Government originally intended to include the Congo State in the agreement, which would have given us the right to pre-emption and have enabled us to penetrate it economically. We refused this offer ostensibly out of consideration for Belgian suscepti-bilities. Perhaps we wished to be economical of successes ?

As regards the practical realisation of the real though unexpressed intention of the treaty—which was at a later date to carry out the actual partition of the Portuguese colonies—the document in its new form showed marked improvements and advantages as com-pared with the old one. Cases had been specified which empowered us to take steps to guard our interests in the districts assigned to us. These were couched in such vague terms that it was really left to us to decide when ' vital ' interests arose, so that, with Portugal entirely dependent on England, it was only necessary to cultivate further good relations with England in order to carry out our joint intentions at a later date with English assent.

Sir Edward Grey showed the sincerity of the British Government's desire to respect our rights by referring to us various Englishmen who wished to invest capital in the districts assigned to us by the new agreement, even before this was completed and signed ; on their asking the British Government for support he informed them that their enterprises belonged to our sphere of influence.

The agreement was practically completed at the time of the King's visit to Berlin in May 1913. At that time a conference took place in Berlin under the presidency of the Imperial Chancellor ; in this conference I also took part, and certain further wishes of ours were defined. On my return to London I succeeded, with the assistance of Counsellor of Embassy von Kühlmann, who was working at the agreement with Mr. Parker, in having our last proposals incorporated, and the whole agreement was paragraphed by Sir Edward Grey and myself in August 1913, before I went on leave.

But now fresh difficulties arose which prevented its being signed, and I did not obtain the authorisation to conclude it till a year later —that is, shortly before the outbreak of the war. It was, alas ! never signed.

Sir Edward Grey was only willing to sign *if the agreement were published together with the agreements of* 1898 *and* 1899. England had, he said, no other secret treaties besides these, and it was contrary to established principles to keep binding agreements secret. Therefore he could not make any agreement without publishing it. He was, however, willing to accede to our wishes with regard to the time and manner of publication, provided that such publication took place within one year from the date of signature.

At our Foreign Office, where my successes had caused increasing dissatisfaction, and where an influential personage, as if re-enacting the part of Herr von Holstein, wanted the London post for himself, I was informed that the publication would endanger our interests in the colonies, as the Portuguese would then not give us any more concessions.

The futility of this objection is apparent when we remember that the Portuguese, in view of the closeness of Anglo-Portuguese relations, were most probably just as well aware of the old agreement as of our new arrangements, and that the influence which England possesses at Lisbon must have rendered their Government completely impotent in face of an Anglo-German agreement.

Another pretext had, therefore, to be found for wrecking the treaty. It was suggested that the publication of the Treaty of Windsor, which had been concluded during the Prince Hohenlohe's Chancellorship—though it was only a renewal of the Treaty of Charles II., which had always remained in force—might endanger the position of Herr von Bethmann-Hollweg, as affording a proof of British hypocrisy and perfidy !

I pointed out that the preamble of our agreement expressed the same thing as the Treaty of Windsor and as other similar treaties, namely, that we would protect the sovereign rights of Portugal and the inviolability of its possessions. In vain ! In spite of repeated discussions with Sir Edward Grey, at which he made many fresh suggestions that the documents should be published, the Foreign Office persisted in its attitude, and finally arranged with Sir Edward Goschen that matters should be left as they were.

The treaty, which offered us extraordinary advantages, was the result of more than a year's work. It was thus dropped [as it would have been a public success for me].

When I mentioned the subject to Mr. Harcourt at a dinner at the Embassy in the spring of 1914, the Minister for the Colonies told me that he was placed in a difficult position and did not know how to act. The present position was intolerable—he wished to safeguard our interests, but was in doubt whether he should proceed on the terms of the old or the new treaty. It was therefore urgently desirable to clear up the situation and to settle the matter, which had dragged on for such a long time.

In reply to a dispatch in this sense I received instructions couched in terms which showed more emotion than civility, telling me to abstain from further interference in the matter.

I now regret that I did not immediately go to Berlin and place my post at the disposal of the monarch. That I still continued to have some faith in the possibility of arriving at an understanding with those in authority was a sinister mistake which was to take its revenge a few months later in a most tragic manner.

However little I even then enjoyed the goodwill of the highest official of the Empire, [as he feared that I was aspiring to his post], yet I must in justice to him say that during our last interview before the outbreak of war, at the end of June 1914, to which I will refer later, he gave me his assent for the signature and publication of the treaty. In spite of this it required repeated applications on my part, which were supported by Herr Dr. Solf [1] in Berlin, before sanction was finally obtained at the end of July 1914. As the Serbian crisis at that time already imperilled the peace of Europe, the completion of the treaty had to be postponed. It, too, is one of the sacrifices of this war.

THE BAGHDAD TREATY

At the same time I was negotiating in London, with the able support of Herr von Kühlmann, about the so-called Baghdad Treaty. The real object of this treaty was to divide up Asia Minor into spheres of influence, although this term was anxiously avoided in view of the rights of the Sultan. Sir Edward Grey, too, repeatedly stated that there were in existence no agreements with France and Russia which in any way aimed at the partition of Asia Minor.

In consultation with the Turkish representative, Hakki Pasha, all economic questions concerning German undertakings were settled in the main according to the wishes of the Deutsche Bank. The most important concession Sir Edward Grey made to me personally was the continuation of the railway as far as Basra. We had dropped this point in favour of the side line to Alexandretta ; up to that time Baghdad had been the terminal point of the railway. An inter-

---

[1] Then Secretary of State for the Colonies. (Translator's note.)

national commission was to regulate navigation on the Shatt-el-Arab. We were also to have a share in the harbour works at Basra and to receive rights for the navigation of the Tigris, which hitherto had been a monopoly of the firm of Lynch.

By this treaty the whole of Mesopotamia as far as Basra was included within our sphere of influence (without prejudice to already existing British navigation rights on the Tigris and the rights of the Willcox irrigation works), as well as the whole district of the Baghdad and Anatolian railway.

The coast of the Persian Gulf and the Smyrna-Aidin railway were recognised as the British economic sphere, Syria as the French and Armenia as the Russian. If both treaties were executed and published, an agreement with England would be reached which would preclude all doubts about the possibility of an ' Anglo-German co-operation.'

THE QUESTION OF THE NAVY

The Naval question was and is the most delicate of all. It is a problem on which a good many wrong views prevail.

The creation of a powerful fleet on the German side of the North Sea—the development of the greatest military power on the Continent into the greatest naval power as well—was bound to prove ' inconvenient ' to England, to say the least of it. No fair-minded person can be in any doubt about this. In order to maintain her advantage and not to become dependent, as well as to secure that supremacy at sea which is necessary for her if she is not to starve, England was compelled to undertake armaments and expenditure which weighed heavily on the taxpayer. Great Britain's international position would be threatened, however, if our policy created the belief that warlike developments might ensue—a state of affairs which had almost been reached during the time of the Morocco crisis and the Bosnian problem.

Great Britain had become reconciled to our fleet *within its then appointed limits*; but the presence of this fleet was certainly not welcome, and was one of the causes—though not the only or the most important cause—of her adhesion to France and Russia ; but on account of the fleet *alone* England would not have drawn the sword any more than on account of our trade, which has been alleged to have produced jealousy and finally war.

From the very beginning I maintained that, *notwithstanding* the fleet, it would be possible to arrive at a friendly understanding and *rapprochement* if we refrained from introducing a new Navy Bill and if *our policy were indubitably pacific*. I also avoided mentioning the fleet, and no reference to it ever passed between Sir Edward Grey and me. On one occasion Sir Edward Grey said at a meeting of the Cabinet, 'The present German Ambassador has never once mentioned the fleet to me.'

During my tenure of office Mr. Churchill, then First Lord of the Admiralty, proposed, as is known, the so-called ' Naval holiday,' and suggested for financial reasons, and probably also to meet the pacific wishes of his party, a year's pause in armaments. Officially Sir Edward Grey did not support the proposal ; in our talks he never mentioned it, but Mr. Churchill repeatedly spoke to me about it.

I am convinced that Mr. Churchill's proposal was honest, as intrigue is altogether foreign to the English nature. It would have been a great success for the Minister if he could have come before the country with reductions of expenditure and freed it from the nightmare of armaments that weighed on the people.

I replied that for technical reasons it would be difficult to agree to his plan. What was to become of the workmen who were engaged for this purpose, and what of the technical staff ? Our naval programme had been decided on, and it would be difficult to alter it in any way. On the other hand we had no intention of exceeding it. But he reverted to it again and pointed out that the sums spent for such enormous armaments might be better employed for other and more useful purposes. I replied that money expended in the naval dockyards also benefited our home industries.

After several interviews with Sir W. Tyrrell, Sir Edward Grey's chief private secretary, I managed to get the question removed from the agenda without causing any ill-feeling, although it was again referred to in Parliament. I succeeded in preventing any official proposal from being made. This ' naval holiday ' was, however, a pet idea of Mr. Churchill's as well as of the Government, and had we fallen in with his suggestion and accepted the formula of 16 : 10 for battleships, we might, I think, have given tangible proof of our goodwill and have strengthened and encouraged the tendency, already prevailing in the Government, to enter into closer relations with us.

But, as I have already said, it was possible to arrive at an understanding *in spite of the fleet* and without a ' naval holiday.' I had always regarded my mission from this point of view, and I had also succeeded in realising my plans when the outbreak of war destroyed everything I had achieved.

COMMERCIAL JEALOUSY

The ' commercial jealousy ' about which we hear so much is based on a wrong conception of the circumstances. Certainly Germany's rise as a commercial power after the war of 1870 and during the following decades was a menace to British commercial circles which, with their industries and export-houses, had held a virtual monopoly of trade. The increasing commerce with Germany, which was the leading country in Europe as regards British exports—a fact to which I invariably referred in my public speeches—had, however, given rise to the wish to maintain friendly relations with their best customer and business friend, and had driven all other considerations into the background.

The Briton is matter-of-fact—he takes things as they are and does not tilt against windmills. Notably in commercial circles I encountered the most friendly spirit and the endeavour to further our common economic interests. As a matter of fact, nobody in these circles took any interest in the Russian, Italian, Austrian or even in the French representative, despite the striking personality of the latter and despite his political successes. None but the German and American Ambassadors attracted public attention.

In order to get into touch with important commercial circles, I accepted invitations from the United Chambers of Commerce and from the London and Bradford Chamber, and was the guest of the cities of Newcastle and Liverpool. I was well received everywhere ; Manchester, Glasgow and Edinburgh had also invited me, and I intended to go there later.

People who did not understand British conditions and who did not realise the importance of ' public dinners,' also people to whom my successes were unwelcome, reproached me with having done harm by my speeches. I believe, on the contrary, that by appearing in public and emphasising common commercial interests I contributed in no small measure to the improvement of relations,—quite apart from the fact that it would have been clumsy and churlish to refuse all invitations.

In all other circles I also met with the most friendly reception and hearty co-operation—at Court, in society, and from the Government.

THE COURT AND SOCIETY

The King is a simple and benevolent man with sound common-sense ; he demonstrated his goodwill towards me and was frankly desirous of furthering my task. Although the British Constitution leaves only very limited powers to the Crown, yet the monarch, in virtue of his position, can exercise a considerable influence on opinion, both in society and in the Government. The Crown is the apex of the social pyramid ; it sets the fashion and gives the tone. Society, which is principally Unionist (Conservative), has always taken an active interest in politics, a habit which the ladies share. It is represented in the House of Lords, the House of Commons and hence also in the Cabinet. An Englishman either is a member of society or would like to be one. It is his constant endeavour to be a ' gentleman,' and even people of modest origin delight to mingle in society and in the company of beautiful and fashionable women.

British gentlemen of both parties have the same education, go to the same colleges and universities, have the same recreations—golf, cricket, lawn tennis or polo. All have played cricket or football in their youth ; they have the same habits of life, and are wont to spend the week-end in the country. There is no social cleavage between the parties, only a political one ; in recent years it had so far developed into a social cleavage that the politicians of the two camps avoided social intercourse with one another. Even in the neutral territory of an embassy one did not venture to mingle the two parties, as since the Veto and Home Rule Bills the Unionists had ostracised the Radicals. When the King and Queen dined with us a few months after my arrival, Lord Londonderry left the house after dinner, as he did not wish to remain together with Sir Edward Grey. But it was not a difference of caste or education as in France ; they are not two separate worlds, but the same ' world ' ; the opinion about a foreigner is formed in common and is not without influence on this foreigner's political position, whether Mr. Asquith be governing or Lord Lansdowne.

There has been no difference of caste in England since the time of the Stuarts ; not since the Guelph and Whig oligarchy, in contrast to the Tory landed gentry, encouraged the rise of an urban middle-class. It is rather a difference of political opinions about questions of constitutional law and taxation. Aristrocrats like Grey, Churchill, Harcourt and Crewe, who joined the people's party—the Radicals—

were especially hated by the Unionist aristocracy ; one never met any of these gentlemen at any of the great aristocratic houses except at those of a few friends of the Liberal party.

We were received in London with open arms, and both parties treated us with the greatest courtesy. In view of the close relationship between politics and society in England, it would be wrong to undervalue social relations, even when the majority of the upper ten thousand are in opposition to the Government.

There is not the same unbridgeable gulf between Mr. Asquith and the Duke of Devonshire as there is between M. Briand and the Duc de Doudeauville. Although they do not consort together in times of party tension and belong to two separate social groups, they feel that they are part of the *same* society, though of different grades, the centre of which is the Court. They have common friends and habits of life ; mostly they have known each other from their youth up and also are frequently related to one another either by blood or marriage.

Phenomena like Mr. Lloyd George—the man of the people, the self-made man who began as a small lawyer—are the exception. Even the self-taught Mr. Burns, the Socialist and Labour leader, sought contact with society. In view of the prevailing attempt to rank as a gentleman, the prototype of whom is still the great land-owner, the value of the verdict of society and its attitude must not be underestimated.

Hence the social adaptability of a representative nowhere plays a greater rôle than in England. A hospitable house run by pleasant hosts is worth more than the most profound special knowledge ; a savant with provincial manners and limited means would gain no influence, in spite of all his learning.

The Briton loathes a bore, a schemer and a prig ; what he likes is a good fellow.

SIR EDWARD GREY

Sir Edward Grey's influence in all matters of foreign policy was almost unlimited. On important occasions he used, indeed, to say, ' I must first bring the matter before the Cabinet,' but the Cabinet invariably agreed with him. His authority was undisputed. Although he does not know foreign countries at all, and had never left England except for a short visit to Paris, he was fully conversant with all the important questions owing to his long parliamentary experience and his natural insight. He understands French but does not speak it. He was returned to Parliament as a young man, and soon began to interest himself in foreign affairs. Under Lord Rosebery he was Under-Secretary of State for Foreign Affairs, and became Secretary of State in 1906 under Mr. Campbell-Bannerman ; he has now held the post for some ten years.

The scion of an old north-country family which had already furnished Earl Grey, the well-known statesman, he joined the left wing of his party and sympathised to some extent with the Socialists and pacifists. One might call him a Socialist in the ideal sense of the term. For, although he has extensive means, he carries the theory into his private life and lives very simply and unpretentiously. Ostentation is foreign to him. In London he only had a small flat, and never gave dinners, except the one official dinner at the Foreign Office on the King's Birthday. On the few occasions when he entertained guests it was at a simple dinner or lunch, with maidservants to wait. He avoided large functions and banquets.

Like his colleagues, he regularly spends his week-ends in the country ; he does not go in for large or fashionable parties. He is mostly by himself in his cottage in the New Forest, where he takes long walks to study birds and their ways, for he is a passionate lover of nature and a distinguished ornithologist. Or sometimes he goes to his estate in the north, where he feeds the squirrels that come in at the windows. In his park he breeds various species of waterfowl.

He was very fond of going to the Norfolk Broads to watch in their breeding season the rare kinds of herons which nest only there.

In his youth he was a well-known cricketer and racquets player ; now his favourite pastime is salmon and trout fishing in Scottish rivers in company with his friend Lord Glenconner, Mr. Asquith's brother-in-law. ' All the rest of the year I am looking forward to it,' he says. He has even published a book on fishing.

On one occasion when we spent a week-end with him alone at Lord Glenconner's, near Salisbury, he arrived on a bicycle and returned to his cottage about thirty miles distant in the same way.

The simplicity and honesty of his ways secured him the esteem even of his opponents, who were to be found rather in the sphere of home affairs than of foreign policy. Lies and intrigue are equally repugnant to him.

His wife, to whom he was devotedly attached and from whom he was inseparable, died in consequence of being thrown from a trap she was driving.   As is generally known, one of his brothers was killed by a lion.

Wordsworth was his favourite poet and he knew much of his poetry by heart.

The calm quiet of his British nature does not lack a sense of humour.   Once when he was lunching with us and the children, and heard them talking German, he said, ' I can't help thinking how clever these children are to talk German so well,' and was pleased with his joke.

This is a true picture of the man who is decried as ' Liar-Grey ' and as the ' Instigator of the World War.'

Mr. Asquith

Mr. Asquith is a man of an entirely different stamp.   A jovial *bon viveur*, fond of the ladies, especially the young and pretty ones, he is partial to cheerful society and good cooking, and his zest for enjoyment is shared by his wife.   Formerly a well-known barrister with a large income, and for a number of years in Parliament, then a Minister under Mr. Gladstone, a pacifist like his friend Grey, and favouring an understanding with Germany, he handled all questions with the cheery calm and assurance of an experienced man of business, whose good health and excellent nerves had been steeled by devotion to the game of golf.

His daughters had been at school in Germany and spoke German fluently.   In a short time we got on friendly terms with him and his family, and were his guests in his small country house on the Thames.

Only on the rare occasions when important questions arose did he concern himself with foreign politics ; then, of course, his decision was final.   During the critical days of July Mrs. Asquith repeatedly came to us to warn us, and in the end she was quite distraught at the tragic turn of events.   Mr. Asquith also, when I called on him on the 2nd of August to make a last effort in the direction of expectant neutrality, was quite broken, though absolutely calm.   Tears were coursing down his cheeks.

Nicolson

Sir A. Nicolson and Sir W. Tyrrell were, after the Minister, the two most influential men at the Foreign Office.   The former was no friend of Germany's, but his attitude towards me was scrupulously correct and courteous.   Our personal relations were excellent.   He, too, did not want war ; but as soon as we advanced against France, he no doubt worked in the direction of an immediate intervention. He was the confidant of my French colleague, with whom he was in constant touch ; also he wished to relieve Lord Bertie in Paris.

Sir Arthur, who had been Ambassador at Petrograd, had concluded the treaty of 1907, which had enabled Russia again to turn her attention to the West and to the Near East.

TYRRELL

Sir W. Tyrrell, Sir Edward's private secretary, possessed far greater influence than the Permanent Under-Secretary. This highly intelligent official had been at school in Germany. He had afterwards been in the diplomatic service, but had only been abroad for a short time. At first he favoured the anti-German policy, which was then in fashion among the younger British diplomatists, but later on he became a convinced advocate of an understanding. He influenced Sir Edward Grey, with whom he was very intimate, in this direction. [Since the outbreak of the war he has left the Foreign Office and found a place in the Home Office, probably because of the criticisms passed on him for his Germanophil tendencies.]

ATTITUDE OF THE GERMAN FOREIGN OFFICE

Nothing can describe the rage of certain gentlemen at my achievements in London and the position that I had managed to make for myself in a short time. They devised vexatious instructions to render my office more difficult. I was left in complete ignorance of most important matters and was restricted to the communication of dull and unimportant reports. Secret agents' reports were sent in on matters about which I could without espionage learn nothing, even had I had the necessary funds, which was not the case ; it was not till the last days of July 1914 that I learned, quite by chance, from the Naval Attaché, of the secret Anglo-French agreement concerning the co-operation of the two fleets in case of war. The knowledge of other important events which had been known to the Office for a long time, like the correspondence between Grey and Cambon, was kept from me.

IN CASE OF WAR

Soon after my arrival I became convinced that under *no* circumstances had we to fear a British attack or British support for any foreign attack, but that *under all circumstances England would protect the French should we attack them.* I expressed this view in repeated dispatches, with minute proof and great emphasis, but did not obtain any credence, although Lord Haldane's refusal to assent to the neutrality formula and England's attitude during the Morocco crisis had been pretty obvious indications. In addition there were the secret agreements which I have referred to, and which were known to the Office.

I always pointed out that in the event of a war between European Powers, England as a commercial state would suffer enormously, and would therefore do her best to prevent a conflict ; but, on the other hand, she would never tolerate a weakening or the annihilation of France, because of the necessity of maintaining the European balance of power and of preventing a German superiority of force. Lord Haldane had told me this shortly after my arrival, and all the leading people had expressed themselves in the same sense.

THE SERBIAN CRISIS

At the end of June I went to Kiel by command of the Kaiser. A few weeks prior to this I had been made an honorary D.C.L. of Oxford, an honour which had not been conferred on any German Ambassador since Herr von Bunsen.[1] Whilst on board the *Meteor* with the Kaiser, I learned of the death of the Archduke. His Majesty regretted that his efforts to win the Archduke over to his political ideas had thus been rendered vain. I do not know whether the plan of an active policy against Serbia had already been decided on at Konopischt.

As I was not instructed about views and events in Vienna, I did not attach very great importance to this occurrence. Later on I could only remark that amongst Austrian aristocrats a feeling of relief outweighed all other sentiments. [On board the *Meteor* there was also an Austrian guest of the Emperor's. He had remained in his cabin all the time, suffering from seasickness, in spite of the splendid weather ; but on receiving the news he was well. The fright, or joy, had cured him.]

On my arrival in Berlin I saw the Chancellor and told him that I considered the state of our foreign relations very satisfactory, as we were on better terms with England than we had been for a long time, whilst in France also the Government was in the hands of a pacifist Ministry.

[1] Count Metternich was made D.C.L. at Cambridge. (Author's note.)

Herr von Bethmann-Hollweg did not appear to share my optimism, and complained about Russian armaments. I sought to reassure him, emphasising the fact that Russia had no interest in attacking us, and that such an attack would never receive Anglo-French support, as both countries wanted peace. Thereupon I went to Dr. Zimmermann, who was acting for Herr von Jagow, and he told me that Russia was about to raise 900,000 additional troops. His language betrayed unmistakable annoyance with Russia, a country which, he said, was everywhere in our way. There were also difficulties in economic policy. Of course I was not told that General von Moltke, Chief of the General Staff, was pressing for war ; but I learned that Herr von Tschirschky had been reprimanded because he reported that he had counselled moderation in Vienna towards Serbia.

On my return from Silesia to London I stopped only a few hours in Berlin, where I heard that Austria intended to take steps against Serbia in order to put an end to an impossible situation.

[I am sorry that at the moment I underestimated the importance of the news. I thought that nothing would come of it this time either and that matters could easily be settled, even if Russia became threatening. I now regret that I did not stay in Berlin and at once declare that I would not co-operate in a policy of this kind.]

Subsequently I ascertained that, at the decisive conference [1] at Potsdam on the 5th July, the Vienna enquiry received the unqualified assent of all the leading people, [and with the rider that no harm would be done if a war with Russia should result. Thus it was expressed, at any rate, in the Austrian protocol which Count Mens-

----

[1] On the afternoon of 5th July, 1914, according to the official German statement now available, the Kaiser, after conferring with the Imperial Chancellor at Potsdam, sent for the War Minister, General von Falkenhayn, and told him that from what the Austrian Ambassador had said, he, the Kaiser, understood that Austria-Hungary intended, 'if necessary,' to march on Serbia. (Cf. the somewhat biassed account given by Count Montgelas in *The Case for the Central Powers*, p. 119.) The Kaiser also received a naval officer the same afternoon and, on the following morning, representatives of the Admiralty and of the General Staff. He informed them briefly of his conversation with the Austrian Ambassador, adding that he 'did not believe that there was any prospect of great warlike developments, as the Czar would not side with the Archduke's murderers, and as Russia and France were not ready for war. So there was no need to make special dispositions.'

Three-quarters of an hour later the Kaiser left for his annual trip to Norway.

It is interesting to note that these conferences at Potsdam gave rise later on to the notorious story of a Crown Council alleged to have been held at Potsdam on 5th July. This remarkable myth had its origin in Germany. After being whispered about for a while as gossip in Berlin clubs, it gradually spread to the Entente countries, where, as was natural, it everywhere found credence. Entente historians now admit that it was a gross exaggeration of the actual facts. (Tr.)

dorff received in London. Soon afterwards Herr von Jagow was in Vienna to consult Count Berchtold about all these matters].

At that time I received instructions to induce the British Press to adopt a friendly attitude should Austria administer the *coup de grâce* to the ' Greater Serbia ' movement, and to exert my personal influence to prevent public opinion from becoming inimical to Austria. If one remembered England's attitude during the annexation crisis of 1908, when public opinion showed sympathy for the Serbian rights in Bosnia, as well as her benevolent furtherance of national movements in the days of Lord Byron and Garibaldi, the probability that she would support the intended punitive expedition against the murderers of the prince was so remote that I found myself obliged to give an urgent warning. But I also warned my Government against the whole plan, which I characterised as adventurous and dangerous, and advised them to counsel the Austrians to *moderation*, as I did not believe that the conflict could be localized.

Herr von Jagow in reply told me that ' Russia was not ready ; there would probably be some fuss and noise, but the more firmly we took sides with Austria the more would Russia give way. As it was, Austria was accusing us of weakness, and therefore we dare not leave her in the lurch. Public opinion in Russia, on the other hand, was becoming more and more anti-German, so we must just risk it.'

In view of this attitude, based, as I found later, on reports [from Count Pourtalès] that Russia would not move under any circumstances, reports that made us spur Count Berchtold on to the utmost energy—I hoped for salvation through British mediation, as I knew that Sir E. Grey's great influence in Petrograd could be used in the direction of peace. I therefore availed myself of my friendly relations with the Minister to request him in confidence to advise moderation in Russia in case Austria, as seemed likely, demanded satisfaction from Serbia.

At first the English Press preserved calm and was friendly to Austria, because the murder was generally condemned. But gradually more and more voices were heard insisting emphatically that, however much the crime merited punishment, its exploitation for political purposes could not be justified. Austria was strongly exhorted to use moderation.

When the ultimatum was published, all the papers with the exception of the *Standard* [—the ever necessitous, which had apparently been bought by Austria—] were unanimous in condemnation. The whole world, excepting Berlin and Vienna, realised that it meant war—indeed, 'the world war.' The British Fleet, which happened to have assembled for a naval review, was not demobilised.

My efforts were in the first place directed towards obtaining as conciliatory a reply from Serbia as was possible, since the attitude of the Russian Government left no room for doubt as to the gravity of the situation.

Serbia responded favourably to the British efforts, as M. Pashitch had really agreed to everything, excepting two points, about which, however, he declared his willingness to negotiate. If Russia and England had wanted the war, in order to attack us, a hint to Belgrade would have been enough, and the unprecedented Note would not have been answered.

Sir E. Grey went through the reply with me, and pointed out the conciliatory attitude of the Belgrade Government. Thereupon we discussed his proposal of mediation, which was to include a formula acceptable to both parties for clearing up the two points. His proposal was that a committee, consisting of M. Cambon, the Marquis Imperiali and myself, should assemble under his presidency, and it would have been an easy matter for us to find an acceptable formula for the points at issue, which mainly concerned the collaboration of Austrian Imperial officials in the investigations in Belgrade. Given goodwill everything could have been settled at one or two sittings, and the mere acceptance of the British proposal would have brought about a relaxation of the tension, and would have further improved our relations with England. I therefore strongly backed the proposal, on the ground that otherwise there was danger of a world-war, through which we stood to gain nothing, but lose all ; but in vain. It was, I was told, derogatory to the dignity of Austria—we did not intend to interfere in Serbian matters—we left these to our ally. I was to work for the ' localization of the conflict.'

Needless to say a mere hint from Berlin would have decided Count Berchtold to content himself with a diplomatic success, and to accept the Serbian reply. This hint was not given ; on the contrary they urged in the direction of war. It would have been such a splendid success.

After our refusal Sir Edward requested us to submit a proposal. [We insisted on war with Serbia.] I could not obtain any reply but that Austria had shown an exceedingly ' accommodating spirit ' by not demanding an extension of territory.

Sir Edward rightly pointed out that even without an extension of territory it is possible to reduce a state to a condition of vassalage, and that Russia would see a humiliation in this, and would not suffer it.

The impression grew stronger and stronger that we wanted war under all circumstances. It was impossible to interpret our attitude on a question that did not directly concern us in any other way. The urgent requests and definite assurances of M. Sazonov, followed by the Czar's positively humble telegrams, the repeated proposals of Sir E. Grey, the warnings of the Marquis San Giuliano and Signor Bollati, my urgent counsels, all were of no avail. Berlin insisted that Serbia must be chastised.

The more I pressed, the less were they inclined to come round, [if only that I in conjunction with Sir Edward Grey might not have the success of averting war].

Finally, on the 29th, Sir E. Grey decided on the famous warning. I replied that I had invariably reported that we should have to reckon with English opposition if it came to a war with France. Repeatedly the Minister said to me : ' If war breaks out, it will be the greatest catastrophe the world has ever seen.'

After that, events followed each other in quick succession. When at last Count Berchtold, who up till then had, at the behest of Berlin, played the strong man, decided to come round, [and when Herr von Bethmann, too, grew afraid], we replied to the Russian mobilisation, after Russia had negotiated and waited for a whole week in vain, with our ultimatum and the declaration of war.

The English Declaration of War

Sir Edward still strove to find some way of avoiding the catastrophe. Sir W. Tyrrell called on me on the morning of the 1st August to tell me that his chief still hoped to find a way out. Would we remain neutral if France did ? I understood that we should then agree to spare France, but he had meant that we should remain altogether neutral—towards Russia also. That was the well-known ' misunderstanding.' Sir Edward had asked me to call in the afternoon. As he was at a meeting of the Cabinet, he called me up on the telephone, Sir W. Tyrrell having hurried to him at once. In the afternoon, however, he talked about Belgian neutrality and the possibility that we and France might face one another in arms without attacking.

This was thus not a proposal at all, but a question without any binding force, as our interview, as I have already mentioned, was to take place soon afterwards. Berlin, however, without waiting for the interview, made this report the foundation for far-reaching measures. Then there came M. Poincaré's letter, Bonar Law's letter, King Albert's telegram. The waverers in the British Cabinet— excepting three members who resigned—were converted.

[Up to the very last moment] I had hoped that England would adopt a waiting attitude. Nor did my French colleague feel at all confident, as I heard from a private source. As late as the 1st August the King had given the President an evasive reply. But England was already mentioned as an opponent in the telegram from Berlin announcing the imminent danger of war. Berlin was therefore already reckoning on war with England.

Before my departure Sir E. Grey received me, on the 5th, at his house. I had called at his request. He was deeply moved. He told me that he would always be prepared to mediate. ' We don't want to crush Germany,' he said. By making this confidential interview public Herr von Bethmann-Hollweg unfortunately destroyed the last chance of gaining peace through the mediation of England.

The arrangements for our departure were perfectly dignified and calm. The King had previously sent his equerry, Sir E. Ponsonby, to express his regrets at my departure and at not being able to see me himself. Princess Louise wrote to me that the whole family were sorry we were leaving. Mrs. Asquith and other friends came to the Embassy to take leave.

A special train took us to Harwich, where a guard of honour was drawn up for me. I was treated like a departing sovereign. Such was the end of my London mission. It was wrecked, not by the wiles (*Tücken*) of the British policy but by the defects (*Lücken*) of our own.

[Count Mensdorff and his staff had come to the station in London. He was cheerful, and gave me to understand that perhaps he would remain there, but he told the English that we, and not Austria, had wanted the war.]

Retrospect

Looking back after two years, I come to the conclusion that I realised too late that there was no room for me in a system that for years had lived on routine and traditions alone, and that only tolerated representatives who reported what their superiors wished to read. Absence of prejudice and an independent judgment are resented. Lack of ability and want of character are praised and esteemed, while successes meet with disfavour and excite alarm.

I had given up my opposition to the insane Triple Alliance policy, as I realised that such opposition was useless, and that my warnings were attributed to ' Austrophobia,' to my *idée fixe*. In politics, which are neither acrobatics nor a game, but the main business of the firm, there is no ' phil ' or ' phobe,' but only the interest of the community. A policy, however, that was based only on Austrians, Magyars and Turks was bound to come into conflict with Russia, and finally lead to a catastrophe.

In spite of former mistakes, all might still have been put right in July 1914. An agreement with England had been arrived at. We ought to have sent a representative to Petrograd who was at least of average political capacity, and to have convinced Russia that we wished neither to control the straits nor to strangle Serbia. ' Lâchez l'Autriche et nous lâcherons les Français ' (' Drop Austria and we will drop the French '), M. Sazonov said to us. And M. Cambon told Herr von Jagow, ' Vous n'avez pas besoin de suivre l'Autriche partout ' (' You need not follow Austria everywhere ').

We needed *neither wars nor alliances* ; we needed only treaties that would safeguard us and others, and secure our economic development, a development that was without precedent in history.

If Russia had been freed in the West, she could have again turned to the East, and the Anglo-Russian rivalry would have been re-established automatically and without our intervention. With no less certainty the old rivalry between Russia and Japan would have revived.

We could then have also considered the question of the reduction of armaments ; we need no longer have troubled ourselves about Austrian complications. Then Austria would have become the vassal of the German Empire, without any alliance—and especially without our seeking her good graces, a proceeding ultimately leading to war for the liberation of Poland and the destruction of Serbia, although German interests demanded the exact contrary.

[I had to support in London a policy the heresy of which I recognised. That brought down vengeance on me, because it was a sin against the Holy Ghost.]

MY RETURN

As soon as I arrived in Berlin I saw that I was to be made the scapegoat for the catastrophe for which, despite my advice and warnings, our Government had made itself responsible.

In official quarters the report was deliberately circulated that I had allowed myself to be deceived by Sir E. Grey. It was argued that if he had not wanted war, Russia would not have mobilized. [Count Pourtalès, whose reports could be relied on, was to be protected, not least on account of his relationship. He had conducted himself 'magnificently,' he was praised enthusiastically, and I was blamed the more severely.]

' What does Serbia matter to Russia ? ' this statesman said to me after eight years in office in Petrograd. [The whole thing was, I was told, a British trick that I had not noticed. At the Foreign Office they informed me that war would in any case have come in 1916. Then Russia would have been ready ; therefore it was better now.]

THE QUESTION OF RESPONSIBILITY

As is evident from all official publications—and this is not refuted by our White Book, which, owing to the poverty of its contents and to its omissions, is [a gravely self-accusing document].

1. We encouraged Count Berchtold to attack Serbia, although German interests were not involved and the danger of a world-war must have been known to us. Whether we were aware of the actual wording of the ultimatum is completely immaterial.

2. During the time between the 23rd and 30th July, 1914, when M. Sazonov emphatically declared that he could not tolerate any attack on Serbia, we rejected the British proposals of mediation, although Serbia, under Russian and British pressure, had accepted almost the whole of the ultimatum, and although an agreement about the two points at issue could easily have been reached, and Count Berchtold was even prepared to content himself with the Serbian reply.

3. On the 30th July, when Count Berchtold wanted to come to terms, we sent an ultimatum to Petrograd merely because of the Russian mobilization, although Austria had not been attacked ; and on the 31st July we declared war on Russia, although the Czar pledged his word that he would not order

a man to march as long as negotiations were proceeding—thus deliberately destroying the possibility of a peaceful settlement.

In view of the above [undeniable] facts it is no wonder that the whole of the civilized world outside Germany places the [entire] responsibility for the world-war upon our shoulders.

THE ENEMY POINT OF VIEW

Is it not intelligible that our enemies should declare that they will not rest before a system is destroyed which is a constant menace to our neighbours ? Must they not otherwise fear that in a few years' time they will again have to take up arms and again see their provinces overrun and their towns and villages destroyed ? Have not they proved to be right who declared that the spirit of Treitschke and Bernhardi governed the German people, that spirit which glorified war as an aim in itself, and did not loathe it as an evil, that with us the feudal knight and the landed gentry, the warrior caste, still rule. It is they and not the civilian gentleman, who set ideals and fix values ; that the love of fighting which animates our academic youth still persists in those who control the destinies of the nation ? Did not the Zabern incident and the parliamentary discussions about it clearly demonstrate to foreign countries the value we place on the rights and liberties of the citizen if these collide with questions of military power ?

The gifted historian Cramb, an admirer of Germany, clothed the German conception in the words of Euphorion :

> Träumt Ihr den Friedenstag ?
> Träume, wer träumen mag !
> Krieg ist das Losungswort !
> Sieg ! und so klingt es fort !
> GOETHE, *Faust*, ii.

Militarism, which by rights is an education for the people and an instrument of policy, turns policy into the instrument of military power when the patriarchal absolutism of the soldier-kingdom makes possible an attitude which a democracy, remote from the influence of the landed gentry, would never have permitted.

So think our enemies, and so they must think when they see that, in spite of capitalistic industrialisation and in spite of socialist organisation, ' the living are still ruled by the dead,' as Friedrich

Nietzsche says.   The principal war aim of our enemies, the democratisation of Germany, will be realised !

BISMARCK

Bismarck, like Napoleon, loved conflict for itself.   As a statesman he avoided fresh wars, the folly of which he recognised.   He was content with bloodless battles.   After he had, in rapid succession, vanquished Christian, Francis Joseph and Napoleon, it was the turn of Arnim, Pius and Augusta.   That did not suffice him.   Gortschakoff, [who thought himself the greater], had repeatedly annoyed him.   The conflict was carried almost to the point of war—even to the extent of depriving him of his railway saloon.   This gave rise to the miserable Triple Alliance.   At last came the conflict with Wilhelm, in which the mighty one was vanquished as Napoleon was vanquished by Alexander.

Political life-and-death unions only prosper if founded on a constitutional basis and not on an international one.   They are all the more questionable if entered into with a partner who is frail and feeble.   Bismarck never meant the Alliance to take this form.

He always treated the English with forbearance ; he knew that this was wiser.   He always paid marked respect to the old Queen Victoria, despite his hatred of her daughter and of political Anglomania ;   the learned Beaconsfield and the worldly-wise Salisbury he assiduously courted ;   and even that strange Gladstone, whom he did not like, really had nothing to complain about.

The ultimatum to Serbia was the culminating point of the policy of the Berlin Congress, the Bosnian crisis, the Conference of London : but there was yet time to turn back.

We eventually succeeded in achieving that which above all other things should have been avoided—the breach with Russia and with England.

OUR FUTURE

After two years' fighting it is obvious that we dare not hope for an unconditional victory over the Russians, English, French, Italians, Rumanians and Americans, or reckon on being able to wear our enemies down.   But we can obtain a peace by compromise only by evacuating the occupied territory, the retention of which would in any event be a burden and cause of weakness to us, and would involve the menace of further wars.   Therefore everything should be avoided which would make it more difficult for those enemy groups who might possibly still be won over to the idea of a peace by compromise to come to terms, viz. the British Radicals and the Russian Reactionaries. From this point of view alone the Polish scheme is to be condemned, as is also any infringement of Belgian rights, and the execution of British citizens—to say nothing of the insane U-boat plan.

' Our future lies on the water.' Quite right ; why seek it, therefore, in Poland and Belgium, in France and Serbia ? This is a return to the days of the Holy Roman Empire and the mistakes of the Hohenstaufens and Habsburgs. It is the policy of the Plantagenets, not that of Drake and Raleigh, Nelson and Rhodes. The policy of the Triple Alliance is a return to the past, a turning aside from the future, from imperialism and a world-policy. The idea of an all-powerful ' Middle Europe ' belongs to the Middle Ages, Berlin-Baghdad is a blind alley and not the way into the open country, to unlimited possibilities, to the world mission of the German nation.

I am no enemy of Austria, or Hungary, or Italy or Serbia, or any other state, but I oppose the Triple Alliance policy, which was bound to divert us from our aims and bring us on to the inclined plane of a Continental policy : this ideal was not German but Austrian and dynastic. The Austrians had come to regard the Triple Alliance as an umbrella under shelter of which they could make excursions to the Near East whenever it suited them.

And what must we expect as the result of this war of nations ? The United States of Africa will be British, like those of America, Australia and Oceania. And the Latin states of Europe, as I predicted years ago, will enter into the same relations with the United Kingdom that their Latin sisters in America maintain with the United States. The Anglo-Saxon will dominate them. France, exhausted by the war, will only attach herself more closely to Great Britain. [Nor will Spain continue to resist for very long.]

And in Asia the Russians and the Japanese will spread and will carry their customs with their frontiers, and the South will remain to the British.

The world will belong to the Anglo-Saxons, Russians, and Japanese, and the German will remain alone with Austria [and Hungary]. His dominion will be that of thought and commerce, not that of the bureaucrat and the soldier. He made his appearance too late, and his last chance of making good the past, that of founding a Colonial Empire, was annihilated by the world-war.

For we shall not supplant the sons of Jehovah. Then will be realised the plan of the great Rhodes, who saw the salvation of humanity in the expansion of Britondom—in British Imperialism.

> Tu regere imperio populos, Romane, memento.
> Hae tibi erunt artes : pacisque imponere morem,
> Parcere subjectis et debellare superbos.

DIPLOMACY AND DEMOCRACY [1]

I

' The Ambassador worries me to death, as I thought he would. He is the most punctilious fool you can imagine, and cautious and fussy as an old aunt—a man who is never satisfied with himself and whom, consequently, no one can ever please. When I am writing, I like to go straight ahead, and when it's down, it's down. Then *he*'ll come along and hand me back my work and say, " It's not so bad, but go through it again. One can always find a better word here and there or a purer particle." It's enough to drive one crazy. A sentence must never begin with " and " or any other conjunction ; and as for inversions, a habit I often slip into, they're his pet aversion. Unless one reels off one's sentences to the usual humdrum melody, he professes not to understand a word of them. It's torture to have to work under such a man.'

' I'm very much afraid that my good Ambassador and I shan't be able to hit it very much longer. He is simply intolerable. His manner of working and the way he runs the place is so ludicrous that I can't help contradicting him and often do things in my own way as the fancy takes me, which of course, doesn't meet with his approval.' [2]

Well, I hope that my diplomatic colleagues in London, excellent officials as they were, will have passed a more favourable verdict on me than did young Werther on his chief in that winter of 1771-72.

Complaints concerning the inefficiency of diplomats are no new thing. Since the collapse of our foreign policy in the summer of 1914, many such laments have been heard in Germany. When anything goes wrong, it is of course the diplomats who are to blame. People take pleasure in finding fault with this privileged class who with their high salaries, their dinner parties, their decorations, orders and distinctions, not to mention their privileged social position, have

---

[1] First published in the summer of 1917 in the *Berliner Tageblatt*.

[2] The quotation is from Goethe's *Sorrows of Werther*.

long since excited envy. Everyone has, no doubt, at some time or other met diplomats of various countries whose brilliance lay rather in externals and in their social talents than in profound knowledge or remarkable shrewdness, men whose interests were mainly confined to Court gossip, invitations, and the order of seats at table, extended, in exceptionally gifted cases, to bridge.

Carl Schurz [1] in the description he gives in his *Memoirs* of his mission to Madrid humorously depicts his first call on a colleague from whom, in consequence of his long experience at the Spanish Court, he expected to get some valuable hints about conditions in Spain. Instead of giving his caller information on political matters, to which he had apparently never devoted any thought, the Minister with an air of mystery and importance showed him a silver casket in which he kept the various Orders conferred upon him by Kings and Emperors, explaining in each case why the special distinction had been granted him.

I, too, well remember the first visit I paid as a young chargé d'affaires at one of the less important Courts to the *doyen* of the diplomatic corps, an elderly bachelor who represented a small southern state. He talked to me not of politics but of the many duels he had fought in his youth, illustrating these reminiscences with scraps of silk and tulle which he had piously preserved.

At forty or so, a German diplomat who does not happen to have a black mark against his name and who possesses the necessary pliability, will as a rule have attained the rank of Minister, often without any extraordinary exertions on his part, most of his feats having been achieved at the festive board or in the ballrooms and drawing-rooms of society. Non-diplomatic officials of the same age will probably not have attained a similar standing even though they have worked harder. This disparity easily leads people to indulge in criticism when mishaps occur. The taxpayer asks why such high salaries should be paid to diplomats who achieve nothing in a career for which only the greatest dunderheads are apparently chosen. In Germany as elsewhere it frequently happens, too, that successful business men suddenly develop a wish to possess an aristocratic title and to prefix a ' von ' to their names, a prefix borrowed from a time when families were named after their ancestral castle or their estate. Once their names have been embellished in this fashion, a privilege

---

[1] Carl Schurz, born 1829, had to flee from Germany in 1848. He afterwards became famous in the United States as a publicist and politician.   (Tr.)

which until a short time back in Austria and Bavaria automatically accompanied the conferring of certain decorations, they form a part of the ' nobility.' The shortcomings of Herr von Maier are much more unsparingly criticised than would have been those of plain Herr Maier,[1] and are of course debited to the account of the nobility.

A great many of Germany's diplomats belong, it is true, to our old aristocracy ; I do not regard this as a disadvantage, except in cases where ' birth has to make up for lack of brains,' and where members of aristocratic families have been unduly favoured at the expense of bourgeois candidates. The fact that most of our diplomats bear a title of nobility is partly ascribable to the circumstance that out of social and financial considerations the choice of candidates for the foreign diplomatic service is limited to the class of the optimates.

Many years ago, as the head of this special department, I had to report on the qualifications of candidates for our diplomatic service. I found it no easy task to select young men who were satisfactory in all respects. I never troubled about pedigree or wealth. Candidates quite without means never applied for admission. Many of these young men had at that time only very modest incomes, but no one was ever turned down because he did not happen to have the pre-scribed £300 a year. I made it a practice to watch the candidate as he entered the room. Then I knew pretty well with whom I had to deal. The conversation that ensued soon showed what sort of intelligence he possessed.

A course of reading in law is undoubtedly the best foundation that candidates for the diplomatic service can have. As a general rule examination marks do not count so much as personality. A know-ledge of the commercial side of political economy is useful though not essential, as the Consulates generally do all the work necessary in this field ; on special occasions, as for instance when commercial treaties are being negotiated, special representatives are sent by the Foreign Office. As a rule the overseas appointments, where commerce plays a prominent part, are filled by a former Consul General who then passes into the diplomatic service. This procedure suits the purpose, as in the states in question we are not often likely to find in their presidents allies of any great value.

Ex-officers, too, may on occasion make quite good diplomats, even without a university training, always pre-supposing, of course, that

---

[1] The German surname ' Maier ' is to be compared with ' Jones ' and ' Smith in English for frequency of recurrence. (Tr.)

they have talent and zeal.   Older military men, however, are seldom
adapted for higher diplomatic posts.   They often lack the necessary
scepticism, a quality best acquired abroad.   Nor do they generally
possess the faculty of judging men and things apart from a hard and
fast schedule.   They fail for the most part to see the different sides of
political questions and find it difficult to get out of the habit of
regarding affairs from the angle of their own particular class.

There is and there can be no such thing as a special prescription for
turning out a perfect diplomat.   In former years we used to lay great
stress upon a mastery of French, and Bismarck relates that he had
often met men among the older generation of our envoys to foreign
courts ' who had reached high place solely through the excellence of
their French, although they had no knowledge whatever of politics.'
Nowadays we are inclined to go to the other extreme and to underestimate the importance of foreign languages.   Russian and Austrian
diplomats, I have noticed, are mostly better equipped in this respect
than ours.

As for methodical study and intellectual training, I consider it
distinctly desirable, if for no other reason than that an uneducated
diplomat is apt to expose his shortcomings and make himself
ridiculous.   I have known men among the older generation, both in
Germany and elsewhere, who, when measured by present standards,
were not well educated, but who, thanks to their tact and wide experience, strong personality, social position and natural gifts, possessed
considerable influence.   One may be an eminent jurist and an authority
on economics and know all manner of things without being able to
take the wide and enlightened view that is essential in a diplomat or
statesman.   The British diplomatic service, which some people
consider to be so superior to ours, certainly does not make higher
educational demands on its members than does ours.   In England
there are even more complaints than here concerning superficiality
and ignorance, and I read not long ago in an English newspaper that a
man high up in the diplomatic service was quite astonished to learn
that Galicia did not belong to Hungary but to Austria.   When
Turkey declared war, there was in the London press no end to the
attacks on the British diplomatic service, which was reproached with
being simple and unsophisticated, while ours was described as crafty
and energetic.

As regards income, it is suggested that salaries should be raised so
that the most able men may be appointed.   But who are the ablest ?

Not necessarily those who come out highest in examinations. Is there to be a still greater disparity between our diplomatic salaries—which, by the way, compared with the British are by no means brilliant—and the modest incomes of the rest of our civil servants ? Can one prevent an ambassador who has a large family but no private fortune from putting aside one half of his salary instead of spending it for representative purposes ? Is it not important, just in the case of a diplomat, that he should possess a certain degree of independence in order that he may be in a position always to act according to his conscience instead of having to tremble for his post, which may be taken from him at any time without the reason being stated ? It is noteworthy that a democratic country like the United States generally sends wealthy men abroad as ambassadors, as they are best able to meet the demands made upon them for representative purposes.

I will not, however, deny that our diplomats' salaries are in many cases quite insufficient and urgently in need of increase. One of the reasons of this is to be found in the present depreciation of our currency, which is hardly likely to improve for some time to come.

Some diplomatic appointments bring with them a salary of £1,500—many less, but few very much more. Out of this sum the Minister, should there be no official building at his disposal, must pay some £900 a year for a suitable residence. From the remainder must be deducted various taxes and a special allowance for his chargé d'affaires during vacations. How can what is left be made to cover all the other items of necessary expenditure ? If he is married he cannot possibly escape the obligation of returning the hospitality shown him. His wife's dressmakers' bills swallow up almost all that is left. The Austro-Hungarian diplomatic service is by no means one of the worst, and its members, despite political troubles, mostly enjoy a good personal position, because as a rule they belong to families in which, as Bismarck put it, a greater degree of self-assurance in Court circles and rather less than the average blockheadedness are products of their education.

To be an efficient diplomat a man must possess, in addition to a good general education and a fairly assured private income, a certain amount of tact, social culture, a natural instinct for men and things, sound commonsense, the faculty of making himself liked and of adapting himself to foreign conditions, ability to understand and appreciate other people's standpoints and, especially in the case of important positions, political judgment.

These things lie outside the pale of rules and regulations for the training of diplomats and beyond the scope of all the praiseworthy orations delivered in the Reichstag concerning the reorganisation of our diplomatic service. ' Give the man of ability a chance to come to the front ' is doubtless an excellent principle, but it has no more value than the usual mottoes on coats-of-arms which everyone interprets to his own taste.

I will not attempt to maintain that our diplomats were all up to the mark, but it is quite an exaggeration to say, as is often done, that they are, one and all, inefficient. On the whole, they are certainly no worse than those of other countries. The conspicuous mistakes that have sometimes been made in appointing the wrong people to important posts are to be traced rather to bureaucratic than to Court influences.

People often confuse diplomacy in the sense of foreign policy with the foreign diplomatic staff. A diplomat is only an organ and a representative. All he can do is to report, to pass on his observations, to counsel and warn. If the men at home refuse to listen to him and if they disregard his advice, he is powerless, and it is unjust to make him responsible for events that he correctly foresaw and predicted. But even should he be wrong, and this is known to have happened at decisive moments, he is not so much to blame as the men who allowed a man to remain at an important post long after his incompetence had been proved beyond a doubt.

Are all doctors clever at their profession ? Or all artists ? All farmers ? And is every honest cobbler to be recommended ? The public can judge by its own experience in such cases, while the authorities, on the other hand, have to remove officials who are inadequate for their posts. Incompetent ambassadors have, I admit, their advantages. They are easy-going and are ready to write and report anything you want to read ; they have no opinions of their own, and best of all, there is no danger of their becoming the competitors of their superiors. Men of this calibre used justly to be held in especially high esteem.

An able and thoroughly competent representative can be of the greatest service provided he succeeds in winning the confidence of authoritative circles in the country to which he is accredited. But he must have the support of his Government. If for some outside reason or other his efforts are consistently thwarted, all his energy is thrown away and he is nothing more than a private gentleman who gives dinner-parties for the glory of the Empire.

II

To rational enthusiasts, foreign policy means love and loathing ; to ignorant romanticists it means tradition and trial by battle ; to simple-minded philistines, loyalty and treason ; to muddle-headed counsellors it is a kind of game played with official documents ; for bored and yawning Courts it is a form of pastime ; to many a diplomat, his career ; to impatient generals, the road to glory ; and for German professors, a *terra incognita*. In reality it is the business our own firm carries on with foreign firms. Foreign policy can be a fine art when it treads successfully new and original paths of its own and embodies an idea, but not when it embodies an error. It is then that the difference is revealed between real statecraft and bureaucratic or diplomatic routine and mediocrity.

In Bismarck's time, too, Germany's ambassadors and envoys were not all shining lights. If we leave out of account Hohenlohe, Schweinitz, Hatzfeldt and perhaps Arnim and Radowitz, there are few who rise above the average.

I intentionally refrain from all personal remarks ; but if I go to the root of the matter, I cannot but ask myself whether it is not the system itself that is at fault.

The system stakes everything on a single card. It plays, so to say, for the first prize in the lottery. The destinies of the nation lie in the hands of a single official and only in rare instances is this official equal to such a task. The English call this the ' one man system.' Whereas in England every question of importance has first to be submitted to the Cabinet—a council consisting of some twenty members which in its turn remains in constant touch not only with the parliamentary majority but also, in all important questions of foreign policy, with the Opposition as well—in Germany every-thing rests in the hands of one single Minister who is advised by irresponsible and mostly incompetent, sometimes not even quite normal, subordinates.[1]

This Minister has, it is true, to take his orders from the Sovereign and it is with the Sovereign that the final decision lies. Considering

[1] This refers to the mysterious and all-powerful Baron Holstein, whom contemporaries nicknamed ' die graue Eminenz,' (the Cardinal in grey). (Tr.)

the manifold demands made upon the Monarch and the manifold interests that claim his attention, it is often impossible for him to go to the bottom of every question and thoroughly understand it.   In practice he has to depend upon the reports that are made to him by his Minister, and the more so since it is the Minister and not the Monarch who has to bear the responsibility.   Should the decision in any important question be given in a sense contrary to the report given by the Minister, the latter knows what conclusion he has to draw.

In spite of occasional outbursts of temperament, the Monarch refrains far more than is generally supposed from autocratic inter-ference.   During the whole of my experience at the Foreign Office and since, I can remember not a single case, either in foreign policy or in important imperial appointments, when the decision come to was not in accordance with the proposals recommended by the Ministers.

Will this system, the system of individualised responsibility and of bureaucratic power, be able to survive the war ?   Would the monarchical idea necessarily suffer if the responsibility were dis-tributed over a broader basis, if a council took the place of the individual and if this council again, without necessarily consisting of members of the Reichstag, kept in close touch and in organic con-nection with the people's representatives and the majority parties ? Will questions that decide the fate of the nation continue to be settled in the bureaucratic, patriarchal manner, without applying the principle of self-administration to the business of the state and the Empire and granting to the nation extended powers of self-determination ?

The spirit of ' true democracy ' will, I am convinced, find its way into Germany, too, no matter whether we may regard this innova-tion as a blessing or the reverse.   Although this be a matter of opinion, it is the inevitable consequence of the stupendous experience that we as a nation have gone through in the past three years.

In future it will be regarded as unthinkable that treaties which may involve a nation in war should be concluded or renewed without the assent of the representatives of the people.   Just as impossible will it be to force on an existing treaty an interpretation that means war, unless Parliament give its assent.   Nor will the despatch of an ultimatum or a declaration of war take place in future without the Reichstag having first been consulted.

If in an age when the democratization and republicanization of nations is proceeding apace we desire to maintain the monarchy uninjured, we must relieve the Crown of some of its dangerous responsibilities, unless we wish it to be subjected to even more criticism than at present. Otherwise it may easily happen that the Crown will be held responsible for mistakes and failures for which it is not to blame.

No matter what fault critics may find with the parliamentary system and with the statesmanlike qualities of the people's representatives, the co-operation and co-responsibility of Parliament will have to be extended. The bureaucratic state, the obedience to the authority of a régime like that of Bismarck, has passed away, never to return ; the days when nations were kept in a state of tutelage are as obsolete as those of theocracy, and it will no longer satisfy a people merely to have the right to say ' Yes ' and to cry ' Hurrah ' when faced with accomplished facts.

Even if the war end for us as favourably as possible, the result will always fall short of the sacrifices we have made, even should we conquer and subjugate alien territory and thereby sow the seeds of new wars. It is, of course, just those people who before the war jeered at the idea of an understanding and preached a preventive war, who have now developed the most rapacious appetite and who are clamouring loudest for ' guarantees.'

No scruples advanced by sticklers for the Rights of the State will in the long run avail to check the onward march of the democratic development of the ideals of the Reich. I am by no means blind to the advantages of the present Federal Constitution and should like to see this form kept as far as possible. The importance of the Empire as the representative of the most vital interests of the nation has grown as the years have passed. Its competence has widened ; like any other big concern, it has gone through a process of organic development. This process inevitably involved the sacrifice of certain rights of the individual states. To-day the Reich is something more than an ' everlasting confederation ' of sovereign states. Nothing in nature remains everlastingly the same, and the forward movement of the Reich was inevitable, unless reaction was to set in and lead to dissolution.

The individual federal states, like the individual citizens, will be obliged to make sacrifices for the sake of the whole. Here, too, there can be no rigid adherence to existing laws and conditions, which will have to be adapted to the new demands. Bismarck is frequently quoted in order to prove that no alteration should be made in the

existing constitution of the Empire.   But the great statesman could
be quoted just as cogently to prove the opposite.   It is wiser,
perhaps, for the present, to leave such quotations alone.   When
Bismarck called the Constitution of the Reich into being, it is pretty
certain that he never contemplated a war against practically all the
remaining inhabitants of our planet, nor did he, when he framed the
Constitution, reckon with the political, economic and social consequences of a war lasting several years.   It is, too, a delicate question
why the Bavarians and the Thuringians, the Oldenburgers and the
Lippians should have a greater right to individual stateship and enjoy
greater consideration for their racial peculiarities, than the Han-
overians, the Schleswig-Holsteiners and the Hesse-Nassauers?   The
particularism that in the one case counts as a virtue in the other
counts as a vice.   The Great Chancellor, to whose authority people
are so ready to appeal, never allowed legitimistic and sentimental
arguments to weigh with him.   In coming to his decisions he was
guided not by principles so much as by considerations of practical
utility.   Although he shrank from interfering with established
institutions, the needs of the moment helped him to overcome
his scruples.   Force of habit and the ramifications of personal
interests that are linked up with tradition and that are cruelly torn
asunder with each new reform, have always been the main obstacles
in the way of necessary changes.

The war with its incalculable national debt and its obscure problems of interest and amortisation has pushed the question of
centralisation into the foreground and created a new situation, new
tasks and problems, which will oust all other considerations and
demonstrate the inadequacy of the present state form to deal with
them.   To-day the Reich is already mortgaged to the extent of
about one-third of our entire national assets.   And wealth means
power.   Economic questions have from time immemorial been the
decisive factor in the life of a nation.

Perhaps the time is coming when we shall see the democratization
of our diplomatic service.   Will such a change prove an advantage ?
Or will the diplomatic service be done away with altogether ?
For the present I should say to any young friend who possessed
everything necessary for the diplomatic career except earthly goods,
' Choose any profession you like, but do not choose diplomacy.
It is not the road that leads to an assured and independent posi-
tion in life.   That is a thing you are expected to bring with you ! '

THE ROOTS OF THE CATASTROPHE [1]

(Some Remarks on the 'Memoirs' of General von Schweinitz, German Ambassador at St. Petersburg, together with a Criticism of Bismarck's Foreign Policy.)

I

ANYONE who reads the *Memoirs* of General von Schweinitz attentively must come to the conclusion that this man, who from 1876 to 1892 was German Ambassador at St. Petersburg,[2] has in these *Memoirs* left behind him a work of unusual importance as an historical source. When the reader lays down the book he will be filled with regret that this diplomat was not Bismarck's successor. It is the greatest pity that there is not a third volume. One regrets this the more on learning that for technical reasons the great mass of material left behind by the Ambassador had to be cut down in order to prevent the work running into a third volume.

I never had the honour to meet General von Schweinitz. I remember that in my youth he was looked upon as the most able ambassador of the Bismarckian era—a reputation his *Memoirs* fully justify. Nor, with the exception of Bismarck's *Reflections and Reminiscences*, do I know of any other book written by a German diplomat that can be compared with it. One feels oneself in the presence of a great and noble man, two qualities that, as we know, were not always found in combination even in those days. The extraordinary value of the book lies, however, more especially in the courageous and unsparing exposition of certain errors which finally led to the great catastrophe and in the frank and fearless criticism of Germany's first Chancellor, a man whom General von Schweinitz reverenced as he did no other and to whose goodwill he mainly owed his successful career. Nowadays a belief in the infallibility of the Iron Chancellor's foreign policy has become an article of faith in Conservative circles, to doubt which is nothing short of impious; but

[1] Originally published in the *Berliner Tageblatt* in the summer of 1927. (Tr.)

[2] He had already held a similar appointment at Vienna and been for a time Military Plenipotentiary at the Russian Court.

this diplomat's candid utterances clearly show that the origins of the present catastrophe date back to the days when our estrangement from Russia first began, an estrangement which, despite all Herr von Schweinitz's warnings, eventually led to the world war.

Schweinitz clearly perceived that an understanding with Russia was the fundamental basis of our position as a Great Power ; he knew that the maintenance of the Czaristic régime, be it what it might, accorded with our interests ; he recognised, too, that the Dictator's treatment of Russia in the 'seventies and 'eighties was marked as much by ingratitude as by petty spite and could not but lead to a dangerous state of tension.   He failed, however, to understand that Germany had to choose between Russia and Austria and that it was impossible to go arm in arm with both.   His strictly Conservative-legitimist convictions led him to overestimate the value of the Habsburg Empire.   Seeing in it an important pillar for the support of the monarchical principle, he overlooked the fact that Austria was an anachronism in modern Europe.

Herr von Schweinitz certainly shows that a man can be an irreproachable patriot and at the same time have the courage of his own opinions.   He has shown, too, that love of country does not necessarily impose upon a diplomat the duty of saying yea and amen to everything done by the men in office or of defending every blunder they may make.

The most notable chapters of Herr von Schweinitz' book deal with the period during which he was ambassador at Petrograd.

The author begins by giving a delightful account of the conditions under which his youth was spent on his father's Silesian estate where he was born in 1822.   We get a glimpse of how the landed gentry of those days had to suffer under the economic consequences of the Napoleonic wars, very much in the same way as their descendants are having to suffer to-day.   It is amusing to learn that, although the Schweinitz family had a clergyman as tutor, young Schweinitz had never known any of his relatives to pray and as a child had never been sent to church.

Then came his time at Potsdam in the First Regiment of the Foot Guards.   We are shown the headquarters of that caste which occupied such an influential position in the Prussia of those days, that it was soon able to infect most of the other classes of society with its medieval ideas.   This organism formed a state within the state. Unfortunately it not only possessed great influence in politics but

also had the chief say in matters at Court. Although this caste undoubtedly accomplished great things, it is also responsible for many
grave errors. Although it produced not a few remarkable men, it
set up a somewhat feudalistic standard of values for the whole of
our state and civic life. Twenty-six years of peace were felt to be an
oppressive burden, merely because military promotion suffered in
consequence, since war offered almost the only chance of a rapid
career. The author gives a vivid account of the change of rulers in
1840 [1] with the inevitable changes of uniform that followed ; he
describes the preparations made for the ' great epoch that led
Germany through various phases of disappointment and humiliation,
through hard work and sanguinary wars to the heights we attained
under the great Kaiser Wilhelm I.' It is the ' spirit of Potsdam '
that here speaks, the spirit that is the corollary of autocracy. It was
this spirit too that Bismarck made use of for his political aims and
that, unfortunately, was henceforth to be so greatly overstressed
throughout the country.

Was not the Great Statesman himself up to a certain point a
personification of the ' Potsdam spirit ' with its Junker-militarist
basis ?

In what other country would a statesman who had never held an
army command have gone about wearing the uniform of a cuiras-
sier ? Where else could he have appeared in this uniform in the
House of Parliament, especially when this Parliament was based on
universal suffrage ? Could anyone imagine a statue of Cavour, or
Gortschakoff, or, to take an extreme case, of Disraeli, showing these
statesmen in military garb ? [2] Is there not something almost grotesque
in the spectacle of an Ambassador or Minister striding about in the
uniform of a lieutenant of Hussars or accoutred as a captain of
artillery, disdaining the ordinary diplomatic uniform, a uniform
which, I confess, is more remarkable for the richness of its embroidery
than for its good taste ?

' Our enthusiasm for hereditary monarchy,' says von Schweinitz,
' was so deeply and firmly rooted that we were filled with hatred and
contempt for any form of nationhood that ran counter to this principle and we especially loathed the new German ideal whose aim was
a united empire on a national basis.'

[1] On the death of Frederick William III. and the accession of Frederick
William IV. (Tr.)

[2] The author evidently has in mind the colossal military statue of the great
Chancellor, set up in front of the Reichstag in Berlin.

The years spent at Frankfort [1] (1854-1857) as adjutant to Count Waldersee brought Schweinitz for the first time into touch with Bismarck. These years may be regarded as the starting-point of his brilliant diplomatic career. It was then that his interests, which had hitherto been chiefly of a military nature, broadened to include the problems of international politics. He became a disciple of Bismarck, the statesman whose intentions he was later on destined to voice on many an important occasion and whom he always admired, but with whom he by no means always agreed.

Schweinitz was for some years adjutant to Prince Wilhelm of Prussia, afterwards Crown Prince, and makes the interesting statement that in the May and June of 1859 we had prepared for war—the Prince Regent having resolved to go to the help of the Austrians, as soon as ever Napoleon should cross the Mincio. In other words, we in those days meant to thwart the aspirations of the Italians for unity just as fifty-five years later we tried to thwart the aspirations of the Serbs. While Bismarck, at that time Prussian Minister at St. Petersburg, as well as certain diplomats of the Liberal school, pronounced against supporting Austria, General Moltke wrote several memoranda to demonstrate that the Mincio line must remain in the hands of the Austrians. Moltke's arguments seem to have convinced Herr von Schweinitz. Although it is quite understandable when we remember the reactionary views of those times, it sounds a little strange to-day to find Schweinitz commenting as follows : ' If we Prussians had in those days, together with the rest of Germany and with Austria, overthrown the Empire of Napoleon, we should have achieved a very fair position in Germany, not, certainly, a supremacy as at present, but we should have had no universal suffrage, no conflict with the Curia and no general confusion of ideas on the subjects of morality and law.'

In those days Bismarck recognised that the real danger for Germany was to be found not in Paris but in Vienna, a fact that he unfortunately later on forgot.

In 1861 Schweinitz became military attaché in Vienna, where he quite capitulated to the charm of Viennese life and society with its aristocratic generals and its noble families who occupied a position with which modest Berlin conditions could not for a moment be compared. The strongly marked feudal character of the Austria of those days was in full accord with his conservative tastes and was at

---

[1] Up to 1866 Frankfort was the seat of the German Federal Diet. (Tr.)

the root of that over-estimation of Austria as a state which continued to colour his judgments, even in later years. ' For I firmly believed that it was only by means of a sincere understanding with Austria that the fight against revolutionary elements and the indispensable reform of the Federal Constitution could be brought to a happy conclusion.' Out of regard for the sensitiveness of the Vienna Court and out of dislike for the Italian revolutionaries, he expressed his disapproval of the Crown Prince's proposed visit to the Court at Turin and contrived while accompanying the Prince on his Italian journey, to prevent all contact with the Italian Royal Family.

We see Schweinitz again acting as adjutant to the Crown Prince from 1863 to 1865. When the Crown Prince and his Consort on a journey through the Altmark paid a fleeting visit to Bismarck at Schönhausen, Bismarck went to meet them and awaited them on horseback on the boundary of his estate. ' The Crown Prince was cool, but polite, while the Princess hardly returned the Prime Minister's greeting and invariably looked the other way when Bismarck trotted up alongside her carriage.'

With his appointment to St. Petersburg as military plenipotentiary, a post which he held from 1865 to 1869, and which brought him into constant touch with Czar Alexander II., the real political career of the future ambassador begins. His remarks concerning the demeanour and motives of Alexander II. at this time are worthy of note : ' Our relations with Russia in 1865 were on the whole quite good, despite our national ambitions which had in the Schleswig-Holstein question, displayed both force and earnestness. Fortunately Czar Alexander shared the general opinion, seeing in Herr von Bismarck a stronghold of conservatism and holding that if he took the weapons of revolution into his hands, he had only done so in order to break them to pieces, and not by any means in order to use them against the other German princes.' A little further on we read : ' The main factor that decided things in our favour was, I admit, to be sought elsewhere, that is to say, in the marked tension that had arisen between France and England on the one hand, and Russia on the other, after the Polish insurrection.'

The following utterances are no less brilliant : ' If the mood which had been fostered by the exchange of civilities at the Paris Congress and at Stuttgart had continued up to the time of the war with Denmark, the annexation of the Duchies would have been impossible. But the Polish Insurrection had altered the whole situation ; Bismarck

had at once perceived this and exploited the situation to the
full.   Scarcely had the insurrection broken out than the Prussian
Prime Minister, in the midst of a violent conflict with the Opposition
in his own country, openly took sides with Russia ; without being
asked, indeed almost against the wishes of St. Petersburg and even
more against those of Warsaw, Bismarck pressed our good services
upon them.   The somewhat clumsily worded Convention concluded
on 8th October, 1863, by General Alvensleben, was severely
criticised both in Russia and in Berlin, even by the Conservatives.
Indeed, so violent was the criticism that the Convention had to
be half and half disclaimed.   In Paris and London it called forth a
storm of indignation.   In Vienna they made fun of it.   Bismarck,
however, knew very well what he was about, and apart from the
somewhat infelicitous wording of the agreement, the Convention is to
be admired as one of this great politician's masterpieces.'

In another passage Schweinitz says : ' On the afternoon of that
15th February, 1763, on the morning of which the Peace of Hubertus-
burg was signed, Frederick the Great wrote to Katherine II., offering
his services in the event of disturbances taking place in connection
with the impending election of a King of Poland.   On this memor-
able day was inaugurated the community of Russo-Prussian interests
in the Vistula area and, as a corollary, the solidarity of the two
countries in most European questions.'

When the war against Austria was being prepared and Bismarck
had shown that he was bent upon it, Alexander II. regarded this
conflict as a misfortune.   He had not yet shaken himself free from
the traditions of the Holy Alliance and, just as his father in 1849 had
helped the Austrians to protect the hereditary monarchy against
revolutionary Hungary, Alexander saw in revolution a common
enemy to whom such a war could only bring advantage.   The
national-orthodox idea which at a later date under Moscow's influence
led to a growing opposition between Russia and Austria, gave way
at that time in St. Petersburg to the legitimist feeling of solidarity
between all dynasties.

At St. Petersburg Schweinitz scored his first diplomatic success.
The weak Count Redern, who was at that time Prussian Minister there,
owing to his Austrophile tendencies was left completely in the dark
by Bismarck, and it fell to von Schweinitz, then a Lieutenant-
Colonel and military attaché, to explain Berlin's policy to Alexander
and to restrain him from bringing to bear on Berlin pressure

that would have been extremely embarrassing at that particular moment.

' I look back with the greatest satisfaction on that difficult time in which I had to defend the standpoint of my Government with a good deal more firmness than people in St. Petersburg had learned to expect from a Prussian diplomat.'

In spite of powerful opposition, especially on the part of German princes related to the Czar, von Schweinitz succeeded in preventing Russia's intervention. Bismarck owes it largely to this military envoy that he was able to carry through unhindered his greatest feat of statesmanship, the solution of the German question, without including Austria in the process.

What Schweinitz says about Alexander II.'s feeling towards Napoleon III. is also of interest : ' Napoleon's action in the Polish affair had soon afterwards estranged him for ever from the Czar, and the latter, from that time up to the day on which Sedan was fought, never for a moment changed his opinion with regard to that " adventurer ".'

Schweinitz describes his own position at that time and the difficulties that he had to contend with as follows : ' Without any instructions from my Court, without a line from Bismarck and without any knowledge of our policy, I had to defend this policy at the Court of a mighty autocrat who was incessantly egged on against us by his Consort, by his sister and by a host of princely German relatives. Our Minister at St. Petersburg maintained a neutral attitude, the Vice-Chancellor was against us, as were also the Russian Ministers at Berlin and Paris. I had but a single ally, a powerful one, in the heart of that noble Monarch who held unquestioned sway over one-seventh of the surface of the earth. His reverence for his mother's memory, the reminiscences of his childhood and youth, which were so intimately bound up with things Prussian, and his admirable understanding of the virtues of the Prussian army, proved stronger than all the hostile words whispered in his ear and the reasoned exhortations of his political advisers.'

With the change of Ministers that took place in 1867, when Count Redern was relieved by Prince Reuss, the abnormal political rôle played by Herr von Schweinitz came to an end.

From 1869 to 1876 he was first Minister and afterwards Ambassador at Vienna. At first he received an exceedingly cool reception as the year 1866 was still too fresh in the memory of both

Court and society. It is a well-known fact that the dislike of the leading Viennese circles for everything Prussian continued even after the conclusion of our fatal treaty of alliance, although, on the other hand, this dislike was gradually countered by the national movement in favour of a *rapprochement*—and even of union—that grew up in bourgeois circles. It was not until the times of Wilhelm II., a monarch who enjoyed a certain amount of popularity in Vienna, that the Court and society adopted a more friendly attitude towards us.

When in 1870 war with France became unavoidable, Count Beust, the Austrian Chancellor, declared that Austria would remain neutral. Schweinitz, however, had good reason to doubt the sincerity of this statement. It was not until Beust had become convinced that Count Bray, the Bavarian Prime Minister, and the other South German states would not oppose Prussia, that the danger of Austria's intervention in favour of France was removed. Schweinitz nevertheless reports that the Emperor of Austria, the Archduke Albrecht and the Minister of War were longing for swift French successes in order to attack Prussia. How much we then owed to the attitude of Alexander II. becomes clear from the remark that Count Beust understood much earlier than anyone else what Austria had to expect from Russia as soon as she showed signs of taking part in the war. ' Count Beust knew, however, without the reports of Chotek, the Austro-Hungarian Minister at St. Petersburg, and without any hints from me, that Russia would not remain inactive if Austria lifted a finger.' ' I, for my part, while in Vienna never breathed a syllable during the whole of the war to reveal that we had the Czar's promise that he would move 300,000 men up to the frontier if Austria entered the war.'

Schweinitz was dumbfounded by the telegram that Wilhelm I. sent to Alexander II. after the preliminary Peace of Bordeaux : ' We are at last at the close of a glorious but sanguinary war which was forced upon us by unparalleled frivolity. Never will Prussia forget that she owes it to you that the war did not assume extreme dimensions. God bless you for this. Yours in lifelong gratitude, Wilhelm.' Schweinitz adds : ' So it was not to the good sense of the Viennese burghers, not to Count Beust's pro-German sentiments and wisdom, not to the Magyar influence that we owe Austria-Hungary's neutrality, but only to the threats of Russia.'

Of gratitude to Russia, however, there was later on but little to be seen. Whatever Wilhelm I. may have felt, his Minister certainly manifested no such sentiment.

The first signs of estrangement between Berlin and St. Petersburg revealed themselves in 1874, when Serrano was appointed President of the Spanish Republic and was recognised as such by Bismarck. Schweinitz makes the following note : ' Then I wrote to Bismarck. I told him that when I remembered how he had bestowed his favour on me for the past twenty years and had graciously helped me forward in my career, I felt that I owed it to him frankly to confess that I should feel regret if Russia, without whose friendship we should never have been able to carry through the national policy of 1866 and 1870, should now suffer affront through Serrano's appointment. Czar Alexander felt outraged. He was furious, and was more than ever inclined to listen to Prince Gortschakoff when the latter tried to increase the distrust that was already for other reasons growing from day to day against Prince Bismarck.'

Concerning the famous ' War in Sight ' affair which marked the actual beginning of that alienation between us and Russia which eventually led up to the world-war, Schweinitz writes : ' On the 10th May, 1875, Czar Alexander reached Berlin on his way to Ems. Some incautious utterances of Herr von Radowitz,[1] together with the notorious ' War in Sight ' article in the Berlin journal *Die Post*, gave Prince Gortschakoff an opportunity to play the rôle of peacemaker. He telegraphed to various embassies that all danger of war was now removed and it was soon bruited abroad in France that Czar Alexander's authoritative words had prevented Prince Bismarck from falling upon France. Czar Alexander, however, later on often told me that he had during his sojourn in Berlin not heard a single word about any danger of war or about any preparation of armaments and that it was only after he got to Ems that he learned with amazement that he was supposed to have prevented a war. From that moment dated the hatred of the German Chancellor for the Chancellor of the Czar, a hatred which was to bring untold suffering to millions of innocent people.

The ' War in Sight ' affair was the first step we took on the road to Versailles ! Both in St. Petersburg and London people henceforth distrusted the Great Chancellor who had really already outlived his glory and whose great period lay between 1862 and 1871.

---

[1] Then at the Berlin Foreign Office ; later on Ambassador to Turkey and to Spain. (Tr.)

II

By far the most important part of General von Schweinitz' book is that dealing with the period between 1876 and 1892 when he was Ambassador at St. Petersburg. It was during this period that despite his warnings the estrangement between Berlin and St. Petersburg became more and more marked. This was the result of Bismarck's grudge against Gortschakoff. The epigones naturally thought it incumbent on them energetically to pursue the same line of action. Thus it came about that the Re-insurance Treaty failed to be renewed. The consequence was the Russo-French alliance of 1892. We see from Herr von Schweinitz' notes that the Czar was at that time still under the spell of the Holy Alliance. The very contrary was the case with the national-orthodox movement in Moscow, led by Aksakoff. This movement, at first known as the Slavophile and afterwards as the Panslavistic Movement, was directed mainly against Austria and Turkey and against Germany only in so far as Germany undertook to act as a shield for the protection of these two states. ' The Monarch,' says Herr von Schweinitz, ' then went on to speak of the topic of the day, the Near Eastern question, and expressed his satisfaction that an agreement between the six Powers had been brought about by the harmonious co-operation of the three great Imperial States. This co-operation between the three Empires, though it no longer went by the name of the " Holy Alliance," had, he said, the same objectives and the same effectiveness. I fully agreed with the Czar when he said that he had complete faith in the policy of Vienna, for the gist of my instructions from Berlin was above all to assent to anything about which Russia and Austria would be likely to agree.'

Bismarck, too, still hugged the idea of bringing about an alliance of the three emperors, not perceiving that in most countries the state idea was gradually being transferred from a dynastic to a national basis, from a conservative and feudal to a liberal and democratic ideal, and that owing to the Near Eastern question there could be no lasting friendship between Russia and Austria.

How eager Prince Gortschakoff was to restore good relations with Bismarck is shown by the following note : ' The unhappy story of the Russian intervention in the cause of peace in 1875 was referred to by Prince Gortschakoff on one of the first days of our meeting. He wanted to explain and justify his attitude at that time and described to me the state of excitement in which he had found the ambassadors accredited to Berlin.   He had not for a moment, he said, shared their apprehensions and his only aim in sending the notorious telegram to Karlsruhe had been to dissipate the prevailing anxiety. " It is, after all, quite natural," added the Prince, " that a giant should be feared."   He repeated again and again his assurances of friendship and admiration for Prince Bismarck, who had called himself his pupil, a joke that could only be taken in the same sense as the statement that Raphael was a pupil of Perugino.'

On the 19th April, 1876, M. de Giers, the Russian Minister for Foreign Affairs, used exactly the same words as M. Sazonov in 1914 : ' Nous n'avons pas de programme, si ce n'est paix, mais nous ne pouvons pas laisser écraser la Serbie.'

We see a general desire, in Russia as elsewhere, to leave things alone as far as possible and to avoid inconvenient situations by maintaining the *status quo* in the Near East.

The Bosnian disturbances of 1876 and the attitude of Serbia and Montenegro on that occasion caused the Powers serious embarrassment.   They played the political game of hiding their heads in the sand and failed to see that the independence and unity of the Balkan peoples could not be frustrated but at most postponed.   Had we but given the Russians a free hand at that time, even with regard to Austria, instead of invariably taking that country under our wing and had we at the same time declared we were completely disinterested, there could never have been a world-war !   This is what Schweinitz reports on this point : ' In Russia they were already beginning to grow distrustful of our policy ; on 3rd June the *St. Petersburg Journal* published a remarkable article in which it said that Prince Bismarck was far from being as considerate towards Russia's wishes and ambitions as Russia had a right to expect.   On the contrary, the German Chancellor had on many occasions rather taken the part of Austria, with the result that Prince Gortschakoff's original programme had undergone important modifications.'

Under the pressure of these circumstances and in order to gain a free hand towards Turkey, Gortschakoff made the fatal mistake of concluding the treaty of Reichstadt which held out to Austria the hope of conpensation in the annexation of Bosnia.

How little trust was to be put in this Alliance of the Three Emperors is clear from the enquiry addressed, to Bismarck's great indignation, by the Prussian General von Werder to Berlin on 1st October, 1876.

The General, as an attaché to the Czar, sent a message from Lividia asking on behalf of Alexander II., what attitude Germany would adopt in the event of Russia's attacking Austria.

Even at that time the rulers of Russia seem to have felt that both the Jugoslav and the Ruthenian questions could only be settled by an appeal to arms, and Alexander II. hoped that the debt of gratitude that we owed him for his support in 1866 and 1870, a debt to which Wilhelm I. had specially referred in a letter he had sent by General von Manteuffel a short time before, would cause Germany to adopt the attitude hoped for by Russia. There was an outburst of fury in Berlin at Werder's letter, although we had with no small success made use of our Military Plenipotentiary von Schweinitz under exactly similar circumstances.

Even at this early stage, previous to the Russo-Turkish War, both the Czar and his Chancellor show chronic dissatisfaction with Bismarck's attitude. They had counted on the German Chancellor's gratitude and support and found themselves bitterly disappointed. Complaints concerning the lukewarm attitude of the Berlin Government in the Near Eastern question are the order of the day. Again and again Germany is reminded of the debt of 1866 and 1870, as if it were a bill she had failed to honour. It was while Russia was still feeling sore at Bismarck's ingratitude, and was being irritated by further pinpricks and reproaches from Berlin, that France put out the first feelers for a *rapprochement* with Russia. Prince Gortschakoff denied that it had any official support, but at the same time added : ' Les empereurs sont d'accord, mais pas les empires.'

Throughout the whole period that preceded the Berlin Congress Bismarck was touchy, easily piqued and inclined to indulge in malicious remarks. The Dictator's ill-humour against Gortschakoff, who had wounded his pride and who had been audacious enough to play the part of peacemaker, finds expression in a thousand ways. On the other hand, Alexander II., conscious of the immeasurable service Russia had done us, without which Bismarck's successes would have been unthinkable, thought that he had a claim on our gratitude and support. Our failure to fulfil these expectations called forth repeated protests and reproaches. Bismarck was trying to steer a course between Russia on the one side and Austria and England on the other, and it was this that St. Petersburg took so much amiss.

During the Russo-Turkish War Russian feeling again veered round in our favour. ' I cannot fail to recognize,' writes von

Schweinitz, ' that in spite of the Slav inclination to arrogance that showed itself at that time, there was a readiness frankly to acknowledge the political services Germany had rendered Russia ; the crossing of the Danube and Gurko's swift advance on Adrianople had roused the more clear-sighted of the politicians in Moscow to recognise that Russia could only venture so far afield, because she was sure of Germany. And thus it came about that at the end of July 1877, it was proposed by Moscow that an address of thanks should be sent expressing the Russian people's appreciation of Germany's friendly attitude ; at the same time a ladies' committee was formed with the object of making preparations to weave a costly carpet for presentation to Prince Bismarck.'

While relations with Berlin and Vienna had improved during the Balkan War and words of appreciation were heard in Russia for our friendly attitude, the Ambassador has again to report an estrangement that came about soon after the end of the war. Alexander II. was furious at a letter received from Wilhelm I. ' That epistle must have been dictated by the Chancellor,' said the Czar. ' There is not a single mention of friendship to be found in it.' It is noteworthy that Prince Gortschakoff had no objection to a Congress, as he still counted on our full support and wanted to avoid a war with England. He was quite prepared to accept Berlin as the place where the Congress should meet. Vienna and London he declined. He formulates his standpoint quite clearly : ' You should now do rather more than hitherto,' said Prince Gortschakoff to Schweinitz. ' You always declare that if Russia and Austria agree on any point, you are prepared to endorse it ; that is not enough ! ' ' And with this,' adds Schweinitz, ' he came back again to what Czar Alexander had done for us in 1870.'

At that time we were at the parting of the ways. The Three Emperors Alliance, which was still officially recognized by Russia as well as the other two Powers, had grown thin and fragile with the increasing estrangement between Russia and Austria. The time had come for us to choose between Russia and Austria, it being no longer possible to go with both. *Bismarck, by deciding in favour of Austria, committed the greatest and most fatal error of his life.*

It has generally been assumed that it was the Congress itself that led to the estrangement between Germany and Russia. The Ambassador's notes show that this was not the case. It was Bismarck's attitude at the Congress that caused ill-feeling and to which Russia's recantation was ascribable. 'Have seen Prince Gortschakoff, who is in the seventh heaven because we have consented to have the Congress in Berlin,' runs one note. Another note says, ' The Czar described the meeting of the Congress and its work as a peacemaker as urgently desirable.'

But Russia's distrust of Bismarck and her feeling of annoyance at the attitude he took up soon again became apparent when he suggested a preliminary conference. England and Austria took up a threatening attitude towards Russia and this made our friendship the more valuable. On 21st March, 1878, Schweinitz reports : ' Several Russian newspapers maintain that Prince Bismarck and Count Andrassy are combining to whittle down the successes that Russia has won in the war.'

While Prince Gortschakoff continues to refer to our attitude in elegiac tones, MacMahon was already trying to bring about a *rapprochement* with Russia, declaring ' qu'il voulait marcher avec la Russie.'

When Schweinitz received orders to induce Russia to make concessions to Austria, so that the latter country might not be driven into the arms of England, he makes the following note : ' I requested M. de Giers [1] to jot down what I had told him and lay the matter before the Czar. He said that it would make a painful impression on His Majesty. It could hardly be otherwise, for since the beginning of the war the Czar, his Ministers and the Press have often enough expressed the hope that they expected that Germany would bring pressure to bear on Austria as Russia had done in 1870 ; the unfortunate telegram of thanks from Versailles and the despatch of Manteuffel to Warsaw in the autumn of 1876 justified them in these hopes ; from the very outset, even in October of that year at Livadia, I set to work to tone down these hopes ; nevertheless it must make a terrible impression on Czar Alexander when he now learns for certain that instead of urging Austria to abate her exorbitant claims, we are calling upon him to support these claims.'

The fact that we were even at that early date engaged in driving Russia into the arms of France can scarcely be put more plainly.

On 22nd June, 1878, Schweinitz writes : ' Prince Alexander of Hesse, the Czarina's brother, arrived here to-day from Czarskoje Selo and called on me. He informed me that things were not going

---

[1] Who had taken Prince Gortschakoff's place. He was afterwards Foreign Minister.—Author's Note.

at all well at the Congress ; Andrassy, he said, is heading straight for war. If Czar Alexander yields to these demands, he cannot possibly remain in power.' The Czar even goes so far as to say : " Si on veut m'acculer, me mettre entre la guerre et l'humiliation de la Russie, mon choix est fait." The decision lies in Prince Bismarck's hand.'

When von Schweinitz was in Berlin during the Congress, Gortschakoff complained of Bismarck's attitude, contrasting it with that of Lord Beaconsfield. After a visit to Herr von Bülow, Secretary of State, Schweinitz writes : ' I could not for a moment fail to observe that my views on our relations with Russia were not endorsed at headquarters.'

In a memorandum written by General von Schweinitz in the autumn of 1883 we read : ' Count Peter Schuvaloff, thanks to the attitude taken up by Germany, achieved in Berlin far more than he could ever have hoped to attain by an attitude of defiance. This success on the part of Russia was, however, branded as a defeat, partly by Prince Gortschakoff and partly by the Press. The latter by stirring up discontent tried to drive the Government to liberal reforms. Since that time it has been a firmly established axiom, not only at the Court, but also in the Russian army and in all classes of society, that Russia was injured and humiliated at Berlin and—just because it was in Berlin that this happened —they lay all the blame on us ; just as senseless and no less universal than was once the cry in France, ' Revanche pour Sadowa,' is now in Russia the desire to avenge the Treaty of Berlin. This mood was artificially created in the weeks immediately following the Congress, when the grey-haired Chancellor on his return from Berlin, spent some time with the Czar at Czarskoje Selo ; the mood was fostered and aggravated during the whole of the following year, when Commissions met in the Balkans to decide various points, to define boundaries and to construct the new states. The questions concerning Arab-Tabia and the Albanian districts that were to be ceded to Montenegro and various other often quite trifling differences of opinion in which the Germans invariably sided with Austria, embittered the Czar and Russian public opinion, as far as one can speak of such a thing as public opinion in Russia, to the utmost. Then came the treaties of Gastein and Vienna in the autumn of 1879. But it was the measures of protection that we, in fulfilment of what we thought to be our duty, took against the Veblyanka Plague

that marked what was nothing short of a turning point in the sentiments of the Russians towards the Germans.'   In February 1879 the
author writes : ' From Berlin we have received unpleasant telegrams
announcing new vexatious frontier measures against Russia, although
plague no longer exists there.'   Another note says : ' The Russian
Press is growing very hostile.   The *Golos* (an important Liberal
organ) refers to the present juncture as offering a favourable opportunity to make sure of France's gratitude by liberating her from her
isolation.   As was natural, I referred in my dispatches to the
language current in the newspapers and added the following note :
" Many Russians who six weeks ago would have scouted the idea of a
rapprochement with France, are to-day inclined to favour some such
measure.   The reason for this change of attitude is to be found in
the fact that the rather painful execution of the terms of the Peace of
Berlin happens to coincide with the closure of the frontier ordered by
Russia's western neighbours, a closure that is ascribed to the
prompting of Germany." '

A little later Schweinitz writes that Bismarck would like another
alleged case of plague, in order to have a pretext for causing Russia
further vexation, as if he has not annoyed her enough already !
Schweinitz also had a talk with M. Valuyeff, the Russian Minister,
who made no secret of the fact that the German frontier measures
against the plague were arousing distrust and annoyance and were
greatly increasing people's inclinations towards ' Frenchification.'

The Czar told General von Werder that all these frontier annoy-
ances were nothing but Bismarck's way of avenging himself for
Gortschakoff's telegram of 1875 concerning Russia's rôle as a peacemaker.   Prince Bismarck, said the Czar, no longer visited the
Russian Ambassador M. Oubril ; when any question concerning
the Near East cropped up, the Russian Ambassador in Berlin was
always told that the German authorities must first consult Vienna !

On the Kaiser's birthday on 22nd March, Schweinitz, angry at the
ill-natured policy pursued by his Government, a policy which ' made
it difficult for Czar Alexander honestly to carry out the terms of the
Berlin Treaty,' and ' incensed at Berlin's manifest intention to
exasperate the Czar into putting himself in the wrong,' delivered a
speech in which he frankly stated these views.   We cannot enough
admire the courage and character of such a man !

It is interesting, too, to read what Schweinitz says about internal
conditions in Russia : ' The opinion that things cannot go on as they

are much longer in Russia is gaining ground both at home and abroad. Autocratic government, people say, is no longer in keeping with the times. But there they make a mistake. More than ever is such a government necessary at the present time. But it no longer exists ; the autocratic system has been so weakened that the dynasty now thinks only of self-preservation. With the increasing decay of the power of the state, the insolence of the Nihilist sects and the discontent of the intelligentsia is increasing ; the great mass of the people still remains stockish and unmoved. Apart from these still unaffected nine-tenths of the population, one may safely say that the remainder—the majority of the propertied classes and the people who can read and think—are now convinced of the necessity of putting new life and strength into the Government by introducing new forces. "Things must have come to a pretty pass," General Trepow recently observed to an acquaintance, "when Schuvaloff and I find ourselves longing for constitutional government." The only radical opponents of such reforms at the present moment are probably the people who batten on the present system. These people are very near to the Throne and keep at arm's length all men of character and talents. They are at pains to strengthen the Monarch's belief that the millions who are loyal to God and the Czar afford sufficient protection against a mere handful of Nihilists. It may be true enough that it would be an easy matter to get the peasants to slay the students at Charkov, but if the autocracy is based only on the stockish, patient masses and on the servile, pleasure-seeking nobility and bureaucracy, then it will not be long before it totters to its fall.'

How eager Bismarck was in his endeavours to bully the Russians is shown by a statement made by Lord Dufferin, the British Ambassador, to Schweinitz. He told him that the German Ambassador in London had explained to Lord Salisbury that the German Government saw no reason why the Turks should not march into Eastern Rumelia. ' This is coming it rather strong ! ' remarks Schweinitz. ' Instead of the *coup d'épaule* the Russians have asked for, we have given Count Schuvaloff a *coup de pied*.'

Count Peter Schuvaloff, the Russian Ambassador in London, who was well known for his pro-German sympathies, begged Schweinitz to ' do everything in his power to prevent the bonds that united Germany and Russia from being untied, or even slackened.' ' Vous voyez,' he said half in jest and half in earnest, ' on me croit payé par l'Allemagne et je ne puis rien faire ; si je leur dis, demandez donc telle ou telle chose par Oubril, on me répond qu'on ne pourrait plus s'exposer à de nouvelles humiliations.'

III

 AMBASSADOR AT ST. PETERSBURG—THE AUSTRO-GERMAN ALLIANCE

The rabid mood with Russia into which Bismarck had argued himself finally led him to the disastrous step of concluding an alliance with Austria.   We find a dramatic record of these events in the notes Schweinitz made after a visit paid to the Dictator on 5th April, 1879.   The first thing that aroused Bismarck's ire was the fact that Prince Francis Arenberg, at that time Secretary at our Embassy at St. Petersburg, in making a fair copy of a report, had made his r's look like w's.   Schweinitz goes on to tell us how Bismarck, after having done everything in his power to drive Russia into the arms of our western adversary, professed great annoyance at what was happening in Russia : ' Gortschakoff's constant coquetting with France, Miljutin's everlasting new armaments, the advanced position of the Russian cavalry in the vicinity of our frontier, the hydrophobic utterances of the St. Petersburg and Moscow newspapers have finally convinced the Chancellor that he can no longer depend upon Russia, or even on the Czar, in the same measure as before.   Germany cannot, therefore, he thinks, afford to make enemies of the other Powers, least of all of England and Austria, for the sake of such an uncertain asset as the friendship of Russia.   With Austria we must try, he thinks, to enter into closer relations and conclude some organic agreement that cannot be dissolved without the consent of the Parliaments of the two countries.'

It is evident that the Great Chancellor was no longer the man he once was and that he now allowed himself to be guided rather by personal moods than by the considerations that alone should move a statesman.   ' At the conclusion of our conversation,' adds von Schweinitz, ' the Prince again referred to the r's and w's in Arenberg's fair copy.   Then the Austrian Ambassador was announced and I took my leave without the Chancellor having asked me a single question about Russian conditions.'   One can hardly believe one's ears !   Was this, then, Germany's Great Man of the post-war period, the Wotan of our Teutons !

Bleichroeder, the great banker, too, confirms Schweinitz's impressions. ' We have undoubtedly got into Russia's black books,' he says. Despite all the pinpricks and humiliations, Alexander II. was still anxious to maintain the old traditional relations. He let no opportunity pass without showing us the usual Court and military acts of courtesy. Regimental festivals, parades and similar spectacles, things of no little importance at the Court of an autocrat, were utilised in order to show his regard for us and his admiration for the successes of our arms. Toasts and references to the memory of Königgrätz and similar well-meant trifles ! He still clung to the idea of a German-Russian community of interests. How systematically Bismarck in those days pursued an anti-Russian policy becomes clear from the words used by Alexander II. on 7th August, 1879 : ' I have received a letter from Lobanoff ; he complains that your delegates regularly vote against ours ; no matter what question crops up, your government declares that the matter is of no interest to it, but at the same time instructs your representative to vote with Austria, even in cases where it appeared to recognize the moral justification of our claims ; this was the case in East Rumelia and the same thing has happened again on the Turkish-Montenegrin frontier with regard to Mrkowitz. The Austrians, without making any great sacrifices, have annexed two provinces while Russia has got nothing beyond the return of her old Bessarabian possessions. Everywhere you take sides with Austria against us, even when we are not asking anything for ourselves. If you really want the friendship that has united us for a century to continue, you ought to alter this. Il est tout naturel que le contrecoup se produise ici ; vous voyez le langage que tiennent les journaux ; cela finira d'une manière très sérieuse. J'en écrirai à l'Empereur quand je lui répondrai à la bonne lettre qu'il vient de m'envoyer.' ' The tone in which this apostrophe was delivered,' says Schweinitz, ' was mild to the point of sadness. There was nothing threatening about it and it is important to remember this, if one is to form a correct estimate of the words " cela finira d'une manière très sérieuse." ' That we found to our cost in 1914 ! Naturally the consequences of this policy soon became evident. ' There are many French visitors in the camp,' writes von Schweinitz ; ' they are treated with becoming respect and politeness, but without any demonstrative preference being shown. A Russian return visit, that has been spoken of for some time, would, however, probably merit our attention. It is said that General Obrutscheff is to be sent to France.'

Alexander's attitude is illustrated by the following notes : ' Czar Alexander would fain distinguish between the person of Kaiser Wilhelm and his government, that is to say, between him and Bismarck ; although we often did exactly the same in the attitude we adopted towards the Czar and Prince Gortschakoff, it was impossible for me to express my agreement with him in this argument. The more testily the Czar now and again expressed himself with regard to Bismarck's procedure, the more demonstrative he immediately afterwards became in his protestations of friendship for our Kaiser and for the Prussian Army.'

In describing how our unfortunate alliance with Austria came about, Schweinitz relates how Bismarck utilised Russia's huff with us, for which he himself was to blame, and which found expression in Alexander II.'s well-known letter of 15th August, 1879, to Wilhelm I., in order to make the alliance with Austria more plausible to the Kaiser. The sending of the Russian General Obrutscheff, whose wife was a Frenchwoman, to the French manoeuvres, Bismarck used to the same end. In the meantime, to Bismarck's great annoyance, the two Monarchs had met at Alexandrovo. This meeting led to the Czar's well-known utterance, ' Thank God, a war with Germany is impossible ! ' Bismarck, however, wrote a long memorandum of thirty pages for the Kaiser ; in this document he sought to explain that the old and tried friendship with Russia was no longer to be relied upon, its only support being the Czar himself, and he, too, could no longer be depended on ! Germany must therefore look about her for support elsewhere and carefully avoid purchasing an unreliable alliance with Russia at the cost of concessions which might estrange Austria or jeopardise the position of Waddington's Cabinet, the maintenance of which meant so much to Germany. On reading this passage, the Kaiser remarked : ' So I am expected to have more faith in M. Waddington than in Czar Alexander.'

Fortunately Count Andrassy did not respond to Bismarck's wish to enter into an organic relationship that could only be dissolved with the consent of both Parliaments. In other words, we now witnessed a return to the old Holy Roman Empire with the Hohenzollerns instead of the Habsburgs and the Balkans instead of the Appenines. The Magyar and Austrian Russophobes in Vienna inaugurated great ovations for Prince Bismarck, in whom they rightly saw the protagonist of an anti-Russian policy. Schweinitz, however, writes : ' In return, we undertook weighty obligations. Although I am ignorant of the full extent of these obligations, I know at least that they may well entangle us in a war with Russia in the defence of interests that do not in any way concern us.   These agreements were, neither from a political nor from a military standpoint, to the old Kaiser's taste ; Bismarck knew this and got General Moltke to write a Memorandum with the object of converting the Emperor to his views.   Count Moltke did as Bismarck wished. He said, ' If the German Empire is not strong enough to deal with France single-handed, it has no right to exist.   It is therefore unnecessary for us to get Austria's promise to stand by us.   On the other hand, an alliance with Austria could be of great value to us in the event of a simul-taneous attack on our eastern and western front.'   All this sounds very fine, but it is mere sophistry and therefore failed to have any great effect on the commonsense of our clear-headed Kaiser.   He had only just exchanged the most cordial assurances of friendship with Czar Alexander II. and it was with a heavy heart that he now had to put his signature to a document that might oblige him to declare war on Russia.   In his simple and touching way, the Kaiser described to me the struggle he had with his own conscience and with the people round him before he could bring himself to give way.   He told me that he had been on the point of abdicating when Bismarck definitely declared that he himself would send in his resignation, ' and Bis-marck is more necessary than I am,' concluded the noble-minded old man.   Finally Count Stolberg, whom Bismarck sent to Baden, got the Monarch to put his name to the treaty.   The only question now was what we were to say to Czar Alexander, to explain the contra-diction between the conversations at Alexandrovo and the Vienna pact, and how we could make it appear as plausible as possible.'

How was it possible that our diplomats and statesmen failed to perceive the mistakenness of this policy.   There was only one man who persistently warned Berlin against an entanglement with Austria, thus gaining for himself the reputation of being an Austrophobe—a dangerous reputation to have at a time when our diplomats were esteemed not only in proportion to their incom-petence but also according to the warmth of their sentiments towards Austria !

It is the curse of belief in authority that it relieves people of the trouble of thinking for themselves.   How few there are who recognise the fact or, recognising it, dare to express it, that Bismarck in the 'seventies and 'eighties was no longer the man he once had been !

Nothing is further from my intention than to withhold from the memory of this great man the respect he deserved. I see, however, no reason why a sincere admiration for his great achievements should be incompatible with a frank criticism of his actions during the period of his subsequent Dictatorship. It is one of the advantages of the British Constitution that one party succeeds the other in power and that it seldom happens that a Minister remains in power more than ten years running.

In the last instructions that Schweinitz got before leaving for St. Petersburg he was given his cue : ' Cool to your heart's core ! ' ' Towards the Czar as well ? ' ' Towards the Czar as well ! '

' The Prince is so irate with the two emperors who exchanged pledges of friendship at Alexandrovo,' writes Schweinitz, ' that such a thing as a placid exchange of ideas is out of the question.' Such a mood would seem scarcely credible but for the fact that one can have absolute faith in the author's statements.

Some idea may be formed of Bismarck's omnipotence at this time from the General's remark : ' Everybody here dances to Bismarck's piping. Everyone is at his beck and call ; never has there been such a complete autocracy ; this docility is not based on fear so much as on admiration. Everyone voluntarily subordinates his will to Bismarck's.'

Germany's demeanour encouraged the notion that she intended to attack Russia. ' The number of Russians who of late have come flocking back to St. Petersburg from abroad, and especially from Germany, have caused the idea to spread that Germany has fully resolved on a war with Russia. But why this should be the case nobody knows, and no argument will convince them that Russia is not going to be treated in the same way as Austria and France.'

Let us try to picture to ourselves the situation at that time. Germany had vanquished and humiliated France, and France regarded the Alsace-Lorraine question as an open wound. It was a wound that could only be healed by time and not by rough interference from outside. Just as the Pope could not afford officially to renounce temporal power, without undermining his ecclesiastical authority, although the Curia knew perfectly well that the Papal States could never again be revived, France was unable officially to renounce Alsace-Lorraine although the French clearly recognized that the tricolour would never again fly over Metz or Strasburg,—unless, of course, as the result of our blundering. They knew that neither

Russia nor England was interested in the question of Alsace-Lorraine and that they could never reckon on the help of either Power in a war of revenge. It was quite possible for us to arrive at a correct *modus vivendi* with France, if we were prepared to treat her sensitiveness on this point with tact and understanding, and if we refrained from making her feel our superiority at every turn. Our representatives at Paris had agreed in stating that people in France did not want a war of revenge, although now and again speeches were made that might lead one to a contrary opinion. The *revanche* idea was for the French what the Messias was for the Jews or the Mahdi for the Arabs. These rallying cries gave the nation an ideal to hope for, but everyone knew that this ideal neither could nor should be realised.

At that time there were no points of friction between England and Germany. The question of naval competition was still in the womb of Time. German Imperialism had not yet entered upon the colonial and commercial stage, or, if so, it was still in its infancy. England, then as later, was anxious to come to an understanding with us, but even at that time, was resolved not to permit an attack on France.

Under Andrassy it was not difficult to arrive at an understanding with Austria, even without an alliance. A return to a policy à la Beust was no longer to be apprehended. Neither the Austrian Germans nor the Magyars would have permitted this. Everything depended on our coming to an understanding with Russia on the old basis of friendship between the dynasties and of a complete absence of any real antagonism between us. What the Czar expected of us was our warm support of the Russian policy in the Near East in recognition of the immense services he had rendered us. Instead of that, Bismarck quite ostentatiously went over to the opposite camp and let no opportunity slip of ruffling Russia, and ended by concluding with Austria an alliance directed against Russia.

In January 1880 Schweinitz writes : ' Czar Alexander bitterly complained about the persistent rumours published in the German newspapers concerning Russian massing of troops on the German frontier and hinted that it looked as if somebody was trying to make the Kaiser distrustful of Russia and gradually accustom him to the idea that a war with Russia was inevitable.' The Czar also said : ' You will easily understand that Prince Bismarck's meeting with Count Andrassy immediately after the meeting at Alexandrovo made a very unpleasant impression on me.' As to the contents of the Vienna Pact, the Czar was mute. All he said was : ' Our common enemies are trying to separate us and now they are happy; I have always been frank and straightforward and have never wavered in my conviction concerning the necessity of good relations between our two countries, and I shall continue to hold this belief to the end of my days.'

Threatened as he was by the ever-increasing danger of revolution at home, deserted by his 'best friend' and deeply disappointed by his attitude, the Czar was also exposed to the attacks of the Russian Nationalists who thought that Russia had been cheated out of the fruits of her victory when she was not allowed to take Constantinople. On this point Schweinitz remarks that the dissatisfaction with the results of the victory, which the Russians describe as a defeat, is directed against the Czar inasmuch as the parties have been trying to put the blame on to Germany and the Czar is regarded by that part of the population that takes an interest in politics as the main representative of the Germanophile policy followed in 1866 and in 1870-71. Every reproach levelled at Germany was at the same time levelled against the Czar.

On 22nd March, 1880, Kaiser Wilhelm's birthday, Schweinitz writes : ' The Czar introduced his toast with a long speech which was in marked contrast with his toasts of former years. It had been carefully revised and committed to memory. In delivering it, the Czar stressed various points. He was manifestly embittered by the latest attacks published in the *Norddeutsche Allgemeine Zeitung* and by the revelations of the Press with regard to the movements of troops in Russia. Warm as were his congratulations and his assurances of friendship for our Monarch, it was no less obvious that his sentiments towards the Kaiser's Chancellor were of a very different nature ; the emphasis he laid on a continuance of the century-old friendship between the two dynasties showed that he thought this friendship jeopardised.'

The growing distrust felt against us had, as is well known, led to Russia's moving certain regiments to her western provinces. Great masses of cavalry were pushed forward. This fact formed the subject of a somewhat angry protest from Prince Bismarck. ' They must be mad,' cried the Czar, ' if they think that I am going to attack Germany ; I shall, however, not alter the disposition of my troops and I hope that I shall hear no more of the matter.' On the 19th August, 1880, Schweinitz makes the following note : ' The language of the Vienna statesmen, which is not always friendly, and which is sometimes even offensive, is here ascribed to the feeling of security with which the relations now existing between Austria-Hungary and Germany has filled them.'

In what a state of nervous excitement Bismarck was at that time (1880) is shown by the following notes, which give the impression of a man in a state of mind little short of morbid. ' The Chancellor next discussed our relations with Austria, relations which, as though in realization of von Gagern's visionary phantasms, were expected to develop into something organic, something independent of the whims of regents and ministers, something that could be dissolved only by the three Parliaments. On my referring to Poland, he answered just as he had done in the spring of 1879 with the horrible proposition that we might again restore Poland for a time, perhaps under the rule of an Austrian Archduke, and later on, after Poland had served its purpose against Russia, could partition it again. Bismarck went on to say that he would rather turn Catholic than Russian orthodox, although he had no particular fancy for either ; he preferred, as he had always done, to perish like a gentleman rather than put up with indignities ; if the sky were to fall, the sparrows would all be killed ; as for trying to conceive a policy that would hold good for the far distant future, such a thing was downright lunacy.'

On the death of Dostoievsky, Schweinitz writes : ' He was really not a Nihilist, but he was one of those writers whose works confuse people's ideas and fill their hearts with morbid fancies, robbing young people of their energy and of the joy of life and filling them with pessimism ; for, like so many of his contemporaries, he prefers with artful acumen to depict men's sufferings and crimes without showing the way to penance, reconciliation and salvation. Such a tousled, muddleheaded martyr, who painted black in grey, was just the man you would expect to find an enthusiastic echo in the Russian society of to-day. No one would have anticipated, however, that people would make such a fuss of him as has just been the case at his funeral. Nearly a hundred deputations took part in the funeral procession ; that a big crowd should follow the procession was natural ; and it was just as natural that the crowd should not know who it was that was being buried. A peasant asked whose coffin it was, and another answered him that it was a general's, while another ventured the opinion that it was that of an old schoolmaster. All eye-witnesses are agreed on one point, viz., that there was a longer procession and more order at this funeral than when the Czarina was buried. It is in the orderliness that accompanied Dostoievsky's funeral that men of experience find a new and menacing note.'

This passage shows that even such a talented and cultured man as Schweinitz could allow himself to be influenced by tradition when he had to form judgments on contemporary events that ran counter to his political tenets and his own literary predilections. One cannot help thinking of Frederick the Great's verdict on Goethe.

IV

AMBASSADOR AT ST. PETERSBURG—WITH RUSSIA OR WITH AUSTRIA ?

Up to the death of Czar Alexander II. on 13th March, 1881, negotiations had repeatedly taken place concerning a renewal of the League of the Three Emperors. People refused to see that it was impossible to reconcile Russia's and Austria's interests in the Near East and clung to the ideal of dynastic solidarity on a conservative-monarchical basis. After the death of the Czar, Schweinitz makes the following comment on this theory : ' I could not conceal from myself, however, that this important matter was being followed up both in Vienna and St. Petersburg in a very half-hearted fashion. Neither there nor here is there any sincere wish for a binding understanding. Such an understanding is, moreover, held to be impossible and both the Vienna and the St. Petersburg Cabinets are wooing our favour at the cost of the third party. Alexander III. for the present is continuing along the lines mapped out for him by his father. He was recently heard to observe, however, " Doesn't all this point to the fact that an understanding with this Austria is quite out of the question ? " '

To-day it seems quite incomprehensible that a man like Bismarck should not have perceived that the Empire of the Habsburgs was an anachronism and that it was impossible for us to march with such an Empire and with Russia simultaneously. People will perhaps retort that the Russia of the Czars was also an anachronism. Doubtless it was, but in Russia there was a national and ecclesiastical idea permeating the whole Empire. This idea, represented, as it was, by an all-powerful bureaucracy, made Russia a much mightier political factor than the crumbling Dual Monarchy on the Danube. Austria-Hungary lacked any uniform state idea except the dynastic. As a witty Frenchman once put it, ' L'Autriche est une unité gastronomique ! ' Nor had we to anticipate any danger of a clash with

Austria or with any other Great Power as a consequence of our supporting Russian policy in the Near East. By supporting Austria, on the other hand, we could not but, sooner or later, drift into a war with Russia, in addition to making Russia disposed to join the Western Powers.

After his fall Bismarck probably saw the mistakenness of his policy with regard to Russia, and constantly pleaded in favour of a Russian orientation, preaching without cease ' Back to Russia ! ' ' With Russia through thick and thin ! ' Although at a later date a sort of understanding was again reached between Russia and Austria, this merely meant that the differences were for the time being patched up but by no means removed.

As early as November 1881 Bismarck discussed with Schweinitz the possibility of a war with Russia and with France. In view of the fact that there were no points of friction whatever between us and Russia and that France alone was too weak, such an assumption not only lacked plausibility but was positively monstrous.

M. de Giers, the Russian Minister of Foreign Affairs, told our Ambassador, Herr von Schweinitz, in September 1883 that even Alexander III., who unlike his father, had not grown up in the old traditions, had nevertheless come to recognize that a sincere friendship with Germany was the only possible basis of Russia's policy.

After Gortschakoff's death Bismarck was anxious to shake hands and be friends again with Russia. Unfortunately the alliance with Austria was nevertheless renewed and everything remained as before.

Russian feeling towards Austria was described by von Schweinitz in May 1884 in the following terms : ' I pointed out in Berlin that the exaggerated tone of affection which since last autumn has taken the place of our former irritating and unfriendly attitude was misleading the Russians into thinking that they could give rein to their ill-humour with Austria. The nationalist agitation of the Slavophile parties, having been checked by our action, has given place to ecclesiastical propaganda, directed against Austria. There are in Russia many well-to-do and influential people—fewer, it is true, in St. Petersburg than in Moscow and in the country—who regard political Pan-Slavism with disfavour on account of its revolutionary character, but who in matters pertaining to the church are aggressive enough and can be sure of having the support of the masses of the people. This is the army that M. Pobjedonoszew commands. Ever since Russo-German relations took an apparently favourable turn, the malicious tone in the Russian Press and in the agitation among the Ruthenians becomes more and more marked in all references to Austria. The friendly responses that our changed attitude meets with here is prompted less by any deep-rooted change in the feelings of the Russians towards us than by the hope that our good understanding with the Habsburg monarchy, which is to-day more necessary than it was during the lifetime of Alexander II., may thereby be shaken.' Why this good understanding was so necessary, Schweinitz does not say. He surely must have known that the Habsburg Empire was entirely dependent on Germany and could find no other protection and no other power to whom it might look for assistance.

We also see how M. de Giers' constant endeavour was to avoid anything that might encourage the urge of the Slavophiles in the direction of the Dardanelles and how official Russia resisted this urge. That is why the Minister did not want Egypt to be separated from the suzerainty of Turkey.

It was at this time, too, that Russia began to show irritation with Austria on account of Serbia. M. de Giers complains about King Milan and is distrustful of Austria. ' I certainly do not want a war with Austria,' said the Russian Minister, ' but believe me, Austria's attitude is not honest ; she has pledged herself to King Milan.' And more to the same effect.

At Skierniewice (1841), where Bismarck had positively forced the Emperor Franz Joseph on the Russians, we find von Schweinitz on the side of the Dictator and his sons. Franz Joseph referred with some anxiety to the Russian policy in the Balkans which, he said, although it had become ' correcter,' would have still further to improve, as otherwise circumstances might arise that would force Austria, in spite of her love of peace, to ' take energetic steps to put a stop to Russia's activities.' He looked upon our support as a foregone conclusion, for without us he was, of course, not in a position to carry out such a threat.

Bismarck's opinion concerning the stability of the German Constitution is shown by a remark which he made to Schweinitz in April 1868. ' The Chancellor referred to the German parliament in the somewhat contemptuous fashion often heard from him of late,' says von Schweinitz. ' " Things may possibly come to such a pass," he said, " that I shall have to smash up the constitution I myself created ; people forget that the same thing may happen to the existing Union (*Bund*) as happened to the Frankfort Bundestag in

1866 ; the Princes may withdraw from it and form a new Federation, this time without the Reichstag." '

In other words, without any co-operation whatever of the representatives of the people and purely on a dynastic basis, the founder of the Empire thought he could force a new constitution on the nation, and this in an age of universal suffrage when there was Parliamentary government everywhere except in Germany, Russia and Turkey.

Rumours concerning a Russo-French *rapprochement*, or even an alliance, kept cropping up with more and more persistency in the autumn of 1886 and were confirmed to some extent by the statements of French Ministers to our Ambassador in Paris. Schweinitz was in a position authoritatively to contradict these reports. He adds, however, that ' the moment has now come when Germany will have to decide either for or against Russia, even though it may mean having to drop Austria for a while.' Schweinitz was backed up in this view by Count Peter Schuvaloff whose words are quoted by the author at some length : ' As long as we go on in this fashion, we shall never reach a state of security ; as long as Prince Bismarck continues to make an understanding between Austria and Russia a preliminary condition for his support, Czar Alexander's distrust will also continue. How pronounced this distrust is, you yourself are aware. He now believes that you want to decoy him into advancing into Bulgaria. And what sort of a Triple Alliance is this, I ask you, in which two of the contracting parties are in league against the third ? For Heaven's sake, write to Prince Bismarck and ask him to get some suitable person to lay before the Czar an historical *remémoration* in which it will be made clear to the Czar that your *rapprochement* with Austria in the autumn of 1879 was purely the result of our mistakes, among them Alexander II.'s letter of 15th August. The Czar, who knows nothing of all these matters, will doubtless at once perceive that if we in future avoid similar errors, the necessity of your alliance with Austria will cease to operate. Why should we not conclude a firm alliance with you in which Russia guarantees you the possession of your newly acquired provinces ? If one day a notice were to appear in the newspapers, announcing that Russia and Germany had concluded a treaty in which they guaranteed each other's present boundaries, no one in Russia would have a word to say against it, but if the arrangement come to between us two and Austria should leak out, all Russia would be filled with indignation. It is no secret that the Czar has set his heart upon the possession of the Dardanelles ; if Germany would refrain from laying obstacles in our way and from invariably supporting Austria in her opposition to our plans, Russia and Germany might form a dual alliance by which you would, once and for all, be relieved of all anxiety concerning France.'

On Germany's refusing to drop Austria, all possibility of coming to an understanding with Russia vanished, and with it the chance of safeguarding the peace of the world.   The offer was afterwards repeated.   On the very eve of the war, the Russian statesmen were still saying to us : ' Lâchez l'Autriche, et nous lâcherons les Français.'

During the Bulgarian turmoil of 1866 Schweinitz reports that the St. Petersburg and Moscow newspapers were accusing us of trying to unite all the hostile powers against Russia, with the result that the Czar had become more distrustful than ever and that Katkoff, in the September of that year, had recommended an agreement with France.   M. de Giers was thus discredited both with his Sovereign and with his colleagues, as well as in the eyes of the public. Schweinitz was informed on behalf of M. Katkoff, the leader of the Pan-Slav movement, that Russia would be Germany's best friend if she would only cut the painter with Austria.   On 3rd February Schweinitz reports : ' The Czar kept me nearly three-quarters of an hour and spoke frankly and in a very friendly tone about Bulgaria and his Hessian relatives, about France, about the German Reichstag and especially about Austria.   As on several previous occasions, he specially emphasised the high esteem he felt for the Emperor Franz Joseph.   He expressed a wish to remain on peaceful and friendly terms with him, but at the same time said that he wanted to have nothing more to do with the Austro-Hungarian Government.'

Soon afterwards Schweinitz writes that he could by no means guarantee that, should it again come to a war between Germany and France, the Czar would this time be able to restrain his people from intervening in favour of France.   Schweinitz adds, however, that he was as convinced as ever that Alexander III. himself was not in the least inclined to have anything to do with the French Republic.

On 27th February, 1887, Schweinitz writes : ' A special messenger has just arrived, bringing the most incredible announcements with regard to a Tariff and Press War ! '

Concerning the oft discussed Re-insurance Treaty, we learn that it was Count Peter Schuvaloff who first suggested it and that his brother Paul, the Russian Ambassador in Berlin, was ready to go much further than Bismarck.

In 1887 Schweinitz writes : ' M. de Giers is powerless to control the Press ; in view of our alliance with Austria, no one can be surprised at the Russians' wishing for a *rapprochement* with France.'   In short, it was our alliance with Austria that drove the Russians into the arms of France.

V

Von Schweinitz leaves St. Petersburg—The Franco-Russian Alliance

It was at this time that Herr von Holstein began to play his influential and disastrous rôle in German foreign affairs. He is described by von Schweinitz in the following words : ' When I saw him in 1864 at Düppel, helping the wounded in the front line of the fighting, I could not help feeling a certain respect for this queer individual. Even now he is said to do many a kind action without saying anything about it. Von Holstein is nevertheless a man of spiteful disposition. He allows himself to be influenced by his personal dislikes and without its ever coming out does harm through his malicious propaganda in the Press. No one can deny that he is a man of more than ordinary intelligence, but although straight of stature he has the mind and character of a hunchback. He clearly perceives the great dangers into which we have drifted as a result of the present policy which, in spite of its factitiousness, is often enough rough and even brutal in its methods

What Schweinitz writes in December 1887, soon after the conclusion of the famous Re-insurance Treaty, sounds nothing short of incredible.   ' I have been shown a memorandum written by Count Moltke in which the great strategist tries to prove that Germany ought at once, in the middle of winter, to declare war on Russia.   This document has been communicated to Vienna and our military attaché there has spoken in the same sense with the Emperor Franz Joseph. I expressed my entire disagreement with this view.   By making such an attack on Russia, we should double her power and halve our own. For while such an invasion would inspire the peace-loving Russian nation with the will to make the utmost sacrifices, it would arouse not the slightest enthusiasm in the Fatherland, for the necessity of carrying on a winter campaign that would involve such unheard-of efforts on our part would appeal neither to the Federal Council nor to the German nation at large.'   And yet we professed surprise that the Russians should show distrust of Germany and make advances to France.   Such things could not be expected to remain a secret for long, in view of the reputation for indiscretion enjoyed by the Austrian diplomatic staff.

As usual the old Emperor Wilhelm showed the soundest common-sense.   He had, it will be remembered, only given his consent to the alliance with Austria under extreme pressure.   He expressed doubts as to the assistance that Italy could render in the threatening war on two fronts and, as Schweinitz points out, smiled with sad scepticism at Moltke's calculations, according to which 150,000 Italians could be transported within three days to the Upper Rhine.

On 29th December, 1887, M. de Giers remarks, ' Ici le sentiment prédomine que nous serons attaqués au printemps.'

Concerning Bismarck's notorious instructions to the Reichsbank, forbidding it to advance money on Russian securities, Schweinitz writes as follows : ' The Russian Minister of Finance, M. Vischne-gradski, called on me and had interesting things to say about the severe blow we had dealt Russia's state credit.   '' I am,'' he said, '' on principle opposed to reprisals and particularly so in a case like the present, mainly, I confess, on the ground that I am unable to adopt them.''   In scrupulously correct tone but with suppressed bitterness, the Minister characterized Bismarck's instructions to the Reichsbank not to lombard Russian securities as an extremely severe and odious measure, one which, in view of the fact that it had been taken immed-iately before the Czar's arrival in Berlin, was nothing short of an act of brutality, and a flagrant insult both to the Czar and to Russian society.   Naturally, he did not express himself quite so outspokenly, but it was obvious that this was what he meant.'

On 5th February, 1888, Schweinitz writes : ' Bismarck has wired to tell me that he is going to speak in the Reichstag to-morrow in a pacific sense ; I went to Giers and told him this.   I found him in rather a gloomy mood ; for the papers here talk disrespectfully of Russian diplomacy which, they say, has for the past ten years allowed itself to be duped by Germany.   In proof of this they cite the German-Austrian treaty which has been published here.   '' C'est une profonde humiliation,'' said M. de Giers, '' nous sommes garottés.'' Another note says that somebody remarked : ' À la Russie il ne reste que le choix entre une grande bêtise et la résignation ; heureuse-ment elle s'est décidée pour cette dernière.'

In a note written on the Emperor's birthday, 22nd March, 1889, Schweinitz remarks : ' We cannot conceal from ourselves the fact that the Russians no longer trust us, even Giers does not ! '   In November 1889 Schweinitz visited Bismarck at Friedrichsruh. ' After lunch,' he says, ' the Prince went for a long walk through the woods with Herr von Helldorf [1] and myself.   I listened in silence with great interest to their conversation about the question of the day, the new anti-Socialist law.   Herr von Helldorf had come to try to induce the Chancellor to withdraw the paragraphs concerning expulsion, for which the National Liberals declined to vote and which even the Conservatives regarded as harmful.   The Prince would not assent and declared that he would have no funking and shirking, that the time was coming for " blood and iron," and more in the same strain.'

' There is no doubt,' writes von Schweinitz in December 1890, after Alexander III.'s visit, ' that the Czar's visit to Berlin has left an excellent impression and that the monarch himself has now been relieved of all anxiety on the score of a German attack.   This is all to the good.   For this fear, diligently fanned by our enemies and strengthened by the intrigues attributed to Count Waldersee, had become almost chronic with Czar Alexander and had made him resort to more and more extensive preparations for war.'

On Bismarck's fall the Czar believed that the Dictator had been dismissed on account of his ' Russophile ' policy and was afraid that Waldersee, whom he knew to have been agitating for a prophylactic war, would be his successor.   In spite of Bismarck's numerous and grave mistakes, his retirement from power was regretted by the Czar. The latter believed that the Great Chancellor would, had he stayed, never have allowed it to come to a war with Russia.   The Czar felt that he now had to confront various completely unknown quantities. He authorised Schweinitz to inform Berlin that he trusted that the retirement of the Prince might lead to no change either in the personal relations between the monarchs nor in the political relations between the two states.

In his comments on the non-renewal of the Re-insurance Treaty, Schweinitz reported that Wilhelm II. had had the Ambassador, Count Paul Schuvaloff, roused quite early in the morning, when he was still fast asleep, and had summoned him to the Castle to tell him that he was ready to conclude the treaty with Russia immediately ! It was Herr von Holstein who wrecked the treaty with the assistance

[1] Leader of the Conservatives in the Reichstag.

of Count Berchem and Baron Marschall. It is unfortunate that Herr von Schweinitz, too, who had previously been in favour of a renewal, allowed himself to be converted to a contrary opinion, mainly by the arguments of the new Chancellor, von Caprivi. This good man had proposed to Wilhelm II. that the Russian treaty should not be renewed, chiefly in order to avoid the odium with which we should be covered should its existence leak out ; were it to be brought to the knowledge of the Vienna Cabinet, either deliberately or by mere chance, it would be bound to alienate Austria ' (!)

O sancta simplicitas ! The Ambassador at Berlin, Count Paul Schuvaloff, was very angry and excited and felt that he had been made a fool of in the eyes of his Government. When Schweinitz returned to St. Petersburg he found M. de Giers ' in a state of consternation.'

Concerning his audience with the Czar, Schweinitz reports : ' The Monarch did not conceal the disdain he felt for our Triple Alliance, thought it would soon fall to pieces, as the burdens it imposed on its members, and especially on Italy, were far too heavy ; but the dissolution of such a treaty would do no harm, for if Russia and Germany only held together, all the other Powers would have to keep quiet. ' L'Autriche continue à faire ses petites cochonneries,' continued the Czar, ' but that is of no consequence if only Germany and Russia are at one.' He enquired concerning General von Caprivi, whether he, too, were not, like Count Waldersee, anxious for a war.'

Schweinitz then adds : ' When the Czar, soon after receiving the news, summoned me to his presence, he did full justice to the great German statesman. Prince Bismarck, he said, had, it must be confessed, often inflicted pain on Russia, but Russia had now come to a right appreciation of his activities at the Berlin Congress ; he himself, the Czar, especially on the occasion of his last conversation with him in Berlin, had become convinced that the Prince harboured no hostile intentions against Russia. The Russian Press Department, at the wish of the Czar, was thereupon ordered to see to it that the Russian Press did not too warmly take sides with Prince Bismarck. The Prince had done the Russians many a bad turn ; he had engineered the Triple Alliance against them ; he had caused the depreciation both of their securities and of the rouble, and had often enough annoyed them beyond measure by such vexatious measures, as for instance, the frontier regulations he had ordered at the time of the alleged plague at Vetlyanka ; it would nevertheless have pleased

Russia better if he had remained in office, for she knew that he did not want a war, and that from political conviction he had remained deaf to the complaints of the Baltic Germans, of the Lutherans and the German colonists in Russia. Many Russians were grateful to him, too, for having protected them through his League of Peace, from their own Pan-Slav and Chauvinist extremists.'

One sees that, in spite of all the friction and provocation, the retirement of the Dictator was regretted in Russia because the Russians refused to believe that Bismarck had wanted war with them. ' L'Empereur,' as M. de Giers several times said, ' regrette pourtant la démission du Prince de Bismarck.' M. de Giers, nevertheless, like his Imperial Master, had the best will in the world to cultivate good relations with Germany and wherever possible to improve them.

Again and again M. de Giers comes back to his old hope that in some form or other an agreement, if possible in writing, should be come to between Russia and Germany. Schweinitz's comment is : ' I must not neglect to express my purely personal opinion that if we completely turn down the very conciliatory advances made by the Russian Minister, either he or his successor will be forced to look elsewhere for the *rapprochement* that he in vain seeks in Germany.'

When Schweinitz was received by the Czar on the Kaiser's birthday, he in accordance with his convictions chose as the theme of his remarks the solidarity of the interests of the monarchies. The Czar responded with some hesitation and agreed only in so far as Germany and Russia were concerned. He did not wish to hear anything about Austria and emphasised the fact that one could not have anything whatever to do with that country.

It is always the same song : ' With you we would fain be good friends, but don't talk to us about these good-for-nothing Austrians.' We persisted in turning a deaf ear to all such asseverations !

Concerning the then nascent *rapprochement* with France, which found expression in the conferring of the St. Andreas Order on President Carnot, Schweinitz writes : ' After what had happened between the 19th and 22nd March last year,[1] Russia's action could scarcely come as a surprise to us. She was not only justified in taking this step but was obliged to take it.'

Other events followed, preluding the conclusion of the Franco-Russian Alliance : ' When I returned on 1st August, 1891, I found all my Russian diplomatic acquaintances under the overwhelming

[1] The non-renewal of the Re-insurance Treaty.

impression made upon them by the enthusiasm of the multitude that had witnessed the spectacle of the French warships entering the Neva and the reception of the French officers at the Town Hall. Cool and experienced observers assured me that in no country had they ever seen such a passionate and at the same time such a childishly cordial demonstration on the part of the masses of the people. It was perhaps not altogether wise of the Russian Government out of mere pique against the Triple Alliance to permit and even to provoke demonstrations on such a huge scale.[1] For through such demonstrations the masses might well learn how to make their weight felt. Although no evil consequences are for the moment to be expected, there is no doubt that the Czar is less free to-day to decide on peace and war than he was a fortnight ago. The conferring of the St. Andreas Order on President Carnot marked the first step, the Marsellaise at the Court banquet at Peterhof the second, and the letting loose of the multitude the third. The greater the frenzy of the masses grew, the plainer it became how far from their thoughts lay any longing for war.' A short time afterwards Schweinitz writes that the Russians feel not only that they are isolated, but also that they are threatened and that they recognise the necessity of organising some sensational demonstration as an answer to the sensational circumstances that had accompanied the renewal of the Triple Alliance.

How great was the distrust still felt against Germany is shown by an utterance of M. Pobjedonoszeff's at the end of 1891 in which this man, the President of the Holy Synod, frankly reveals his apprehension of a German attack. M. de Giers says that this apprehension is felt by almost all Russian statesmen, although he himself does not share it.

When he comes to the close of his career as Ambassador at St. Petersburg, von Schweinitz writes in a strain that is almost elegiac. He felt that the year 1892 was to be the last he was to spend in St. Petersburg, and that his programme, based as it was on dynastic tradition and community of interests, could no longer be upheld.

---

[1] Eckardstein in his *Memoirs* tries to show that Bismarck's famous embargo on further German loans to Russia (1887) was based in part at least on the argument that if Berlin continued to take up Russian stocks with the avidity then being displayed for this class of investment, Germany would soon be Russia's principal creditor and thus become financially dependent on a country with politically divergent interests.   On Bismarck's decision becoming known, Russia turned to France for money and the foundations were laid for the Entente between the two Powers. (Tr.)

He saw the complete collapse of his life's labours. 'Our provocative behaviour at the renewal of the Triple Alliance had driven Russia into the arms of France,' he writes. 'As I rode into the camp at Krasnoje Selo after witnessing the visit of the French Fleet at Kronstadt, I felt like a Don Quixote entering the lists to champion legitimism.'

In reply to an enquiry addressed to him from Berlin asking whether there were a War Party in Russia, Schweinitz wrote : 'Neither at the Court nor among the higher officials nor in the Imperial Council and least of all among the men in the Russian Foreign Office do I know of a single personage of whom it could be said that he was consciously an advocate of war.' To a further enquiry as to whether the apprehensions expressed by Russian statesmen with regard to German or Austrian plans of attack were meant seriously or were only bluff, Schweinitz shortly before his retirement replied that Alexander III., in spite of all his esteem for the Emperor Franz Joseph, felt a deep-rooted distrust of Austro-Hungarian policy and had a very poor opinion of the Vienna Cabinet's ability to resist the aspirations of Hungary and Poland. He adds that 'the Minister of War and Generals Dragomiroff and Gurko are acquainted with the monarch's views on this subject and are doing what they can to encourage them ; the demands for new supplies of money for increased armaments, for the shifting of troops from one part of the country to another, for fortifications, and for railway and road building are always explained to His Majesty on grounds that have become almost an axiom, viz. that Austria-Hungary, relying on Germany's support, intends to attack Russia.' Von Schweinitz explains that M. de Giers' repeated and reluctantly abandoned efforts to get something in writing, even if it were only a few lines, which Russia might regard as a guarantee against such an attack, were only to be explained on the ground that he shared this hypothesis. 'Our persistent refusal to meet this wish strengthened the Russians in this delusion and made them finally decide to join hands with France.' 'M. de Giers,' says Schweinitz, 'does not go so far in his distrust as the Czar, nor in his apprehensions so far as the generals ; he is, however, not strong enough to put a stop to the imputations they are continually casting on the policy of the Ballplatz ; and it was especially for this purpose that he so urgently needed the " few lines " that he begged for.'

At the end of these important *Memoirs*, which close with his

retirement in 1892, Schweinitz once more lays stress on the fact that
he had received many proofs that people in the highest circles
in Russia conjectured that Germany meant to attack Russia. ' Unfounded as these suspicions against us and Austria may be, they are
to be regarded as genuine and not merely as feigned ; and the Russian
distrust is wrought up to serious apprehension through the tone in
which the Austro-Hungarian and a part of the German Press is discussing the famine and want prevailing in Russia. This does harm,
as it leads not only to a more zealous cultivation of French friendship
—which was already beginning to cool—but also to an increased
activity in military matters, of which signs are by no means lacking.'

On his retirement from the Diplomatic Service, Herr von
Schweinitz warns the Chancellor, General von Caprivi, concerning
the lines on which business is conducted at the Foreign Office. He
frankly tells the Chancellor that a personage who is ' not quite right
in his head ' wields too powerful an influence there. He means
Herr von Holstein, and this official, whose character Herr von
Schweinitz accurately describes, and whom recent revelations have
also exposed in other directions as well, was throughout the whole
post-Bismarckian epoch the man who really guided Germany's foreign
policy, the most important of all branches of state affairs. Even
after von Holstein's retirement and even after he was in his grave,
right up to the year 1914, his system was clearly traceable.[1]

On the last pages of his book von Schweinitz mentions the fact
that Germany could at any moment restore her old relations with
Russia by seceding from the Triple Alliance.

Against whom, one may ask, did we at that time need these
alliances ?   Against whom were these insane armaments directed ?

The *Memoirs* of this Ambassador have helped to shatter the general
faith in the infallibility of the Great Chancellor. For they show that
the catastrophe of the Great War is to be traced back to his mistakes.
It is an unspeakable tragedy that the men who came after Bismarck
should have done their best to wreck the splendid but shortlived
empire that he had set up .

---

[1] Bismarck, just before retiring from office, predicted the muddle that
Holstein would cause at the Foreign Office. ' This man,' said the old Chancellor to Guido Henckel, ' knows foreign affairs inside out and will mightily
impress the new hands whom the Kaiser has expressly forbidden to come to
me for advice. After I am gone Holstein will contrive to get the whole office
under his thumb and will make a complete mess of things.' (Tr.)

LETTERS

I

Friedrich Naumann to Prince Lichnowsky.[1]

Berlin, 30th July, 1917.

I have read with interest Your Serene Highness's article on ' The Austrian Problem.' I agreed with most of it until I came to the last few sentences. The passage about which I should like to write to you runs as follows :

' We should, however, be on our guard not to urge the Austrians with fantastic programmes such as that of " Middle Europe " [2] to sacrifice their economic and political independence. Rather should we leave it to the Austrians to supply the Balkan markets in free competition with Germany. Everything from which the most favoured nation clause excludes third parties would be bad for them and bad for us! Any attempt to revive the old Holy Roman Empire would be a mistake, even if a Byzantine took the place of a Roman orientation, and if the new institution were given industrial instead of sacerdotal unction.'

As a publicist I should like first of all to compliment you on the delicate ease with which you have in this passage managed to compress a whole series of arguments and ideas into a short and apparently cogent line of defence. If I may, however, be permitted to criticize, I should say that in this little paragraph, side by side with genuine art, you also display skill in juggling with ambiguous terms. This, while doubtless contributing a brilliant touch to your style, by no means makes for lucidity. I refer more especially to the last sentence about the old Holy Roman Empire and its projected modern counterpart. What is meant by the word ' Byzantine ' in this

---

[1] An open letter originally published in the *Berliner Tageblatt*.

[2] Herr Friedrich Naumann published his sensational work *Mitteleuropa* in 1915. The Greater Germany which he advocates in it was to include Austria and thus form a Germanic Central Europe. (Translator's note.)

connection ?   Is it only a poetic synonym for the Turkish Alliance,
or are the words Roman and Byzantine meant to awaken reminiscences that stretch even further back into the past ?   Is the expression ' industrial unction ' meant to arouse in us an antipathy of an
ethical and aesthetic nature ?   In short, what mysterious literary
concoction have we here ?   Nobody will deny that a mere revival of
the Holy Roman Empire of the German Nation is impossible.   But
there is no particular need to assure us of that fact.   If, nevertheless,
at the present moment, reminiscences of the old historical bonds that
once existed between us and Austria are being somewhat strongly
stressed, this does not give anyone a right to try to hamper the new
association from the very outset by laying upon it the burdensome
heritage of its olden counterpart.   It is a mistake, too, to represent
the industrialist tendency as the essential part of this new constella-
tion ; for although in the present age all historical facts automatically assume an industrial and capitalistic character, the genesis of the
aspirations for a Middle Europe is traceable not to an economic but
to a political source.   This brotherhood in arms, already tested and
proven on the field of battle, must now be lifted on to a still higher
plane and made into a permanent institution.

The manner in which the word ' fantastic ' is applied to the programme known as ' Middle Europe ' strikes me, too, as open to
criticism, for in the word ' fantasy ' the ideas of creation and illusion
are so commingled that the reader has some difficulty in deciding on
which of the two elements he is expected to lay the stress.   If it was
your wish to stress the element of illusion and to point out its inadequacy and impossibility, then there was scarcely need for such an
expenditure of energy in bringing out the contrast.   You also
appear to regard the term ' Middle Europe ' as connoting a sort of
intellectual power, a formative idea, but nothing more than an idea,
and as such not necessary for you to combat.

In the passage referred to, you do not go into details concerning
the constitutional considerations that have led you to oppose a
permanent and closer connection with Austria-Hungary, and I am
thus prevented from pursuing the matter here.   It is clear, however,
from the earlier sentences in the passage quoted that you are by no
means opposed on principle to a political alliance between Germany
and Austria-Hungary.   Who could be ?   It is plain, then, that we
differ only as to degree and as to the closeness of texture of the
treaties to be concluded.   You for your part hold that the Austrians

should not be forced into ' sacrificing their economic and political independence.' In these words is contained the gist of the questions at issue between us. The words, at the same time betray what seems to be an incredible misunderstanding on your part.

As I am kept supplied by a neutral press-cutting agency with the English and French newspaper cuttings dealing with *Middle Europe*, I am quite familiar with the line of thought which you here develop. The Entente Powers are trying methodically to disturb the union between Austria and Hungary and to set the two nationalities by the ears. Simultaneously the Dual Monarchy is warned with the greatest solicitude not to allow itself to be degraded into the position of a vassal state. As you yourself remark, there is in Austria a ' Court aristocracy with English tastes and English habits,' and this English method of sowing seeds of distrust is, when regarded from an English standpoint, not such a bad one. What amazes me is not that the line of thought should be met with among us, but that it should be championed by Your Serene Highness.

Your Serene Highness states in another place in writing,—and, I am convinced, not without due deliberation,—that it was the incapacity of statesmen that brought about the world-war, I may therefore assume that you would be the first to deprecate any wrong methods of handling the relations between the two Central European Empires. Must it not make a most painful impression to find a highly placed member of the German Empire coming forward to endorse the daily accusations made by the English Press ? The English Press Department knows quite well what it is doing and what it is aiming at ; but I ask myself in vain what rational grounds there can be for lending it assistance. Doubtless I should have a certain understanding for the risky procedure of inculpating one's own fellow-countrymen if it were true, even in part, that Austria (and Hungary) were to be urged to sacrifice their economic and political independence. For that would be a crime against the spirit of comradeship and mutual loyalty. But who in the world harbours such a dangerous intention ? Is it by any chance the author of the book *Middle Europe* that is meant ? Or is it the German delegates who have been sent to Vienna ? I may safely say that I am thoroughly familiar with every aspect of the Middle Europe movement and on the strength of my knowledge I can assure you that in this instance the matter has been represented from quite a wrong angle.

Not a single one of us who are working for the Middle Europe ideal is so blind or petty as to assume that an Austria that had been forced to subordinate herself to us could be a firm and loyal ally. On the contrary, with all our heart we wish for an Austria-Hungary that shall stand proud and straight and strong. For the league of good-will that we need is only possible between strong states that have a mutual respect for each other. Not only must the forms of state suzerainty be retained in each country, but there must be a far better mutual understanding and more cordial esteem for each other than there is at present. We step forward together into the world's history as one great family of states and peoples and we link ourselves together each of his own free will for the attainment of an intenser life. This union is for all who participate in it the best possible way to increase their powers and capacities. Your Highness may, if you like, describe this as fantastic. I, for my part, believe that it is one of those fantasies out of which new epochs in history are born.

It is clear that when the states of Middle Europe have once combined in a closer union, the Central Treaty will be surrounded by a number of secondary treaties,—I mean, for instance, treaties dealing with such questions as the Balkan markets and the most favoured nation clause. When I describe agreements on such matters as secondary treaties, this must not be taken to imply any depreciation of their objective importance. It merely means that each party, before passing over to the economic treaties which round off the agreement, must first know whether the State Treaty and Military Convention have been satisfactorily concluded. When both parties once recognise their historical political community of interests, they can save themselves much unnecessary friction in connection with debatable questions of commercial policy. Anyone reading Your Serene Highness's sentences might get the impression that the Austro-Hungarian industrialists would prefer that there be untrammelled German competition in the Balkan markets, as though it meant a sacrifice of Austria's economic independence for her to conclude agreements with us which would amount to a kind of zone system. Anyone familiar with the actual facts knows that exactly the contrary is the case. Austria and Hungary in their very necessary industrial extension in the Balkans wish to be hindered as little as possible by interference from Germany. How far Germany can concede to this wish and how far such concessions are to be reconciled with the justifiable aspirations of individual German export industries are among the many questions included in the economic problem of Middle Europe. But there is not in the remotest degree any question of seeking an opportunity of robbing either Austria or Hungary of her independence. As for the most favoured nation clause, it has as a result of the numerous declarations of war, become almost mythical. Whether the economic world will, after the war, again be built up on the most favoured nation system, not even the most far-sighted of us can say. But even assuming that there were a wish to revive the system, the economic union of the two great industrial areas of Middle Europe would certainly not be an obstacle. We should then grant most favoured nation treaties on a common basis, just as other groups of states will probably do. But there is still plenty of time to discuss that. We do not yet know what will be the upshot of the conference now being held. These conferences are, moreover, nothing but subordinate stations in the long process by which Germany and Austria are to grow together.

It was the passage concerning the sacrifice of Austria's independence that prompted me to write to Your Serene Highness. This passage I look upon as a blow that ought not to have been dealt. I felt it my duty to tell you this.

Yours very obediently,

FR. NAUMANN.

II

TO HERR FRIEDRICH NAUMANN, Member of the Reichstag.[1]

BERLIN, 1st August, 1917.

I should like first of all to thank you for your letter in which you express your concurrence in the main with the views contained in my article on Austria's internal problems. , I am sorry that we do not agree concerning the question of Middle Europe which you have so brilliantly championed.

When I hinted that economic dependence generally brought political dependence in its train, it was, of course, not my intention to deal with the whole complex of economic and political questions associated with the project of a Middle Europe. One does not willingly tell a friend that one considers oneself the stronger—unless, perchance, one wishes to forestall unfriendly suggestions on his part ! It would therefore have been a little tactless if I had said that I regarded Germany as the strongest partner in the limited liability

[1] An open letter originally published in the *Berliner Tageblatt*.

company which you so warmly champion. I imagine, moreover, that this partner would inevitably have to be given the leadership if there were to be satisfactory and harmonious collaboration. But between leadership and dependence there is, as is well known, a certain connection,—this being the result not so much of the end aimed at as of the causes at work. I can quite appreciate the indignation with which you repudiate any suspicion of disloyalty towards our tried and trusty ally and companion in misfortune, and I deeply regret that you should have imagined that I intended to charge you with an intention which would have been little short of a crime. Nothing was further from my mind, and I should like to assure you that I am in full agreement with the views you have so eloquently voiced concerning the spirit of ' comradeship in arms and loyalty,' even though I have not yet been able to convince myself that your ideal and mine of an alliance can be transferred from the realm of the ideal to the material region of commercial policy. It is generally maintained that in money matters there is no room for sentiment, and I cannot help feeling that the perfect harmony, as a champion of which you have rightly described me, has in no way suffered owing to the complete separation of accounts and cashboxes that has hitherto prevailed. A union on the basis of a common economic policy towards the outside world, that is to say, towards our present foes as well as towards the neutrals, would pre-suppose the sacrifice of important interests of individual members of such a union in favour of the interests of the association as a whole. It would take for granted, too, the renunciation of important sources of revenue, and would in short involve sacrifices that might easily be looked upon by one party or the other as prejudicial to their interests and lead to a cooling off in their fraternal feelings. Especially might this be the case if the business circles affected, who do not always look at things from as ideal a standpoint as do you and I, should openly oppose the agreements on the ground that they were burdensome or should even try secretly to evade them.

You are, of course, aware of the difficulties already existing within the Dual Monarchy, which has a common economic policy that applies to both halves of the Empire. In spite of the fact that the whole region forms one single customs area, the Hungarian Government has already tried to set up a customs frontier. The complaints of the Austrian industrialists concerning the efforts of the Hungarian Government to protect its young and less developed industries at the expense of the Austrian, have already repeatedly disturbed the harmony of the two states, to say nothing of the anxiety regularly caused by the renewal of the compromise, both states fancying their interests prejudiced in the calculation of the so-called ' Key ' to their common expenditure.   Without wishing to criticize the sentiments of comradeship entertained by our Magyar friends, I would never- theless be inclined to doubt whether they would be more willing to throw open their gates and markets for the importation of German industrial products which, owing to Germany's own protective tariff and the older development of her industries, might easily compete successfully with Austrian goods.   If it is difficult for the various parts of the Dual Monarchy, in view of the disparate stages of their economic development, to find a uniform basis for their economic policy, how much more difficult will it be to find a solution when the problem is made still more complicated by the admission of such a mighty economic unit as the German Empire, a country moreover whose export trade has found overseas markets in the discovery of which our allies have played a comparatively insignificant part.

You say that ' we step forward together into the world's history as one great family of states and peoples.'   These inspiring words would move me far more than they do but for the feeling I have that we have already for some time past been treading the stage of world history.   Before the war Austria and Germany got on very well together and we had no reason to complain of any lack of affection on the part of our allies.   That, at least, has been my personal ex- perience and the impression I have always got during my annual sojourn on my Austrian estates.

Genuine altruism, a quality which I, like yourself, regard as the basis of political ethics, finds utterance in your wish to restrict the sale of German goods in Balkan markets in favour of Austro- Hungarian competitors, and I am quite of your opinion when you say that ' Austria and Hungary wish to be hampered as little as possible by Germany in their necessary industrial expansion in the Balkans.'   That is my conviction, too.   I am somewhat more sceptical, however, with regard to the zone system that you propose. Such a system would amount to subdividing the Balkans into spheres of interest, somewhat after the fashion that we wanted to have introduced in Asia Minor before the war, but did not dare officially to define out of regard for the justifiable sensitiveness of the Sublime Porte.   Only in remote parts of Africa and Asia has this system hitherto been employed.   Unlike the Balkan States in question, these Asiatic and African communities are not young, independent and ambitious states that resent subdivision in any shape or form, even when it is purely economic in aim, but are regions where foreign interference in their affairs has been made possible only by their helplessness.

I do not like having to differ from such a famous economist and parliamentarian on a question like most-favoured-nation treatment. Statistics show, however, that even before America came into the war on the side of our enemies, about fifty per cent. of Germany's two thousand five hundred million dollars worth of exports went to what are now enemy countries.   This was about four times the value of the goods taken from us by our present allies.   The British Empire was our best customer, taking twenty per cent. of our exports.   I had hitherto been under the impression that one of the most important tasks that awaited us on the conclusion of peace would be to sweep away the obstacles in the way of the resumption of trade relations that have been destroyed by the war.   I regard as the chief of these obstacles our exclusion from most favoured nation privileges or any tariff discrimination against us such as that which is apparently contemplated by the Paris Economic Conference.

Although, unfortunately, I do not, like you, subscribe to a neutral agency for press cuttings about *Middle Europe* I nevertheless fancy that I have remarked that various references to the Middle Europe movement have been, no doubt wrongly, interpreted in an imperialistic sense and that the term is being used as an effective weapon for agitation in favour of an economic union against us.   Nor do I think that we should be in a position to demand for ourselves either the minimum tariff or most favoured nation treatment, if we refused to grant them to others.

With regard to your question as to the meaning to be attached to the word ' Byzantine,' I need hardly say that it refers not to bureaucratic but to geographical tendencies.   Your declaration to the effect that the ' genesis of the aspirations for a Middle Europe is not economic but political in character ' makes comment on my part superfluous, since analogies and reminiscences press upon one's mind almost automatically, directly the political character of the projected union is admitted, even though we may not for a moment confuse ' Middle Europe ' with the Middle Ages.

Before concluding, you must permit me a personal remark.   I am

no admirer of either brag or braggarts.   This need not prevent me
from remarking that I possess courage enough to confess to holding
an opinion even when by doing so I run the risk of seeing some
similar view expressed in an English newspaper and of then being
taxed by you with helping to support English accusations.   I have
already mentioned that your ' Middle Europe ' propaganda is being
exploited by our enemies to our injury.   It is even possible that this
may have been attempted in more senses than one.   I cannot,
however, see why I should on that account be expected to get up any
enthusiasm for the project.   Nor does the fact that my opinions are
combated with admirable eristic skill incline me the more to do so.

Yours very faithfully,

LICHNOWSKY.

III

To The Prussian Upper Chamber.

BERLIN, 20th April, 1918.

Under Paragraph 9 of the Ordinance of 12th October, 1854,
a vote of censure has been proposed against me.   Although I little
imagined that I should ever have to answer a charge of having in the
affair of the much talked of Memorandum behaved in a manner not
in keeping with the dignity of this High House, or that I should ever
have to defend myself against the slanderous and distorted versions
of the matter that have appeared in the Press, I nevertheless feel
myself bound to expound the actual circumstances of the case to the
Commission that has been appointed to examine the proposal before
the House.   Through a monstrous indiscretion my reflections were
spread abroad and published.   The document will probably be
known to most of the members of this House, either in the form of
excerpts published with malicious comment in the columns of the
Press, or in the form of copies, made at the instigation of some person
unknown, and bearing the garbled title : ' The Guilt of the German
Government in the World War.'   The title alone is sufficient to
brand this private and confidential document of mine with a tendency
it was never intended to have.

My private secretary typed out the Memorandum, making at the
same time a few carbon copies.   The document bore the title, ' My
Mission to London, 1912-1914.'   It was meant to be a justification of
my personal attitude as German Ambassador at London against

unobjective and unfounded attacks and was written for my own satisfaction and for that of my family. It was, furthermore, meant to be a record both of my impressions and experiences in London and of my ideas on the politics of the time. These notes were intended for my family archives and were shown by me only to a small number of intimate acquaintances.

As the document was of a confidential character it was to be expected that I myself should be the central figure of the statements contained in it. This being so, it naturally creates a painful impression that anyone should venture to choose for the memorandum the forged title quoted above.

The printed document represents me as saying that the failure of my Mission was due to the *Tücken* of our policy. My own copy speaks not of *Tücken* (tricks) but of *Lücken* (gaps).

With regard to the publication of my Memorandum, I have not even to reproach myself with carelessness. No politician will regard it as a transgression on my part that I should have discussed my ideas in a circle of intimate friends and under the pledge of strictest confidence, especially when it is remembered that I was being unjustly attacked at the time, even by people in official circles.

All the men to whom I showed my Memorandum had treated it as strictly confidential. One of them, however, was incautious enough to entrust it for twenty-four hours to Captain von Beerfelde of the Political Department of the General Staff, who frequently came to him for information on political and economic questions. The Memorandum was lent to Captain von Beerfelde on the express condition that he should only read it himself and that he should return it next day. This officer, contrary to his promise and in spite of repeated reminders, kept the document one or two days longer in his possession. In his naïve ignorance of the world, he failed to recognise the importance of the memorandum. Under the delusion that it might help to bring about peace, he had had some fifty cpoies made of it. These he sent to His Imperial Highness the Crown Prince, the Duke of Brunswick, Prince Max of Baden, Field-Marshal von Hindenburg, General Ludendorff, Dr. Solf, Secretary of State for the Colonies, Count von Roedern, Secretary of the Treasury, to the General Staff and other official departments in addition to a number of eminent personages in public life. Apparently nothing was done by any of these gentlemen to prevent the contents of the document from being bruited abroad. I myself only got wind of what had happened some weeks later and immediately set to work to collect the copies that had got about. Unfortunately Captain von Beerfelde had in the meantime sent the Memorandum to various members of Parliament and journalists, so that all my efforts were in vain. I thereupon reported the matter to the Chancellor, Dr. Michaelis, and have since been in constant touch with the German Foreign Office in my endeavours to prevent the further circulation of the document. I especially endeavoured to prevent it finding its way abroad.

I think I am justified in saying that I could not possibly have foreseen such an indiscretion.

All these facts have been discussed in detail before a Berlin court at the legal investigation ordered against me by the Crown Attorney. I have therefore instructed my legal adviser, Dr. von Gordon, to ask this High House to disregard any immunity I may enjoy as one of its members, and to authorize the Crown Prosecutor to take proceedings against me. The trial will, I hope, still further exonerate me from having been guilty of any breach of official secrecy.

There can here be no question of any act of mine having injured the dignity of this House.

Is it then the views contained in my Memorandum that are called in question ? I feel sure this is not the case. For I have not expressed a single idea that is not shared by numerous politicians, even within this House itself.

The ideas to which I wished to give expression were in brief the following :

In the first place I wanted to show that an understanding with England, which was the pronounced object of my Mission, was quite within reach and that such an understanding had almost been achieved when the world war broke out. I wanted to show, too, that the British Cabinet was most willing to help towards this end. The treaty concerning the Portuguese colonies was drawn up ready to be signed, as was also the treaty concerning the Bagdad Railway. In both cases the London Cabinet had shown the greatest willingness to meet us halfway. The Anglo-French understanding in 1904 had been introduced in much the same way with a treaty concerning the interests of the two countries in North Africa and the Anglo-Russian treaty of 1907 with a similar agreement concerning interests in Asia. I also tried to show in my Memorandum that England did not want the war, but that she had, as I had reported in my dispatches, only intervened in order to protect France and Belgium.

In his replies to my dispatches, Herr von Jagow confirmed my views on all essential points by declaring that ' he, too, believed in Sir Edward Grey's love of peace and in his earnest desire to arrive at an understanding with us.'

Von Jagow also confessed that the ' English Government had pursued a policy that aimed at an understanding.' He expressly stresses the fact that he himself ' considered an Anglo-German *rapprochement* as desirable and an understanding on the points in which our interests clashed as attainable.' He further declared that ' it was not correct to say that the reports that England would under all circumstances protect the French had failed to find credence in the German Foreign Office.'

The second idea that I wished to make clear was that our political orientation since the Berlin Congress or at least since the denunciation of the Re-insurance Treaty, was based on an error which in time was bound to lead to a European war. I wanted to prove that the present world-war did not originate in a defective understanding with England, but in the long years of neglect that characterized our relations with Russia. I can appeal to Bismarck for support in this attitude. He earnestly warned Germany against allowing any irreparable breach to arise between the two Powers.

Thirdly and lastly, seeing that up to the end of July 1914 we had not realized the gravity of the situation but had believed that a localization of the conflict was possible, I wanted to show that although we had not actually willed the war, yet our attitude was such as everywhere to give the impression that we really wanted war. The English offer of mediation, the acceptance of which I earnestly recommended, was turned down by Germany, and the Russian suggestion that the dispute should be submitted to the Hague Tribunal was left unanswered. But it was our brusque refusal to allow any Power to intervene in the Serbian question that did us most harm in the eyes of foreign countries. Furthermore, we took up the attitude that we would only permit mediation between Austria and Russia if the Serbian question—which was the real point at issue—were excluded. The fact, too, that we declared war on Russia without Austria-Hungary having been attacked, and at the very moment when Count Berchtold [1] wanted to give way, could not but strengthen foreign countries in their impression. Austria-

[1] Cf. English Blue Book (Documents No. 137 and No. 61) ; Austrian Red Book (Documents No. 53 and No. 56) ; French Yellow Book (Document No. 120).

Hungary, it will be remembered, did not enter the war till 5th August.

'From the very beginning of the conflict, we adopted the standpoint that it was a purely Austrian affair which Austria alone would have to settle with Serbia. We therefore directed all our efforts towards localizing the war and towards convincing the other Powers that Austria-Hungary in justifiable self-defence and compelled by circumstances, had had to decide on an appeal to arms. We emphatically contended that no civilized state had a right to attempt to hold Austria back in this fight against barbarism and a criminal code of political ethics or to save the Serbs from righteous punishment. In this sense we instructed our representatives abroad.' German White Book. Memorandum of 3rd August, 1914.

The conflict was simply to be localized. It was, however, only the statesmen at Berlin and Vienna that believed in the possibility of such a localization. The reproach has been levelled against me that my statements might prove harmful to the prestige of the German Empire. The following passage in the German White Book of 3rd August, 1914, will, I think, suffice to refute this criticism :

'Under these circumstances, Austria could not but say to herself that it was compatible neither with the dignity nor with the security of the Monarchy to look on inactive any longer at the doings on the other side of the frontier. The Austrian Government informed us of their conception of the matter and asked for our opinion. We were able to assure our Ally of our cordial acquiescence and to inform her that any action deemed necessary by her to put a stop to the Serbian movement directed against the very existence of the Dual Monarchy would meet with our approval. In giving her this assurance, we were well aware that any warlike steps taken by Austria-Hungary against Serbia might bring Russia into the arena and thereby in accordance with our treaty obligations involve us in a war. In recognition of the vital interests of Austria-Hungary that were at stake, we could neither advise our Ally to make concessions that were incompatible with her honour, nor deny her our support in her moment of need.'

From these official statements concerning the causes of the war the following facts become clear :

(a) That Austria-Hungary intended to have recourse to ' deeds ' in dealing with Serbia (in other words, she meant war) ;

(b) That she ' informed ' us of this intention ;

(c) That we ' out of the fullness of our hearts ' declared our
acquiescence and assured her that ' armed action ' against
Serbia would meet with our approval.   In other words,
we encouraged Austria-Hungary to go to war with Serbia ;

(d) ' That in doing this we were well aware that any warlike action
on the part of Austria-Hungary against Serbia would bring
Russia into the arena and might possibly, ' in accordance
with our obligations to our ally,' involve us in a war.
According to this, we knew perfectly well that we had to
expect a world war, for I had continually pointed out in my
dispatches that England would come in on the side of
France ;

(e) That we did not ' counsel Count Berchtold to moderation,' but
that we assured him of our support under all circumstances.

In the circular note issued by the Chancellor to the Federal
Government this statesman furthermore says :

' If, however, contrary to our hopes, the conflagration should be
extended through Russia's intervening, we should in loyalty to
our treaty obligations have to support our neighbour, the Dual
Monarchy, with all the forces at the disposal of the Empire.'

According to this, the German official declarations state quite
unambiguously that we were not attacked, inasmuch as we were con-
fessedly prepared, even at the cost of a world war, to use all the
forces at the disposal of the German Empire for the glory of Austria
and for the dynastic interests of the Lothringians.

*Whilst I, for my part, argue that we did not believe that Russia would
intervene, in other words, that we did not actually will the war, the
German White Book declares that we steered deliberately into the world
war, fully realising what might be the result of our attitude.*

This, I think, proves beyond a doubt that the official documents
are far more damaging for us than are the statements contained in
my Memorandum.

A nation may doubtless will a war without this necessarily being a
crime.   The only question in such cases is whether such a war is
regarded as a practical necessity or not.   That, of course, is a matter
of opinion.   Bismarck, in his *Reflections*, says that he had ' given his
counsel in favour of three wars ' ; so that on those occasions, too, it
was not we who were the attacked.

The telegram addressed to Herr von Tschirschky on the evening of
29th July, which became public through Herr von Bethmann-

Hollweg's speech of 19th August, was, so far as is known, the only message sent by us to Vienna advocating moderation. This message shows that at the last moment when Berlin finally recognised the seriousness of the situation, we were ready to make concessions. Then came the Russian mobilization, our ultimatum and our declaration of war on Russia, and the world war was let loose.

Every citizen has the right to criticize his Government. If it holds good that he may find fault with his Government's home policy, the same must apply in the case of foreign policy. The Conservative Party itself has, as is well known, submitted the internal policy pursued by Herr von Bethmann to the sharpest criticism. I, to my no small regret, am unable to appreciate the foreign policy of this statesman as highly as other members of this House apparently do. But I fail to see how the dignity of the Chamber can in any way be affected by my holding this view.

It goes without saying that my criticisms were not intended for the public or even for wide circles. No one can regret more than I do that my intimate and candid discussions should through an unfortunate concatenation of circumstances have been made accessible to friends and foes alike. I think I am, however, entitled to state that the assumption that the publication of this document did serious harm to the interests of the Fatherland is, to say the least of it, greatly exaggerated. All the essential facts had long since become known from the various official publications, and our own White Book was, as I have explained above, in reality much more unfavourable to us than were any views expressed by me.

General Smuts in a recent speech declared that Herr von Jagow's reply was much more damaging than either my notes or the revelations made by Dr. Mühlon, a gentleman, by the way, with whom I am not acquainted. In a London letter printed in the foreign Press, moreover, it is stated that in British parliamentary circles the outspokenness of the former German Ambassador is regarded with distrust, as it is suspected that the German Government is behind the publication of the Memorandum, its object being to pave the way for an understanding with England and to strengthen the hands of Lord Lansdowne.

I may in conclusion point out that after my return from London I refrained, though not without a struggle, from answering the attacks made upon me on many sides by people who had no real knowledge of the facts of the case. I have always declared that as long as the world war was still going on I should not reply to any such accusations. I am convinced that the members of the Commission will not shut their eyes to the fact that my strictly confidential statements expressing the view that the world war might have been avoided contain nothing inconsistent with the dignity of a member of this House. Nor do I fear that any member of this Chamber, to which I have had the honour to belong for the past sixteen years, will have the slightest misgiving as to the genuineness of my patriotism.

I confidently hope that the explanations I have given will help towards a calm and objective judgment in this painful affair. I feel sure that the astonishing motion laid before the House, a motion that was probably influenced by the malicious and libellous attacks made against me in certain organs of the Press, will be satisfactorily dealt with.

IV

AN APPEAL TO THE BRITISH NATION [1]

BERLIN, 14th November, 1918.

In this hour of distress and defeat I turn to the British nation and to its leading statesmen, not in any official capacity but as a private individual, as a friend of England and as one of the innumerable Germans who from the very outset have condemned this unhappy war and who, despite all the horrors we have witnessed during the past four years, have never lost faith in the British people's sense of justice or in its straightforwardness and have never doubted its sincere wish to offer us the hand of reconciliation as soon as the fratricidal strife was over. I turn to my many personal friends, first and foremost to Lord Lansdowne, Lord Grey and Mr. Asquith, and beg them to throw into the scale their high personal reputation, which raises them above all differences of Party, on behalf of the lofty ideals of humanity and justice which characterise their political past.

Now that the aims have been attained for which England entered the war, viz. the protection of Belgium and France and the transformation of Germany into a state with a democratic basis, I still find it impossible to believe that the thirst for revenge, the wish to strangle the German nation, will oust all those other feelings which

[1] Originally published in *Vorwaerts*.

actuated the British as a people before the war and which I personally witnessed on so many occasions.

If since the beginning of the war I have never hesitated to declare
that it was not, as a noisy Press declared, the will to destroy that
drove the British Government into the war, I have based my hopes,
as have various political friends, on the belief that England's attitude,
once the struggle was over, would justify my view and demonstrate
that England's humanity and justice would outlive the chaotic
passions of war and refuse to lay upon the German people, which
has made and must still make, such terrible sacrifices, burdens
that would amount to strangulation and make the re-knitting
of the lacerated bonds of friendship with England for ever impossible.

The terms of the armistice now laid upon us are animated by a
spirit for which one can find no other name than revenge ; for if
these terms were conscientiously observed, they would infallibly
bring in their train misery and famine, anarchy and chaos. No
Government, however strong, would be able to ward off the consequences of such conditions or to guard Europe against the danger
of infectious tendencies that run counter to all law and order. Nor
could any Government prevent Russian terrorism, the greatest and
most dreaded foe of democracy and freedom, from spreading to all
the other members of the comity of nations. In their own interests,
our former opponents and, at their head, the great British nation,
must now see that they ought to help us to maintain law and order
and not make it impossible for the German people to do so, a people
the great majority of whom did not will the war and are now filled
with a sincere desire that Germany shall tread the path of reconciliation and peaceful labour as a diligent member of the great family
of nations. The foundations without which there can be no reconstruction after such an unexampled catastrophe must not be
begrudged to this nation, if it is to build up a new peaceful and
democratic state.

Is it necessary that I should point out that a peace violently
imposed upon us, entailing the cruel exploitation of our plight, would
endanger the ideal of the League of Nations and the future peace of
the world? Must I point out that a peace containing conditions which
would not only ruin us both financially and economically but would
also dismember the Fatherland by separating from it geographically and economically indispensable areas which owe their prosperity

to German administration and to the German sense of order, would mean the annihilation of the work of many generations and the sacrifice of German provinces that form part of one organic whole ?

As a German patriot and at the same time as a friend of England's, I speak to the British people and to all Englishmen who despite the horrors of this war have managed to preserve their feeling for humanity and justice. I appeal to all those whose political far-sightedness has not been dimmed by passion and I ask them whether they will help us to create a state of things which will, on new foundations, later on permit of reconciliation and *rapprochement*, the restoration of the trade relations indispensable to both nations, and of mutual peaceful work in the service of a common humanity, or whether they would rather destroy this foundation, cripple the German people and surrender it to chaos, thereby making our dream of a world peace and a world of law and order a sheer illusion.

I make my appeal not to the British nation's sense of pity, but to its commonsense and insight, and I sincerely hope that my appeal will not remain unheeded.

V

To Herr Theodor Wolff, Editor of the *Berliner Tageblatt*.

Kuchelna, 26*th May*, 1925.

May I be permitted to say a few words on the wretched flag question ?

Like many others, I deeply regretted that it was thought necessary at Weimar to abolish the black, white and red flag which was known all over the world and beneath whose glorious colours we had conquered the world markets. The change was made chiefly at the instance of the Austrian representative, Professor Hartmann, who thought the prospects of a union more promising under the black, red and gold banner. Quite apart from the consideration that the desirability of a union is a much disputed question, it is very doubtful whether the Allied and Associated Powers would permit it. The union is a question which, in my opinion, depends not on colours but on material interests, and it would, to put it mildly, be an exaggeration if out of what its advocates profess to be consideration for a population numbering little more than one tenth of that of Germany we went so far as to replace for their sake the flag of the newly united German Empire by the colours of the Greater-Germany party [1] of the Frankfort Parliament of 1848.

Even the citizen-kingdom in France did not in 1830 abolish the revolutionary tricolour : La Tricolore a fait le tour du monde.

As, however, according to the Constitution, the black, red and gold is now a flag in being, it will not do simply to ignore it, especially as it has developed into the symbol of the republican state. On the other hand, we cannot fail to recognize that all Germans living abroad, as well as the bulk of all the middle-class parties, and even many members of the Centrum and the Democrats, cling to the old colours of the North German Confederation and the German Empire, and will not hear of such a thing as a change of flag.

A flag conjured up out of the imagination and designed on some entirely new pattern could not, even though it possessed all the international virtues of Esperanto, rescue us from this dilemma. Such a flag would satisfy nobody and would merely increase the present chaos. The only result would be that we should then have three flags instead of two.

I therefore agree with those who think that the question ought to be decided by a referendum. Should a majority of the German people pronounce in favour of one or the other of the two flags, the question would be decided for ever. I see no other solution.

Yours, etc.,

LICHNOWSKY.

VI

To His Excellency The Grand Admiral von Tirpitz.

KUCHELNA, 3rd November, 1926.

Your Excellency has done me the honour to publish in your new Collection of Documents a confidential letter which I addressed to you under date 26th September 1914.[2] I have no reason what-

---

[1] This party, as distinguished from the Smaller-Germany party, was in favour of establishing a new German Empire which should include *all* German-speaking states, including Austria. (Tr.)

[2] Cf. page 179 *et seqq.* of *Deutsche Ohnmachtspolitik im Weltkriege ;* von A. von Tirpitz ; Hamburg and Berlin, Hanseatische Verlagsanstalt, 1926. (Tr.)

ever to repudiate the opinions I then expressed when I said that we should not succeed in ' dictating peace ' and that therefore the goal we ought to aim at was a peace by understanding arranged with England as mediator. Throughout the war I advocated, unfortunately without success, this line of action in opposition to Your Excellency and most of the other political and military people of influence. Events have shown only too clearly how right I was. Hitherto it has always been the custom, unless the consent of the writer has first been obtained, to refrain from publishing documents that possess neither an official nor a business character. In the present case I should have acquiesced with special pleasure, but should naturally have wished that the ironical remarks concerning a diplomatic friend at the close of the letter should have been omitted as superfluous.

My surprise at the publication of my letter has been increased by reading in a letter of yours to Admiral von Capelle, published in the same work and dated 16th October, 1914, your views concerning my ability to judge character and on my capacities in general. I am naturally loth to regard the confidence I placed in Your Excellency on various occasions as one of the reasons why you reproach me with a lack of judgment. Our opinions of the leading statesmen in the Wilhelmstrasse and of their policy previous to the outbreak of the war so completely coincide that we should have a great deal in common.

We were at one, too, in the conviction that our Fleet was not responsible for England's taking part in the war, and we agreed that England, even apart from the Fleet question and even had there been no violation of Belgian neutrality, would never have permitted a second Sedan. I had constantly reported in this sense without finding credence at our Foreign Office. If nevertheless I, as will become clear from the dispatches printed along with your other documents, up to the last moment hoped that England would adopt a waiting attitude, I did so because I was convinced of the unqualified desire for peace that animated both the British Government and the British nation, and because I knew, moreover, that the feeling of the Cabinet was divided.

Your Excellency will, however, admit that my judgment, not only concerning the upshot of the war, but also concerning the necessity of a peace by understanding and especially concerning the effect of unrestricted submarine warfare, turned out to be more correct than the programme of the so-called 'Fatherland Party ' [1] which led us to the Peace of Versailles.

    With the assurance of my highest consideration, I remain,

        Your Excellency's very obedient servant,

                LICHNOWSKY.

VII

TO THE EDITOR of the *Schlesische Zeitung*, Breslau.

        BERLIN, 10*th December*, 1916.

    Under the heading ' German Diplomacy in England ' you publish in your columns a letter from a correspondent in which the writer states that what he calls my ' sin against the Fatherland ' is especially heinous because through my Memorandum, which by a regrettable indiscretion was published during the war and re-published at the close of the war with the consent of the Foreign Office, the ' fiction ' that the German Government wanted the war was put in currency. The gift for fiction in this case, should, I imagine, be attributed not to me but to your correspondent, in whom I think I recognise a former colleague who has long since been placed on the retired list. If the writer—who, by the way, rightly seeks the short-comings of German policy of those days where alone they are to be found, viz. in the central office at Berlin, and not on the periphery— had taken the trouble to read my Memorandum carefully, he would have discovered that I nowhere either suggest or state that our Government willed the world war. ' The whole world—everyone, in fact, except the statesmen at Berlin and Vienna—understood that this (the ultimatum to Serbia) meant not only war, but the world war.' I by no means wish to deny that in my Memorandum I bring grave charges against the men who were at that time in charge of the Berlin Foreign Office. For these men, in spite of my persistent warnings that we were on the brink of a world war in which we stood to lose everything and gain nothing, apparently allowed themselves to be influenced by reports to the contrary and believed up to the last moment that the conflict could be ' localized ' and that Italy would remain faithful to her German and Austrian allies in the event of the general European war coming about, a war which they persisted in regarding as improbable. I merely point out that the brusque demeanour of our Government in those critical days of July 1914

    [1] Of which Admiral von Tirpitz was President. (Translator's note.)

could not but be interpreted abroad as a will for war. Nor could it fail to weigh heavily against us in the war-guilt question. That the men at the helm did not want a world war is evident, however, from the mere fact that they were ready to enter into negotiations when the seriousness of the situation at last dawned upon them. Then came the Russian mobilization and our declaration of war on Russia and France. Herr von Jagow said that there was sure to be some ' fuss and noise ' raised. He regarded the unambiguous language of M. Sazonov as mere ' bluff.'

Hoping that you will find space in your columns for these lines,

I remain, etc.,

PRINCE LICHNOWSKY.

VIII

To PROFESSOR ALBRECHT MENDELSSOHN-BARTHOLDY and
DR. FRIEDRICH THIMME.

BERLIN, 21st December, 1926.

May I make the following remarks with regard to the footnotes on pages 622 and 633 of Vol. XXXIX. of the *Grosse Politik der Europäischen Kabinette* ?

1. During my official sojourn in London I learned nothing whatever either of the arrangements come to between the English and French Naval and General Staffs or of the correspondence between Grey and Cambon. On the contrary, the German Foreign Office had intentionally withheld from me all information concerning the material collected by its secret agents, published in the *Norddeutsche Allgemeine Zeitung* on 16th October, 1914, some time after the outbreak of the war.

2. It was not through information given me by my chiefs that I received the first hint of an Anglo-French Naval Agreement, but through a jeering remark made during the latter part of my stay by Herr von Müller, our naval attaché, who had been informed of it by the German Admiralty.

3. If the Foreign Office was of opinion that I was letting myself be ' taken in ' by Grey, and if statesmen in Berlin had grounds for supposing that Sir Edward Grey was not an ' honest, and truth-loving statesman,' it was the duty of the Chancellor and of the Foreign Office to inform me and to warn me by laying the necessary material before me.

4. This was not done either on the occasion of my visit to the Chancellor on the 29th June or when I called upon Herr Zimmermann, the Under-Secretary of State, or at any other time. Herr von Bethmann-Hollweg merely complained of the Russian armaments and pointed out the painful impression caused by certain things that had come out with regard to Anglo-Russian agreements.

5. Your contention that I had been informed of the correspondence between Sazonov and Benckendorff or of that between Grey and Cambon is therefore incorrect. Neither the Chancellor nor anyone else ever told me about it.

6. You refer to a statement made by Herr von Jagow to the effect that I had not been left in ignorance concerning the most 'important things,' so far as they had a bearing upon my mission.[1] The statement in question is an untruth. Herr von Jagow must know perfectly well that 'important things' of which I should undoubtedly have been informed, things that were of the greatest importance for my mission, were withheld from me purposely in order if possible to lead me astray and to make me appear a fool. The conduct of our foreign policy lay at that time almost entirely in the hands of Herr Wilhelm von Stumm, the worthy successor of Herr Fritz von Holstein. Herr von Stumm was guided by the notion that he might become my successor in London. He therefore endeavoured with the willing support of Herr von Jagow, to paralyse and thwart my efforts with all the means at his disposal. Among other things, he proposed with this end in view to wreck the Colonial Treaty that had been drafted some time before. Does Herr von Jagow perhaps not reckon the Grey-Cambon correspondence and the Anglo-French Naval Agreements among the 'important matters' he refers to? Does he really consider that Ballin's mission to Grey and Haldane in July 1914, undertaken apparently with the object of undermining my position in London, an incident of which I remained in ignorance until 1915, was merely another of the 'unimportant things' that had no 'bearing' on my mission?

As witnesses to the truth of the above statements, I might, if need

[1] For von Jagow's statement on the question, see *Norddeutsche Allg. Ztg.* of 23 March 1918. (Tr.)

be, name the two Secretaries of State who have now retired, Dr. Zimmermann and Herr von Kühlmann, my Counsellor of Embassy in London.

With the request that you will be good enough to append this correction to the next volume of your publications,

I remain, etc.,

LICHNOWSKY.

IX

To Professor Albrecht Mendelsshon-Bartholdy and Dr. Friedrich Thimme.

BERLIN, *22nd December*, 1926.

With reference to my letter of yesterday, may I, in connection with your footnote on p. 129, Vol. XXXVII., point out that I can also cite Dr. Rosen, at that time German Minister at Lisbon, and Dr. Solf, then Secretary of State for the Colonies, as witnesses to the correctness of my statement that Herr Wilhelm von Stumm, who at that time wielded such absolute power in German foreign affairs, did his best to prevent the Colonial Treaty from coming into effect.[1]

With the request that you will publish this supplementary note as well,

I remain, etc.

LICHNOWSKY.

X

To Dr. Friedrich Thimme, Berlin.

DAVOS PLATZ, *4th January*, 1927.

DEAR DOCTOR THIMME,

Many thanks for your letter of the 28th ult., which has been forwarded to me here. May I make the following comments ?

First of all I must point out that the Grey-Cambon correspondence has nothing whatever to do with the Anglo-Russian Naval Agreements. Consequently the Chancellor could, on 29th June, 1914, have told me about the Anglo-Russian Agreements had he chosen to do so, without necessarily touching upon the correspondence in

---

[1] This letter is discussed in a hostile article published by Colonel Schwertfeger (formerly of the German General Staff) in the *Tägl. Rundschau* of 29 Dec. 1927. (Tr.)

question. My conversation with Herr von Bethmann-Hollweg on that occasion lasted scarcely half an hour. He confined himself, as I have already stated, in the main to generalities and to complaints about the Russian armaments, and in passing just touched upon the subject of the Anglo-Russian Agreements which had already been published in May in the *Berliner Tageblatt*. He did not communicate to me facts of any kind, and the somewhat oracular statement to the effect that I had been given the ' main outlines ' can therefore not be regarded as correct, as his utterances contained neither anything new nor anything at all positive. I must therefore emphatically deny that the Chancellor on the 29th June gave me information of any real importance.

As far as I myself am concerned, the real question is not whether he touched upon the Anglo-Russian Agreements already published in the Press or not, but whether he brought to my notice, as it was his duty to do, the secret facts of which the Foreign Office had a precise knowledge, that is to say, the Anglo-French Naval Agreement, the Sazonov-Benckendorff correspondence, the Grey-Cambon correspondence and other similar matters. It would be very remarkable, too, if Herr von Bethmann-Hollweg had left behind him no notes concerning such an important conversation. That he, as you say, gave me clearly to understand that there must be some truth and authenticity in the articles published about the Anglo-Russian Naval Agreements may be correct, but even that was only given in the form of vague hints, or, as you yourself put it, in ' general outline.'

I never demanded proofs or names of the sources from which the secret information had come, but I certainly did object to the intentional withholding from me of information that would have been of the greatest importance for my mission, such for instance as that contained in the various secret documents published in the *Norddeutsche Allgemeine Ztg.* after the outbreak of war. It seems to me very remarkable, too, that the famous Grey-Cambon correspondence should, as is alleged, not have come to the knowledge of the Foreign Office until June 1914. It is somewhat strange that this correspondence that took place in November 1912, should so long have remained a secret while the Benckendorff-Sazonov correspondence was known after the lapse of only a few weeks. This fact would, to say the least of it, throw an extremely unfavourable light on the efficiency of the secret service of the Foreign Office. According to information I have received, the Foreign Office came into possession of the above correspondence in the winter of 1912-13. Unfortunately I have not the necessary documents at my disposal here, but I think I remember that the correspondence referred to is to be found in the series of secret documents arranged in chronological order and published in the *Norddeutsche Allgemeine Zeitung.*

I gladly accept your offer once more to consult the men whose names I have mentioned and if necessary to add a further note to your correction. I should like to say in conclusion that I have full confidence in Herr von Schubert, the present Secretary of State at the Foreign Office, who was at that time Second Secretary at the London Embassy. He is no doubt in a position to give you any information you may require and to confirm my statements.

I remain, etc.,

PRINCE LICHNOWSKY.

MY LONDON DISPATCHES

PREFATORY NOTE

Unfortunately I am no longer in a position to make use of a number of extremely interesting letters of an official character addressed to me by Herr von Bethmann-Hollweg, Herr von Jagow and Herr von Stumm. These letters I lent in the original to one of the editors of the so-called Kautsky Documents who wished to make use of them.[1] Soon afterwards they mysteriously vanished from his Berlin residence.

[1] The culprit was Count Max Montgelas. In the December issue of the *Kriegsschuldfrage*, 1927, in answer to Prince Lichnowsky's statement, this gentleman expresses his extreme regret that the very important documents entrusted to him by the Prince should have got lost " either in moving or in some other unaccountable way." Unfortunately, Prince Lichnowsky had kept no copy of these official papers. He seems to have implicitly trusted the orderliness of the man to whom he lent them. For had Graf Montgelas by his researches, his methodology and his associations, not won the right to be regarded as an unbiassed and trustworthy seeker after truth in the question of " War Guilt " ? Herr Kautsky, the Socialist publicist who had been originally entrusted with the collecting and editing of the War Guilt Documents, took a different view of the Count's leanings, and was anything but pleased when this ex-Oberquartiermeister of the Great General Staff was appointed " to assist " him in his work. Kautsky frankly expressed his distrust of the Count's goodwill and thought that his purpose was to delay publication.

Count Montgelas, who with Herr Kautsky thus came to co-edit the *Docs. relating to the Outbreak of the War*, had had a curiously mutable career. After having commanded a German Division on the Western front at the beginning of the war, he, for some reason or other, had retired or been retired to Switzerland at an early stage of the war. He had not been long in that land of freedom ere he professed himself an ardent pacifist and a believer in Germany's war guilt. The theory that Germany had been forced into a war of defence he pronounced to be " a lie." " Germany," he told the author of *J'accuse*, " had deliberately brought about a preventive war only to transform this preventive war, in September, 1914, into a downright war of conquest." (Cf. R. Grelling's article in the *Weltbuehne*, 1928, p. 625.) Despite these and numerous other denunciations he was not trusted by men like De Muehlon and Dr. von Schlieben, the pacifist editor of the *Freie Zeitung* (published by German refugees at Berne during the war), nor did his attempts to get into touch with the British Legation at Berne meet with the faintest encouragement.

At the end of the war Count Montgelas again changed his coat and has ever since been the most zealous apologist for the old military régime and champion of the spotless innocence both of the General Staff and of his Excellency Gottfried von Jagow. (Tr.)

MY LONDON DISPATCHES

THE AUSTRO-SERBIAN DISPUTE

To The Foreign Office.   London, 14*th November*, 1912.

Sir Edward Grey, who received me this afternoon, repeatedly expressed to me his satisfaction that the tension which had marked the last few days had considerably slackened and that there was no longer any reason to fear serious complications. He had authorized the British Minister in Belgrade to try to influence the Government in the direction of moderation and to represent to them that they would forfeit all sympathy among the Great Powers of Europe if they persisted stubbornly in a one-sided demand for an extension of territory in the direction of the Adriatic. There was, he said, in the opinion of the British Cabinet still another way of satisfying the justifiable wishes of the Serbian people and that was to give them a safe commercial route with a port to correspond, or some line of connection with the Aegean. He knew for certain that the Russian Cabinet had brought its influence to bear on the Serbian Government in the same direction, so that the Belgrade Government would now clearly perceive that they could no longer reckon on any support from outside. The Austro-Hungarian Government had hitherto, he said, shown moderation, and one could only hope that it would not allow itself to be carried away into adopting any violent measures against Serbia in the event of the latter, in spite of warnings, insisting upon seizing possession of some point on the Adriatic coast. The Belgrade Government also knew that the creation of a *fait accompli* in this direction would in no way influence the final settlement of the frontiers, as no delimitation of frontiers could take place without the assent of the Great Powers. In principle, said Sir Edward Grey, everyone was agreed that Albania must come out of the present disturbances as an autonomous state.

In answer to my remark that, in accordance with the wish of Great Britain, we should be quite willing to associate ourselves with the step under consideration—the purpose of which was to prevent Constantinople's being seized by the Bulgarians—provided that Great Britain would continue to use her influence in St. Petersburg in the direction of moderation in the Serbian question, the Minister told me that negotiations between the Turks and the Bulgarians were already going on and that the war might be regarded as over. An occupation of Constantinople was, he said, no longer to be feared and the St. Petersburg Cabinet, so far as the Serbs were concerned, was in full agreement with London.

I took this opportunity to lay stress on the fact that we were in complete accord with Mr. Asquith's statement when that statesman said that it was desirable that none of the Balkan questions should be dealt with separately, but that it would be better to wait and settle them all together. I explained that the brusque behaviour of the Serbian Government had obliged us to take up a position with regard to one particular danger by which Austria-Hungary felt herself specially threatened. The Minister quite concurred. He also expressed the hope that by the time that the various Balkan problems had been settled as the result of our common action, the present excited mood would have had time to cool down. He hoped that by then we should have succeeded in getting rid of all inflammable material. In conclusion he expressed profound satisfaction that it had proved possible to go hand in hand with us in this question and he hoped that in the future this might more and more be the case.

My French and Italian colleagues whom I met at the Foreign Office spoke in a similar strain. They, too, had received quietening news. LICHNOWSKY.

TO THE IMPERIAL CHANCELLOR VON BETHMANN-HOLLWEG.

LONDON, 15*th November*, 1912.

In a chance conversation I had with him, Sir A. Nicolson remarked that the attitude of Austria in the present crisis deserved every recognition. Vienna had, he said, in the face of Serbian provocations, observed a dignified calm that one could not but admire. The Serbs had alienated all sympathy with their noisy megalomania. The best thing for the Great Powers to do was to take Serbia's arrogant talk humorously. LICHNOWSKY.

To The Foreign Office.   London, 18th November, 1912.

My Russian colleague told me to-day that the Russian Note to Belgrade had turned out to be much sharper in tone than the one sent by the British Government.   He thought that Russia's influence in Serbia was greatly overrated abroad and that this was especially the case at the present moment when the Serbs, fresh from their military successes, were declaring their intention of freeing themselves from any kind of tutelage, either on the part of Russia or of Austria.   It was therefore difficult to calculate what they would decide to do in the existing dispute with Austria.   Fortunately, he said, the relations between Sazonov and Count Berchtold, as the former recently told Count Benckendorff in London, are excellent. The confidence that marks them promises well for a peaceful settlement of the questions in dispute.

Fortunately conditions now were not like those that prevailed when Aehrenthal and Isvolsky were at the helm, or the outlook would be much graver.   If Austria had opposed the occupation of the Sandschak, the St. Petersburg Government would hardly have been able to resist public opinion.   But nobody would want to go to war over Albania, a state which in the unanimous opinion of the Great Powers ought to become independent.   The British Government, too, said Count Benckendorff, was absolutely opposed to a war and had in Belgrade supported the wishes expressed by Austria, well knowing that any other attitude would have rendered the danger of war considerably more acute.

In conclusion Count Benckendorff told me that the well-informed Bulgarian Minister had expressed the opinion that his Government did not want to keep, or even to take, Constantinople, as it held the view that Bulgaria could not ' digest ' it.   In other words, that it feared the bloodshed and the religious difficulties that would follow such an occupation, although it must at the same time be remembered that the victorious army might prove an incalculable factor and perhaps force its will on the Bulgarian Government, unless the Cabinet soon succeeded in re-establishing a direct understanding between Turkey and Bulgaria.   Lichnowsky.

To The Foreign Office.   London, 19th November, 1912.

At the banquet following yesterday's audience, granted me at Windsor that I might present my credentials, I had a long conversa-

tion with Sir Edward Grey.   He seemed less confident with regard to
the foreign situation than he had been on the occasion of our first
talk.   The treatment to which the two Austrian consuls had been
submitted by the Serbs had made an unpleasant impression on him
and he seemed to fear further difficulties.   Austria-Hungary would
be fully justified, he thought, in demanding satisfaction.

He was afraid, however, that if it came to a collision between
Austria and Serbia, public opinion in Russia might disastrously
influence the Government, which had hitherto behaved in an exem-
plary fashion and had recently given the hotheads at Belgrade the
benefit of a cold douche.   Sir Edward Grey in answer to a question
said that he had not received any unfavourable news on the point in
question from the capitals concerned ; he was, however, as I could
see, worried about the insecurity of the situation.   He seemed to
attach special importance to finding a way out, some course that
might prove acceptable to both parties, and suggested with a show of
conviction that a very narrow strip of land along the Montenegrin
frontier as far as the Adriatic might be handed over to the Serbs.

I told him that this solution seemed to me risky, since it was
scarcely likely that the Austrian Government, after the resolute
attitude it had hitherto taken up in the question of a Serbian port on
the Adriatic, would consent to such a proposal ; it would be difficult
for Austria to retreat without sacrificing prestige.   The irredentist
movement in the South Slav provinces of the Monarchy was far too
serious to make it desirable to allow Serbia to encircle Austria in this
way.   There were, too, I pointed out, in those mountainous regions
technical obstacles that made it seem improbable that Serbia was
prompted by purely economic considerations in her desire to reach
the Adriatic.

The Minister admitted this, but repeatedly declared that he had
not contemplated the cession of the whole of Northern Albania, as
Serbia had originally demanded, but only of a very narrow strip of
territory.   If Montenegro were allowed access to the sea, Austria
could well afford to let Serbia get there too.

I did my best to talk him out of this idea and pointed out to him
that not only had the other two members of the Triple Alliance
supported the Dual Monarchy in its attitude of refusal, but that the
British Government, as well as the St. Petersburg Cabinet, had also
fully appreciated Count Berchtold's standpoint.

In this conversation I again got the impression that the British

Cabinet is anxious above all to prevent any serious European complications and that this anxiety outweighs all other considerations in the question of finding a final solution of the Balkan problem. It is at bottom a matter of comparative indifference to the British Government how the Turkish booty is divided up, as long as the distribution does not give rise to a European war which would force Great Britain to take sides. The British Government would also like to see peace, or at least an armistice, concluded as soon as possible, and is therefore not particularly delighted at the latest Turkish success at Tchataldja, since it is feared that this success may strengthen the Turks' confidence and make them less ready for peace.

Sir Edward Grey promised to use his influence to get the disputes that had arisen treated in the most dilatory manner possible, experience having shown that delay blunts their sharpness. He also promised to do what he could to have the various questions dealt with in the aggregate and not each one separately.

The Minister has asked me to come and see him to-morrow afternoon when among other things we are to discuss colonial questions.

LICHNOWSKY.

TO THE FOREIGN OFFICE.   LONDON, 25th November, 1912.

During my visit to Sir Edward Grey to-day, I brought up for discussion M. Sazonov's utterance, at the same time referring to England's wishes in the matter. I suggested that influence should be brought to bear in St. Petersburg in the direction of greater restraint. The Minister replied that he was not aware that the Russian Government had made any definite promises with regard to a Serbian port ; on the contrary, so far as he knew Russia had always counselled moderation and calmness in Belgrade ; M. Sazonov had probably been trying to find some middle course between the exaggerated Serbian demands and the brusque attitude of refusal adopted by Austria-Hungary in the question of an Adriatic port for Serbia ; he thought that Sazonov had done so without definitely taking sides with either party. He, Sir Edward Grey, had also had visions of some such compromise as a solution of the problem. This time he spoke of a neutralised strip of territory under Serbian control as the connection between the Kingdom of Serbia and the sea. The Minister seemed to me to have none too clear an idea as to the constitutional basis of his proposal ; he said that for the present he would prefer not to take any definite attitude towards the question, but to leave the regulation of the whole matter till after the conclusion of peace when it could very well be dealt with along with the other questions.

When I pointed out to Sir Edward Grey that the British and German Governments were united by the common wish to maintain peace and to avoid anything that might add to the acuteness of the situation, he quite agreed with me and declared his readiness to continue his efforts along these lines. Far from being nervous about the situation, he is distinctly optimistic and sees in the Russian and Austrian armaments purely preparatory measures. He hopes that once peace has been successfully concluded between the Turks and Bulgars, the remaining questions will be settled peacefully among the Great Powers. Among these remaining questions he includes that of the islands, of Albania and of the Serbian port ; for the rest, he is of opinion that the Great Powers will be able tacitly to accept the agreements come to by the belligerents. He also told me that he had advised the Turks not to negotiate first for an armistice, but to begin right away by discussing peace, as peace would not involve a discussion of the Tchataldja line, whereas the first armistice had come to grief through the Turks declining to hand over this line and thus deliver themselves defenceless into the hands of the victor.

As for the islands in the Aegean, England would put forward no claims, as long as this was not done by any other of the Great Powers. The Minister seemed to be inclined to hand over some of the islands to the Greeks.

He declared that he felt little interest in what happened to Macedonia. LICHNOWSKY.

To The Foreign Office. LONDON, *26th November*, 1912.

My Russian colleague told me yesterday that military measures were being taken in Russia. Mobilization in that country, he said, always proceeds more slowly than in Austria and very much more slowly than in Germany. The Government felt that it was necessary to be prepared for any emergency. M. Sazonov was thoroughly peaceful in his intentions. He had sharply reprimanded the Serbian Minister here and had protested against Serbia's impudent pretensions. Sazonov was apt, he said, to flare up in a rage and to use much sharper expressions than he really intended. It was therefore quite on the cards that he had expressed himself to foreign diplomats concerning the present crisis in a form that did not correspond with the impression he had intended to give.

Count Benckendorff, who is a relative of mine and who has shown me marks of special confidence during my stay here, thinks that a solution will probably be found for the Serbian question. The possibility of new Turkish successes causes him far more anxiety. Judging by reports that have reached him from Russia, he is inclined to fear that in such a case public opinion in Russia might bring pressure to bear in favour of the Balkan States, in other words, against Austria, pressure that no Government could well withstand. He was of opinion that Russia had by no means seen the last of the spectre of Revolution. Every Russian Government feared it. It was therefore very difficult to count with any certainty on official circles and it was impossible to say who it was that was actually guiding the destinies of the Russian Empire.

My impression was that these statements made to me by Count Benckendorff, who attaches importance to maintaining good relations with the German Embassy here, were quite sincere and based upon an exact knowledge of the actual conditions in Russia. They are, I think, worthy of serious attention.

LICHNOWSKY.

To The Imperial Chancellor von Bethmann-Hollweg.

LONDON, 15*th November*, 1912.

Mr. Acland, Under-Secretary of State for Foreign Affairs, and a close friend of Sir Edward Grey's, delivered a speech at Rochdale on Saturday, in which he emphasized the fact that from the beginning of the Balkan crisis up to the present the Governments of Germany and England had stood together uninterruptedly in close and friendly relations. If difficulties had arisen, they were not of the British Cabinet's making, but could at most have arisen, if at all, through the utterances of irresponsible persons like Lord Roberts. Later on in his speech Mr. Acland returned to Lord Roberts' well-known propaganda speech and expressed his satisfaction that the Field-Marshal had disclaimed as erroneous the interpretation that had been put upon his statement that Germany would attack Great Britain as soon as she was strong enough to do so. Mr. Acland said that he would nevertheless have preferred to have seen Lord Roberts unambiguously withdraw his utterances as there was a danger that such speeches would often be used by Chauvinists in Germany as a weapon against England. He could at least assure them that England would never embark upon an aggressive policy of violence such as had found expression in Lord Roberts' words. Just as little did he believe that Germany would ever contemplate such a thing.

LICHNOWSKY.

To The Foreign Office.   London, 27th November, 1912.

Our discussion to-day, which took place at the Foreign Office after a luncheon with Mr. Asquith, was introduced by Sir Edward Grey with the remark that he had received satisfactory news from St. Petersburg about the audience given by the Czar to the Austro-Hungarian Ambassador. The prospects of a peacful solution of the differences between the two countries had thereby been considerably improved. He knew, he said, that M. Sazonov was untiring in his efforts to find some way of settling the disagreement between Austria and Serbia, and had been at special pains to appear as impartial as possible. The Russian Ambassador in London, too, had told him that the Russian Government cherished the hope that some economic outlet in the direction of the Adriatic which would prove acceptable to Austria would be found for Serbia.

To him, personally, the question of Serbia getting a port on the Adriatic was a matter of indifference. His own efforts were solely directed towards finding a solution that would prevent one or other of the Great Powers from being drawn into the quarrel. The consequences of such an extension of the war would be incalculable *and no mortal man could predict what Powers might then be involved in the struggle.*

I told him that ever since my arrival I had had the impression that our two countries, guided by a common wish for the maintenance of European peace, had in the present crisis gone hand in hand and that I cherished the hope that this association might be continued throughout the further course of this affair as well as in future. It therefore seemed desirable, I said, that we should in common bring our influence to bear on friendly Powers in the direction of moderation and dissuade them from measures which ran counter to our common goal, the maintenance of peace. Russia's military preparations, for instance, could not but seem calculated to call forth counter measures.

Sir Edward Grey mentioned,—somewhat extenuatingly, I thought, —that the visit of the Austrian Chief-of-Staff in Berlin had made a rather unfavourable impression on the Russians, and seemed to justify new armaments.

Whether the Minister will make representations in the desired direction in St. Petersburg I cannot, of course, judge. I believe, however, that what I told him made some impression, and that he will continue to use his influence in the direction of moderation and the maintenance of peace. He regretted that peace had even yet not been concluded in Turkey and that the belligerents were still negotiating for an armistice. He thought that it would be an easy matter to arrive at an understanding between the Powers once peace was concluded. Questions such as the Macedonian problem, for instance, could be excluded from the negotiations between the Great Powers, and attention could be concentrated on those questions that interested them. England would place the three questions already mentioned by me in the foreground, the Serbian port, Albania and the Aegean islands. It was for the other Powers to put forward any questions in which they in their turn were specially interested.

Herr von Kiderlen-Waechter had suggested, said Sir Edward in the course of our conversation, that there should be an exchange of opinion on the weightiest points, before the Conference assembled for its final deliberations. He, Sir Edward Grey, thought that it would be advisable for the various Ambassadors to meet informally in one of the European capitals to discuss the points at issue, according to the instructions received from their respective Governments and if possible come to some understanding. It was a matter of indifference what capital was chosen. M. Poincaré had suggested that the representatives of the Balkan States should be present, but this would not be possible until after the conclusion of peace. A preliminary discussion of the character he had mentioned seemed to him to be better adapted for the achievement of their aims than a never-ending exchange of opinions between the Cabinets—a procedure which would not exclude misunderstandings and delays. The assurance that Austria-Hungary had no intention of intervening in Serbia's military operations in Albania was accepted by the Minister, I may remark in conclusion, with evident satisfaction.

LICHNOWSKY.

To The Foreign Office.   London, *4th December*, 1912.

Sir Edward Grey sent for me to-day and opened our conversation with the remark that he was delighted at the cordial words spoken in the Reichstag by the Secretary of State for Foreign Affairs concerning the relations between England and Germany. The words used by the Secretary of State had been in complete accord with his own views and wishes. He had, he said, unfortunately no very good news to report from Austria-Hungary, as information had reached him of further mobilization on a larger scale in that country. He then asked me whether we still adhered to the old standpoint that had been repeated by Herr von Kiderlen-Waechter, by which we undertook to deal with no question separately but to handle all questions in the aggregate, after peace had been signed. I hastened to assure him that this was the case, and expressed my astonishment that he should for a moment think that we could abandon a programme which had been put forward by Mr. Asquith and most willingly accepted by us. He replied that he feared that the speech of the German Chancellor, who to his surprise had even at the present stage emphasised the possibility of a war between the Continental groups, had induced him to put this question, and he asked me whether my impression was that this speech could be interpreted to mean that Germany was willing to guarantee to protect Austria's rear, in other words, to give her a blank cheque for all emergencies and for whatever steps she might think it in her interest to take. He feared, he said, that such a far-reaching support of Austrian policy would be incompatible with our common goal, which was to maintain peace and ensure moderation on either side, as it would only stiffen Austria's spirit of resistance.

Sir Edward Grey said that he wished above all that there might be no repetition of the situation that had arisen in 1909.[1] For he was convinced—and this sentence he twice repeated, with special emphasis—that Russia would not a second time beat a retreat but would rather take up arms. It was therefore of supreme importance that the Serbian port question should not become so acute that one or other of the two Great Powers concerned would be forced to give way. All his efforts were concentrated on getting the Austro-Serbian dispute treated in common with all the other questions at

---

[1] This refers to the crisis which followed the annexation of Bosnia-Herzegovina by Austria in 1908 in violation of the Treaty of Berlin (1878) to which Great Britain, France and Russia were signatories. (Translator's note.)

issue, so that it might be possible to create compensations by including the Sandschak and other territories in the bargaining. He could not, he said, suppress a certain anxiety lest the speech delivered by Your Excellency, despite the fact that this speech had in general been favourably commented on here, might contribute towards bringing about a separation between the Austro-Serbian dispute and the other questions at issue, and thus stress the sharp opposition between the two European groups whose confrontation of each other in two opposing camps he had so anxiously sought to avoid. For he particularly wished that no question of honour or of party should arise out of the dispute between the existing groups, so that England and Germany, the two countries which had hitherto to a certain extent worked hand in hand as non-participants and with the same interest in the maintenance of peace, should continue to work together as mediators at Vienna and St. Petersburg and also make it possible to create a basis for further political collaboration. If, however, a European war were to arise through Austria's attacking Serbia, and Russia, compelled by public opinion, were to march into Galicia rather than again put up with a humiliation like that of 1909, thus forcing Germany to come to the aid of Austria, France would inevitably be drawn in *and no one could foretell what further developments might follow.*

This is the second time that Sir Edward Grey has given me this hint, a hint that cannot be misunderstood. Various people in close touch with him have in the last few days corroborated his statement and told me that the British Government was particularly anxious to avoid European complications, as it feared that such complications might again jeopardise the *rapprochement* with us for which the way had been paved ; for, despite the fact that there were no secret agreements with France, it was for England of vital necessity *to prevent that country from being crushed by Germany* ; England, they said, would have no alternative but to come to the aid of France should Germany, as is expected here, prove victorious over the French.   LICHNOWSKY.

To The Imperial Chancellor von Bethmann-Hollweg.

LONDON, *9th December*, 1912.

In order to prevent any misunderstandings I should like to sum up the impressions that I have received in London and from time to time expressed in my dispatches. Not only the British Government but also the great majority of those people in England whose opinions count in political matters, are most anxious to live on good terms with Germany. Every opportunity of giving expression to this desire and of publicly testifying to the existence of an understanding between us is therefore gladly utilised. The general wish is to live in peace and friendship with us, and the echo aroused here in all circles by the utterance of the German Secretary of State, as well as by my own recent speech, shows the correctness of this opinion. The attitude of the English Press during the last crisis corroborates this view. The Press, almost without exception, avoided any reference to the clash of interests in the Serbian question.

In his foreign policy, and especially in dealing with the delicate questions at present occupying the attention of Europe, Sir Edward Grey is guided by the wish to maintain peace and to go hand in hand with the German Government in all important affairs. Nothing would therefore be less welcome to him than that the differences should assume such an acute form that a peaceful issue was no longer possible without the moral defeat of one or other of the two parties. In making his proposal not to treat any of the questions separately but to settle them all together by means of mutual compromises, he was prompted by the idea that in this way alone could the retreat of one of the two parties be rendered unnecessary. For although official Russia may not identify herself with the Serbian demands, it is nevertheless clear, he thinks, that there is in Russia strong feeling in favour of the Serbs, and that for this reason everything should be avoided that could be interpreted as a threat or as pressure, so as to make it easier for the Russian Government to maintain the moderate attitude it has hitherto adopted. Austria's reinforcement of her armaments seemed to him on this account to be inopportune and has caused him some uneasiness.

Although M. Isvolsky's retreat in 1909 was not the result of pressure brought to bear by Germany, the not very brilliant rôle played by Russian diplomacy on that occasion and the incident of the ' gleaming armour ' are still too fresh in people's memories for the British Government not to feel a certain amount of justifiable anxiety lest a similar situation should again arise. I once more repeat that the main object of this Government is to avoid any complications on the Continent. In other words, the British Government wishes to avoid anything that might be interpreted as meaning that the Russian Government would have to yield to pressure from without, and has suggested a Conference of Ambassadors so that in the end there may be neither victors nor vanquished and so that the Serbian question may through a conciliatory attitude on both sides find a solution equally acceptable to both Austria and Russia.

These are the reasons why it is not desired here that participation in these discussions shall be coupled with stipulations from any side whatever, as it is thought wiser that all such stipulations should, outwardly at least, appear to be the outcome of the discussions ; in other words, it is felt here that it would be a mistake for the Powers concerned to contribute to a *petitio principii*. It was for this reason, too, that Your Excellency's speech in the Reichstag caused uneasiness here. The reference to Germany's 'loyalty to her allies' was looked upon as a blast on a trumpet at a moment when everyone would have preferred to hear the tones of an organ.

We have to reckon with the fact, and in this matter no change has recently taken place—nor is any change to be anticipated—that England's policy towards us is one of peace and friendship, but that no British Government could reconcile it with the vital interests of the country if it permitted France to be still further weakened. This attitude is based neither on secret treaties nor on the intrigues of Edward VII. nor on the after-effects of the Morocco crisis, but solely on the consideration, which seems so natural to the English from their standpoint, that after a second collapse of France like that of 1870, the British nation would find itself confronted by one single all-powerful Continental nation, a danger that must be avoided at all costs.

Although it is always a delicate task to make predictions in politics, I nevertheless venture to say that England will only attack us after we have marched into France and fought our first successful engagement, but even a declaration of war on France or of France against us would bring in its wake the mobilization of the British Fleet, while a war with Russia alone, if such a thing were thinkable, would not necessarily involve the intervention of the British Naval forces.

This is the situation with which we have to reckon. It is one, however, which makes it possible for us to continue developing and fostering our mutual relations without any sacrifice of our own interests, provided we show ourselves ready to meet the British half-way and avoid treading on their corns. It is for these reasons, too, that Sir Edward Grey and the whole Cabinet are so anxious to see a peaceful settlement of the Serbian dispute.

LICHNOWSKY.

SECOND SECTION

BEFORE THE CONFERENCE OF AMBASSADORS AND THE PEACE CONFERENCE

SECRETARY OF STATE FOR FOREIGN AFFAIRS VON KIDERLEN TO THE AMBASSADOR AT LONDON, PRINCE LICHNOWSKY.

BERLIN, 18th November, 1912.

May I ask you to call on Sir Edward Grey and give him the following message : The danger of the situation, as I see it, is that at the impending Conference of the Powers arising out of the conclusion of peace in the Balkans, individual Powers may give support to certain pretensions put forward by the Balkan States, pretensions that may be described as unacceptable by other Powers. It seems to me that it is essential for the maintenance of peace that before the beginning of the negotiations with the Balkan States the Powers should agree upon a definite programme, and especially that they should agree as to what demands of the Balkan States are in their opinion admissible and what are not.

First of all there is Albania, a country in which our allies, Austria and Italy, may have especial interests which they wish considered. The self-restraint shown by Austria in the face of Serbia's direct provocations deserves recognition, but this self-restraint is only possible on the assumption that Serbian garrisons could not be regarded as having created the right to definite possession. It would be useful if at this stage this could be made clear to the Serbs from some other quarter. As the autonomy of Albania is apparently desired by all parties, it does not seem possible to cut the country into two parts by running a strip of Serbian territory through it. We think, however, that an understanding may be possible on some such basis as the following :

It would be a good thing if Austria would state as precisely as possible and communicate to the Powers what concessions she thinks she can make to Serbia, so that there may be a firm basis for the negotiations that are to be anticipated at the conclusion of peace.

According to information so far received from Vienna, a suitable basis for an understanding with Serbia might, we think, be the granting of an assured railway line.   This line, while to a certain extent independent of Albanian territorial suzerainty, would run to a harbour on the Adriatic guaranteed for Serbian exports without thereby involving any acquisition of territorial rights by Serbia ; further, safe transit for Serbia on Bosnian railways and safe transit for Austria to Salonica, both on the Serbian railways and on the Sandschak line after it has been built.   Russia also has wishes, as far as we know, with regard to Constantinople and Adrianople, and also with regard to Mount Athos.

Before beginning peace negotiations with the Balkan States, it would be useful to formulate precisely all these wishes and to come to some agreement in advance concerning a programme which is to be supported by all the Great Powers.

This would fall in with Mr. Asquith's idea of not dealing separately with any particular question beforehand.   Austria has observed this principle in her dealings with Serbia and we assume that Russia is also doing so in the case of Bulgaria.

In the event of Sir Edward Grey's falling in with these ideas, it might perhaps be useful if he would try to get St. Petersburg and Paris to see things in the same light, while we would do the same at Vienna and Rome.   I am looking forward with interest to a wire from you telling me how Sir Edward Grey takes these suggestions.

KIDERLEN.

To The Foreign Office.   London, *20th November*, 1912.

In accordance with your instructions I have just had an interview with Sir Edward Grey.   The Minister seems on the whole to acquiesce.   He said, however, that for the moment he could not give me a definite answer as he would have to think over the various points.   He asked me to come again to-morrow when he would tell me what he thought of the suggestions.

Speaking generally, he remarked that my communication contained two separate questions, firstly, the question of the preliminary discussions which were to be undertaken with a view to coming to an agreement concerning a common programme, and second, by the request that England should back up the suggestion that the Serbian garrisons could not be regarded as creating a right to definite possession. Without going any deeper into this question, he merely declared that the principle of an autonomous Albania included in itself the question of the definition of its frontiers.   It seemed to me as if he wished in this way to avoid broaching the delicate matter of Serbia's wishes on the Adriatic.   For the rest, he made notes concerning our standpoint, without urging any objection to our proposals.   Another wire follows to-morrow.

LICHNOWSKY.

To The Foreign Office.   London, 21st *November*, 1912.

On my visiting him to-day, Sir Edward Grey told me that he quite shared Your Excellency's idea with regard to the necessity of an early exchange of opinions between the Great Powers.

As for the questions to be discussed, three points seemed to him of essential importance :

1. The autonomy of Albania,
2. Serbia's connection with the Adriatic, and
3. The Aegean Islands.

As regards Constantinople and Adrianople, this question seemed to him to drop out to judge by the armistice negotiations that had been reported between the Bulgars and the Turks, as the two belligerents seemed likely to come to an agreement on this point.   Assuming that this was so, the British Cabinet could hold itself just as aloof from the solution of this question as Germany was evidently doing. Russia would probably also be satisfied with this attitude.   Mount Athos occupied a special position nowadays and would probably continue to do so.

From the further utterances of the Minister I gathered :

1. That the fate of the Greek islands was a matter of especial interest to the Government.
2. That the idea, already dealt with elsewhere, of finding a possible solution for the Serbian problem by granting Serbia a narrow strip of territory along the Montenegrin frontier, is gaining ground here.   The Minister, it is true, admits that this solution is not by any means the only and final form in which Serbia's wishes might be met.   He was, however, of opinion that in spite of Austria's misgivings, to which I had again referred, the idea was one that should not be summarily dismissed without closer examination.   On my asking whether

Paris and St. Petersburg shared this view, he evaded my question with the remark that so far as he knew the opinion was general that this solution was one that was at least worth discussing.

As the Minister had apparently already come to some understanding with his friends of the Entente and as I had yesterday learned from my French colleague, whom I met before seeing Sir Edward Grey, that he had been informed of our suggestion by way of Paris, I considered that, in view of the divergent view taken by the British Cabinet in the critical Serbian question, it would be better to refrain from any special request to support our proposals in Paris and St. Petersburg.

For the rest, the Minister repeatedly declared that his main object was to find some way out that would guarantee the maintenance of peace in Europe and avoid a conflict into which one or more of the Great Powers might be drawn. The views that he had expressed should therefore be regarded merely as providing a basis for further discussions.   LICHNOWSKY.

TO THE IMPERIAL CHANCELLOR VON BETHMANN-HOLLWEG.

LONDON, 1st December, 1912.

My Italian colleague called on me yesterday to explain the following matter.

Italy desired, he said, perhaps even less than Germany, to be involved in a war over the Serbian affair, especially as it was a question only of a commercial harbour. Rome's chief interest was in Valona and the Italian Minister had given the Greeks to understand that the occupation of this bay could not be tolerated. It was therefore absolutely necessary that a compromise should be found between the Austrian and the Russian standpoints. The longer one waited, the more difficult would it become to find a solution that would not entail a humiliation for one party or the other, as public opinion in both countries was becoming more and more excited by the continued mobilizations which made it increasingly difficult to avoid war. According to his information, it would be a dangerous mistake to assume that Russia's mobilization was mere bluff. Count Thurn's audience had proved fruitless, the Czar having confined himself to polite and friendly phrases, without giving any kind of assurance. Neither Sazonov nor any other Russian Minister would venture publicly to express views that ran counter to opinion in Russia, *which was definitely on the side of the Serbs*. If he did, he would be swept from office.

We must reckon with these facts, he said, if we wanted to avoid war, and must try to bring about an agreement as soon as possible. Only in this way was a general European war to be avoided. Marquis Imperiali compared the affair with the meeting that takes place annually at Naples at the Feast of St. Januarius between the Cardinal and the Mayor of the city. Neither of the two may compromise his dignity in the eyes of the other and both have to take exactly the same number of steps so that they may meet exactly in the centre of the church.

Before this compromise is agreed upon, he said, it would be dangerous to proceed to the Conference of Ambassadors proposed by Sir Edward Grey, as the Conference would run the risk of remaining without result. Until both Austria and Russia had given way a little and shown some readiness to meet each other's wishes, it was useless to come together and discuss matters about which the Ambassadors would after all not be able to arrive at an understanding. Marquis Imperiali has also told Sir Edward Grey much the same thing, and has, he tells me, reported to Rome. I am inclined to think that his opinions coincide in the main with those of Marquis San Giuliano.

I did not omit to point out to my Italian colleague how important it was that Germany and Italy should in the interest of peace back up the Austrian standpoint, so that our opponents might not be encouraged by our want of unity, and the danger of war thus be increased. Marquis Imperiali fully admitted the justification of this standpoint, but repeated that *it was a mistake to suppose that St. Petersburg was only bluffing*. The situation was extremely grave and he considered war inevitable unless Austria was inclined to show a somewhat more conciliatory attitude in the question of the Serbian harbour. He asked me to use my influence in this direction in Berlin, as no Power but Germany could have sufficient weight with Austria. The personality of the British representative at Vienna was not such that he would be likely to achieve very much in the direction desired by the British Government, while Count Mensdorff, although popular in London society, had no great influence either in Vienna or here. Nor should we make the mistake of supposing that the mood in France was different to-day from what it was three years ago. The victories of the Bulgarians over the Turks had also helped to increase the self-confidence felt by the French and there was no doubt that in the event of complications with Russia, the French would join in. It was also certain that the English, in spite of the leaning towards Germany that was specially marked at the present moment, and in spite of England's pronounced need of peace, could not hold aloof. If the powers of the Triple Alliance were to prove victorious, *the English would not tolerate Germany's oppressive preponderance on the Continent.*

As for the place at which the Conference of Ambassadors should be held, I gather from utterances of my Russian and Italian colleagues, that Sir Edward Grey is inclined to favour Paris, on the ground, apparently, that he does not speak French. Marquis Imperiali thinks that London would be a suitable place and considers Paris dangerous on account of M. Isvolsky. A small place like The Hague he thinks unsuitable, as it would mean sending special delegates and the meeting would then take on the form of a Congress and would no longer correspond to the intentions of the British Cabinet.

I should like to associate myself with the utterances of my Italian colleague which are probably based on instructions from Rome. I feel sure that a proposal emanating from Germany to the effect that London should be chosen as the place for the Ambassadors' preliminary discussions would make a favourable impression here and would be regarded by the public as evidence of our closer relations. The rôle of mediator which would then devolve upon Sir Edward Grey would have the further effect of strengthening him in the impartial attitude which he has hitherto shown himself inclined to adopt.

LICHNOWSKY.

THE SECRETARY OF STATE FOR FOREIGN AFFAIRS VON KIDERLEN TO KAISER WILHELM II.

BERLIN, *6th December,* 1912.

I beg most obediently to inform your Imperial and Royal Majesty that on receipt of Austria's and Italy's acquiescence I to-day despatched the following reply to Sir Edward Goschen with regard to the enquiry concerning the conversations that are to take place between the Ambassadors :

' The Imperial Government notes with lively satisfaction Sir Edward Grey's proposal that the Ambassadors of the six Great

Powers accredited to one of the European capitals should be authorised to meet for the informal discussion of several aspects of the
Balkan problem which are of special importance from an international standpoint.   The Imperial Government sees in the proposed meeting a suitable method of simplifying and speeding up
business procedure, and would welcome the choice of London as the
place for these conversations, seeing that the suggestion emanated
from that city.   Should this proposal be endorsed by Sir Edward
Grey, the Imperial Government declares its readiness forthwith
to furnish Prince Lichnowsky with the necessary instructions.   In
so doing it acts on the assumption that in these conversations of the
Ambassadors, anything that might give outsiders the impression of a
formal conference will be avoided.

As Rumania, owing to its important position and interests in the
Balkans, is in the same situation as the Great Powers, and as it is the
only Balkan State that will have no voice in the peace negotiations of
the belligerents, the Imperial Government would suggest that the
Rumanian Minister be also invited to take part in the Ambassadors'
discussions.   KIDERLEN.

To The Foreign Office.   London, *7th December*, 1912.
        Provided Paris sees no discourtesy, Sir Edward Grey agrees to
London, as it is known there that he proposed Paris and as it was
Poincaré who first mooted the idea of a conference.   I replied that
we, so far as I knew, would have been quite content with Paris, but
that misgivings had been expressed, not only by us but by others as
well, as to the personality of M. Isvolsky.

I am convinced that if some form can be found that will avoid
hurting M. Poincaré's feelings, a ready assent will be given here, as
people here are by no means blind to the drawbacks of Paris.

The Minister seemed to have no objection to the Rumanian
Minister's being invited to take part ;   he repeated, too, that any
appearance of a formal Congress was to be avoided and that for this
reason there should be no opening ceremonies.   We should, he said,
simply take our seats at a Round Table.

In accordance with Berlin's suggestion he had drawn up the agenda
for the first discussion :

   1. Those points to be fixed which were to be excluded from the
      discussions, as being better left to the belligerents alone.

2. The points to be fixed that would interest the Powers participating in the Berlin Treaty and which the Ambassadors would deal with.

3. Discussion of these latter points for the purpose of coming to an agreement concerning them, whereupon corresponding proposals would be laid before the Governments represented.

A dispatch couched in these terms which the Minister had sent to Vienna he handed to me to look through. His message closed with the touching wish that Christmas might bring peace to the world as the result of the Ambassadors' discussions.

He also told me as a curiosity that the Balkan States had decided to hold their Peace Conference in London without asking his opinion on the matter and that the Bulgarian Government was the only one that had given him any official intimation of the fact.

LICHNOWSKY.

To THE FOREIGN OFFICE.   LONDON, 10*th December*, 1912.

Sir Edward Grey, whose mood is a sure index of the state of peace prospects, was again very cheerful when he received me to-day. The Minister declared that in response to the generally expressed wish he was quite ready to fall in with the suggestion that the Ambassadors' discussions should take place in London. He to-day told several of my colleagues the same thing. Sir Edward Grey attaches especial importance to the earliest possible commencement of the discussions, as he is of opinion that there will then be less danger of unforeseen occurrences between Austria and Serbia. When once the discussions have begun, it is improbable, he thinks, that the Austrians will allow their feelings to betray them into taking any impulsive step that might lead to the interruption of the Ambassadors' negotiations. Austria's attitude was still causing the Minister some anxiety. He showed me a telegram from Vienna reporting new movements of troops in the direction of the Serbian and Russian frontiers. He would not, he said, attach too much importance to these military measures, but one could never tell what they might lead to, especially as the affair of the Consul who had suffered ill-treatment had not yet been settled.

Count Mensdorff leaves for Vienna to-morrow morning, having been summoned thither by Count Berchtold. Sir Edward Grey wishes particularly to impress upon him the necessity of counselling

Vienna to calmness and moderation, so as to prevent the occurrence of incidents before the Ambassadors' conversations begin.

The Minister has counselled the Serbian chargé d'affaires to calmness and circumspection. The chargé d'affaires had asked the Minister's advice in view of the rumours concerning impending Austrian measures. The Minister reminded him that none of the Powers had any wish to jeopardise the peaceful settlement of the affair. Serbia's wisest course was to submit to the verdict of the Powers.

In the meantime Sir Edward Grey, influenced apparently by the attitude of Russia, is less uneasy about the stipulation made by Vienna. He is of opinion that the boundaries of Albania will come up for discussion at one of the first meetings and that it will present no small difficulty. Provided Count Mensdorff is back by Monday and provided that all the Ambassadors have received their instructions by then, he would like to begin on that day.

LICHNOWSKY.

To The Imperial Chancellor von Bethmann-Hollweg.

London, 10th December, 1912.

As I hear from a well-informed journalistic quarter, M. Poincaré until quite recently energetically opposed the choice of London as the place of the Ambassadors' Conference, as he could not bring himself to renounce his favourite idea of enhancing the brilliance of his term of office at the Quay d'Orsay by an international conference. The French Minister thus made it very difficult for Sir Edward Grey, who knew his French colleague's weakness, to accept London as the place of the Conference. Poincaré's attitude did not help to diminish the tension between himself and M. Cambon. The latter, from the outset, was in favour of London, as he considered the composition of the diplomatic corps in this capital as being more likely to bring about a reasonable solution than would be the case if the conversations had been held in Paris.

M. Poincaré, probably not without good reason, reproaches the French Ambassador in London with having up to the last moment declared in his dispatches that the outbreak of a Balkan war was improbable and of having thus been partly responsible for the manner in which the French Foreign Office was taken by surprise.

LICHNOWSKY.

To The Imperial Chancellor von Bethmann-Hollweg.

London, 13*th December*, 1912.

Sir Edward Grey has during the last few days busied himself in detail with the forthcoming Conference in London. He wishes to strip it as far as possible of any formal character. No minutes are to be kept. Nothing will be put down in black and white until the informal exchange of ideas has led to some result in the individual questions.

According to Sir Edward Grey's intentions, the Conference should proceed at once, without losing time over trifles, rapidly to debate the main points, and then adjourn on the understanding that it is to meet again directly new and important material for debate is available.

The Minister hopes to get through the main part of the work in four or five sittings and seems to contemplate the possibility of handing over to special commisions all questions that are likely to render extensive discussions necessary, as for example such questions as the Dette Publique and the railways.

Sir Edward Grey seems in the last few days to have been carrying on an exhaustive exchange of ideas with the Russian Cabinet. In private conversation he has expressed his satisfaction with the result, as he is now convinced that Russia will pursue a thoroughly peaceful and conciliatory policy.

The mood towards Austria in government circles here continues favourable ; the justification of the Austrian standpoint in many directions is recognised, although at the same time stress is again and again laid upon the fact that it might lead to the gravest dangers if Austria in her dealings with Serbia were to try to bend the bow too far. Austria's continued armaments are still causing considerable uneasiness here.

Of the Balkan nations, Bulgaria is the only one that enjoys any marked sympathy here ; the Serbs by their noisy behaviour and by interviews such as that given by the peace delegates to the *Temps* have somewhat offended people here. They will probably hear some plain English from Sir Edward Grey.   Lichnowsky.

To The Foreign Office.   London, 16*th December*, 1912.

Sir Edward Grey has just proposed to the Ambassadors taking part in the Conference, that the first discussion should take place to-morrow at 3.30 p.m. The negotiations are to be regarded as confidential and no minutes are to be kept. Only when resolutions are actually passed are they to be committed to paper. The Minister thinks to begin with the Albanian question and to fix in rough outline the boundaries of Albania which is to reach up to Montenegro. This done, he wishes to pass on to the question of Serbia's economic connection with the Adriatic quite in the sense of Telegram No. 217. The resolutions which as far as possible are to be unanimous will then be submitted to the Powers. By dealing with these two points at the very outset the Minister hopes to settle as quickly as possible the questions fraught with most danger.

The internal delimitation of their newly acquired territories he wishes to leave to the belligerents themselves and not to discuss the question of the Aegean Islands till later.

Sir Edward Grey, who had already spoken with my colleagues with the exception of Count Mensdorff, who does not get back until this evening, again seemed to be very sanguine, and told me that he hoped that a favourable result would be reached. We two, Germany and England, had, he observed, worked in the same direction all along, and he would be very glad if our common efforts were crowned with success.

LICHNOWSKY.

THIRD SECTION

THE BEGINNING OF THE CONFERENCE OF AMBASSADORS AND THE COLLECTIVE DÉMARCHE OF THE POWERS AT CONSTANTINOPLE

To The Foreign Office.   LONDON, 17th December, 1912.

At the first sitting of the Ambassadors which took place to-day and at which Sir Edward Grey took the chair, Count Benckendorff on the strength of his instructions was able to take up a very conciliatory attitude. The following points were unanimously agreed on :

1. Albania independent and able to support herself ; guaranteed and supervised exclusively by the Powers ; under the Suzerainty of the Sultan. It was my Russian colleague who suggested this, his proposal being accepted after the amendment 'with a limited number of Ottoman troops, whose strength would remain to be fixed ' had been dropped, as it

gave rise to misgivings. In the same way the words 'a Governor appointed by the Powers and confirmed by the Sultan' were omitted ; instead of this my Austrian and Russian colleagues were asked to get their Governments to formulate ' their views concerning the future organisation of this independence ' and then to lay these projects before us.

2. It was unanimously resolved that Albania should be neutralised. Count Benckendorff had only proposed the neutralisation of the ports and the sea-coast, but declared his acquiescence with the changed wording.

3. The following resolution was passed :

   ' It is agreed that in any case the boundaries of independent Albania shall in the north touch those of Montenegro, in the south those of Greece.'

Count Benckendorff expressed his agreement with this wording which excludes Serbian sovereign rights on the Adria. Difficulties arose only in so far as Count Mensdorff wished to establish as a principle the boundary of Montenegro as the northern boundary of Albania, while Count Benckendorff declared that his Government did not wish to interfere in the negotiations of the belligerents with Turkey with regard to their future boundaries ; he was therefore not in a position to bind himself to the present southern boundary of Montenegro. Count Berchtold, however, abides by his claim that Scutari shall belong to Albania on the principle of ethnographical delimitation. Marquis Imperiali declared that he was without instructions and has asked for them for to-morrow. The further discussion of the Albanian frontiers is therefore to take place to-morrow and Count Mensdorff will then bring forward his proposal. With regard to Serbia's connection with the Adriatic, the following text was unanimously adopted :

' Access for her commerce is reserved for Serbia by means of a free and neutral Albanian harbour which will be served by the international railway under European control and under the protection of an international military force with freedom of transport for all commodities, including munitions of war.'

Here, too, a Russian proposal had served as a basis and Count Benckendorff was requested to suggest to his Government that they should draw up a plan giving details.

It was agreed to regard the discussion as confidential ; no minutes. Sir Edward Grey will continue to preside in person. LICHNOWSKY.

To The Foreign Office.   London, 17*th December*, 1912.

Sir Edward Grey has just informed me that our discussions are to come to an end on Friday evening.   He hopes that by that time the material in hand will have been dealt with.   On Saturday the Minister, like most of the other members of the Cabinet, intends to go on leave for ten days and not return to London until the 30th, the day when Parliament again assembles.   If necessary our meetings will then be resumed.

LICHNOWSKY.

To The Foreign Office.   London, 18*th December*, 1912.

The leader of the Serbian delegation, M. Novakovitch, has just been to see me.   He asked me for my advice as to whether I thought he could confidently leave the Powers to deal with Serbia's wishes with regard to the Adriatic and whether he would do well to exclude this point from the peace negotiations.   I encouraged him in this opinion and told him that the Powers were well-disposed towards Serbia and would undoubtedly be the readier to consider Serbia's wishes, the calmer and more conciliatory the attitude of the Serbian representatives was.   He complained of the attitude of the neighbouring Monarchy which continued to keep the Serbian population in a state of alarm.   He seemed to fear that people would begrudge his country any extension of territory whatever.   He also wished to know whether all the Powers were agreed as to the granting of an economic line of communication to the Adriatic together with a neutral harbour there.   I explained to him that I could not talk about our deliberations, but that I believed I could set his mind at rest on these two points.

LICHNOWSKY.

To The Foreign Office.   London, 18*th December*, 1912.

Sir Edward Grey opened to-day's sitting by telling us that the Serbian chargé d'affaires had informed him of the instructions received by the Serbian delegates.   These are the same as those M. Novakovitch had already imparted to me.   The chargé d'affaires had also added, said Sir Edward Grey, that he hoped that the wish of the Powers would be communicated to Serbia in a form which would render it easier for public opinion in that country to give way.

It was thereupon unanimously resolved to ask our Governments whether in the event of their assenting to our resolutions of yesterday, they would agree to Sir Edward Grey's communicating these resolutions next Friday to the Serbian chargé d'affaires as the result of our deliberations and as the united will of the Powers, on the assumption that Serbia would abide by her decision to forgo any extension of territory on the Adriatic. We hoped by this means to speed up the peace negotiations and to get Serbia definitely to fix her standpoint. Simultaneously with this a communiqué is to be published in the London Press on Friday evening, just before our deliberations are adjourned, which will announce as the result of our discussions Albanian autonomy and the granting to Serbia of a free economic line of communication to a neutral harbour on the Adriatic. The publication of this communiqué, to which I would ask your telegraphic approval, will, Sir Edward Grey hopes, help considerably to relieve public opinion, which, if nothing were published, might easily imagine that our deliberations had come to naught.

The delimitation of Albania was adjourned till Friday, as Marquis Imperiali was still without instructions concerning Scutari and Count Mensdorff did not wish to lay before the meeting the map he had brought back with him from Vienna, the existence of which he revealed only to me and my Italian colleague. On this map is marked the Austrian conception of Albania's new boundaries. The map represents Prisren as having been given up. Count Mensdorff thinks to represent this as a concession for Scutari. He was invited to lay the wishes of his Government before the meeting on Friday.

Sir Edward Grey told me in confidence that should difficulties arise in connection with Scutari, he would be unable again to bring his influence to bear on the Russian Government. The latter, under the combined influence of the British and French Governments, had already made many concessions. It was now for the German and Italian Governments to bring their influence to bear on Austria, in case Russia, whose standpoint he did not yet know, should insist upon the cession of Scutari to Montenegro. Count Benckendorff was still without instructions, but the question would probably be brought up at Friday's meeting. Sir Edward Grey spoke with my Italian colleague in a similar sense.

Thereupon the Aegean Islands came up for discussion. Count Benckendorff, speaking on behalf of his Government, said that

Austria did not wish that any Power should take possession of the islands of Tenedos, Imbros, Lemnos and Samothrace, to all of which autonomy should be granted. A motion put forward by Great Britain was then unanimously adopted :

' Whatever be the future status of the islands in the Aegean Sea, we are of opinion that they must be neutralised under the guarantee of the Powers.'

With regard to the question of ownership, there were no motions put forward, but the feeling of the meeting was predominantly in favour of autonomy.

In the case of Crete, it was agreed that, in the event of the island being ceded by Turkey to the Greeks under the terms of the Peace Treaty, no exception was to be taken to this arrangement.

My French colleague made the following declaration : ' With regard to Constantinople, the French Government firmly upholds the standpoint of the maintenance of the *status quo*. This city must therefore remain in the possession of the Ottoman Empire. Turkey must, moreover, retain in Europe a strip of territory along the Sea of Marmora and the Dardanelles.' This declaration met with general assent.

My Austrian colleague declared : ' We consider that the position of the port of Salonica and of the railway line that terminates at that port should be regulated with a view to maintaining intact Austria's commercial interests.' This concept met with no contradiction.

Next meeting Friday afternoon. Then adjournment till the New Year. Sir Edward Grey will go to his estate in Northumberland.

LICHNOWSKY.

To The Foreign Office.   LONDON, 18*th December*, 1912.

M. Daneff has declared to several of my colleagues here that the Allies would act together in their negotiations with Turkey and would demand from her the cession of her European possessions to the west of a line between the Aegean and the Black Sea, thus including Adrianople. Should Turkey refuse to give way, Bulgaria would inexorably continue the war. The partitioning of the ceded territory, with the exception of Albania, would then be undertaken forthwith by the Allies.

LICHNOWSKY.

THE SECRETARY OF STATE FOR FOREIGN AFFAIRS VON KIDERLEN TO
PRINCE LICHNOWSKY, GERMAN AMBASSADOR AT LONDON.

BERLIN, 20th December, 1912.

According to your telegram No. 207, Turkish sovereignty or
suzerainty over Albania was accepted without demur. We hear,
however, from another source that a lengthy argument first took
place on this subject, in the course of which the Russian Ambassador
specially championed the suzerainty of the Sublime Porte in which
he received your warm support.

KIDERLEN.

TO THE FOREIGN OFFICE.   LONDON, 20th December, 1912.

Long negotiations took place in connection with all the
resolutions passed, but I only reported to you *in extenso* about such
discussions when they gave rise to misgivings and had to be considerably amended. The proposal upon which resolution ad I was
based was brought forward by the Russian Government and I
supported it because, in view of the exceedingly conciliatory attitude
of the St. Petersburg Cabinet in the important question of the
Adriatic harbour, I thought it the more advisable to back up the
Russian wishes, seeing that Count Mensdorff had only taken exception to the presence of Turkish troops and because the instructions
given me in telegram No. 217 expressly referred to the autonomy of
Albania, which surely presupposes the suzerainty of the Sultan, even
though this should be only nominal. I further pointed out that
should Macedonia not remain in the possession of Turkey, Albania
would be completely separated from Turkey and as a matter of fact
removed outside the Ottoman sphere of power.

In the question of the Turkish troops, I took up the standpoint
that it was not so much a question of their admission on principle as a
question of their numbers which could, perhaps, be limited to a kind
of bodyguard for the governor.

In conclusion I should like to remark that the suggestion mentioned
at the end of my telegram 207 that the Russian Government should
be asked to work out a plan concerning the Serbian line of connection
with the Adriatic has been allowed to drop and that we are now in
expectation of Austrian and Italian drafts concerning the organisation of Albanian autonomy.

LICHNOWSKY.

To The Foreign Office.   London, *20th December*, 1912.

To-day's sitting, which was again presided over by Sir Edward Grey, first dealt with the text of the communiqué which is to be published this evening and with the message to the Serbian chargé d'affaires.   The latter will correspond to the text mentioned in my telegram No. 207, sub 1 and 3 ; it will not, however, contain the second point as Count Benckendorff has not yet received the assent of his Government to the total neutralization of Albania.   The communiqué will, however, appear in an abridged form.

Count Benckendorff had previously declared that his Government would assent to the above agreements on the following condition :

' That Serbia be recognised as having the choice of direction in the case of the railway line and the choice of the terminal port.   Every guarantee to be given of freedom for the necessary studies in connection with the choice of the track and the surveying of the line for the Serbian Government against any difficulties that the future Albanian Government might make.   Serbia to have the right to take part in the international control of the railway line and of the harbour.'

All the Ambassadors with the single exception of Count Mensdorff regarded these conditions as justified and voted their assent.   My Austrian colleague, however, declared that he could not express an opinion on the matter and seemed to regard the concessions made to the Serbians as going too far.

The amendment was therefore taken *ad referendum*.   This was done on the express understanding that the text accepted did not exclude the amendment.

Hereupon Count Mensdorff brought forward his wishes with regard to Albania, comprising not only Scutari but also Ipek and Prisren. Count Benckendorff mentioned the Drin as the eastern boundary ; he has promised to show us a map at the next meeting.   He declared it to be impossible at present to carry the ethnographical principle to its logical conclusions, as this would lead to impossible groupings. The general view was that frontiers would have to be rounded off and compromises made on the basis of the ethnographical conditions. No resolutions were passed and the next meeting has been fixed for 2nd January.

At the close of the meeting, Sir Edward Grey once more asked me to make representations in Berlin with the object of getting Germany to induce the Austrian Government to show a readiness to give way in the question of Scutari. This matter did not come up to-day for discussion. Sir Edward Grey said that so far he had achieved everything we wanted, and that it had cost him no small trouble to carry it through. Should difficulties arise in this case, he would be unable again to help us and would be obliged to take the other side. He told my Italian colleague the same thing.

On my taking leave the Minister expressed to me his cordial satisfaction that our deliberations were proving such a success and that relations all round had so much improved in the last few weeks.

LICHNOWSKY.

To The Imperial Chancellor von Bethmann-Hollweg.

LONDON, 20th December, 1912.

Now that the Ambassadors' discussions have been temporarily brought to a close, I should like to emphasize the fact that the favourable impression that I have received during my stay here, both as to the attitude of the British Government and the intentions of Sir Edward Grey, has been strengthened in no small measure as a result of the manner in which he has presided over our deliberations. As sponsor of the idea of toning down the differences that divide the two opposing parties by means of a personal exchange of opinion between friendly diplomats, Sir Edward Grey was manifestly at pains during our discussions to avoid the faintest suspicion of partiality and to act as mediator whenever it became necessary.

We have to thank his love of peace and the British people's need of peace for it that English public opinion in the exciting weeks that have just passed has so decisively cast its weight in favour of a calm and moderate attitude on the part of England's political friends. I feel that I may safely conclude from this that we can reckon on a similar attitude on the part of the British Government for the future as well, for there is no reason to suppose that Great Britain, had she really harboured any intention of taking up arms against us, would have let such a favourable opportunity pass or that after the settlement of the Continental quarrel, she will suddenly and without reason conceive a desire to fall upon us.

On the contrary, Anglo-German relations have, as authoritative members of the British Cabinet have declared in private conversation, not for a long time been so favourable as they are to-day, and there is reason to suppose that the *rapprochement*, strengthened by co-operation during this last crisis, will continue to develop unless something very unexpected should occur. The attitude which leading people here have without exception taken up towards me and the mood observable in the British public, all point to a wish to live in unclouded harmony with us. This wish is both sincere and general. I may perhaps be told that the English naval armaments with their inevitable agitation against the foe on the other side of the North Sea reveal a different aspect of British policy, that new demands are again about to be brought forward and that the fact that the British Empire is a member of a group of nations which, to put it mildly, is not very favourably disposed towards us, all point to a less amiable side of British foreign policy.

I do not intend to go into the details of the naval question at this moment, especially as the facts are already well known and have been frequently discussed. To me it seems quite obvious that the British Empire, depending as it does on imports from overseas, should regard the protection of its trade routes as indispensable. It is equally natural that the growth of German naval power should be utilised as a welcome argument in support of new naval demands. Great Britain as a world-power stands and falls with her predominance at sea. If we ourselves were responsible for the safeguarding of an empire like that of Great Britain, we should without doubt strive to maintain our sea-power with the same solicitude as that now shown by the British Ministers.

As for the so-called Entente policy, I am of opinion that its solidarity varies in inverse ratio to the cordiality of England's relations with Germany and that the only way of loosening this friendship is in all our dealings with the English to ignore their Entente friendships as far as possible, at the same time avoiding anything that might possibly give rise to distrust and uneasiness. England will never formally break off her engagement with France and Russia and penitently fall into the arms of Germany, unless we have first been defeated. The powerful of this earth have at all times regarded each other askance, and throughout the course of her history England has never willingly tolerated any very powerful nation on the Continent, and when any such Power threatened to establish a hegemony, England has invariably gone to war with it. To guard her security and influence in the rest of Europe, England will therefore continue to insist on a certain ' balance of power,' a counterpoise to this or that powerful group, and *under all circumstances will hold a protecting hand over France.*   We are respected here ; we are highly esteemed, perhaps even overrated, and from this feeling, that some people have been inclined to regard as fear, proceeds England's endeavour to hem us in, which is quite a different thing from a wish to go to war with us.   Our common interests are too colossal, our economic ties too close and too important and the material losses involved, even in a victorious war, too vast for that.   And people in Great Britian have grown too comfort-loving to want a war.   The nation loves peace and does not care to be disturbed in the routine of its daily life.   A war with us would therefore not be popular, but in spite of all this *the English would wage such a war if France were threatened* by us, for the opinion is general here that France would not be able to stand up against the superior might of Germany without British help.

In all this I am the less able to see any menace for us, since we have no intention of going to war with France, and since recent events have shown that among the French as among the Russians, the desire to live at peace with us outweighs all else.   The protection afforded to the French by England corresponds roughly to the protection that we should give the Austrians and Hungarians in the event of a Russian attack, and we, too, should fail to understand why Russia should regard that as a threat.   The adverse criticism that the Anglo-German *rapprochement* has met with in Paris in the last few weeks and the uneasiness betrayed by such journals as *Le Temps* may be taken to show that a development of trustful relations between England and Germany is regarded in France as a weakening of the Entente.

LICHNOWSKY.

A NOTE ON THE CONFERENCE.

BERLIN, *22nd December*, 1912.

During the three days of the Ambassadors' deliberations, I made it my special duty to mediate between the Austrian and the Russian standpoint and to try to avoid giving the impression that Russia was to emerge from our negotiations in any way humiliated or vanquished.   When therefore at the first meeting Count Bencken-dorff brought up the Russian proposal with regard to the autonomy of Albania, thus jettisoning the Serbian wishes for a port on the

Adriatic, I thought it my duty to support the Russian proposals for the construction of an autonomous Albania—in order, so to say, to build a golden bridge for the Russians. I sought in this way to influence Count Mensdorff. When, however, the question of the admission of Turkish troops to Albania and the appointment of the Governor led to misgivings and lengthy discussions, I pointed out that the Turkish suzerainty would, after all, be only a matter of form, as the exercise of actual authority presupposed the autonomy of Macedonia. When once the partition of Macedonia had taken place, Albania would be completely severed from the rest of the Ottoman Empire and it would therefore be highly improbable that the sovereignty of the Sultan would prove at all disturbing. I mentioned this especially in order to dissipate the misgivings of my Austro-Hungarian colleague and at the same time to show a readiness to meet Russia's wishes. It goes without saying that I did not broach any such proposal, if merely because the future of Macedonia was not down on the programme for discussion. This seems, therefore, to have been a misunderstanding on the part of the Russian Ambassador. The latter is well known for his absent-mindedness which in this case is perhaps explained by the fact that in London the report was current that Bulgaria wished for autonomy in the case of Macedonia, in order by this means to keep out the Greeks and thus later on get hold of Macedonia for itself the more easily.

As for Scutari, I tried in this case too to act as mediator and represented to Count Mensdorff that it would scarcely be advisable to risk the exceedingly favourable results already produced by our deliberations through insisting too strongly on this point, especially as the most important of Austria's wishes had already been attained. I, too, think that it would be a good thing both in this question and in that of the northern and eastern delimitations of Albania, to advise moderation in Vienna. Sir Edward Grey sided with the Triple Alliance in the dispute about the Serbian harbour. He will not, however, as he repeatedly told me and my Italian colleague, oppose Montenegro's wishes in the matter of Scutari.

LICHNOWSKY.

To The Foreign Office.   London, *2nd January*, 1913.

Osman Nisami Pasha visited me this morning to tell me that an agreement had been reached among the Turks—or at least that an understanding was possible on all points but one, viz. Adrianople. To give way on this point was for Turkey an absolute impossibility, not only on military grounds, which make it urgently necessary to keep this fortress which was less than two hundred miles from Constantinople, and not have the frontier pushed even closer. Adrianople was for the Turks much the same as Moscow was for the Russians, he said. It was the former residence of the monarch, a city with numerous sacred relics and mosques, and no Government could risk sacrificing it. His Majesty the Sultan, too, who did not otherwise meddle in the details of the negotiations, was inexorable on this point. Turkey wishes after peace has been signed to live on good terms with Bulgaria, but this would be impossible if Adrianople fell into Bulgarian hands, as the wish to reconquer it would lead to new wars.

Unless the Powers bring pressure to bear on the Bulgarian Government, and such pressure would be particularly effective if it came from Austria, the failure of the negotiations in London and the resumption of hostilities was definitely to be expected. In accordance with my instructions, I told him that we could only advise the Turks to moderation and that we should not understand it if the prospects of peace were brought to naught by the abruptness of the Ottoman attitude. Turkey could then certainly not expect support from any side. He replied that in giving up the whole of European Turkey with the sole exception of the district round Adrianople, the Turks had shown a very conciliatory spirit and that more could not be expected of them.

LICHNOWSKY.

To THE FOREIGN OFFICE.   LONDON, *2nd January*, 1913.

Sir Edward Grey asked me to call on him at noon to-day in order to have a talk with him before the sitting. In the first place I conveyed to him Your Excellency's thanks for his message of condolence. He took occasion to say a few cordial words about the deceased statesman von Kiderlen-Waechter, dwelling especially on his attitude during the last crisis and on the assistance he had given in furthering Anglo-German co-operation.

He then told me that, if I had no objection, the delimitation of Albania would not be discussed to-day, as a short postponement of the debate on this subject was desired, especially by the Italians.

The Scutari question is still causing the Minister anxiety. He nevertheless hopes that a direct understanding may be achieved between Vienna and St Petersburg.

He proposed to discuss the islands this afternoon and said that he thought that negotiations were taking place between Count Benckendorff and M. Venizelos. Sir Edward Grey said that if Russia would give up her original objection to letting the four islands that command the entrance to the Dardanelles fall to Greece and would content herself with their neutralization, the British Government, too, would accept this solution.

I replied that we had only a secondary interest in the question and would therefore associate ourselves with the English standpoint, and that I would this afternoon support the view that an acceptable solution of the island question might perhaps be found in giving autonomy to all the islands hitherto belonging to Turkey, with the exception of Crete, perhaps under a Greek Protectorate and with neutralization, provided such a solution seemed desirable and were put forward in the form of a motion.

LICHNOWSKY.

TO THE FOREIGN OFFICE.   LONDON, *2nd January*, 1913.

On opening to-day's sitting Sir Edward Grey on behalf of the assembled ambassadors and himself expressed his deep regret at the death of Herr von Kiderlen and asked me to convey this expression of condolence to Berlin.

When the Aegean Islands came up for discussion, Count Benckendorff at once declared : ' Russia does not oppose the union of all the islands of the Aegean Sea with Greece. provided that the four islands are neutralized under the following conditions :

1. Greece undertakes to raze the existing fortifications, both military and maritime.

2. Greece undertakes never to erect new fortifications or other defence works.

3. Greece undertakes not to use the islands for military operations or for strategic purposes, no matter with what Power she may be at war.

4. Greece undertakes not to cede to any other Power rights of possession or exploitation or any other rights which she may obtain through the union of the islands with the kingdom.'

My Austro-Hungarian and Italian colleagues declared that they wished first to obtain the assent of their Governments to the above proposal, while my French and English colleagues declared : ' that they would not oppose the union of all the islands with Greece under the conditions stated.'   I said that we were not directly interested in the fate of the islands and that I would therefore refrain from voting, although I believed I could say that my Government would associate itself with the resolution of the other Powers regarding the fate of the islands.   As my purely personal opinion, I gave it to be understood that the extension of the Russian reservations with regard to the four islands at the entrance to the Dardanelles to the remaining Aegean Islands in the event of the latter being incorporated with Greece would be in harmony with the resolutions adopted at the session of the 18th ult. with regard to the neutralization of the Aegean Islands.

My French colleague raised the question whether the Island of Thasos should not be incorporated with Bulgaria on account of its proximity to the coast which after the conclusion of peace would become Bulgarian.   Sir Edward Grey replied that the Greeks and Bulgars must themselves come to an agreement on this point. My Russian and French colleagues thereupon declared that their Governments had no objection to Thasos being incorporated with Bulgaria.

With regard to Crete, Sir Edward Grey and my French and Russian colleagues declared themselves ready to propose the cession of the island to Greece.   The Marquis Imperiali agreed, with the reservation that Italy would then expect that Greece should moderate her claims to southern Albania.

In conclusion, the possibility was discussed that to-morrow's meeting of the peace delegates might prove fruitless and that the delegates might then find themselves compelled to turn to the representatives of the Great Powers with a request for mediation in the dispute about Adrianople.   As a resumption of hostilities was under all circumstances to be avoided, we thought it as well to give them an opportunity of discussing their wishes and the next meeting was fixed for 11 a.m. on Saturday.   I may mention that it was resolved to admit the newly appointed Rumanian Minister M. Misu, as soon as opportunity offered, in order to hear his views.

LICHNOWSKY.

To The Foreign Office.   London, 6th January, 1913.

Sir Edward Grey, at the close of the Ambassadors' discussions, told us that he had just learned that the Turkish delegates had offered new negotiations on the basis of further concessions in the vilayet of Adrianople, without the city of Adrianople entering into the discussions. Thereupon the president, M. Novakovich, had immediately closed the meeting without fixing any date for further negotiations. The breaking off of peace negotiations is probably imminent, but according to the above news this has not yet definitely taken place.

LICHNOWSKY.

To The Foreign Office.   London, 6th January, 1913.

At to-day's sitting of the Ambassadors, I informed the meeting that my Government agreed to the proposed text of a *démarche collective* at Constantinople should there be a breakdown of the peace negotiations. My Italian colleague made a similar statement, adding that the Italian Ambassador at Constantinople had already been instructed to speak to the same effect should his colleagues receive identical instructions. At the same time Marquis Imperiali drew attention to the fact that Point 5 is understood by Italy to mean only that this point does not include assent to the cession of all the islands but refers only to the cession of Crete ; it was admitted on all sides that Point 5 by no means included any obligation to cede all the islands to Greece. Count Mensdorff was without instructions ; the Russian Government had also given its assent and had added a remark that the four conditions mentioned in Telegram 4 should apply only to the four Dardanelles islands, and that Greece must renounce the right to cede to other Powers any other islands it might acquire.

M. Poincaré sent word that he concurred on Points 1, 2 and 3, and that he had no objection to a *démarche collective* nor to supporting such a step by sending warships, but that he would prefer that the steps taken by the Powers should be confined to the following two points :

1. The cession of Adrianople.
2. The regulation of the cession of the islands question by the Powers.

For the present it did not seem to him to serve any practical purpose to discuss with the Turks the financial question, the future position of Constantinople or the possibility of warlike developments in Asia Minor. In answer to our remark that it was not a question of entering into obligations towards Turkey, but merely of convincing the Turks of the seriousness of the situation and of the advantages of a conciliatory attitude, M. Cambon declared himself ready to report and endorse the opinion of the meeting in this sense.

Sir Edward Grey intends to instruct his Ambassador to be prepared to take part in the *démarche collective* on the basis of the agreement come to with regard to these points. The Ambassador should, however, note the reservations made by M. Poincaré and together with his colleagues agree with the French Ambassador upon a text. At the same time Sir Edward Grey told us that, in order to be ready for all emergencies, he would send two warships to Besika Bay, in case a *démarche* should prove necessary.

Merely as a personal suggestion, at the same time emphasising the fact that I had no instructions on the point, I put forward the following suggestion, after having first obtained the assent of my Austro-Hungarian and Italian colleagues :

1. It seems to me too early to think of pressure or of a naval demonstration before Constantinople in the event of a *démarche collective* of the Powers failing in its effect.

2. It seems to me advisable that we associate ourselves with the idea put forward by M. Poincaré in conversation with M. Jonescu, viz. to let the *démarche* be followed by an analogous step in Sofia in favour of a conciliatory attitude towards the demands put forward by Rumania.

3. It seems to me (1) that considerations of fairness and neutrality are opposed to the idea of taking from Turkey both Adrianople and all the islands and (2) that provided Turkey yields in the case of this city, she might be guaranteed the possession of the four islands off the Dardanelles, as well as Mitylene and Chios or that the Sublime Porte should be granted the possibility of keeping at least some of these islands.

In connection with Point 1 the remark was made that it was certainly advisable not to treat the Turks with unnecessary harshness, but that one should be prepared for all emergencies. In connection with Point 2, M. Cambon declared that he knew nothing of

M. Poincaré's alleged remark. Thereupon the following text was agreed upon : ' After discussing the German Ambassador's remarks, the meeting raised the question whether it would not be advisable to get Bulgaria to give a pledge that in the event of her receiving through the good offices of the Powers, the Peace conditions desired by her, she would manifest a conciliatory attitude towards Rumania.' The discussion of Point 3 was adjourned. Next meeting to-morrow afternoon.

LICHNOWSKY.

To The Foreign Office.   London, *7th January*, 1913.

Judging by my impressions I do not altogether believe in the far-reaching conjectures of Marquis di San Giuliano concerning the future intentions of the Triple Entente with regard to the islands. The Franco-Russian attitude is explained, perhaps, by the wish for a final settlement of the island question and by the desire to do Greece a favour, while England, as Sir Edward told me in confidence yesterday, is afraid lest if some of the islands were left in the possession of the Turks, there should be excesses on the part of the Ottoman troops, while the introduction of an autonomous régime would probably soon lead to situations that would be embarrassing to the Powers, situations that would follow on the inhabitants declaring, as they doubtless at once would do, their adherence to Greece.

The suggestion that I made yesterday in this connection was by no means turned down by the representatives of the Entente without careful consideration. Misgivings were, however, expressed, and the motion was finally shelved. Perhaps an agreement could be come to under some arrangement whereby only the four islands of the Dardanelles should remain Turkish, as M. Venizelos, who has just been with me, has told me that what Greece specially wants is to have possession of Chios and Mitylene, which are the most important of the islands and the most capable of development. After them would come Samos, Kos and Rhodos. Should the two first-named islands not be assigned to Greece, the King would prefer to have none at all, as the others would be a burden rather than otherwise and would be reckoned among Greece's acquisitions when Turkey came to be divided up. To the three Dardanelles islands, he seemed to attach but little importance. For the rest, the Greek Minister declared that when he recalled the difficulties caused by autonomy in

Crete, he was terrified lest there should be a repetition of similar conditions in the case of the other islands.

I shall wait for the Italian proposal to be brought in, as Marquis Imperiali was yesterday still without instructions.

LICHNOWSKY.

To The Foreign Office.   LONDON, 7th January, 1913.

At to-day's meeting we began by discussing whether it was advisable to proceed with the *démarche collective* at Constantinople forthwith. The general view was that collective action on the part of the Powers would not be regarded as unwelcome by the Sublime Porte, as such action would be an argument on which the Porte could base its surrender by explaining that it was only bowing to the will of Europe. It was high time, too, for the step to be taken, if it were to be taken at all, as when once relations had been completely broken off, war would recommence and it would then be more difficult than ever for Turkey to give way. Agreement was no longer to be expected. It was therefore necessary to act without delay.

The question of a naval demonstration was also discussed and the conclusion was come to that ships were in any case to be held in readiness. I said that I must for the present deprecate carrying out any demonstration or even threatening one ; and in this attitude I was supported by my colleagues of the Triple Alliance.

On the proposal of Sir Edward Grey, the following text was then agreed upon :

' The meeting is of opinion that the Ambassadors at Constantinople should receive instructions to come to an understanding as to the drafting of a Note by discussing the remarks of their respective Governments, and that they should as soon as possible present this Note in a *démarche collective.*

' In view of the possibility of the resumption of hostilities and of the riots that might follow in Constantinople, it is necessary that the Powers should be prepared to safeguard the lives and property of their nationals by sending warships to Besika Bay, so that these may be at hand for any emergency.'

Thereupon M. Cambon declared that M. Poincaré desired some such wording as the following for the warning to be addressed to Turkey, advising her to give way :

' Be warned in time.   If you resume hostilities, the question of
Constantinople and perhaps of Asia Minor will be unrolled.   In order
to develop this part of your Empire, which from now on will constitute your only strength, you will not be able to count on the
financial help of Europe if you prolong the war through your resistance to the counsel given you by the Great Powers.'

It was agreed that the Ambassadors at Constantinople should
meet and agree upon an exact and identical text.

Thereupon the island question came up for discussion.   My
Austro-Hungarian and my Italian colleagues put forward the view
that the islands lying off the Dardanelles and the coast of Asia
Minor should remain in the possession of Turkey.   Sir Edward Grey
declared that he would discuss the matter to-morrow in the Cabinet.
For the present he let it be understood that he thought that England
would not be inclined to admit Turkish troops to the islands or to
undertake the responsibility for the consequences.

During the interval for tea, I asked Sir Edward Grey in confidence
why France was in favour of giving the islands to Greece.   He
replied that it was in order to do the Greeks a favour and for fear lest
the Italians might hit on the idea of establishing themselves on one of
them.   The suggestion was also mooted that the Turks should also be
promised the possession of a few islands if they gave way, but it was
agreed that it was impossible owing to the shortness of the time, to
come to any agreement on this question.

The suggestion was also made by my colleagues of the Triple
Alliance and supported by me that pressure should be brought to
bear in Sofia in favour of Rumania.   The idea was not greeted with
hostility by the other group, but the tone was distinctly lukewarm ;
I nevertheless believe that should opportunity arise it will be possible
to get the meeting to sanction friendly representations in Sofia.

Count Benckendorff, as an addendum to the recent clause concerning the islands, proposed to add the following condition :

' Neither the sovereignty nor the occupation is to be ceded to
another Power.'

Next meeting Thursday afternoon.   LICHNOWSKY.

To THE FOREIGN OFFICE.   LONDON, 8th January, 1913.

     I regard the Italian standpoint in the islands question as quite
hopeless, as the British Government is determined not to give way in

this matter but to let the Greeks have the islands.   The apprehensions expressed by the Marquis San Giuliano appear to me, as I said, very much exaggerated.   I have reason to believe that the British Government expects us to meet them halfway in this matter.   As a *quid pro quo*, Sir Edward Grey will, I learn confidentially, try at St. Petersburg to get a solution of the Scutari question that will prove satisfactory to Austria.

An exact drafting of the Note is to be agreed upon at Constantinople by the Ambassadors in which the French wishes are to be taken into consideration ; I therefore think that it would serve no useful purpose to open up the question again at to-morrow's meeting.

Point 3, in the English view, should contain a threat to Turkey, but should not dwell upon any regulation in principle of the Dette question as regards the Balkan Allies.

M. Poincaré, as M. Cambon has repeatedly pointed out, wished specially to avoid giving the impression that we wanted to hold out to Turkey any prospects of financial assistance.

Should opportunity offer, I shall express my views.   I scarcely think, however, that any final form will be agreed upon here.

LICHNOWSKY.

To The Foreign Office.   London, *8th January*, 1913.

Sir Edward Grey asked me to go and see him.   He told me that he had just had a long talk with Reshid Pasha and Tewfik Pasha and that he had left these gentlemen in no doubt as to the gravity of the situation and had impressed upon them that their position could only become worse if they were to suffer new defeats in the field.

The Turkish delegates replied that it was impossible to give way, not only on military grounds but also on grounds of internal policy. Sir Edward Grey told me that Mr. Babington Smith of the National Bank in Constantinople had come to him with an enquiry as to whether he had any objection to Turkey's receiving money from this financial institute.   The Ottoman Government had also applied to the Banque Ottomane and the Deutsche Bank.   He wanted to know what advice we should give the Deutsche Bank in this connection.   He himself had hitherto adopted the principle of leaving it to the British financial institutes to act on their own responsibility and at their own risk.   Both in the Japanese War and in the present war he had strictly adhered to this principle.   Now, however, the question arose whether money should be lent to Turkey before the dispute concerning Adrianople had been satisfactorily settled. On the other hand, however, it was dangerous to refuse the necessary financial help, if this entailed the collapse of the Turkish customs administration, etc.

The Minister then told me that at the Cabinet meeting to-day the mood had been much more pronouncedly in favour of a radical solution of the island question than had been the case in his own utterances on that subject. His colleagues would hear nothing of any violent measures for preventing the autonomous islands from joining up with Greece and still less of any measures that would sacrifice the population to the Turkish troops. The Cabinet also apprehended vexatious Court meddling from various relatives of the Greek Royal Family. The British Cabinet would on no account hear of a repetition of the Cretan troubles in a new form.

I shall, of course, support my Italian colleague, who by the way is still without instructions. I think it my duty, however, again to point out that I consider it unlikely that his proposals will prove acceptable. Sir Edward Grey also said that he would speak to Marquis Imperiali or through Sir Rennell Rodd to Marquis di San Giuliano and try to dissipate the misgivings of the Italian Cabinet. These misgivings were mainly ascribable to the attitude taken up by *Le Temps* and other newspapers in France, where people still seemed to believe that Italy wanted to annex Rhodos. He, Sir Edward Grey, had some time ago explained to M. Cambon that all the rumours with regard to England's having designs on Syria were sheer invention.

LICHNOWSKY.

To The Foreign Office.   London, *9th January*, 1913.

At to-day's Conference of Ambassadors, M. Cambon brought up the question whether it would not be better to draw up the text of the identical Note for Constantinople in London, and to lay this text before the respective Governments. To judge by his own experience, he said, a Note drawn up by the local Ambassadors would not have the same effect. The Conference would moreover be in a better position to ascertain the various details. After lengthy negotiations we agreed to ask M. Cambon to draft a text to be submitted to the meeting to-morrow. I took this opportunity of making use of the remarks made in Telegram No. 14 to Point 2 of the English proposals.

The question of the naval demonstration is to come up next. The following declaration was agreed upon :

' The Conference of Ambassadors wishes to know what warships and how many of them the Governments intend to send to Besika Bay and when they are to arrive there.'

England is sending two ships of the pre-Dreadnought class, one of them to be the *King Edward VII.* ; they have, however, not yet been despatched. France is also sending two ships which are to await orders in the Piraeus or elsewhere. Austria-Hungary agrees in principle. The wish was expressed that the arrival at Besika Bay might be timed to take place simultaneously.

I then made the following declaration :

' The Imperial Government is of opinion that it is essential that the *démarche* of the Powers in Sofia in favour of the Rumanian demands should not follow the *démarche* at the Sublime Porte but should take place simultaneously. Any friendly intervention in Sofia in this order of sequence which, like that in Pera, aimed at staving off the danger of war, would at the present juncture find an even more favourable reception, seeing that Bulgaria could then justify her action in the view of the public, by letting it be supposed that the concessions were made to Rumania as a consequence of the weighty advantages that the Powers were about to secure for Bulgaria at the Sublime Porte.'

In this I received cordial support from my colleagues of the Triple Alliance. Count Berchtold had, it is true, not pointed out to Count Mensdorff the necessity of simultaneous action, but had reserved his decision as to the time.

Count Benckendorff raised objections. According to his information, the conversations between M. Daneff and M. Jonescu had by no means come to a deadlock. As was usual in eastern countries, there was a good deal of exaggeration and lying on both sides. In principle he had nothing whatever against the plan, but the present stage seemed to him unsuitable as Bulgaria was ready to meet Rumania halfway and Rumania was quite unnecessarily threatening to march into the other's country. Under these circumstances, representations ought at least to be made to both parties. The upshot was that no decision was come to and the meeting was adjourned.

My Russian colleague explained in conclusion that he had not spoken on the basis of instructions ; he was not, however, in a position just at present to recommend his Government to accept the proposal I had put forward.

Hereupon Sir Edward Grey read out the following declaration that had been handed to him by the Serbian chargé d'affaires :

' In order to show her respect for the unanimous will of Europe and to show what sacrifices she is prepared to make in the interests of European peace, Serbia makes the following declaration : When the time comes, that is to say, when peace has been concluded and the questions connected with it settled, Serbia will submit to the will of Europe and withdraw from the Serbian shores of the Adriatic those military forces which with superhuman effort and at the cost of gigantic sacrifices have reconquered her old territory bordering on the Adriatic, a territory the possession of which would have guaranteed her free connection with the other States ; while, however, taking on herself these unspeakable sacrifices—for rivers of blood have been shed and her best sons have been lost—Serbia expects the Great Powers justly to estimate the importance of these sacrifices, sacrifices that she lays on the altar of European peace, in the hope that the Great Powers will not permit that still further sacrifices be demanded of her, for after all that she has suffered, she has neither the strength nor the means to make further sacrifices, and to expect such a thing would be to drive the country to despair and create a state of things the consequences of which no man can predict.'

To this the Ambassadors drew up the following reply which is to be handed to the Serbian delegates after the text has been approved by the Powers :

' The Powers have duly noted this declaration. They consider that Serbia will be expected to evacuate the coast and the territory of Albania after the boundaries of this State have been fixed by the Powers and as soon as the said Powers communicate their decision to Serbia.'

Next meeting to-morrow, Friday afternoon.

LICHNOWSKY.

To THE FOREIGN OFFICE.   LONDON, 10th January, 1913.

Last evening after a banquet given by M. Cambon as the doyen to the peace delegates, M. Daneff again told me that he was ready to resume negotiations with M. Jonescu, but that he would urgently ask that I should use my influence to get Rumania to desist from her threatening attitude. Otherwise it would be impossible for the Bulgarian Government to meet Rumania's wishes halfway.

I spoke to-day to M. Jonescu to this effect and he promised to report the matter to Bukarest. I also arranged with him that he would under no circumstances leave London at present, but wait here to hear what M. Daneff had to say. If nothing should come of the negotiations, I said, the moment would have arrived to bring the question before the Powers and I should then suggest the admission of the Rumanian representative to the meeting of Ambassadors, and also bring up afresh the question that had been temporarily adjourned concerning a *démarche collective* in Sofia.

Under these circumstances, I should like to suggest that the latter question be temporarily allowed to rest, while we await further developments.

M. Jonescu also told me that Bulgaria was not in a very pleasant position, partly on account of her heavy losses and partly because the Bulgarian soldiers in the Tchataldja Line were beginning to desert. A quarrel with Greece was also brewing over Salonica and another with Serbia over Monastir, this town being claimed by Serbia. Serbia had also withdrawn her troops from the lines outside Adrianople on the pretext that she wanted to strengthen her Austrian frontier.

LICHNOWSKY.

To The Foreign Office.　　　 London, 10th *January*, 1913.

M. Cambon has just submitted to us the following text of the identical Note which is to be delivered at Constantinople. The text was unanimously accepted and is to be submitted to the respective Governments. Sir Edward Grey gave preference to M. Cambon's text, rather than to that sent in by Mr. Lowther. The latter text had been drafted by the Ambassadors accredited at Constantinople. Sir Edward Grey will therefore authorise his representative to take part in the delivery of this Note.

Draft of the Collective Note :

' The undersigned Ambassadors of Austria-Hungary, England, France, Russia, Germany and Italy are authorised by their Governments to make the following communication to His Excellency the Minister of Foreign Affairs of His Imperial Majesty the Sultan :

' Prompted by the wish to prevent the resumption of hostilities, the

Powers mentioned must draw the attention of the Imperial Ottoman Government to the grave responsibility it would take upon itself if through its resistance to their wishes it should frustrate the restoration of peace.   The Ottoman Government would then have itself to blame if the prolongation of the war should result in jeopardising the fate of the capital and of extending the hostilities, perchance to the Asiatic provinces of the Empire.   In the latter case, the Imperial Ottoman Government will not be able to count on the benevolence of the Powers to protect it from dangers against which the Powers had already warned it . . . and they again warn it against exposing itself to such risks.

' Whatever happens, the Imperial Ottoman Government will, after peace has been concluded, need the moral and material support of the Great Powers, in order that it may again make good the damage done by the war, that it may consolidate its position in Constantinople and develop the great provinces in Asia, whose prosperity will constitute its main strength.   In order to inaugurate and put into execution this great and necessary task, the Imperial Ottoman Government would only then be able to reckon on the benevolent support of the Powers, should it follow their advice, which is inspired by the general interests of Europe and Turkey.

' Under these circumstances, the Great Powers of Europe feel impelled once more unitedly to advise the Imperial Ottoman Government to agree to the cession of the city of Adrianople to the Allied Balkan Powers and to leave to the Great Powers the task of deciding the destiny of the islands in the Aegean Sea.

' In return for these concessions, the said Powers would endeavour to ensure the safety of Moslem interests in Adrianople and respect for the mosques and religious buildings and property in that city. They would do this in order that the solution suggested by them in the question of the islands of the Archipelago may exclude any threat to the security of Turkey.'

LICHNOWSKY.

To The Foreign Office.   London, 10th January, 1913.

At to-day's sitting, which lasted only about an hour, Sir Edward Grey informed us that the Turkish delegates had assured him that they could not possibly give way with regard to Adrianople ; the Bulgarian delegates, on the other hand, maintain that it is useless to call a new meeting unless the cession of Adrianople, the details of which were still open to discussion, had been already resolved upon. Under these circumstances Sir Edward Grey, as Honorary President of the Peace Conference, is not in a position to come forward with proposals as to a date for the next meeting.

Sir Edward Grey is still striving to prevent the complete break-down of the peace negotiations, but anticipates the resumption of hostilities, should the steps taken by the Powers in Constantinople prove fruitless.

The dispute between Bulgaria and Rumania also came up for discussion. The general opinion was, I regret to say, that personal differences between M. Daneff and M. Take Jonescu were playing a part, and that it was urgently necessary to advise the Rumanians to be calm and moderate. There was still a hope, however, that thanks to my mediation and to similar proposals with which Sir Edward Grey promised to support me, that a way might yet be found of putting the negotiations on the right track.

The text of the identical Note, already referred to by me, as having been drafted by M. Cambon, was formally approved by the meeting.

Next meeting Monday afternoon.   LICHNOWSKY.

To THE FOREIGN OFFICE.   LONDON, 13th January, 1913.

At to-day's sitting I brought the remarks contained in Telegram No. 24 from your end to the notice of the meeting. They were placed *ad referendum* and met with no contradiction. I then declared in accordance with your Telegram No. 22 that we did not wish to take part in any naval demonstration. At the suggestion of Sir Edward Grey, who pointed out that it was nevertheless advisable to consider the idea of sending ships to Besika Bay, in order that they might be ready to protect Europeans in the event of a state of anarchy prevailing in Constantinople, the text of the following declaration was agreed to :

' From the remarks made by the German Ambassador with regard more especially to the technical difficulties, the possibility of a common naval demonstration seems to have come to naught. The assembly of Ambassadors asks the Governments to make known their views with regard to the advice which was submitted to them on the 7th of January concerning the despatch of warships to Besika Bay, in view of the possibility of a resumption of hostilities and of riots which might threaten the lives and property of their nationals and do harm to European interests at Constantinople.'

Count Benckendorff informed the meeting that his Government, at the wish of the Bulgarian and Rumanian Governments, had agreed to mediate.

Communications from M. Daneff and M. Jonescu seemed to point to the fact that the possibility of an understanding being reached was nearer than before. M. Daneff has also informed Sir Edward Grey that his Government, or the Allies, immediately on delivery of the collective Note, intended to denounce the armistice and that the resumption of hostilities was to be expected for next Monday.

I then, in accordance with document No. 50,[1] brought up the question of the Turkish State creditors. Sir Edward Grey declared himself in agreement with my proposal, while my colleagues assented in principle, but expressed a wish to submit the three points laid before them to their Governments. I laid special stress on the fact that Germany attaches importance to the said agreement being included in the peace treaty.

Next meeting Wednesday afternoon.   LICHNOWSKY.

To The Foreign Office.   London, 15th *January*, 1913.

Before to-day's meeting began, I seized the opportunity of informing Sir Edward Grey of the contents of Telegram No. 28.[2] The Minister declared himself in agreement with our view and said that he would await the course of events. The chief thing was that the Note should be delivered immediately, so that Turkey might not count on the Powers being divided in their counsels.

The sitting was opened by M. Cambon, who stated that he had taken the opportunity urgently to advise M. Daneff not to send the proposed Note concerning the breaking off of negotiations with the Turkish delegates, but to await the effect of the step agreed upon by the Powers in Constantinople. Other colleagues had spoken to M. Daneff and to other Balkan delegates in a similar strain. The effect of this advice was, as Sir Edward Grey was able to inform

[1] The gist of the German proposal was that the question of the Turkish State debts should be dealt with by the London Conference of Ambassadors and be proclaimed to the peace delegates as the will of the Great Powers. (Author's note.)

[2] This referred to instructions from the German Foreign Office to refuse assent to any measures against Turkey on points in which these measures went beyond the *démarche* agreed upon. (Author's note.)

the meeting, that the Bulgarian delegates had resolved for the present at least, not to leave London. In another quarter it had been said that even should the negotiations with Turkey be broken off the Balkan delegates would continue to discuss their affairs in London.

Negotiations between Rumania and Bulgaria have also failed to make any headway. But whereas M. Take Jonescu, who has again resolved to remain here, declares that he is still without news from M. Daneff, the latter maintains that he sent proposals to M. Take Jonescu some days ago. Perhaps I may manage at the banquet which Count Mensdorff is giving to-morrow in honour of the Balkan delegates, to learn further particulars concerning the stage negotiations have reached. My suggestion that M. Misu should be summoned to appear before the Conference, though accepted in principle, was considered by Count Benckendorff and M. Cambon to be premature at the present moment. For it would mean inviting the Bulgarian representative as well, who would want to explain Bulgaria's standpoint. The Conference ought at least to wait until the negotiations had broken down.

The Conference was unanimous concerning the usefulness of an immediate delivery in Constantinople of the Collective Note agreed upon.

The meeting then proceeded to discuss the question of Mount Athos about which I shall report elsewhere.

At the conclusion of the meeting M. Cambon stated that M. Poincaré agreed in principle with our wishes concerning the desirability of protecting the interests of Turkey's creditors, but that the wording of the proposal that I had submitted on the basis of the first three articles of the enclosure to your message No. 50 would on the one hand anticipate the work of the Paris Commission while, on the other hand, it seemed to him to go a little too far for it to be embodied in the Peace Treaty. He would therefore lay a modified text before the Ambassadors at their next meeting. Next meeting on Friday. On Wednesday Albania is to come up for discussion.

LICHNOWSKY.

To The Imperial Chancellor von Bethmann-Hollweg.

London, 15th January, 1913.

Count Mensdorff asked me to come and see him yesterday to talk over the Albanian question and to get an idea of the material that he had at his disposal on this question. He and Baron Giesl, the Austrian Consul at Cettinje who has been called to London as an expert in Balkan affairs to assist the Ambassador, explained to me the Austrian standpoint with the help of an ethnographical map which had been drawn by the Baron on the basis of personal investigations made on the spot.

First of all Austria would, come what might, remain firm in the question of Scutari. Scutari and the surrounding country were, I was assured, Albanian and must on no account be handed over to Montenegro. *Vienna would rather let it come to a war than hand Scutari over to Montenegro.* The London Cabinet, he said, seemed no longer to attach decisive importance to the incorporation of Scutari with Montenegro, while Count Benckendorff on the other hand had hitherto evaded any discussion of the matter, and did not wish to see the Albanian question brought before the Ambassadors' Conference yet awhile ; he, Count Mensdorff, was ready to negotiate concerning it. Count Mensdorff asked me to speak to Count Benckendorff and explain to him the Austrian standpoint in the matter. I replied that I did not think that my good offices would have much effect as Count Benckendorff already knew the Austro-Hungarian standpoint and the Russian Ambassador could not act on his own responsibility but only on instructions from St. Petersburg.

Count Mensdorff dwelt especially on the fact that it was dangerous to give a welcome pretext in the form of the Scutari affair *into the hands of the party in Austria that was urging an appeal to arms.* On my asking what Austria had to gain by adopting such a course, both gentlemen replied that although it was not territorial acquisitions that Austria wanted, she was anxious for certain frontier rectifications which would give the Dual Monarchy advantages of a strategic nature, not to mention a bridgehead at Belgrade and other measures of security. ' *If we should then be attacked by Russia, that would mean the* casus foederis *for Germany.*'

I naturally promised my Austro-Hungarian colleague my support when the question comes up for discussion. At the same time I did not conceal from him that the prospects of going to war for the sake of Scutari would arouse little enthusiasm. He quite agreed with me, but insisted that war could only be avoided if Scutari were given to Albania.

I am not in a position to judge whether it would be advisable to give Vienna a hint in view of the bellicose mood that seems undoubtedly to exist in certain circles there. These people's idea, I have repeatedly been assured, is ' to get a little peace and quiet by way of a change.' Should you decide to give Vienna a hint, please refrain from making any mention either of me or of the conversation I had with my Austro-Hungarian colleague ; I want to avoid any possibility of a purely official matter being shifted into the sphere of the personal.

With regard to Albania's other boundaries, both gentlemen told me that Austria was ready to renounce Ipek and Prisren in favour of Serbia, but not Diakova. Furthermore, the boundary should follow the line of hills to the east of the Drin and the Drin itself, should include Dibra and Lake Ochrida, also Koritza and finally follow the course of the Kalamas which flows into the sea opposite Corfu. For the rest, as both declared, the Vienna Government would be ready to listen to argument with regard to the southern frontier.

In the meantime Count Benckendorff has intimated that he will be ready to negotiate concerning Albania next Wednesday.

LICHNOWSKY.

To The Foreign Office. LONDON, 17th January, 1913.

Before the meeting began to-day, I explained to Sir Edward Grey in confidence the standpoint taken up by the Imperial Government as contained in Telegram No. 32.[1] The Minister concurred with our views on all points and remarked with regard to Besika Bay that he would leave it to Sir Gerald Lowther to judge whether and when it might be necessary to send ships for the protection of British interests. He expressed keen regret that the delivery of the identical Note should have been delayed owing to the German Ambassador's having no instructions. I was able to inform him of the authorization that I had in the meantime received.

At the meeting M. Cambon gave us the contents of a dispatch received from the French Ambassador at Constantinople, according to which the Turks were considering whether they should ask the Powers, in the event of Turkey's giving a favourable reception to the advice of the European nations, to grant her certain concessions in respect of release from a war indemnity, permission to cancel the exemption from taxation enjoyed by foreigners, the imposition of

---

[1] The telegram here mentioned referred to the satisfaction with which Germany had learned that a naval demonstration against Turkey was to be abandoned and expressed a wish to observe strict neutrality. (Author's note.)

higher customs duties, loans, etc.   Sir Edward Grey said that on the whole he was in principle in favour of such concessions, without, of course, being in a position to contemplate any binding promises. Most of the Ambassadors present spoke in the same sense, but misgivings were heard concerning the possibility of giving practical form to such concession and concerning the undertaking of obligations before the actual close of hostilities.

Should the Turkish answer have arrived by Monday, an answer which, it is conjectured, will be evasive and ambiguous, the next meeting is to take place on that day.   Otherwise on Monday with Albania as the agenda.   Cambon told me he had up to the present heard nothing from Poincaré concerning the finance question ; he had, however, no doubt that the principles laid down by us would meet with approval, although they might perhaps be slightly modified in form.   LICHNOWSKY.

FOURTH SECTION
THE BALKAN ALLIANCE

To THE FOREIGN OFFICE.   LONDON, *9th June,* 1913.

At to-day's sitting the first matter discussed was the abrupt attitude of Bulgaria which had led to M. Geshoff's resignation.   The prevailing view was that Daneff was the driving force in the war party which is determined not to give way on any point and not to submit even to Russia's arbitration.   The Balkan delegates here, according to a statement made by Sir Edward Grey, are on the point of leaving London.   Sir Edward Grey has advised them to come to an agreement on all points where an agreement is possible and to leave the rest to the negotiations between the Cabinets concerned.

The question of the Serbian railway was then brought up by M. Cambon, concerning which a report follows.

Next sitting on Wednesday.   LICHNOWSKY.

To THE FOREIGN OFFICE.   LONDON, *10th June,* 1913.

My Turkish colleague told me yesterday in confidence that one of the Serbian delegates here suggested to him yesterday that Serbia and Turkey should come to an agreement to make common cause against Bulgaria and had in this connection made the remark that the Balkan mountains were the natural boundary of Turkey. Tewfik Pasha declined to discuss the matter, and answered that Serbia ought to have thought of this sooner. It was now too late for an understanding and Turkey was not going to plunge into any further adventures. The attitude of Bulgaria, which declines to make any concession to Serbia, and the intimate *rapprochement* between Sofia and Vienna seemed, he said, to have driven the Serbs to this desperate step. It is thought here that an understanding has been reached between Bulgaria and Greece, on the basis of which Bulgaria, for the present at least, renounces all claims to Salonica.

LICHNOWSKY.

To The Imperial Chancellor von Bethmann-Hollweg.

London, *27th June*, 1913.

I have just returned from a talk with Sir Edward Grey who had sent for me to tell me about the result of his conversations with the French statesmen.[1] What they had told him he thought very satisfactory. He had been able to ascertain that the French were as anxious for the maintenance of peace as was the British Cabinet, and were just as ready to co-operate with a view to limiting as far as possible the war in the Balkans should a fresh outbreak occur. All the conversations had been on the basis of the after-dinner speeches whose contents are already known and contained nothing to prevent the collaboration of other Powers. In this connection he pointed particularly to an analogous statement in M. Poincaré's[2] speech at the Guildhall and hinted that this utterance had been made by common agreement.

The discussions with the French statesmen had not been limited to the question of peace in general, but had also dealt with Turkey and her future, that is to say, with the question of Asia Minor. There were two possible alternatives : Either the Powers would unite to restore Turkey, making her financial burdens as light as possible or even giving her financial help and assisting her in the re-organisation of her administration, or they could come to an understanding with regard to spheres of interest ; the latter method would, however,

---

[1] On the occasion of King Edward's visit to Paris. (Author's note.)

[2] M. Poincaré had said that the friendship between Great Britain and France contained nothing that excluded the entrance into it of others. (Author's note.)

mean for Turkey the beginning of the end.   M. Poincaré and M. Pichon agreed with him that the first of the two alternatives was the right one to take ; and that Europe would have to keep Turkey alive and help her to her feet again (*rétablir*).   Concerning Syria not a word was said.   I took this opportunity to assure the Minister that we, too, shared and would continue to share this view as long as we were able to feel sure of Great Britain's concurrence.   All contrary opinions corresponded perhaps to this or that private or commercial interest, but not to the views taken by the Government authorities. The news concerning the mood in Arabia, Syria and other non-Turkish provinces was not, I remarked, exceedingly promising, but we thought that with the collaboration of the Powers it would be possible to keep the Turkish Empire alive in its present form.   Sir Edward Grey took occasion to assure me afresh that should it ever come to a question of breaking up Asia Minor, our interests would have to be taken into consideration.

LICHNOWSKY.

To THE FOREIGN OFFICE.   LONDON, *3rd July*, 1913.

Sir Edward Grey has just told me that he is quite in agreement with the views expressed by the German Secretary of State to Sir Edward Goschen, and that he, too, will endeavour to localize as far as possible the hostilities that have broken out afresh in the Balkans.   It is especially desirable, he says, that Austria-Hungary should continue to exercise self-control and not intervene in favour of one of the belligerents, as this would mean the intervention of Russia also.   Austria's attitude during the last crisis had unfortunately, whether rightly or wrongly he was unable to discover, aroused the suspicion that she was encouraging Bulgaria in her anti-Serbian attitude.   So too did the refusal of the Vienna Cabinet to associate itself with the steps that were to have been taken in Sofia to call upon Bulgaria to disarm.

He has, he says, also been in negotiation with the French statesmen and has found them ready to maintain the strictest reserve.

LICHNOWSKY.

To THE FOREIGN OFFICE.   LONDON, *7th July*, 1913.

At to-day's sitting Sir Edward Grey declared that occurrences in the Balkans forced the Powers again to formulate their attitude towards the events taking place there and the question arose whether intervention seemed advisable.　As far as he had been able to ascertain, all the Powers were averse to such a step and shared his wish for strict reserve and localization of the conflict.　He would like to receive from us definite assurances in this direction and he would therefore request us to ask our Governments for the necessary authorization.　I declared at once that this was quite in accordance with the views of the Imperial Government.　　　LICHNOWSKY.

To THE FOREIGN OFFICE.　　　　LONDON, 17th July, 1913.

Sir Edward Grey asked Count Mensdorff to come and see him in the hope of arranging an understanding between Russia and Austria-Hungary concerning the terms of the peace to be concluded between the Balkan States.　He is already apprised of the Russian views and has reason for assuming that between them and the views of Vienna there is no very great disparity.　He hopes that if the two Governments are agreed, the belligerents will bow to their authority and make peace.

　　　　　　　　　　　　　　　　　　　　LICHNOWSKY.

FIFTH SECTION

THE SECOND BALKAN WAR

To THE FOREIGN OFFICE.　　　　LONDON, 21st July, 1913.

Before to-day's sitting began, Sir Edward Grey discussed with me the present situation in the Balkans and expressed the opinion that the Balkan States ought as soon as possible to agree with one another concerning the peace terms, which could then be submitted to the Powers for approval.　He hoped on this basis to bring about an agreement and believed that Russia would also assent to this.　He thought that an understanding existed between Vienna and St. Petersburg with regard to the most essential points.

With reference to Turkey's action, he said that he regarded it as necessary that all the Powers should agree that the Enos-Midia line should be insisted upon as a boundary.　There was, however, another question, namely, what means should be employed in the event of Turkey's refusing to give way and of the Powers finding themselves forced to take action against her.　If all the Powers pronounced themselves in favour of a naval demonstration, England would not remain outside. The difficulty would then arise, however, of forcing the passage through the Straits or of causing Turkey to give way, in the event of her disregarding the naval demonstration. For the present, Turkey could perhaps be intimidated by withholding from her support of any kind, financial or otherwise.

At the meeting, the Minister brought up the same question, but omitted to say that England would, if necessary, take part in a naval demonstration, confining himself to asking us to request our Governments to express their views.

I declared that I could assume that my Government was in full accord with the Minister's views, but that I thought that it would suffice for the present if we agreed in principle on the Enos-Midia question and postponed the decision as to the employment of forcible methods, a matter with regard to the difficulties of which all Governments were in agreement. Events in the Balkans had shown, I said, that one must always be prepared for surprises. The question of the naval demonstration might for the present be postponed and further developments awaited.

Count Benckendorff hinted that his Government attached special importance to swift and energetic action on the part of the Powers, and my colleagues are inclined to fear that Russia may take action alone against Turkey.

The following report of the meeting was agreed upon :

' Sir Edward Grey expresses the opinion that the belligerent states, Rumania, Serbia, Greece, Montenegro and Bulgaria, must be encouraged to let their plenipotentiaries meet and put an end to hostilities. They might draft the terms of an agreement concerning the restoration of peace. The agreements with regard to the intervention will be submitted for scrutiny and approval to the Powers, who will then come to an understanding in the matter.

' Sir Edward Grey's view meets with no objection on the part of the Ambassadors who will submit it to their Governments for approval.

' Sir Edward Grey expresses his personal opinion that the Powers cannot withdraw from their pledge to fix the Enos-Midia line as the boundary between Turkey and Bulgaria. The fact that Turkish troops have advanced beyond this line opens up a question that Sir Edward Grey must submit to the Cabinet and he wishes that the Ambassadors may assure themselves as to the views of their Governments.' LICHNOWSKY.

To The Foreign Office.   London, 22nd July, 1913.

Sir Edward Grey told me to-day that, according to news he had received, the Turks still seemed to be occupying Adrianople ; he had, he said, no clue to the Turks' intentions. He again spoke against leaving Adrianople in the hands of the Turks and seemed to be not without anxiety lest the Russians might interfere. He was of opinion that the boundary, while keeping Enos and Midia as end-points, would now probably turn out to be concave instead of convex and nobody would wish any longer to contest the Turks' right to secure for themselves strategically favourable points. He quite agreed with me that it was at present not advisable to consider the question of a naval demonstration, if only on the ground that no one would be willing to take the responsibility of losing a few ships in forcing a passage through the Dardanelles. The Powers might try to bring Turkey to her senses by withdrawing their support. On the whole the Minister took a more favourable view of the situation to-day and appeared to foresee an early termination of hostilities.

LICHNOWSKY.

To The Foreign Office.   London, 25th July, 1913.

At to-day's sitting the question of bringing pressure to bear on Turkey was the first matter discussed.   I did not fail to repeat my recent declarations and to point out that it would be premature to broach this subject at present, if for no other reason than because of the not inconsiderable difficulties that lay in the way of carrying out a naval demonstration. Sir Edward Grey spoke in a similar sense, whilst my colleagues said that they would only be in favour of it if all the other Powers joined in. The idea was not taken up very warmly on any side and was soon allowed to drop, although Count Benckendorff made repeated references to Russian public opinion.

Sir Edward Grey next suggested that the Turco-Bulgarian dispute should be submitted to the Powers for their decision at the same time as the agreements of the Balkan States, that is to say, that Turkey should be measured by the same standards as the belligerent king-doms ; he expressed the hope that they would submit to the united will of the Powers. Count Benckendorff remarked that it was to be feared that Russian public opinion might become impatient.

The question of diplomatic coercion then came up for discussion, coupled with promises that might meet the Turkish wishes. I warmly supported this idea, pointing out that it might apply not only to rectifications of frontier but also to war indemnity. I tried to get the latter included in the declaration that was to be delivered at Constantinople, my object being to get the Powers to commit themselves to a definite statement on this point. But Sir Edward Grey was against it. He said that our object was to invite Turkey herself to come forward with her wishes. We did not want to make offers to the Turks ourselves. It is not improbable that he allowed himself to be guided to some extent by consideration for Russia and by the fear lest by accepting the point in question the delivery of identical declarations might be delayed. Count Benckendorff also said at once that St. Petersburg would not agree to such a proposal. The following resolution was thereupon passed :

' According to the replies of all the Governments to the question laid before them by the Ambassadors after their last meeting, the Powers are unanimous in the opinion that it is essential to emphasize the necessity of the maintenance of the stipulations laid down in the Treaty of London and that the Turco-Bulgarian frontier should be a line starting from Enos and ending in Midia.

' On the proposal of Sir Edward Grey, the assembly is of opinion that the Powers, by a unanimous resolution, should remind the Ottoman Government to adhere to the terms of the Treaty of London and especially to the stipulation with regard to the Enos-Midia line.

' At the same time the Ottoman Government could be informed that the Powers in determining this boundary will be inclined to take into consideration the conditions which Turkey may regard as indispensable for the security of this frontier.'

My Italian colleague had expressed the wish that the words ' ces frontières ' should be substituted for ' cette frontière ' in the last line of the resolution and had, in a state of great excitement, requested that this change might be made, apparently with the intention of utilising this opportunity in order to retain for Turkey the islands that had been occupied by Italy. His suggestion was overruled by Sir Edward Grey, who thought it undesirable that the island question should be dragged in, as he did not wish to make any allusion to this matter in the document to be handed to the Turks. I suspect, however, that Italy will come back to the question and repeat her wish that the occupied islands be offered to the Turks as a sort of compensation and should be glad to have instructions as to the attitude I should take up in this question. To-day I gave my support to the formal wishes of my Italian colleague, without committing myself definitely in the island question.

LICHNOWSKY.

SIXTH SECTION

FURTHER NEGOTIATIONS OF THE LONDON AMBASSADORS' CONFERENCE

To The Imperial Chancellor von Bethmann-Hollweg.

LONDON, 5th June, 1913.

At to-day's sitting Count Benckendorff suggested that it would be advisable to demand the immediate demobilization of the belligerents. The Allies were still mistrustful of one another and were therefore unwilling to lay down their arms, whilst Turkey likewise felt that this prevented her from discharging her troops. The following resolution was adopted on this matter :

' On the proposal of the Russian Ambassador the Conference considers it advisable that the belligerents be summoned to reduce their mobile forces forthwith.'

The question of the Albanian constitution was then discussed. M. Cambon, supported by Count Benckendorff, again represented that it was undesirable on practical grounds to proceed at the present juncture with the despatch of a Prince to Albania, as he would be out of place for the time being in view of the uncertain state of affairs in that country and the lack of any ordered administration. The question whether a Prince should even be appointed at all, and, if so, when, was left untouched, as M. Cambon absolutely refused to discuss the matter. All that was done, therefore, was to decide upon the early appointment of a ' Commission de Contrôle ' and the establishment of a gendarmerie to be supplied by one of the smaller Powers. The following resolution was adopted :

' Without taking into consideration for the present the establishment of a final constitution in Albania, the Conference considers it desirable to proceed to the appointment of an international Commission consisting of delegates of each of the Great Powers together with an Albanian representative. This Commission should study the progressive organisation of the country on the spot and take the necessary measures for the maintenance of order. The first of these measures should be the establishment of a gendarmerie which would have to be instructed and commanded by European officers. These officers should be supplied by a neutral Power to the exclusion of the six Great Powers, the Balkan States and those Powers which have a direct interest in the Balkans.

'Sir Edward Grey observes that it is difficult to imagine a provisional Government without executive authority prior to the establishment of a final constitution; he suggests the appointment by the Powers of a special delegate, who would be charged with the execution of the measures taken by the Control Commission.

'The French and Russian Ambassadors support this idea, whilst the Austro-Hungarian and Italian Ambassadors cannot express any opinion, as they are awaiting the replies of their Governments to the observations made by the French Ambassador in a previous sitting. Prince Lichnowsky accepts Sir Edward Grey's suggestion, while expressing the opinion that the final settlement must include the appointment of a Prince.

'The Conference wishes to draw the attention of the Governments to the necessity of keeping in mind from the outset the provision of the requisite funds to guarantee the service of the international control and gendarmerie.'

Finally, Sir Edward Grey announced that for reasons of internal administration the naval authorities had decided to leave Admiral Burney in Scutari, but to replace the 300 marines there by 300 soldiers from Malta and to withdraw the warships concerned.

Next sitting Monday.

LICHNOWSKY.

To THE IMPERIAL CHANCELLOR VON BETHMANN-HOLLWEG.

LONDON, 9th June, 1913.

At to-day's sitting M. Cambon, as I have reported elsewhere, proposed to notify the Serbian Government in writing of the agreed draft of 17th December as to the Serbian railway to be built across Albania, as the Serbian representatives here were pressing for this and had only signed the peace in consideration of this assurance. Further delay would be tantamount to a breach of honour on our part and would necessarily lead to doubts being cast on our goodwill by Serbia. To this Count Mensdorff replied that his Government made its consent to the contemplated notification dependent upon a *previous* understanding being reached as to the interpretations of certain provisions in the agreed draft, which it thought ambiguous. Negotiations had already taken place between St. Petersburg and Vienna on this subject, which had not, however, attained the desired result. The most important point in dispute is, as Count Mensdorff and Count Benckendorff both agreed, the question whether Serbia is to be permitted to transport war material over the railway in *times of war* as well as in times of peace.

Both Sir Edward Grey and M. Cambon shared the view of the Russian Government that such a restriction of Serbia's rights was difficult to reconcile with the spirit of our agreements. But they were particularly of the opinion (and here they had the tacit concurrence of my Italian colleague, in which I would like to join) that it was hardly possible to postpone the prospective notification until a satisfactory solution had been found for all doubtful points, which include among others precise provisions as to the neutrality of the port, or even to make the declaration dependent upon an understanding at all.

It was therefore on Sir Edward Grey's proposal suggested that the Vienna Cabinet be urged to consent, on condition that it receives the right to stop the transport of arms and munitions in the event of a war between Austria and Serbia.

This clause should suffice if Austria-Hungary is solely concerned with the protection of her *own* interests ; but there is good ground for suspicion that the wishes of Bulgaria play a part. I learn, indeed, confidentially, that the belated objections of the Austrian Government are due to Count Mensdorff having, in the pressure of business, inadvertently given the consent of his Government to the agreement in question too soon, so that he was not in a position to bring up certain conditions and misgivings.

The following report of the proceedings was adopted :

' The French Ambassador having proposed the discussion of the declaration to be given to the Serbian Government on the international railway, Sir Edward Grey states that the declaration adopted on 17th December must be confirmed and that the Powers are on their honour in this question.

' The Austro-Hungarian Ambassador states that it is necessary to have an explanation of certain points which were not defined in this declaration.

' After a short discussion Sir Edward Grey suggests the Austro-

Hungarian Government might say that on agreeing to the renewal of
the declaration it desired to have it established that in case of a war
between Serbia and Austria-Hungary, the latter Power should have
the right to use her navy to prevent the passage of war material
through the neutral port.

' The Austro-Hungarian Ambassador announces that he will convey
this suggestion to his Government and declares that according to his
instructions it is for the Ambassadors' Conference to express its
opinion on the points raised in the exchange of views between the
Russian and Austrian Governments, of the tenor of which the Conference will be advised, and on the manner in which they should be
interpreted.

' The Russian Ambassador declares that his Government is likewise
of opinion that the Conference should be consulted on certain points.

' It is resolved that Count Mensdorff and Count Benckendorff shall
inform Sir Edward Grey and their colleagues as soon as possible of
the various points which might give rise to a discussion.

' Sir Edward Grey observes that in no case may the declaration
to the Serbian Government be made conditional upon the reaching
of an agreement on certain points which are not yet sufficiently
elucidated.'   LICHNOWSKY.

To The Imperial Chancellor von Bethmann-Hollweg.

London, 11th June, 1913.

At to-day's sitting the island question was first of all discussed, on which Marquis Imperiali made the following statement :

' His Majesty's Government is bound by the provisions of the
Treaty of Lausanne and pledged to hold the islands occupied by the
royal troops at the disposal of the Ottoman Government.

' His Majesty's Government therefore does not think it can participate in a discussion between the Powers as to the fate of the said
islands and join in any possible steps which the Powers might take at
the Sublime Porte to convey their decision.

' In view of the interest which all the Powers have in the maintenance of the integrity of the Ottoman Empire and in the security
of its Asiatic Provinces the Royal Government has no doubt that
the Powers, in the general settlement of the fate of the islands in
the Aegean Sea, will share its view as to the necessity of guarding
the interests and prestige of Turkey as far as possible.'

In accordance with my instructions I emphasized that we should do all we could to safeguard the rights of Turkey in the island question and should, therefore, whatever happened, advocate the retention by Turkey of the two islands of Imbros and Tenedos covering the entrance to the Dardanelles. As regards Chios and Mitylene we should also in principle be inclined to leave them to Turkey, but should have to insist on their neutralization in any case, if the course of the negotiations should result in their union with Greece. Since our Allies desired to associate the island question with the Southern Albanian question, we wished to support their wishes in the latter question also. I avoided, however, going into details as to the frontiers of Southern Albania as I have not yet received definite instructions on the matter.

My Italian colleague, vigorously supported by Count Mensdorff, at once reiterated that Phtelia and Koriza were the Pillars of Hercules for his Government, beyond which it could not go. On this very definite reassertion of the Italian standpoint Sir Edward Grey asked Marquis Imperiali what his Government thought of doing if the Greeks refused to evacuate Southern Albania, to which he replied that Italy would not in that case evacuate the occupied islands and might even compel the evacuation of Southern Albania by force.

Count Benckendorff adopted an attitude of reserve, whilst M. Cambon after some hesitation declared that he was not in a position to adhere to the Italo-Austrian view. No definite proposal, however, was made either by him or by any other member of his group.

Sir Edward Grey then declared that it would be as well, before going further into the frontier problems of Southern Albania, to consider the question of what was to be done if Greece refused to comply with the decisions of the Powers. At Scutari we had already had experience of the difficulties to be met in overcoming opposition, and against Greece it would be a still more delicate affair. From what the Greek representative in London had said he gathered that Greece would rather renounce a portion of the islands than evacuate Southern Albania, so that the still further question arose as to who would expel the Greeks from the islands which they occupy should they refuse to yield in the Southern Albanian question. He was convinced that the majority of the Powers would not participate in forcible measures against Greece, and he for his part could only countenance a decision if he were in a position to declare in the name of the Cabinet that England was ready either to put it into effect or to leave its execution to other Powers. But in that case the decision must be of so reasonable a character as to place Greece clearly in the wrong if she refused to comply.

At the next sitting the Minister may define his own standpoint and that of his Cabinet. Up to the present he has refrained from any expression of opinion and has only told me in confidence that it would hardly be possible to induce the Italians to abandon views which they have upheld in such positive tones.

Should I be asked at the next sitting what our attitude would be towards the application of forcible measures against Greece, my best plan, I think, will be to reply evasively that we could not define our standpoint in this matter before having concrete decisions to go upon, and would, if the worst came to the worst, leave it to our Allies to proceed alone or independently.

I think that the Greek Government can hardly anticipate any vigorous support of its desires on the Albanian coast, since Russia can scarcely want to incur the displeasure of Italy and M. Cambon has never mentioned Cape Cephali again, but lays the main emphasis on Koriza, in other words, seeks compensation for Greece in the *interior*. Sir Edward Grey will presumably endeavour to bring about an agreement on this basis and in conjunction with the island question, but afterwards perhaps leave Austria and Italy to take common measures. *The effort to spare Italy and possibly to draw her closer to the Triple Entente no doubt plays a prominent part*, and our well-known Greek sympathies may well be vigorously exploited in this connection.

The following report was adopted :

' Respecting the proposal of the Austro-Hungarian and Italian Ambassadors as to the southern frontier line of Albania, Sir Edward Grey states that he cannot be a party to any agreement unless he is ready to join in measures for its forcible execution and until he has gone into the question whether it would be possible to enforce it on Greece. This is a very grave decision to have to take and he must discuss the matter with the Prime Minister and his Cabinet colleagues. He desires to be able to state definitely whether, in recommending Greece to accept an agreement reached between the Powers, Great Britain could, if necessary, add that Greece must be prepared to face the consequences of rejecting it, or whether, on the contrary, Great Britain must declare that she cannot be a party to the proposed agreement.

' The French Ambassador states that his instructions do not permit him to concur in the proposal of the Austro-Hungarian and Italian Ambassadors, especially as regards the assignment of Koriza to Albania.   He must first consult his Government.

' The Austro-Hungarian and Italian Ambassadors declare it impossible to alter their proposal.'

LICHNOWSKY.

To the Secretary of State at the Foreign Office, von Jagow.

LONDON, 12th June, 1913.

I endeavoured to support the standpoint of our Allies in the Ambassadors' Conference yesterday by declaring at the very outset (as already reported) that I was willing to recognize the connection between the island question and the Southern Albanian question, on which Italy lays so much stress, and to acquiesce in the wishes of our Allies regarding Southern Albania.   In view of the Kaiser's attitude, which has become a matter of common knowledge here also, I confined myself to this very general statement, and in order to avoid an open and abrupt opposition to the views of the Sovereign I refrained from participating in the further discussion or having my assent to the statements of my two colleagues registered in the protocol. This attitude is also in accordance with your instructions, which in the last authoritative dispatch evade the delicate question and merely express the hope that agreement may be reached between Vienna, Rome and Athens.   That this pious wish would not be fulfilled was doubtless already clear to you then, and I took it that I was to support the desires of our Allies, but to avoid expressing myself too openly in this sense or taking the lead.

My attitude of restraint was thus in conformity with your wishes and those of the Chancellor, but was of course not altogether pleasing to my two colleagues.   Marquis Imperiali told me yesterday that everyone here was talking to him about the Kaiser's sympathy for Greece, while you are said to have told Bollati that we were in complete agreement with the Italian standpoint.   I replied that my waiting attitude was only a matter of form, but that had the Southern Albanian question come up for immediate discussion on the motion I had put forward in the sitting, which, as you know, was prevented by Sir E. Grey's opposition, I should definitely have supported Italy's desire.   The question was therefore merely one of a certain formal reserve ; in practice we should not leave our Allies in the lurch.   I also told Grey that we were on the side of our Allies, but that I must leave them the initiative in the whole question.

As you see from my report of yesterday Cambon appears to modify his previous opposition, and Russia appears to be adopting a more accommodating attitude towards the Italians.   I very much doubt whether Grey, who at present maintains complete reticence, will manifest an isolated opposition, if only because he fears that the Italians might then establish themselves in Rhodos, which would be extremely unpleasant for him.   It will probably result in the Triple Entente trying to compensate Greece in the interior, that is, mainly at the expense of Austria's wishes (Koriza).   That is more or less the course of events I foresee, and we shall naturally be the losers, for people will tell the Italians that they owe the fulfilment of their wishes not to us but to the Entente, and will represent to the Austrians that their failure is due to our half-hearted support !

It is at any rate remarkable that Grey has not consulted the Cabinet before, but has preferred to await the course of yesterday's sitting, which gave the clue to the attitude of the various Powers. For he must long ago have made up his mind how far he means to go and what line he considers so ' reasonable ' that he would be prepared to uphold it with British armed forces.   He raised the matter yesterday, but did not desire to discuss it in detail and immediately closed it by saying that he must first make up his mind as to the application of force.

Please, therefore, let me have your views by Wednesday and tell me particularly whether I am to support the Austro-Italian point of view in full and, if necessary, consent to forcible measures against Greece.

LICHNOWSKY.

To THE FOREIGN OFFICE.   LONDON, 15th June, 1913.

Even if we succeeded in reaching an agreement here as to the Cutzowallachians, whom Vienna would like to leave in Albania out of regard for Rumania, that would hardly be sufficient to console Greece for the loss of both the Cape Cephali line and Koriza.   M. Cambon, out of regard for Italy, has now ceased to demand the former, but is all the more insistent upon Koriza, which Austria equally insists must belong to Albania.   The Triple Entente is thus in any case able to offer Greece more than we, unless we want to fall out with Italy completely.

The solidarity between Greece and Serbia, which has recently become so conspicuous, and their common opposition to Bulgaria and Albania, both of which are favoured by Austria, must unavoidably draw Greece closer to the Triple Entente, for all the solemn assurances of M. Venizelos.

For the sake of a problematical friendship with Greece we should fall into opposition with our Allies, without after all being able to achieve as much for Greece as the Triple Entente holds in prospect.

On Wednesday, therefore, I shall unambiguously support the standpoint of our Allies, but shall previously try to reach an understanding with M. Misu over the Cutzowallachians, and if necessary propose that they be given to Greece.

LICHNOWSKY.

To THE FOREIGN OFFICE.   LONDON, 16th June, 1913.

I have just had a discussion with M. Misu in which we went into the question of the Cutzowallachians in detail. The Minister declared that he had so far received no mandate to negotiate with me on the question, but would telegraph our discussion to Bucharest and ask for instructions.

I endeavoured to make it clear to M. Misu that it was in the interests of Rumania to reach an understanding with Greece, since the strengthening of Greece could have no disagreeable consequences for Rumania and would form a welcome counterpoise to the power of Bulgaria. The Cutzowallachians had no actual political significance for Rumania, and, besides this, M. Venizelos promised to guarantee their national rights. We were bound to make concessions to Greece somewhere, and it was therefore a matter of expediency not to insist on the Cutzowallachians belonging to Albania.

M. Misu replied that he was by no means blind to this consideration, but his Government was in a difficult position for reasons of internal politics. If they abandoned the Cutzowallachians they would immediately be accused of betraying a national cause. The Minister ran the risk, moreover, of being assassinated, as was shown by the Cutzowallachian attempt on Jonescu. The bitterness aroused against the Greeks owing to the continuous Hellenisation, especially in some districts, at the hands of the clergy was not to be underestimated, and no one trusted Greek promises. The Government appeared to want to thrust this delicate question on to his shoulders through fear of public opinion. At the moment fresh negotiations were being carried on in Athens by the new Rumanian Minister, on the course of which M. Majorescu's further decision would in any case depend.

General impression : M. Misu appears not disinclined to let the Cutzowallachians go to Greece, but is afraid the Rumanian Government will not be able to agree for fear of public opinion.

LICHNOWSKY.

To The Foreign Office.   London, 18th June, 1913.

The most important event at to-day's sitting was the announcement made at the outset by Sir E. Grey that all the Powers had agreed that the Greek frontier on the coast was to begin at Cape Stylos. Differences of opinion now only existed as to the interior. On this question he did not want to make any definite proposals for the present, but would rather negotiate with each of us separately during the next few days, in order to reach an agreement. He then left the sitting, being called away by the Marconi affair in the House of Commons and left Sir A. Nicholson in the chair. Serbian questions were then discussed, on which I am sending a written report.

Next sitting probably on Monday.

LICHNOWSKY.

To The Foreign Office.   London, 20th June, 1913.

Sir E. Grey has just told me that after mature reflection he had reached the conclusion that the best solution for Greco-Albanian difficulties lay in the appointment of an international delegation to make investigations on the spot and ascertain the ethnographical conditions.

This would enable a fair middle line to be drawn within the disputed zone comprising the area between the frontiers demanded respectively by both parties. He desired in the course of to-day to make the same proposal, to which France and Russia have apparently already agreed, to my two Triple Alliance colleagues, and only bring it before the Ambassadors' Conference when its acceptance was more or less assured.

I replied that we desired to spare Greek susceptibilities as far as possible and would therefore certainly be ready to adhere to his idea, should Austria and Italy do likewise.　My impressions hitherto, however, led me to fear that Vienna in particular was strongly averse to such a plan and that it would scarcely be possible to induce the Austrians to yield once more.　Vienna insisted on Koriza going to Albania unconditionally and would regard a new retreat as humiliating to the Monarchy.　I therefore saw a possibility of agreement only on the basis of giving the Cutzowallachians to Greece, and hoped that an ultimate understanding with Rumania would be reached on this question, since that country had a special interest in good relations with Greece.　This had not, however, been achieved up to the present and since Vienna also felt bound to support Rumania's wishes I was not in a position to come forward officially with such a proposal, and must confine myself to confidential representations.　Should, however, he, Sir E. Grey, be willing to prepare the way for an understanding in this sense I did not consider the plan entirely hopeless when taken in conjunction with the islands.

The Minister replied that he did not think agreement could be reached on the above-mentioned basis, if only because Greece would not acquiesce.　The question would then again arise, who was to expel the Greeks from the areas occupied by them.

I should like to mention that the Minister once again designated Cape Stylos as the point where the frontier is to begin and also assumed that Argyrocastron would belong to Greece, so that Albania would only be left with a narrow strip of coast in the South.　He said in conclusion that if, as appeared probable, war broke out between the Balkan States, that might again alter everything.　For Bulgaria would possibly demand the abandonment by Greece of territory in Southern Albania.　From what Sir E. Grey said it is at any rate evident that he anticipates as probable a war between Bulgaria on the one hand and Serbia and Greece on the other, with the Bulgarians as victors.　In this event a Hellenophile policy would not only bring us into opposition with the most powerful and promising of the Balkan States, but also set us at cross purposes with our Allies, who for obvious reasons are pursuing a policy of avowed friendship with Bulgaria.

LICHNOWSKY.

FURTHER NEGOTIATIONS OF THE LONDON AMBASSADORS' CONFERENCE

To The Imperial Chancellor von Bethmann-Hollweg.

LONDON, 18th June, 1913.

As reported elsewhere, our main subject of discussion to-day was Serbian affairs. M. Cambon began by raising the question of the Serbian Government's well-known desire to receive written confirmation of the promise already given regarding the building of the railway and of a harbour on the Adriatic. Count Mensdorff thereupon declared, with the concurrence of Count Benckendorff, that agreement was in process of being reached on the disputed interpretation of the accepted text, especially in regard to the transit of war material in time of war, and was being worked out by the experts on both sides. It might therefore be as well to wait till a definite proposal could be laid before the Conference. This suggestion was agreed upon. M. Cambon took occasion to repeat the view he had already expressed to the effect that the promise given to the Serbs must in all circumstances be made good independently of any agreement which might be reached between the Powers as to the interpretation of details.

My Austro-Hungarian colleague, with the support of myself and Marquis Imperiali, took this opportunity of pointing out on behalf of his Government that it insisted on the retention of the original draft regarding the protection of the Mussulman, Catholic and Albanian inhabitants of the territories to be ceded to Serbia and Montenegro. He must therefore oppose the alteration of wording, ' pour assurer la liberté du culte,' made at the request of the Serbian Government with the support of Russia. Agreements once made must also be kept in this case and could not be varied at will merely because they were irksome to the Serbs and to Herr von Hartwig. As against that Count Benckendorff pointed out that the text of March 22 might rightly give offence in Belgrade, seeing that it might, in accordance with precedents set under the Turkish régime, be interpreted as admitting the feasibility of foreign intervention in Serbian internal affairs. After a long discussion, a text on Sir Arthur Nicholson's proposal was agreed upon, to be submitted for approval in St. Petersburg and Vienna. This text takes the wishes of both sides into account as far as possible and avoids all ambiguities. The proposed draft runs as follows :

' The six Powers might insist categorically upon the Serbian and Montenegrin Governments taking urgent measures to assure to all sections of the population in the territories to be ceded to Serbia and Montenegro without distinction of religion the freedom and effective protection of their religious observances and education.'

Whether this construction will satisfy Vienna is uncertain, since it concedes Serbia's main objective of denying Austria all power to take charge of the interests of the *Albanian Catholics in Serbia* or even to work for a kind of protectorate over them.

Count Mensdorff finally also raised the point that Serbia was displaying a regrettable delay in evacuating Albanian territory in accordance with her treaty obligations. The Conference took note of his statement, M. Cambon repeating his known view that the total withdrawal of foreign troops was only possible if accompanied by the speedy formation of a provisional Albanian Government. Otherwise the land was in danger of chaos, and one could not wait till the Powers had agreed upon the final form the Albanian State was to take.

LICHNOWSKY.

TO THE FOREIGN OFFICE.   LONDON, *23rd June*, 1913.

At to-day's sitting the question of Albania's southern boundary was not again discussed, since, as Sir E. Grey told us afterwards in confidence, there was for the time being no prospect of agreement and he wanted to wait and see whether a renewal of warlike complications in the Balkans might not produce a changed situation which would render a solution possible. Otherwise he would be bound, as he half jokingly remarked to Marquis Imperiali, to leave Italy the task of driving the Greeks from Southern Albania.

Serbian questions were discussed at the actual sitting, upon which I am making a written report.

Next sitting Tuesday, 1st July.

LICHNOWSKY.

To The Imperial Chancellor von Bethmann-Hollweg.

LONDON, *23rd June*, 1913.

At to-day's sitting Sir Edward Grey again adopted the standpoint that the written declaration which had been promised to the Serbs on the railway and the Adriatic harbour should be delivered in Belgrade as soon as possible, as this was more or less a debt of honour on the part of all the Powers. Count Benckendorff and Count Mensdorff, however, were not yet ready with an agreement on the disputed points, so the matter was again postponed.

The discussion was then resumed from the previous sitting of the question of the declaration concerning the protection of national and religious minorities in the newly acquired territories to be addressed to Belgrade and Cettinje in accordance with the text of the agreement of 22nd March. As the Vienna Cabinet rejected the extended formula agreed upon at the previous sitting and insists on the repetition of the original text unchanged, it was arranged as a way out that the original text should be retained, but that it should be supplemented by a further declaration to be presented at the same time as a kind of explanation calculated to avoid misunderstandings. The resolution adopted was as follows :

' In presenting the declaration to the Serbian and Montenegrin Governments proposed by the Conference on 22nd March, the Conference intends this declaration to be interpreted in the sense that the measures to be taken by the Governments of Belgrade and Cettinje in the territories acquired by Serbia and Montenegro as a result of the war shall have the object of guaranteeing the freedom of religious observances and education, the protection of churches, monasteries, mosques, schools and religious institutions of every kind, and the rights of property against injury through acts of a prejudicial character arising out of the war.'

Count Mensdorff declared that he could make no definite statement on this proposal and would report to his Government, while Count Benckendorff as well as Sir Edward Grey and all the other representatives supported this solution. I, too, had upheld it as calculated to remove all scruples.

Count Mensdorff then brought up for discussion the protest of his Government against the occupation of the Ljuma district by Serbian troops and against the encroachments they had made. It was decided to make representations in Belgrade on the lines of the

Austrian complaint *simultaneously* with the pending notification
regarding the railway.   LICHNOWSKY.

To The Imperial Chancellor von Bethmann-Hollweg.

LONDON, *27th June*, 1913.

At to-day's discussion Sir Edward Grey referred among
other things to the Albanian question and our Ambassadors' Conference.   Count Berchtold had expressed the desire that we should
settle the final constitution of Albania before the summer holidays.
Sir Edward thought that quite impossible.   For he would under no
circumstances remain here beyond the end of June.   He required a
rest after a very strenuous winter, and wanted if at all possible to go
into the country, even before the end of the Parliamentary session,
which would last till the middle of August.   The final settlement of
the Albanian constitution would, however, require a long time, and
he thought it of little use at this juncture to proceed with the appointment of a Prince and with the establishment of a regular administration which would incur grave difficulties with rebellious sections of
the population.   The experiences of the provisional Government
would be of benefit to its successor ; this Government they had no
intention of relegating to the region of pious hopes, as Count Berchtold appeared to assume.   Besides they had already reached agreement on the introduction of a gendarmerie from a neutral State, as
Austria had desired.

I should like to suggest your trying to persuade Vienna to be
satisfied for the time being with an agreement on principle as to the
appointment of a Prince, but to consent on practical grounds to the
formation of a provisional preparatory Government somewhat on
the lines of M. Cambon's latest proposals, as well as the immediate
introduction of a foreign gendarmerie.   This would mean a concession in as far as France has hitherto never been definitely in
favour of setting up a Prince at all.

I take the liberty of enclosing a copy of a telegram handed to me
by Sir Edward Grey which he has sent to the British representative
in Vienna.

It includes a reference to the dispute concerning the Southern
Albanian frontier.   Sir Edward Grey proposes that Count Berchtold
should state on what conditions he would assent to the formation of
a commission to draw up boundary proposals on the spot.   I did not

fail to bring to his notice that Count Berchtold would only entertain such a proposal on conditions which would render the consent of the opposite party more difficult. The Minister nevertheless did not seem to have entirely given up hope, from which it may be concluded that France might possibly prove more amenable to the wishes of Austria than had hitherto appeared likely. He is not ready to come forward with any definite boundary proposal, nor did he say how far France was willing to go, but only that a good deal had been said about Koriza and Argyrocastron and that it would be difficult for him at this distance to form a fair judgment of the conditions obtaining there.

The Minister finally mentioned the difficulties which might arise for the financial discussions in Paris in case war broke out between the Allies. It was scarcely feasible for the Allies to take part in them while at war with one another. All that could be done then would be for the Powers to continue the discussions with the Turks without the Allies.

LICHNOWSKY.

To The Imperial Chancellor von Bethmann-Hollweg.

LONDON, 1st July, 1913.

At to-day's sitting my Russian and Austro-Hungarian colleagues were able to lay before us the promised agreement on the interpretation of certain doubtful points regarding the future Serbian railway to the Adriatic. No objection was raised from any quarter. It was decided that Sir Edward Grey on behalf of the Powers should hand to the Serbian chargé d'affaires here the convention of 27th December last together with the interpretation now agreed upon.

The text is as follows :

' With reference to the declaration regarding the international railway and the neutral Adriatic port, which the Powers are pledged to make officially to the Serbian Government, the Conference resolves that Sir Edward Grey shall be authorised to confirm to the Serbian chargé d'affaires on behalf of the six Powers the decision taken at the Ambassadors' Conference of 17th December, 1912. Its terms are as follows : Access for her trade will be reserved for Serbia through a free and neutral Albanian port, which will be served by an international railway under European control and under the protection of a special international corps of troops, with freedom of transit for all goods, including war material.

Sir Edward Grey will at the same time present a memorandum explaining this declaration. The terms of the memorandum are the following :

1. Special Neutralisation of the Port.

Should the neutrality of the future Albania permit the erection of defensive fortifications, then the trading port served by the international railway is to be made subject to a special regulation disallowing the fortification of this place.

2. International Railway and Freedom of Transit.

The six Great Powers together with Serbia and Albania will participate financially in the formation of an international company for the construction and working of the said railway conceded by the Albanian Government ; they will enjoy joint power of control in proportion to their participation.

The free use of the railway and of the port will be guaranteed by the signatory Great Powers to all States alike under equal conditions and at all times.

3. Control and Protection of the Railway.

The international control will be exercised by a Commission composed of representatives of the six Great Powers, Serbia and Albania, on the lines of the control provided for in Article 8 of the Suez Convention of 1888, but with variations corresponding with the difference in the situation.

The protection of the railway will be entrusted to the gendarmerie, the militia or any other regular Albanian force under European control (six Great Powers).

4. Transport of War Material.

The freedom of transport of war material is in principle subject to no objections ; the right of search and capture is accorded to belligerent States in respect of all trading vessels before entry into the port served by the international railway.

Sir Edward Grey will at the same time remind the Serbian chargé d'affaires of the communication, to which his attention had been drawn on 29th March, insisting on the necessity of proceeding without delay to the evacuation of the territories allotted to Albania.

A like communication will also be made to the Montenegrin Government.

Sir Edward Grey proposes that on presenting this communication the representatives of the Powers in Cettinje should mention that the promised assistance in the regulation of the irrigation question and in the provision of financial support is dependent upon the evacuation of the territories allotted to Albania.'

At the request of Count Mensdorff and in accordance with assurances given at previous sittings the above mentioned notification is to be accompanied by the demand for the immediate evacuation by Serbian and Montenegrin troops of the territory allotted to Albania.

Since there is no accredited Montenegrin representative here it was decided that the communication to the Montenegrin Government should be made by the representatives of the Powers in Cettinje. At Sir Edward Grey's suggestion the above-mentioned subsidies already promised to Montenegro are to be linked with the above declaration. In accordance with my instructions I endeavoured to raise the question whether the promised loan might not be applied to the regulation of the Bojana River and Lake Scutari, but came up against the unanimous view that the two matters could not be associated together, since they had been promised to King Nicholas on different occasions and without any connection.

The question of the declaration to be made in Belgrade and Cettinje regarding the Albanian minorities was now raised. Since the declaration agreed upon at a previous sitting is not acceptable to the Austrian Government the new proposals known to Your Excellency were presented by Count Mensdorff. The sentence under section 4, ' The juridical existence of the Albanian nationality is expressly recognized by Serbia and Montenegro,' aroused particular apprehension in the minds of M. Cambon and Count Benckendorff, as it appeared to found a claim to autonomy. Both Marquis Imperiali and myself supported the Austrian proposals, whilst Count Benckendorff declared that he could express no opinion at that juncture. The following is the agreed text :

' Count Mensdorff says that his Government finds the resolution of 23rd June incomplete and puts forward a detailed plan which, as he says, is the subject of discussions between Vienna and St. Petersburg. Sir Edward Grey remarks that if agreement is reached on the detailed interpretation of the resolution of 23rd June it should take the form of an annexe to this resolution.'

Sir Edward Grey further handed us the enclosed report by Vice-Admiral Burney on the administration of Scutari up to the present.

Count Mensdorff also raised the question of the constitutional position of Mount Athos, whereat everyone pointed out that the autonomy under the protection of the Powers decided upon by us at a previous sitting had been accepted and had thereby acquired a legal status.

Next sitting Monday.

Sir Edward Grey again told me to-day that he would under no circumstances hold sittings after the end of this month. All questions subsequently arising could be settled in the ordinary way by understanding between the Cabinets.

LICHNOWSKY.

To THE FOREIGN OFFICE. LONDON, 3rd July, 1913.

At to-day's discussion Sir Edward brought up the Albanian question and regretted that so little progress was being made. Count Berchtold appeared unable to come to a decision even on the agreed establishment of a foreign gendarmerie taken from a neutral State. My Austro-Hungarian and Russian colleagues had indeed brought forward proposals for the future constitution of Albania, in which it was suggested that the Commission de Contrôle should work out proposals. But there was not a word about the necessity of setting up an immediate provisional administration.

As regards the southern frontier Count Berchtold's proposals had now been received ; they were based on the Phtelia-Koriza line. If this were to be entertained, a concession must be made as to the Cutzowallachians. I replied that this harmonized entirely with the views of Your Excellency, but that Rumania had so far shown little disposition to yield, and that M. Majorescu desired to move the centre of the negotiations in this direction. I urged him to speak to M. Misu, and my impression was that the Minister did not consider an ultimate agreement on this basis impossible.

LICHNOWSKY.

To THE FOREIGN OFFICE. LONDON, 7th July, 1913.

Discussed the marked matter [1] confidentially with Sir E. Grey, who agrees. Could not, however, bring the question up at to-day's meeting, as Count Mensdorff still without instructions.

---

[1] Dealing with certain not very important wishes of Austria regarding the southern frontier of Albania. (Author's Note.)

Sir E. Grey has answered the Austro-Italian scheme handed to him by my colleagues representing those countries with counter-proposals for the establishment of a Commission de Contrôle as provisional Government and the fixing of the date for the selection of a Prince. As soon as the answer is to hand joint proposals will be submitted to the Ambassadors' Conference, probably next Thursday.

A new Austrian proposal that the future constitution of Albania should be worked out by Austrian and Italian plenipotentiaries on the spot was rejected by Sir E. Grey owing to the unfavourable impression it would make on other Powers. He wants to have this question dealt with by the provisional Government.

The Vienna Cabinet still appears to be opposed to the universally desired establishment of a provisional Government invested in the Commission de Contrôle till the Prince is established and the final organisation fixed, as it suspects this to be a mere attempt to frustrate a permanent settlement altogether. M. Cambon told me to-day that his Government entertained no such intention, but considered it on purely practical grounds necessary to establish a temporary governmental authority with the least possible delay.

As regards Koriza, Sir E. Grey pointed out that it was an important matter for Greece to have a direct link with Serbia, who also desired communication with the Aegean Sea through Greece. That might, however, perhaps also be achieved via Salonika, more or less on the lines of the trade route formerly desired by Austria. To my remark that events in the Balkans might bring new solutions for existing difficulties, the Minister replied that quite a number would perhaps be facilitated thereby, a view which I have found shared by several of my colleagues. Sir E. Grey emphasized in this connection, as he had also done in session, that the strife between the former Allies could make no difference to the decisions taken by the Powers. As regards Koriza, that might go to Albania provided that the Islands fell to Greece, with the exception of Imbros and Tenedos, which Turkey should retain, and Thasos, which Bulgaria was getting. He did not mention Samothrace. One or two of the smaller ones, whose populations were mainly Mohammedan, might also perhaps remain to Turkey.

LICHNOWSKY.

To The Foreign Office.   London, 11*th July*, 1913.

It is anticipated that Sir E. Grey will bring up for discussion at the Ambassadors' Conference next Tuesday the establishment of a provisional Albanian Government with a time limit for the selection of a Prince and for the delimitation of Southern Albania on the basis already announced, as with further procrastination a settlement of the matter before the end of the month appears more and more doubtful.

It would be extremely desirable to put pressure on Vienna so that Count Mensdorff may be enabled by that date to declare the standpoint of his Government. Marquis Imperiali has not yet received any final instructions from his Government either and does not venture to participate in the discussion without express directions.

The attitude of the Austrian Government, which always makes fresh difficulties and can never make up its mind, is creating a painful impression. *Sir E. Grey thinks that Vienna is in a state of extreme nervousness on account of the Bulgarian defeats and of the request addressed to St. Petersburg to take over the office of arbitrator.*

Sazonov, he believes, will not permit the annihilation of Bulgaria, but is displaying in his attitude towards Rumania and the other Balkan States a desire to establish a balance as far as possible.

LICHNOWSKY.

To The Foreign Office.   London, 15*th July*, 1913.

At to-day's sitting Sir E. Grey first of all expressed the hope that before the end of this month, that is, before the close of the sittings, it would be possible to come to decisions both on the organisation of Albania and on the delimitation of the frontier, as this would materially contribute towards consolidating the position in the Balkan Peninsula in view of recent events. The Austro-Italian proposals on Albanian constitutional questions were then discussed which my two colleagues had drafted in conjunction with Sir E. Grey.

Report follows. Next sitting Monday.   LICHNOWSKY.

To The Imperial Chancellor von Bethmann-Hollweg.

London, 15*th July*, 1913.

At to-day's sitting, as already reported, the plan drawn up by my Austro-Hungarian and Italian colleagues in agreement with their Governments and with the partial co-operation of Sir Edward Grey for the settlement of the most important questions as to the future constitution of Albania was submitted and discussed in detail.

The first four articles were passed without opposition.

Concerning Article 5 Count Benckendorff, with the support of M. Cambon, remarked that he missed any provision for the continuance of European supervision. It was precisely on the assumption of an international control designed to prevent Albania from falling under the exclusive influence of one or other foreign State that their Governments had agreed to the abandonment of the Sultan's suzerainty. It had, moreover, been held in prospect from the very beginning, and their Governments would consent to no scheme which did not contain binding assurances regarding the continuance of the supervision of all the Powers.

M. Cambon went the furthest when he declared that his Government had agreed to the appointment of a Prince only on the assumption that the Powers as a whole would form a kind of suzerainty over the country. The Powers henceforth take the place of the Sultan. He conceives the Commission de Contrôle as the actual Government of the country exercising supreme authority and control over both finance and administration and entitled practically to the rights of guardianship over the Prince, so that his position must sink to that of an ornamental head.

Both my colleagues were obviously anxious lest Albania should fall into a position of dependence upon Austria unless the influence of all the Powers was guaranteed in an effective manner. If the activity of the Commission ceased after five years without the assurance of its prolongation that would jeopardize all right of objection.

Count Mensdorff gave the meeting to understand that his Government would not entertain the idea of international control *ad infinitum*, and that the whole project might possibly break down on this question.

I emphasised the fact that I was authorized to support the proposals of my Austrian and Italian colleagues, and that I could not view with favour the notion of entrusting the actual exercise of governmental authority in perpetuity to an international commission, especially after the appointment of a Prince. This was inconsistent with the idea of establishing a Monarch, who must after all have the right of appointing his own Government. Besides, I knew of no other country in the Balkan Peninsula, not even Greece in her original form, hardly larger or any better off, where a similar authority was provided limiting the governmental power of the ruler. There was an enormous difference between protecting Powers and Powers which exercised so far-reaching an influence on the Government of a foreign State. Without entering upon the fundamental question whether the claim to supreme control without time limit was permissible, I pointed out that this might be confined to the right of the consuls and diplomatic representatives to take cognizance of the affairs of the country. The main thing therefore was to reach agreement as to what was meant by the control of the Powers. I think, however, that it will be very difficult to reach agreement on this point, as Austria is against any control lasting longer than five years, while France and Russia want to bring all the affairs of the country, and especially the foreign policy, under their supervision.

The following report on the matter was agreed to :

' Count Benckendorff observes that it was agreed under the resolution of 20th December, that the independence of Albania should be exclusively guaranteed and controlled by the six Powers, and that this control should not cease if after the expiry of five years the powers of the Control Commission are not renewed.

Upon this observation of Count Benckendorff Marquis Imperiali expresses it as his personal opinion that the five-year time limit might be replaced by one of ten, instead of abiding by the permanence of the Commission.'

In order to evade the delicate dispute as to whether the supervision should be permanent or only temporary, my Italian colleague had proposed the extension of the Commission's duration from five to ten years. On this proposal I observed that, particularly in view of the far-reaching powers which would be claimed for the Commission from various quarters, an extension appeared to me open to objection and that five years was already more than sufficient.

Article 6 raised a long discussion for the same reason as Article 5, as the final sentence speaks of an organisation of the control of the Powers *for the period of the Commission's activity*. Count Benckendorff moved that the concluding words, from ' pour la durée ' on, be struck out. As this proposal met with opposition the concluding words, from ' et de l'organisation ' on, were struck out. The legal position and sphere of action of the Commission de Contrôle after the appointment of the Prince is thereby left to arrangement among the Powers.

Regarding Article 7 Count Benckendorff was of opinion that it would be advisable to proceed with the appointment of the Prince a year instead of six months hence, as the proposed interval was insufficient to reduce the country to the necessary state of order before the Government takes over.

M. Cambon very strongly objected to the reference to the existing national authorities as implying *de facto* recognition of the so-called provisional Government in Valona, which had not been convoked, established or chosen by anybody, and whose competence rested solely on its own self-appointment. This was another point in which the opposition between the Austrian and Franco-Russian views was thrown sharply into relief, as Vienna was known to be desirous of supporting this Government and leaving it where it was, while Paris and St. Petersburg will not tolerate it at any price, since they suspect it, as M. Cambon told me confidentially, of being in Austrian pay.   M. Cambon proposed the following alteration :

' Till the Prince has been determined upon, the Control Commission appoints the executive organs of administration and will act in co-operation with the local authorities.'

The subsequent articles were passed without opposition, except that in Article 9 the names of all the countries but Sweden were struck out.

In brief, the fundamental difficulties lie in the question of the Powers' right to supreme control, in the competence of the Commission de Contrôle and the period of its duration, and in the question of the admissibility and recognition of the existing provisional Albanian Government.

ANNEXE.

1. Albania will be constituted an independent, sovereign, hereditary Principality according to the law of primogeniture, under the guarantee of the six Powers.   The Prince will be appointed by the Powers.

2. Turkey renounces all rights of suzerainty over Albania.

3. Albania is neutral ; its neutrality is guaranteed by the six Powers.

4. The control of the civil and financial administration of Albania

L.H.A.   Q

will be entrusted to an international Commission composed of delegates of the six Powers and a delegate of Albania.

5. The authority of this Commission will last for five years and may be prolonged in case of need.

6. This Commission will be authorized to work out a detailed scheme of organisation for all branches of the administration of Albania. Within a period of six months it will render a report to the Powers on the result of this work together with its resolutions regarding the administrative and financial organisation of the land and of the organisation of the Powers' control during the period of the mandate of the Commission.

7. The Prince will be appointed within a period not exceeding six months. Prior to his appointment the activity of the national authorities who are provisionally and *de facto* administering the land will be controlled by the above-mentioned Commission.

8. Public order and security will be ensured by the international organisation of the gendarmerie. This organisation will be entrusted to foreign officers, who will have actual supreme command of the gendarmerie.

9. These officers will be taken from European armies, those, namely, of Sweden, Belgium, Holland, Switzerland, Norway, Spain, but not from the armies of the six Powers, of the Balkan States and of Governments which are directly interested in Balkan questions.

10. The sending of foreign instructional officers does not affect either the uniformity of the service or the employment of native officers, non-commissioned officers and gendarmes.

11. The salaries of these officers may be defrayed out of the resources of the country under the guarantee of the Powers.'

To The Foreign Office.　　　　　London, *22nd July*, 1913.

During my visit to-day Sir E. Grey mentioned among other things the question of the Islands and told me that Italy apparently desired to receive the occupied Turkish islands, in order that, on the collapse of Turkish power which may be expected sooner or later, she may be in a position to occupy them and use them as a lever to assert further claims on the mainland of Asia Minor. That accounted for the vacillating attitude of the Italian Government in the question of linking the island problem with the boundary problems in Epirus and Thrace. At the present moment, when Greece is obtaining abundant satisfaction on the mainland she will be glad to see the two matters associated, whereas formerly, when it was a question of Greek concessions towards Albania, she was not content with receiving all the islands by way of compensation. Difficulties would, however, arise in any case, because Rhodes, for instance, on being restored to Turkey, would immediately declare its union with Greece.

LICHNOWSKY.

To The Imperial Chancellor von Bethmann-Hollweg.

LONDON, 21st *July*, 1913.

At to-day's sitting, after the settlement of the questions on which I have already reported elsewhere, Albania again came up for discussion. At the previous sitting M. Cambon had, as I have reported, proposed an alteration of Article 7 of the Austro-Italian proposal for the establishment of an Albanian Government. The text of the article was as follows :

' 7. The Prince will be appointed within a period not exceeding six months. Prior to his appointment the activity of the national authorities who are provisionally and *de facto* administering the land will be controlled by the above-mentioned Commission.'

The proposed alteration was as follows :

' Till the Prince is determined upon the Control Commission will appoint the executive organs of administration and will act in co-operation with the local authorities.'

He was supported by Count Benckendorff, and his object was to avoid the reference to the existing provisional national authorities, since the Triple Entente Powers were against recognizing the provisional Government of Ismail Kemal in Valona and Essad Pasha had incurred their displeasure by journeys to Vienna and Rome. Count Berchtold, however, had objected to the proposal of my French colleague as an undue encroachment on the independence of the country. In order to meet all objections Sir Edward Grey has made the new proposal given below.

Both our Allies also declared their consent, under certain conditions, to the extension of the term of office of the Commission de Contrôle from five years to ten.

The following report on the sitting was adopted :

' Count Mensdorff says that the French Ambassador's alteration to Article 7 would not be likely to be accepted by his Government.

Both he and Marquis Imperiali declare the acceptance of the extension of the Control Commission's mandate to ten years, provided the proposals are accepted in their entirety. Sir Edward Grey proposes that Article 7 should read as follows : " The Prince will be appointed within a period not exceeding six months. Until the Prince is determined upon the administration including the gendarmerie will be controlled by the international Commission in co-operation with the local authorities." '

Lichnowsky.

To The Imperial Chancellor von Bethmann-Hollweg.

London, 24th July, 1913.

At to-day's sitting Count Mensdorff proposed to alter in the manner given below the latest draft put forward by Sir E. Grey of Article 7 of the Albanian Statute.

For the sake of clearness I repeat the various proposals in order :

Count Berchtold : ' The Prince will be appointed within a period not exceeding six months. Prior to his appointment the activity of the national authorities who are provisionally and *de facto* administering the land will be controlled by the above-mentioned Commission.'

M. Cambon : ' The Prince will be appointed within a period not exceeding six months. Till the Prince is determined upon the Control Commission will appoint the executive organs of administration and will act in co-operation with the local authorities.'

Sir Edward Grey : ' The Prince will be appointed within a period not exceeding six months. Until the Prince is determined upon the administration including the gendarmerie will be controlled by the international Commission in co-operation with the local authorities.'

Count Berchtold : ' The Prince will be appointed within a period not exceeding six months. Until the Prince is determined upon and the national Government finally constituted the activity both of the provisional, national authorities and of the gendarmerie will be subject to the control of the international Commission.'

The reference to the ' autorités nationales ' again aroused the opposition of M. Cambon, who was supported by Count Benckendorff, since it implied, in their view, the recognition of the existing so-called Government of Ismail Kemal. After a long discussion a proposal was accepted for submission to the Government replacing the words ' nationales provisoires ' with ' existantes.' Count Mensdorff did not consider himself in a position to agree, but declared his readiness to submit the proposal to Count Berchtold, which in fact is not merely a tolerable way out of the difficulty, but in the circumstances the only possible one. . I too should like to take the liberty of urging that pressure be put on Vienna to accept, as otherwise it may be regarded as certain that the negotiations will break down and that we shall fail to reach any conclusion at all on the Albanian Statute.

Sir Edward Grey concluded by expressing the hope that the present draft would be accepted by the Powers by the next sitting, which he provisionally fixed for Thursday, and which will possibly be the last, so that the Albanian Statute could be finally settled and, after the formation of the Commission de Contrôle, the Swedish Government approached with a view to nominating and placing at disposal the officers required for the formation of the Albanian gendarmerie in accordance with our resolutions of 15th July and Article 9 of the Statute.

Whether under these circumstances we shall still succeed in settling the Southern Albanian frontier question and the Island question before the conclusion of our sittings appears to me highly doubtful.

LICHNOWSKY.

To The Foreign Office.   London, 28th July, 1913.

Sir E. Grey told me that in addition to to-morrow's sitting he would hold a further final sitting probably on Friday, and would then not conclude the sittings but only adjourn them, in order not to convey the impression that our Conference had broken down owing to the disunion of the Powers. He could not tell for the moment whether the Conference of Ambassadors would be resumed in the autumn or winter. He hopes that it will at least be possible to settle the Albanian Statute and the southern frontier of Albania before the adjournment. Owing to the new situation in the Balkans, the Minister is disinclined to have any further discussions for the moment. He intends going into the country next week, returning here occasionally for a day or two.

LICHNOWSKY.

To The Foreign Office.   London, *29th July*, 1913.

At to-day's sitting the Austrian wording of Article 7 of the Albanian Statute with ' indigène existence ' was adopted, and the extension of the Commission's mandate from five years to ten again confirmed. This finally settles the question of the Statute. Full report follows. Next sitting Friday, in which the Southern Albanian frontier question and the island question will be discussed.

LICHNOWSKY.

To The Imperial Chancellor von Bethmann-Hollweg.

London, *29th July*, 1913.

As reported elsewhere the Albanian Statute was finally settled at to-day's sitting of the Ambassadors' Conference, after the Austrian proposal had been accepted to the effect that the words ' indigènes existantes ' should be inserted after ' autorités ' in Article 7. The following resolution on the subject was adopted :

' Having agreed upon the constitution of Albania and especially upon the conditions pertaining to the establishment of the international Control Commission, the Conference recommends that the Governments proceed to the appointment of their representatives for this Commission and take the necessary measures to ensure payment of their salaries. These salaries will be guaranteed to the members of the Commission by their Governments. The Conference considers it desirable that all of them should receive the same salary.

The Conference recommends that the Swedish Government be approached at once to arrange for the appointment of the officers to be charged with the instruction and command of the gendarmerie. It appears necessary first of all to name a higher officer who in conjunction with the Control Commission and with due regard for the exigencies of the service will fix an estimate of the number of officers to be appointed.'

From what the two British representatives and my colleagues have said, I conclude that members of the consular service will probably be designated for the Commission de Contrôle. From a remark of Sir Arthur Nicholson's an English Consul-General might possibly be considered.

As to the salary of the officials in question no definite proposals are made, but general opinion favoured 25,000 to 30,000 francs.

The declaration still to be made to Serbia and Montenegro then came up for discussion. The question of the protection of the Albanian minorities in Serbia and Montenegro was first of all settled, as my Austro-Hungarian and Russian colleagues were able to lay before us an agreement on this subject, which I respectfully enclose in an annexe. The following report was drawn up on the matter :

' The Russian and Austro-Hungarian Ambassadors acquainted the Conference with the agreement between their Governments regarding the protection of the minorities incorporated in Serbia and Montenegro, which they had announced at the sitting of 1st July to be under discussion. The Conference accepts the view there laid down. On Sir Edward Grey's proposal it recommends that the Serbian and Montenegrin Governments be notified of the above view by the representatives of the Powers.

At the instance of Count Benckendorff it recognises that the enjoyment of the liberties granted to the minorities is subordinate to the general rights belonging to all Serbian and Montenegrin subjects.'

On the proposal of my Austro-Hungarian colleague the question of the evacuation of Albanian territory by the Serbian troops was also discussed. In this connection the written declaration to be addressed to the Serbs regarding their Adriatic railway as already agreed upon was confirmed. The resolution adopted was as follows :

' Sir Edward Grey proposes that the representatives of the Powers shall urgently remind the Serbian Government of its obligation to evacuate Albanian territory without delay, and to respect the northern and north-eastern frontiers of Albania as defined by the Powers and communicated to the Serbian Government on 15th April, 1913.

The representatives of the Powers shall at the same time reiterate and confirm in writing the engagement of the Powers regarding the railway and commercial access to the Adriatic in accordance with the declaration of the Conference of 1st July and the explanatory memorandum to this declaration of the same date.'

Then at the instance of M. Cambon the question of the Montenegrin loan was discussed in connection with the notification of the Montenegrin Government to the effect that the evacuation of Albanian territory has already been completed. I did not consider it opportune again to revert to the idea of associating the loan with the regulation of the Bojana River and Scutari Lake waters, as I foresaw no inclination in this sense. I would however urge the discussion of details of the loan with the Vienna Cabinet, as it also appears little disposed to grant it unconditionally. At Count Mensdorff's desire the following draft was agreed upon, speaking only of ' prendre en considération ' and not of a definite engagement.

' As regards Montenegro, which has reported the total evacuation of Albanian territory, the Conference takes note of this evacuation and is of opinion that the representatives of the Powers in Cettinje should inform the Montenegrin Government that the Powers will take into consideration the necessary measures for the regulation of the irrigation question and for financial support.'

Sir Edward Grey then expressed the hope that it would be possible to settle before our adjournment the Albanian frontier question and in connection therewith the question of the islands. Austria, he said, had announced that on condition that Stylos and Koriza went to Albania she was willing for the frontier to be fixed by an international delegation, provided the Rumanian representative is invited to the negotiations here. Since, however, Rumania had intervened in the Balkan chaos in conjunction with Greece this condition was no longer operative, as otherwise the Greek representative would also have to be invited.

As regards the Islands question Marquis Imperiali had advised him (Sir Edward Grey) that his Government had no objection to the cession of the remaining islands to Greece, provided those occupied by Italy in accordance with the Treaty of Lausanne were withdrawn from discussion. Italy did not desire to retain these islands, but was bound by her obligation and must return them to Turkey.

After the close of the sitting the question was also discussed whether on the conclusion of our programme, for which further sittings should if necessary be held next week, it would be advisable to adjourn our meetings *sine die* with a stipulation to the effect that Sir Edward Grey should summon us again if necessity arose, or whether it would be advantageous to make the adjournment renewable from fortnight to fortnight, in order to avoid the impression of disagreement among the Powers. The latter alternative was favoured in particular by M. Cambon, the former by Sir Edward Grey. Whilst several of my colleagues supported M. Cambon, I took Sir Edward Grey's view, as I could see no use in fixing dates for meetings without any intention of keeping them. In the event of important things happening this method would be precisely calculated to arouse attention and give rise to misconstructions. Sir Edward Grey moreover emphasized the fact that he had no intention of holding further sittings, partly because he wanted to go on leave, and partly because Sir Arthur Nicholson would also be absent and on his return would be too busy to have any time for Ambassadors' Conferences.

I finally agreed with Sir Edward Grey, as did also M. Cambon subsequently, that a communiqué should be issued to the effect that on the completion of our allotted work we had adjourned till further orders, and that we should meet again as soon as necessity arose. The maintenance of concord is thus in principle assured as the expression of co-operation among the Powers, without in any way committing ourselves to further meetings.

I have just received from the Foreign Office a copy of the present text of the Albanian constitution in its final form, which I have the honour to enclose. LICHNOWSKY.

Confidential. ANNEXE.

ALBANIA'S CONSTITUTION.

1. Albania will be constituted an independent, sovereign Principality under the guarantee of the six Powers. The succession shall be hereditary according to the law of primogeniture. The Prince will be appointed by the Powers.

2. Turkey renounces all rights of suzerainty over Albania.

3. Albania is neutral ; its neutrality is guaranteed by the six Powers.

4. The control of the civil and financial administration of Albania will be entrusted to an international Commission composed of delegates of the six Powers and a delegate of Albania.

5. The authority of this Commission will last for ten years and may be prolonged in case of need.

6. This Commission will be authorised to work out a detailed scheme of organisation for all branches of the administration of Albania. Within a period of six months it will send in a report to the Powers on the result of this work together with its resolutions concerning the administrative and financial organisation of the country.

7. The Prince will be appointed within a period not exceeding six months. Until the Prince has been chosen and the national Government finally constituted, the administrative activities both of the existing native authorities and of the gendarmerie will be subject to the control of the international Commission.

8. Public order and security will be ensured by the international organisation of the gendarmerie. This organisation will be entrusted to foreign officers, who will have actual supreme command of the gendarmerie.

9. These officers will be taken from the Swedish army.

10. The sending of foreign instructional officers does not affect either the uniformity of the service or the employment of native officers, non-commissioned officers and gendarmes.

11. The salaries of these officers may be defrayed out of the resources of the country under the guarantee of the Powers.

To The Foreign Office.   London, 31st July, 1913.

Sir E. Grey has just informed me of the lines on which he will seek to bring about agreement on the questions of the Southern Albanian frontier and the Islands at the coming sittings. He intends to associate the two questions together in such a way that Koriza and Stylos will be left to Albania, with an international delegation to examine the intervening territory on the basis of nationality, as against which the islands will be given to Greece, except Imbros and Tenedos, which are to be reserved for Turkey, and Thasos and Samothrace, which are among the questions to be settled between the Balkan States themselves subject to confirmation by the Powers. This settlement, however, which leaves out of account the islands occupied by Italy, presupposes as a condition of acceptance that concurrently with the cession of Koriza and Stylos to Albania Italy restores those islands to Turkey irrespective of the non-fulfilment of provisions of the Lausanne Treaty. He gave me to understand that only on this condition would France and England consent to the wishes of Austria and Italy regarding the Southern Albanian frontiers. Italy had so often changed her standpoint in the question of the islands occupied by her that she had aroused the mistrust of other Powers as to her intention of evacuating the islands at all.

I replied that from our point of view there was scarcely any objection to this plan. We desired indeed to support the standpoint of our ally so far as she was unwilling to permit islands which she had occupied by special treaty to be included in the general bargaining. Nor could we oppose the desire of Italy to restore to Turkey the islands in question, and must abide by the repeated assurance of the Italian Government that it does not intend to annex the islands.

LICHNOWSKY.

To THE FOREIGN OFFICE.   LONDON, 31st *July*, 1913.

Sir E. Grey intends holding further sittings of the Ambassadors' Conference next week in order to settle the Southern Albanian and Islands questions. Before the close of Parliament, however, that is at the beginning of the week after next, he wants to make an announcement to the effect that on the completion of our programme he has adjourned our meetings in order to resume them, if necessary, in the late autumn. He himself will then finally leave London and not return till after the middle of October.

On my asking whether he intended the Balkan question to be finally settled by the Ambassadors here he replied in the negative and referred to the possibility of solving these questions by direct exchange of opinion between the Powers.

LICHNOWSKY.

To THE FOREIGN OFFICE.   LONDON, 31st *July*, 1913.

I have just heard that Marquis Imperiali, whom Sir E. Grey received after me in order to give him like information, declared in great excitement that Italy could not accept the idea of evacuating the islands before Turkey had fulfilled her obligations under the Lausanne Treaty and had evacuated Cyrenaica. Sir E. Grey replied that this might be a very long business, as in the case of most Turkish treaty obligations, and that it was not feasible to wait. In these circumstances, and since my Italian colleague must first receive instructions from Rome, it will not be possible to discuss this question by to-morrow. There is, however, a danger that the whole result of our conferences may be jeopardised by this new difficulty. If by the end of our meetings, that is by the middle of August at the latest, we have not settled the frontier question the statute, the gendarmerie and everything else may be endangered.

Count Mensdorff tells me that Vienna is determined to press for the settlement of the frontier at all costs. That, however, is again inseparably bound up with the settlement of the Islands question.

It would perhaps be advisable, in order to prevent the breakdown of our Conference, to urge Rome to accept the Grey proposal on condition that the islands occupied by Italy are kept excluded from the general bargaining. The Italian islands could be conceded to Turkey in return for the evacuation of Adrianople on the basic understanding that she is pledged to withdraw simultaneously from Africa in accordance with the Lausanne Treaty.

I will try to raise the matter with Sir E. Grey and Marquis Imperiali in this sense in order to prevent all the agreements so far reached from being upset and the mistrust in Paris towards Italy's intentions from being still further accentuated.

LICHNOWSKY.

To THE FOREIGN OFFICE.   LONDON, 1st *August*, 1913.

At to-day's sitting it was first of all decided, in view of Sweden's refusal to supply the Albanian gendarmerie, to apply to the following States in the order given : 1. Holland, 2. Denmark, 3. Switzerland.

Then at the instance of Count Mensdorff the following resolution was adopted regarding the assistance to be accorded to Montenegro :

' Count Mensdorff states that his Government desires to know where the agreement regarding the financial aid to be granted to Montenegro is to be discussed between the Powers and the Montenegrin Government. Count Benckendorff holds that the representatives of the Powers in Cettinje could be entrusted with these negotiations. The Conference makes no objection to this procedure.'

I observed that in our view this financial question was one which should come before the Paris Commission, though it was temporarily adjourned, but that as the Vienna and Rome Cabinets had agreed to the above procedure I would not oppose it.

Sir E. Grey then stated that he would only hold sittings during next week and must make a statement in Parliament as to the progress of our work to date on the 12th or 13th before the close of the session. He hoped, however, that mutual accommodation between the Governments would enable us to settle the Southern Albanian frontier and Islands questions by then. The Minister then propounded a basis for understanding on the lines of the views given below. He emphasised the fact that the view had been held from the very beginning that Greece should have all the islands in case she had to renounce Stylos and Koriza. The refusal of Italy to surrender the islands unconditionally was an obstacle to an understanding. Marquis Imperiali replied that Italy did not desire to retain the islands, but would restore them to Turkey on the fulfilment of the conditions of the Lausanne Treaty.

At the beginning of the sitting I had suggested it as my personal opinion that a way out might be found if the islands held by Italy together with certain other advantages to be accorded to Turkey were used to secure the evacuation of Adrianople by Turkey and remained subject to the Powers' decision with all the other questions awaiting eventual settlement as a whole. At the same time Turkey should be summoned to comply with the provisions of the Lausanne Treaty. This proposal met with no opposition, though M. Cambon and Count Benckendorff emphasized that their Governments would only sanction the cession of Koriza to Albania provided *all* the islands except Imbros, Tenedos and Thasos, went to Greece. As may be seen from the following text Sir E. Grey fell in with my proposal.

' Sir Edward Grey expresses the opinion that agreement might be reached on the following points :

1. An International Commission will carry out the delimitation of the southern and south-eastern frontier of Albania, with instructions to give Koriza, Stylos and the island of Sasseno to Albania.

2. Neutralization of the Corfu Channel.

3. Subject to certain conditions of neutrality Greece will retain possession of the islands inhabited by a majority of Greeks and occupied by Greek forces, with the exception of Tenedos, Imbros and Thasos.

4. Italy declares that as soon as the Ottoman troops and Ottoman artillery have evacuated Cyrenaica in accordance with Article 2 of the Lausanne Treaty, she will evacuate the islands occupied by her and restore them to Turkey.

5. The Powers will settle the fate of these islands in the final settlement.

Prince Lichnowsky expresses his personal view that the question of the islands to be restored to Turkey should be made dependent upon certain concessions, as for instance the evacuation of Adrianople.   Sir Edward Grey recognizes that a settlement in accordance with the five points given above would modify the views previously expressed by some Governments, but he nevertheless hopes to reach an agreement before the adjournment of the Conference at the end of next week.   He thinks that certain changes in the situation and especially the occupation of Adrianople by the Turks justify the Powers in reserving their decisions regarding the fate of the islands occupied by Italy after their restoration to Turkey.'

Marquis Imperiali stipulated that he must obtain the sanction of his Government, though he appeared to accept the proposed agreement as far as he personally was concerned.

Next sitting Tuesday.   LICHNOWSKY.

TO THE IMPERIAL CHANCELLOR VON BETHMANN-HOLLWEG.

LONDON, 5th August, 1913.

The following report was drawn up on to-day's sitting :

' Sir Edward Grey enquires of the Ambassadors whether they have received the answer of their Governments on the five points which he had formulated in the last sitting.

The French Ambassador replies that his Government is ready to accept the delimitation of the Southern Albanian frontier from Cape Stylos at one end to Koriza at the other on condition that all the islands in the Aegean Sea except Imbros and Tenedos, but including those at present occupied by Italy, should be allotted to Greece, the last-named on their evacuation.

The Italian Ambassador observes that this standpoint did not harmonize with the views of his Government.   He confined himself to the following statement, which did not imply either an obligation respecting the transfer to Greece of the islands occupied by Italy or an acknowledgment of the connection between the question of the islands and the question of the Albanian frontier :

" His Majesty's Government holds that the question of the islands of the Dodekanese, which arose out of the Italo-Turkish War, is settled juridically by the provisions of the Lausanne Treaty. Under these circumstances the Italian Government reaffirms that it will restore these islands to Turkey as soon as the Ottoman Government on its part has completely fulfilled the obligations imposed on . it by Article 2 of the Lausanne Treaty.   It need hardly be said that as soon as the restoration of the islands to Turkey has taken effect the Italian Government will join with the other great Powers in any unanimous decisions that may be discussed and adopted regarding the ultimate disposal of these islands in connection with the general settlement of all outstanding questions and with due regard for the general European interest in the integrity and security of Asiatic Turkey."

The Austro-Hungarian and German Ambassadors supported the statement of the Italian Ambassador.

The Russian Ambassador declares that his Government is ready to accept the five points provided they are agreed to by all the Powers, but with a reservation regarding the island of Sasseno, which belongs to Greece and the cession of which to Albania might result in Greece demanding compensation.

Marquis Imperiali observes that the Greek claim to the island of Sasseno is disputable, since this island must be regarded as a part of the Bay of Valona and consequently share the fate of this Bay. Count Mensdorff and Prince Lichnowsky supported Marquis Imperiali's observation regarding Sasseno.

Prince Lichnowsky has instructions to demand that the small island of Castellorizo lying between Rhodes and Cape Chelidonia on the south coast of Asia Minor should remain Turkish. (My Italian colleague had requested me to put forward the proposal.)

The Austro-Hungarian and Italian Ambassadors supported this proposal, against which the Conference does not feel called upon to raise any objection owing to the small importance of the island and its proximity to the coast.

The German Ambassador declares that his Government accepts the five points.

The Austro-Hungarian Ambassador declares that his Government is likewise ready to accept them, but under the following reservations:

1. The Vienna Cabinet desires an exact definition of the line between Stylos and Koriza.

2. As regards the Cutzowallachians it demands the inclusion in the resolution of a provision entitling Rumania to look after the rights and interests of the Cutzowallachians in Epirus.

3. The Vienna Cabinet further considers it necessary to establish the following points :

(i) The exact dates when the Boundary Commission shall begin and end its labours.

(ii) That for the purposes of its task the Commission shall divide into sections the areas to be demarcated.

(iii) That the demarcation of the frontier shall be carried out on ethnographical and geographical principles.

(iv) It would be desirable that the Conference should agree to demand the immediate evacuation by Greece of the districts allotted to Albania and of the other areas as and when they are allotted to Albania by the Boundary Commission.

Marquis Imperiali and Prince Lichnowsky support these proposals.

Concerning paragraph 1 of the Austro-Hungarian proposals Sir Edward Grey observes that the work of defining the frontier between Stylos and Koriza belongs to the Commission, and that it was very difficult for the Conference to agree upon the precise line in detail since it did not possess the material information.

The French, Russian and German Ambassadors share this view, while the Austro-Hungarian and Italian Ambassadors reserve their opinion till they have consulted their Governments.

Concerning paragraph 2 Sir Edward Grey observes that as Rumania and Greece are allies it is for them to come to an agreement as to the guarantees to be vouchsafed to the Cutzowallachians in the territories annexed to Greece, without the Powers having to take any initiative. The French, Russian and German Ambassadors believe that this opinion is shared by their Governments. The Austro-Hungarian and Italian Ambassadors reserve their opinion till they have consulted their Governments.

Concerning paragraph 3 :

(i) The Conference is agreed as to the advantages of fixing the exact dates for the commencement and conclusion of the Boundary Commission's work : it proposes 1st September and 30th November respectively.

(ii) The Conference raises no objection to the division into sections of the areas to be demarcated.

(iii) It holds the same view.

(iv) Sir Edward Grey, the French and the Russian Ambassadors are of opinion that Greece may not defer the evacuation of the areas ceded to Albania beyond the time when the demarcation of the frontiers is concluded.

Sir Edward Grey is of opinion that if the Austro-Hungarian and Italian Governments accept this wording a joint warning might be addressed to Greece to refrain from any intimidation of the population of the districts occupied by her.

The Austro-Hungarian, Italian and German Ambassadors withhold the expression of their opinion till they have informed their Governments of the suggested changes in paragraph 3 of the Austro-Hungarian proposals.'

Count Mensdorff had brought with him a comprehensive document which set forth the wishes of Austria-Hungary in much greater detail and laid down still further conditions especially with respect to the frontier. Sir Edward Grey, however, indicated that he had only with difficulty succeeded in restraining M. Cambon from bringing forward a set of conditions of his own in addition and in inducing him to leave the settlement of all details to the Commission. At Sir E. Grey's instance therefore Count Mensdorff confined himself to giving only extracts from his instructions, the geographical details of which have most likely been derived from his experts here. If Vienna does not decide to accept to-day's proposals Sir Edward Grey will hardly be in a position to give Parliament a satisfactory report next Tuesday on the conclusion of our negotiations. It would perhaps be advisable to lay stress on this in Vienna, and I also hope that the influence of Sir Edward Grey will succeed in effecting an agreement between Paris and Rome on the Island question.

The attitude of M. Cambon at to-day's sitting has at any rate once again shown how much importance France attaches to the strengthening of Greece, which she would like to develop as far as possible into a Mediterranean sea power. The language of the French press, especially of the *Temps*, is another valuable indication in the same direction. French statesmen can reckon with certainty that the ever-growing opposition between Greece on the one hand and Austria-Hungary and Italy on the other, will necessarily drive Greece into the arms of France, and that France therefore in case of war will have a valuable support in the Greek fleet and Greek harbours against Austria-Hungary and Italy. This circumstance alone, apart from consideration for our Allies, should suffice, despite all Greek professions of friendship, to dispose us unfavourably towards demands tending unduly to weaken Bulgaria. For these professions would, if occasion arose, prove worthless against the force of facts.

LICHNOWSKY.

L.H.A.　　　　　　　　R

To The Foreign Office.   London, *8th August,* 1913.

At to-day's sitting it was only the stipulations as to the Cutzowallachians (in the latest Austrian proposals on the Southern Albanian frontier question) that caused any difficulty. A new proposal on the matter was agreed to whereby the settlement of the actual frontier is left to the Powers on the basis of the investigations made by the Commission ; only the privileges to be granted to the Cutzowallachians are reserved for direct agreement between Rumania and Greece.

No decision could be taken on the Islands question as Marquis Imperiali was without instructions. M. Cambon announced that an agreement had been reached between M. Pichon and Signor Tittoni.

Next and last sitting Monday.

Lichnowsky.

To The Imperial Chancellor von Bethmann-Hollweg.

London, *8th August,* 1913.

The following report was drawn up on to-day's sitting :

' The French Ambassador informs the Conference of a conversation between M. Pichon and the Italian Ambassador in Paris of the 6th inst., the effect of which is that the French Minister of Foreign Affairs is prepared to give his consent to Article 5 of the formula proposed by Sir Edward Grey on 1st August, provided that in the final settlement the Powers decide the fate of the islands occupied by Italy. This consent would be accorded on condition that Italy leaves it to the Powers to decide on the assignment of the Dodekanese and does not challenge the decision taken unanimously by the six Powers. The Italian Ambassador declares that he is without instructions and can express no opinion on the subject.

Count Mensdorff makes the following communication : The Imperial and Royal Government makes its consent to the appointment of an international Commission to determine the southern frontier of Albania conditional upon the following points :

1. The area for demarcation by the Commission must not remain indefinite. Its boundaries in the west are the mountains which separate the coastline allotted to Albania as far as Phtelia from the Valley of Argyrocastron ; in the north-east the boundary line of

the former Ottoman Kasa Koriza.   The intervening area for demarcation by the Commission is bounded on the north by the line given in M. Venizelos' memorandum, and on the south and south-east by the line proposed by Austria-Hungary.

2. It is settled in advance that the coastline as far as Phtelia, including the Island of Sasseno, the areas north of the Greek line and the former Ottoman Kasa Koriza together with the western and southern banks of Lake Ochrida from the village of Lin to the Svet Naum Monastery shall belong to Albania entire.

3. The Commission shall begin its work on 1st September and conclude it on 30th November this year.

4. The Commission shall complete its work in sections, taking into account the natural formation of the valleys.

5. The delimitation of the frontier shall follow ethnographical and geographical principles ; ethnographical affinity shall be determined by the mother tongue of the population, that is, by the language spoken in family life ; the Commission shall ignore all attempts at a plebiscite or other political manifestations.

6. As regards the district inhabited by Wallachians the Commission has to establish their nationality. The question of its assignment to Albania or Greece shall be the subject of a direct understanding between Rumania and Greece.

7. The evacuation by Greek troops of the areas allotted to Albania shall take place not later than one month after the conclusion of the Commission's work.

Marquis Imperiali and Prince Lichnowsky agree with this statement.   The French and Russian Ambassadors reserve their opinion till they have consulted their Governments.

Sir Edward Grey observes that Article 6 withdraws from the Powers the delimitation of the areas inhabited by the Cutzowallachians and assigns it to Greece and Rumania.

If, as has already been proposed, it could be left to these two Powers to come to a direct agreement as to the guarantees to be given to the population of this district, it would be a good thing if the Powers retained in their own hands the delimitation of the frontier.   He therefore proposes the following draft of Article 6 :

As regards the district inhabited by Wallachians the Commission has to establish their nationality. Its assignment to Albania or Greece is to be decided by the Powers after examination of the international Commission's report.   As regards the guarantees to be granted to the Cutzowallachian population they are to be settled by direct agreement between Greece and Rumania.

Count Benckendorff and Count Mensdorff observed that the omission of Thasos from the report of the last meeting did not mean that this island went *ipso facto* to Greece.

Sir Edward Grey recalls that in December Thasos was assigned to Bulgaria, though he remarked that in case the Powers had to consider the fate of Kavalla the question of this island should be reopened.

The French Ambassador states that his Government regards the possession of Thasos as dependent upon that of Kavalla.'

It would thus appear that Italy and France have come to an agreement on the Italian islands whereby the settlement of their future is reserved for the Powers without any pledge being required as to their transference to Greece.

I had always made a point of upholding the view of my Italian colleague and had gone to the extent of associating the surrender of the Italian islands to Turkey with the Adrianople question. Marquis di San Giuliano's request for energetic support rests, as Marquis Imperiali told me, on a misunderstanding and on an incorrect interpretation of the report of the last meeting.

As regards the southern Albanian frontier question I endeavoured to support the Austrian proposal by referring to the assurances previously given to Rumania ; so far-reaching an intervention by Rumania, however, aroused some apprehension and was opposed by the majority of my colleagues present. Sir Edward Grey's proposal was therefore adopted as a compromise, whereby Greece and Rumania are to agree between themselves only as to the privileges to be granted to the Cutzowallachians, whilst the decision as to the actual frontier is to rest with the Powers on the basis of the Commission's investigations. Should this proposal be accepted in Vienna there is a prospect that the remaining points will be settled in accordance with the wishes of Austria, and that would put us in a position to close the Albanian question finally next Monday.

As regards the island of Thasos the view generally prevailed that it was closely connected with the Kavalla question, though no binding resolution in this sense was adopted.

Next and final sitting Monday.

LICHNOWSKY.

To The Foreign Office.   London, 11th August, 1913.

At to-day's sitting the draft proposed by Sir E. Grey at the last sitting of Article 6 of the Austrian conditions for participation in the international Commission for the delimitation of the southern Albanian frontier was accepted.   This settles the Albanian question as far as the Ambassadors' Conference is concerned.

As regards the Islands question no complete reconciliation has been effected between the French and Italian standpoints, as the draft advocated by M. Cambon at the last sitting has not met with the approval of the Italian Government. Marquis Imperiali proposed the following wording :

' When in accordance with the first part of the Italian declaration of 5th August, Article 2 of the Lausanne Treaty is carried out in like manner by both contracting parties, the six Powers will come to a unanimous decision as to the future fate of the islands of the Dodekanese, taking into account Europe's interest in the integrity and security of Asiatic Turkey.'

My Italian colleague, however, declared himself ready to drop the concluding words from ' en tenant compte ' onwards, having apparently been authorized to do so.   M. Cambon hopes to receive an answer from Paris by to-morrow midday, and Sir E. Grey has also proposed the following compromise :

' When . . . , the six Powers will express their views as to the assignment of the Dodekanese and settle the matter by common agreement.'

Both Ambassadors still hope to have answers from their Governments in time for the statement which Sir E. Grey is to make in Parliament to-morrow afternoon.   Should this, however, not prove to be the case, Sir E. Grey will nevertheless make his statement, adding that there now only remain small differences of a more or less formal character in a single outstanding question.

Both my colleagues reckon with certainty on agreement.

No further sittings for the time being.

Full report follows.

Lichnowsky.

To The Imperial Chancellor von Bethmann-Hollweg.

London, 11th August, 1913.

At to-day's sitting the southern Albanian frontier question was first of all settled.   The following report of the meeting was adopted :

' Count Mensdorff informs the Conference that Sir Edward Grey's proposed alteration of Article 6 of the Austro-Hungarian proposals respecting the international Commission for the delimitation of the southern Albanian frontier has been accepted by his Government on condition that the remainder of the proposal is accepted. As all the Ambassadors are authorised by their Governments to accept the Austro-Hungarian proposal with the alteration of Article 6 proposed by Sir Edward Grey in the sitting of August 8th, the Conference unanimously concurs in acceding to this proposal.'

Count Mensdorff then returned to a proposal regarding the market conditions in Diakova, which he had made in the previous sitting. The following is the report :

' Count Mensdorff had in the course of the last sitting made the following draft declaration :

Free access to the markets of Diakova and Dibra will be assured to the inhabitants of the adjacent districts of Albania, as both these towns have at all times served the said inhabitants as markets indispensable to their economic existence. They must therefore be able to come to these towns, take their products to market there and purchase there the goods they require without being subject to any kind of restriction, or being limited in this freedom of access by any kind of conditions. It is nevertheless agreed that they must submit to the laws in force and to the customs and police regulations.

The Conference considers it desirable to accept this proposal and thinks that it should be communicated to the Serbian Government by the representatives of the Powers.'

The Islands question then came up for discussion, in which the issue is really one of more or less formal differences between the French and Italian texts. M. Cambon declared that his draft rested upon promises which Signor Tittoni had made verbally to M. Pichon, and which contained a pledge that no opposition would be raised to the transfer of the Italian islands to Greece provided the French consented to the cession of Koriza to Albania. It was on the basis of this arrangement that the formula proposed by him at the last sitting omitted any reference to Greece. He could make no departure from this formula without the consent of his Government.

Sir Edward Grey used the occasion to declare with emphasis that English public opinion was much more interested in the Islands than in Albania and could not tolerate one of the Powers finally establishing itself there. The following report was drawn up :

' Sir Edward Grey asks the Italian Ambassador whether he has received an answer from his Government regarding the formula proposed by the French Ambassador at the last meeting on the subject of the islands occupied by Italy. Marquis Imperiali replies that this formula appears to his Government to contain some contradictions, and in conjunction with the first part of his declaration of 5th August he proposes the following text, which in the opinion of the Italian Government corresponds with the expressed views of the French Government :

" When in accordance with the first part of the Italian declaration of 5th August, Article 2 of the Lausanne Treaty is carried out in like manner by both contracting parties, the six Powers will come to a unanimous decision as to the final fate of the Islands known as the Dodekanese, taking into account Europe's interest in the integrity and security of Asiatic Turkey."

Sir Edward Grey observes that if Turkey is mentioned Greece must also be mentioned. He thinks that the concluding words, from " taking into account . . . " on, should be eliminated.

Though not authorized to accept the elimination of these words the Italian Ambassador declares that, in order to facilitate an understanding, he accepts personally the suggestion and will propose it to his Government.

The French Ambassador is not authorised to accept any formula other than the one he laid before the Conference at the last sitting. He will inform his Government of the draft proposed by the Italian Government and of the omission accepted by Marquis Imperiali pending consultation with his Government.

Sir Edward Grey proposes the following draft, which he thinks satisfies the views of both Governments :

When . . . , the six Powers will express their views as to the assignment of the Dodekanese and settle the matter by common agreement.

The French and Italian Ambassadors will inform their Governments of this proposal.'

The question of the salaries of the members of the Commission de Contrôle was then discussed. It was agreed that £1,200 to £1,500 appeared reasonable. Sir Edward Grey stated that the present British Consul-General in Salonika, Mr. Lamb, was proposed for this post.

It was further mentioned that M. Misu, the Rumanian Minister, had expressed on behalf of his Government the desire that Rumania should also be represented on the Southern Albanian Frontier Commission, but that this request could not be granted out of consideration for Greece.

Finally there came up for discussion a request made by the Montenegrin representative here, Conte Voinovitch, that Montenegrin wishes should be taken into account in the settlement of the Montenegrin-Albanian frontier ; report as follows :

' The Montenegrin representative has requested the French, Russian, Italian and German Ambassadors to direct the attention of the Conference to the expediency, when settling the Albanian-Montenegrin frontier, of taking into account the necessities of irrigation and drainage, for which assistance has been promised to the Montenegrin Government. The French and Russian Ambassadors propose that the attention of the Governments should be drawn to this request. The other Ambassadors state that they will communicate it to their Governments.'

LICHNOWSKY.

TO THE IMPERIAL CHANCELLOR VON BETHMANN-HOLLWEG.

LONDON, *8th August*, 1913.

Sir Edward Grey is likewise of the opinion that it will be desirable for Governments to exchange opinions among themselves as to the agreements reached in Bucharest between the belligerents, and has given up the idea of leaving the matter to the representatives of the Powers in Bucharest. The most difficult point will doubtless be the question of Kavalla, in which he has decided, after consulting his Cabinet, to remain neutral and to support the majority. He inclines, however, to the view that it would be difficult to force the Greeks out of Kavalla. He appeared to be especially pleased that a new grouping had arisen on this question, and regards this circumstance as proof of the friendly relations subsisting between the Powers and as ground for the conviction that the solution of the Eastern question will not cause any aggravation of the international situation. He always displays satisfaction and cheerfulness over every symptom of relaxation in the antagonism between the groups.

The Minister has let the Turks know that if they keep quiet in

Adrianople and make no further advance on Bulgarian territory the question of the concessions to be granted to them in the evacuation of the town will be solved as favourably for them as possible. Should they, however, press any further forward they will lose all the advantages which they otherwise stand to gain. By what means, indeed, the Minister imagines the Turks could be forcibly expelled from Adrianople he has given no indication. He intends for the time being at any rate to adopt a waiting attitude in the matter and hopes that after the settlement of all other questions it will be easier to reach an understanding with Turkey.

LICHNOWSKY.

SEVENTH SECTION

THE ALBANIAN THRONE

To The Foreign Office.　　　London, 14th February, 1914.

I think it would be a very good thing for Prince William of Wied to show himself here, too, before taking over the Government. A short visit here would be sure to make a good impression and would dispel the idea that he regarded himself as the protégé merely of the Triple Alliance. Regard for the impartial and conciliatory attitude displayed by Sir E. Grey in the foundation of the Albanian State would in itself be sufficient reason to recommend such a visit. And I think too that he would create a favourable personal impression. He might perhaps make the return journey via Paris.

LICHNOWSKY.

To The Imperial Chancellor von Bethmann-Hollweg.

London, 19th February, 1914.

Prince William of Wied made an excellent impression here upon all the leading personages with whom he came into contact during his short visit. Sir E. Grey has just told me so expressly and I hear from a good source that His Majesty King George also spoke very highly of the Prince. Sir E. Grey informed him that he could feel assured of the sympathy of the British Government provided everything was avoided which might create the impression that Austria-Hungary and Italy were being permitted to enjoy undisguised precedence over the other Powers in Albania. The Minister also told me explicitly that he was quite prepared to advocate in Parliament the assumption by the British Government of one-sixth of the guarantee for the Albanian loan. He would, however, find it difficult to meet the objection that Great Britain had no direct interest in Albania and must therefore, in return for assuming obligations of that kind, at least demand corresponding participation in the Albanian Bank, in which Austria-Hungary and Italy were to hold the majority. Great Britain must also demand that the advance to be made to the Prince on account of the loan and repayable out of same must likewise be made subject to the supervision of the Commission de Contrôle. He did not intend discussing this question with me, but only desired to let me know his point of view confidentially. I replied that I had no precise information on the matter, but assumed that all the Powers had a like interest in the development of Albania and in the maintenance of peace in the Balkans, and that this interest was served by the undertaking to grant and guarantee to the young State the requisite resources to enable it to take the measures indispensable to the organisation of a modern State. An undue restriction of the rights and authority of the young Prince and his subjection to the financial tutelage of the Control Commission would from the very outset still further increase the difficulties of a task already sufficiently delicate in itself. Sir Edward understood this perfectly, and I do not think that serious difficulties are to be anticipated from him in the two outstanding questions of participation in the Bank and of the control of the loan.

LICHNOWSKY.

To The Imperial Chancellor von Bethmann-Hollweg.

London, 29th May, 1914.

Sir Edward Grey had, as I have already reported elsewhere, given me clearly to understand that he was not in a position to advocate the despatch of British troops from Scutari to Durazzo. The plan could not, he stated, be carried out without the consent of the Cabinet, but he was not disposed to support the proposal in the Cabinet.

Meanwhile the Minister has gone away for several days and is not expected back till next Thursday. As regards the aggravation of the situation at Durazzo I wanted to ascertain whether the London

attitude had undergone any change in the interval. I had occasion
to learn that the Minister has stated quite recently in a letter that
despite the renewed pressure on the part of Italy he sees no reason
to alter the attitude of refusal which he has hitherto adopted. The
British Government doubtless views the development of affairs
in Albania with grave anxiety and is perfectly aware that the great
Powers, who created Albania, have an interest in preventing it from
falling into chaos, and that in the long run therefore Great Britain
could not confine herself to the passive rôle of a bereaved mourner.
The British representative, Mr. Lamb, I learn confidentially, takes
the view that it will eventually be impossible to avoid the despatch
of international troops, and that on a more or less extensive scale,
something on the lines of the Chinese expedition. But it is just this
recollection of China which produces a somewhat deterrent effect
here and makes the Government anything but anxious to go to
Parliament and ask the British people for soldiers and money for
objects that are utterly remote from Britain's real sphere of interests.
There is little to be achieved by the despatch of a few troops from
Scutari, it is declared here, and the embarkation of a large force
could only be resolved upon, if at all, when all other means of establishing order have been exhausted.

In the British Government's view one of the best means of consolidating the position of the Prince and opening the way to an
effective administration lies in the earliest possible settlement of
the loan and of the related Bank question. The slow progress that
has been made in the last two matters is thought here to be the
fault of the Austrian Government, whose obstinacy prevents an
agreement with France. London is also inclined to ascribe a good
deal of the blame for the untoward state of affairs to the behaviour
of the Austrian agents in Albania, who are considered here to have
gone far beyond their official instructions. The Albanians, it is
declared, wanted to be ruled by all the Powers together and not by
Austria and Italy. The occupation of Albania by Austria and
Italy, however, should it become necessary, would leave both
Government and public opinion here fairly undisturbed except for
the fear that it might give rise to disputes between the two Powers.
But all these considerations are being pushed into the background
by a sense of disgust with the Albanian problem and by a disinclination to expend British forces for Albanian ends beyond the minimum
necessary for the maintenance of European peace. LICHNOWSKY.

To The Imperial Chancellor von Bethmann-Hollweg.

London, 15*th June*, 1914.

Sir Edward Grey told me to-day that he had not yielded to the urgent request of the Italian Government for the landing of troops in Albania, as British interests there were too slight, and it was impossible to measure the consequences of a military intervention. Five hundred men would be asked for at the start, and as soon as they proved to be insufficient a further instalment would be required. Once you had begun it was difficult to refuse subsequent reinforcements and still more difficult to withdraw from the country. He had therefore contented himself with despatching a British warship to ensure the safety of the Prince's family if necessary. That was all he was willing to do.

I did not gain the impression that this attitude on the part of the Minister was brought about by any discomposure. I am rather of the opinion that he thinks it undesirable, in the absence of any real British interests, to become involved more than is absolutely necessary in Albanian complications.

Lichnowsky.

To The Imperial Chancellor von Bethmann-Hollweg.

London, 15*th June*, 1914.

In the course of my visit to-day Sir Edward Grey again raised the question of Albania, where the situation appears to occupy his constant attention. He repeated in effect his recently expressed view that England had no direct interests there and was therefore unwilling to despatch troops by way of participating in an international occupation of the country. Italy and Austria did not want to act alone for fear of misunderstandings and other Powers would doubtless be as little inclined as England to join in. It was therefore difficult to know what to do. He personally would have no objection to the transference of the Government to Scutari, though to avoid giving offence in any quarter he would take no sort of initiative. The Austrians in particular were averse to this idea.

The Minister had to admit my objection that such a measure would look like a flight from the rebels and would therefore damage the prestige of the Prince, but said his idea was to obviate the Prince's abdication.

As regards the correct mode of addressing the Prince Sir Edward said that ' Highness ' was the customary English term, and that he considered this title appropriate provided we agreed.

LICHNOWSKY.

To The Imperial Chancellor von Bethmann-Hollweg.

London, 24th June, 1914.

Sir Edward Grey had invited me to come and see him to-day in order to discuss the political situation with me before my departure. He mentioned first of all the collision that was threatening between Greece and Turkey, and thought that events had momentarily taken a more favourable turn, so that there was some hope that the worst might be avoided. As he had already explained to me he particularly desired the avoidance of fresh complications through the closing of the Dardanelles, though he did not see how he could undertake to forbid the Turks taking such a step, since we were not in a position to assume any corresponding responsibility on our part ; but he hoped, as already indicated, that war might still be avoided.

Turning to the question of Albania the Minister again took up the same attitude as before, namely, that he could not justify to the country his sending British forces against the Albanian rebels. Public opinion in England would never tolerate such a step and Parliament would not fail to declare its opposition forthwith. In these circumstances there was nothing left but to look calmly on and let things take their course. Should the Prince be compelled to abdicate it had been proposed that the Government be transferred to the Commission de Contrôle. He would have no objection to this, only it would have to be realised that the Commission de Contrôle could not put its will into effect unless it had force at its disposal. From his own point of view he would not mind at all if Austria and Italy, as the most interested Powers, were to unite in establishing order in Albania. This idea, however, broke down, he said, on the unwillingness of the two Powers to be left alone there.

LICHNOWSKY.

EIGHTH SECTION

THE ANGLO-GERMAN COLONIAL CONVENTION.

Note.—From the outset the British Government, for reasons both of home and foreign policy, laid it down as a *sine quâ non* for the conclusion of a new treaty that both the new treaty and all the old ones should be published. Sir E. Grey also considered it of great importance that ' this treaty should demonstrate the unanimity between the two Governments and show the world that it was possible to reach agreement in such fields.' Despite this plain statement it was not till shortly before the outbreak of the war that the German Foreign Office could be induced to permit the publication and ratification of the new treaty, long after it was complete ! One pretext after another was sought in order to find some way of rendering the treaty abortive.—The whole attitude of the British Minister, at any rate, showed his sincere desire for a *rapprochement* with us.

TO THE IMPERIAL CHANCELLOR VON BETHMANN-HOLLWEG.

LONDON, 20*th November*, 1912.

I have just had a detailed discussion in the House of Commons with Sir E. Grey on the Portuguese Colonial Convention, in which Mr. Lewis Harcourt also took part. With the aid of the maps with which I had been provided and of the instructions received in Berlin I endeavoured to turn to account every line of argument tending to justify our claim to the left bank of the Zambesi. I spoke of the small economic value of the Angola enclave, of the inferiority of the port of Loanda, and no less of the accommodating spirit in which we had met the British Government by renouncing Timor, as otherwise this part of the treaty might have become a source of embarrassment to the London Cabinet. They replied that Timor was of no importance to them and they renounced it too. I soon saw that by dwelling longer on this question I should merely put both Ministers out of humour without the prospect of making any advance along this road towards our main goal, the territory north of the Zambesi.

The enclave in Angola, they maintained, was by no means without value to England, containing as it did the Ambacca railway and the port of Loanda. It formed, moreover, North Rhodesia's outlet to the Atlantic. To surrender the other approach to the sea in the Indian Ocean direction as well was impossible. The disputed territory should be annexed to British Nyassaland and the remainder of Mozambique, of course, to South Africa. The Government could not go to the public with a treaty on the lines of our latest proposals. If we insisted on the Zambesi triangle, that was the end of the matter ; alternatively, we could advance the southern boundary of the Angola enclave northwards as already indicated by Herr von Kühlmann, leaving England with the northern part of Angola.

Being convinced that further insistence upon our wishes respecting the Zambesi triangle would not only bring the whole matter to the ground but arouse a certain ill-feeling towards us in the minds of the present Government, I considered that I was acting upon my instructions when I did not go into further details as to the last offer just mentioned, but agreed that the British Government should prepare draft memoranda in which the old treaty together with the present additions should be combined into a fresh agreement. As soon as I receive this draft I shall not fail to submit it to Your Excellency.

As regards São Thomé and Principe, the Ministers declared themselves against including these islands in the existing treaty as they did not wish to have the obligation to take common defensive measures against foreign attack extended to the said islands. It would be sufficient, they thought, if the British Government declared its disinterestedness in a separate note ; we in return should give up Timor, which would then be struck out of the old treaty.

As a further condition, which they designated as the sine quâ non of a new treaty, the Ministers laid down the publication of the entire treaty, and that on grounds both of home and foreign policy. It was impossible, they held, to put off indefinitely answering further enquiries as to the contents of the treaty. They had already had to communicate the main contents to the South African Government, and if the secrecy were maintained it would be impossible in the long run to prevent encroachments by the one nation on the preserves of the other. *Sir E. Grey also said that he was most anxious that this treaty should demonstrate the unanimity between the two Governments and show the world that it was possible to reach agreement in such fields.*

I should like to point out at once that it is not only a question of informing the Portuguese Government but also of laying the treaty before the British Parliament, and I do not think that London would agree to postpone the date of publication for very long. Reasons of party politics may also play a part in the matter, as the Government is being attacked by its own party, especially by the ' National Liberal League,' which accuses it of neglecting its relations with Germany for the sake of its friendship with France.

In the situation as it stands I do not think it would be advantageous to attempt any substantial alterations in the English proposals. It would have no prospects of success, and would not only bring about the breakdown of the Colonial Agreement, *but also ruin a favourable opportunity of considerably improving the relations between the two countries.* I would also like to suggest for your consideration that it might be desirable, in view of the general political situation at present existing, and *of the urgent desire which obviously animates the London Cabinet to conclude the matter with us as soon as possible, that you should meet them in this respect.* As I have said, there is nothing more to be gained, and London will certainly not be disposed to renounce publication. *I also have the feeling that a quick settlement of the matter would put Sir E. Grey in a much more favourable mood to listen to our other political wishes.*

Finally, I might observe that the Ministers gave me the assurance that the South African Union would do nothing against Mozambique without the consent of the Mother Country, and that any step taken from that quarter was to be regarded as within the framework of the treaty and in fulfilment of same. The Minister has, however, given no indication as to how he conceives giving effect to the treaty, and I had the impression that he would rather refrain from binding himself in this matter for the moment.

LICHNOWSKY.

TO THE IMPERIAL CHANCELLOR VON BETHMANN-HOLLWEG.

LONDON, 17*th January*, 1913.

Sir Edward Grey some days ago handed me the enclosed draft of a new agreement on the Portuguese Colonies, which is to replace the former treaty, the secret treaty and the secret note of 1898.

As regards the territorial question it is stipulated in Article 11 that England shall receive that part of the Province of Mozambique lying south of a line drawn from the mouth of the Lukugu or Likungo River along this river to its confluence with the Lugera or Luzhella River, thence along this river to its source, northwards from there to the 16th parallel of south latitude and along it to the British Nyassaland Protectorate. Similarly in Angola all the territory east of the 20th meridian of east longitude and south of the 11th parallel of south latitude. All other territory in the two Portuguese Colonies goes to Germany's share.

Article VI. contains England's renunciation of the above territories, and also of the islands of São Thomé and Principe ; a like renunciation is expected of Germany with regard to England's share, including the Portuguese portion of the island of Timor.

Article IX. contains, in view of publication, a modification to the extent that mention is now only made of acquiring influence or supervision over the administration, whereas in the original treaty the wording was, ' in case Portugal renounces her sovereign rights over Mozambique, Angola and Portuguese Timor or loses this territory in any manner.'

All details as to the proposed alterations may be seen both from the enclosed copy of a letter I have received from Sir E. Grey and from the parallel texts also enclosed. I bring to your notice in addition a draft note to the Dutch Government on Timor which has been handed to me.

On the same occasion I endeavoured, without being able to go into closer detail, to point out as instructed that *we still continued to have serious misgivings on the question of publication.* I hinted, however, that under certain conditions we should not be disinclined to align ourselves more closely with the desires of the British Government. The principal condition I indicated to be an arrangement whereby, if one of the two Governments or their Colonies were compelled to safeguard its interests by occupying Portuguese Colonial territory or taking over its administration, the other contracting party would be entitled to take analogous measures in the area assigned to it by the treaty.

Sir E. Grey made no reply to my observation and I had the impression that he wanted to avoid the discussion of this question for the moment or was not properly prepared to negotiate. He also appeared to consider it important that the British draft should first of all be examined and accepted.

I think, however, that I ought already at this stage to express

L.H.A.   S

my doubts as to whether the British Government will accept an arrangement giving both states equal liberty of intervention with corresponding rights as to analogous measures. Sir E. Grey's political conscience would probably feel it an open violation of the Anglo-Portuguese Treaty if the fate of the Colonies were thus placed in our hands and left to our discretion.

It would not, however, conform with our interests if the future execution of the treaty were left, as far as we are concerned, exclusively dependent on whether and when the Cape Colony thought fit to take drastic steps in Mozambique. I think, therefore, it would be of advantage if two further agreements, both of which Sir E. Grey has discussed in outline with Count Metternich and Baron von Marschall, were drawn up in the form of an exchange of notes. The first would lay down that should the whole or part of a Portuguese Colony declare its independence treaties between England and the Mother Country should be held inapplicable to such territory, while all the provisions of the Anglo-German agreement would remain in full force. The second would lay down that, should the maladministration of their Colonies by the Portuguese occasion the intervention of third Powers, Portugal could not invoke the protection of the treaties of alliance nor expect assistance from England. I think Sir E. Grey would raise no objection and would embody these three points in an exchange of notes ; also that he would undertake to communicate the last of them to Portugal when notifying her of our agreement.

Should the London Government reject the first proposal the three provisions above mentioned would nevertheless enable us to take independent measures of our own. If we could gain influence over the administration of substantial areas in Angola through the establishment of a Chartered Company or in Mozambique by acquiring the majority in the Nyassa Company, it might perhaps be possible to apply the paragraph about Colonies or portions thereof becoming independent. It might also become easy to give practical application to the paragraph about the endangering of important interests through maladministration once we have proceeded with energy to the creation of economic interests, especially in railway matters. Economic penetration, I take it, will be the first thing to be taken into consideration by way of preparing for the possible assumption of political control later on. It will, I think, be as well for the time being not to lay too much stress on political acquisition in dealing with Sir E. Grey and the British. For though no one has any doubt as to the practical meaning of the treaty it is repugnant to their feelings to abandon too openly to another Power a small and defenceless people with whom they are after all in alliance, and it could only serve to promote our relations in general if we showed some kind of consideration for their prejudices and sensibilities in carrying out these changes in the ownership of colonial territory.

I am increasingly gaining the impression that *Sir E. Grey and the British Government desire as far as possible to meet our wishes in colonial matters, partly in order to demonstrate their goodwill, partly to create some sort of outlet for what is called Germany's need for expansion and new territory.* I think, therefore, that the acceptance of the British draft in its essential points will create a favourable opportunity of getting our other desires met in a spirit of understanding and accommodation.

LICHNOWSKY.

To THE IMPERIAL CHANCELLOR VON BETHMANN-HOLLWEG.

LONDON, 21st *February*, 1913.

Sir Eyre Crowe has given me the following confidential information on behalf of Sir Edward Grey :

The Portuguese Minister had stated on behalf of his Government that considerable uneasiness had been caused by the news as to Anglo-German negotiations concerning the Portuguese Colonies which had appeared in one or two organs of the European Press, especially as there were numerous signs of a political *rapprochement* between Germany and England.

The Minister then enquired in detail whether a revision of the treaty of 1898 was really being considered, whether the statements in the Press as to the convocation of a conference for the discussion of African affairs were correct, whether Sir Edward Grey intended, in accordance with his promise previously given in the House of Commons, to publish the secret treaty of 1898 in the Blue Book now being prepared, and finally, whether the joint Anglo-German declaration of March 1912 could still be regarded as legally binding. Sir Edward Grey had sent the following answer to the Minister : Certain changes in the treaty in question had proved necessary and were being considered. Neither England nor any other country as far as the Foreign Office knew had ever thought of convoking a conference of the kind indicated. Sir Edward Grey still held the publication of all secret treaties as desirable in principle ; he could not at that moment say whether and when the treaty of 1898 was to be published. At any rate it would not be in the Blue Book now in preparation, which dealt exclusively with contract labour. None of the changes proposed in the existing agreements of 1898 had the slightest effect on Portugal's relation to this treaty, so that there was no ground for assuming that the above-mentioned Anglo-German declaration did not still hold good.

The Portuguese Minister finally enquired whether the Portuguese Government could answer Parliamentary interpellations in this sense, to which Sir Edward Grey replied that the Portuguese Government was free to declare whatever it thought best.

LICHNOWSKY.

To The Foreign Office.   London, 3rd March, 1913.

I consider an early reply to Sir E. Grey's note of 11th January, on Colonial questions urgently desirable. The successful conclusion of these negotiations would further improve our position with leading circles, whilst too long a delay might easily put them out of humour and lead to misunderstandings.   LICHNOWSKY.

To The Imperial Chancellor von Bethmann-Hollweg.

London, 20th March, 1913.

I have just had a discussion with Sir Edward Grey at the Foreign Office on the question of the Portuguese Colonies. Mr. Lewis Harcourt, the Colonial Secretary, was also present. Following my instructions I began by referring to the two supplementary articles with which we want to complete the draft treaty prepared by the British Government.

No objection was raised to using the Stanford map of Africa as a basis. As regards Kabinda both Ministers deferred any definite expression of their views, as they appeared unacquainted with the territory.

In Article II. they agreed to the elimination of the words ' or Likungo ' and ' or Luzhella.' Nor was any objection raised to the other alteration on page 1 of Article II.

The acceptance of the Kassai Valley as the boundary caused no difficulty. Mr. Harcourt merely observed that no one knew the exact position of the upper reaches.

The omission of the provision as to the island of Timor was refused, owing to the importance attached to that neighbourhood in Australia. The intention, I should explain, is to publish not the old treaty itself, but a short summary giving its territorial provisions. This is no doubt being done on Parliamentary grounds so that they can use Timor in order to meet a possible Unionist charge that the Government had carelessly surrendered the important western outlet to the sea, which would have formed the most convenient line of communication with Rhodesia and Cape Colony.

In pursuance of the above I handed the two Ministers a copy of the draft containing the necessary modifications, together with the letter, of which I enclose a copy, and in which I explained the grounds on which our desires were based. It also includes the two articles the acceptance of which Your Excellency has made a condition of our agreeing to the publication of the treaty.

Article I. immediately aroused various misgivings. Both Ministers declared that the concept of maladministration was difficult to define, and that it was contrary to the spirit of the Anglo-Portuguese Treaty to hand over the fate of the Portuguese Colonies to arbitrary disposal. I replied that independent intervention had already been anticipated in conversations with Baron Marschall, but that if the British Government objected to this formulation it would perhaps still be possible to replace mutual notification with mutual consent. They both answered that they must reserve their final decision, but could consent to no formulation which necessitated a portion of our agreements being kept secret. The original treaty was based on the presumption of a voluntary renunciation by Portugal of her sovereignty by alienation or through the secession of the Colonies from the Mother Country. An act of force, however, would be contrary to the principles on which the treaty had hitherto been based.

Article II. was accepted by both Ministers, but with the express limitation that the reciprocity should only be applicable to the Colony concerned. Should, for instance, the southern portion of Mozambique be annexed to Cape Colony the northern portion would have to pass to us. The annexation of the entire Colony to Cape Colony was ruled out of consideration, and likewise the possibility of taking another Colony as indemnification for such annexation.

Both Ministers promised to submit our desires to close examination and to inform me shortly of the result.

LICHNOWSKY.

To The Imperial Chancellor von Bethmann-Hollweg.

LONDON, 13th May, 1913.

I have the honour to enclose a draft just received of a new convention between us and Great Britain on the Portuguese Colonies,[1] together with an explanatory covering letter in reply to my last proposal. As Your Excellency may observe, the British Government meets our wishes in the main points. It is only in regard to Timor that it insists on retaining the provision struck out by us, and supports this attitude mainly on the ground that Timor must be received in compensation for São Thomé and Principe.

The chief innovation, however, is the acceptance of the two supplementary articles proposed by us, which under certain conditions should prepare the way for the execution of the treaty. In the first article, indeed, the British Government desires the omission of the last sentence concerning the appeal to the Anglo-Portuguese treaties of alliance, but I think that, in view of the rest of the wording, which affords the freest scope for reaching an understanding as to joint action in case of maladministration, we could without misgiving withdraw the proposed addition, which is regarded here as a violation of the existing treaty with Portugal.

The second Article has also been accepted by the British Government, with the limitation, however, that the other party is only entitled to annex the corresponding portion of the same Colony assigned to it by treaty.

As he has already told me before, Sir Edward Grey desires to communicate to the Portuguese Government a summary of the agreements of 1898 and then publish this summary simultaneously with the new treaty. He attaches particular importance to this, as he is anxious to demonstrate that the present treaty introduces no new policy, but rather continues that initiated by the Unionists under Balfour. It will be quite impossible to dissuade him from this course.

In these circumstances there is bound to be some mention of Timor, and I would advocate that we accept the draft note to be

[1] See annexe, page 279 and cf. pp. 285-288.

transmitted jointly to the Dutch Government. A recognition of Holland's right of preemption is likely to cause much less dissatisfaction in Germany than the idea of half Timor being acquired by England or Australia.

There is no doubt the present occasion has again shown what great pains the British Government is taking in order to meet our wishes and reach an understanding with us on all important questions. The early conclusion of the proposed agreement will be certain to contribute materially to the further strengthening of the *rapprochement* that has been growing of late. Both on general political grounds, therefore, and also in view of the possible outbreak of serious disorders in Portuguese Mozambique or Lourenço Marques I would strongly urge that we notify our acceptance of the draft at the earliest possible moment.

Convention.

In view of the possibility that Portugal may require financial assistance from some foreign Power or Powers, and in order to obviate the international complications which such a condition of things may produce and to preserve her integrity and independence the undersigned, duly authorized by their respective Sovereigns, have agreed as follows : [1]

For Articles I to VIII, see pages 285-287.

Article IX is identical with Article IX on page 287 as far as the words ' of which the customs revenues would be assigned to it under the present convention.' It further contains the following passage which was afterwards dropped : ' His Majesty's Government recognizes that the treaties of alliance between it and the Portuguese Government do not apply to colonies or parts of colonies of which the independence has been declared and recognized by both the high contracting parties.'

Articles X and XI correspond to Articles X and XI on page 288.

Articles XII and XIII correspond to Articles XIII and XIV on page 288 ; Article XII on page 288 having been inserted later is not found in the original draft here referred to.

LICHNOWSKY.

---

[1] As the final text of the Convention as given on pages 285-288 is practically identical with that here referred to, it has been thought unnecessary to print the text of the Articles twice over. In the case of Article IX, however, the final paragraph, which was eventually dropped, is quoted here. (Translator's Note.)

To The Imperial Chancellor von Bethmann-Hollweg.

London, 13th June, 1913.

I have just had a discussion with Sir Edward Grey and Mr. Lewis Harcourt on our wishes regarding the latest British draft of the Anglo-German secret treaty on the Portuguese Colonies destined for publication. Immediately on my return I had handed the Foreign Secretary our proposals in writing and explained the reasons, and was invited to-day to go to him and receive the British Government's reply.

As regards the introduction, both Ministers rejected any alteration of the present wording. It would not be a good thing, they argued, to extend the scope of the plan further and make it more general. Even supposing the probability of a financial collapse were not imminent, the main object of the plan was after all to create separate areas for the activity of British and German capital and enterprise. The financial assistance referred to in the introduction related, therefore, not merely to the pledging of the Colonies themselves or parts of them, but also to private activity in the districts concerned with a view to their being opened up and developed. Sir Edward Grey has already spoken in this sense with the former Portuguese Minister, Marquis de Soveral, who appeared to have precise information as to the details of the treaty. He is as anxious as ever to prevent the treaty from containing any edge directed against Portugal, and would rather have it appear as supporting Portugal's colonial development. He also wants to be in a position to tell Parliament that there has been no change in the principles of the treaty. Both Ministers therefore declared that they could not discuss any change in the introduction.

On the other hand both of them are willing to meet our wishes respecting Article VIII to the extent of accepting the addition of the words ' or the vital interests of the adjoining British and German Colonies and Protectorates.' That would mean our gaining our most important point with the British Government. The inclusion of an anti-slavery clause was, however, rejected on the ground of its absence from the previous treaty ; presumably with the object of creating as little offence as possible in Lisbon.

In Article IX the Ministers agreed to the elimination of the last clause in accordance with our desire.

This was the utmost that could be gained in the matter from the

British Government, and I should like to urge the desirability of our giving our final consent to the treaty as now formulated. The date of publication and of communication to the Portuguese Government could no doubt be settled by a further arrangement.

LICHNOWSKY.

To The Secretary of State at the Foreign Office.

LONDON, 1st July, 1913.

Now that the negotiations on the Portuguese Colonial Treaty are complete and no further alterations in the drafting can be obtained, it would be extremely desirable on political grounds if I could receive full powers to sign at the earliest possible moment.

To The Secretary of State at the Foreign Office, von Jagow.

LONDON, 2nd July, 1913.

Only a few words to-day to thank you for letter of the 29th just received. I will discuss the Armenian question again with Grey to-day or to-morrow and think he will be prepared to join us in opposing the exaggerated Russian plans for the reorganisation of Armenia, as he still continues to reject all proposals for partition.

The main object of my letter, however, is to ask you to be good enough to see that both the Colonial Treaty and the Baghdad Agreement, which are in Berlin for approval, are settled as soon as possible. I telegraphed about both questions yesterday, and consider it essential that we should not keep the British Government waiting much longer for an answer. It is urgently to be desired that both matters should be settled and the documents signed before my leave and before Grey goes away, that is to say, in the course of the present month. We have got about as much as we ever can get in both questions. The most we might stand to gain would be one or two minor improvements as to Baghdad. Procrastination will not help the matter ; on the contrary it would merely create a painful impression here. In the Portuguese bargain there is nothing more to be extracted. The sooner I receive full powers to sign the better.

As I have already told you, a definite tendency exists here not only to place no obstacles in the way of our colonial expansion but to facilitate it as far as possible, in order to divert our attention from the

*North Sea, by directing what they thus assume to be our land hunger to
regions which would not seem to affect Britain's power.* But they will
not be willing to include anything in the treaty which puts England
in the wrong as regards Portugal, and are therefore trying to avoid
everything which might be interpreted as giving away Portuguese
possessions.

LICHNOWSKY.

TO THE FOREIGN OFFICE. LONDON, *7th July*, 1913.

Have just thoroughly discussed contents with Sir E. Grey
and read over to him the Introduction and Article 3 of the secret
convention of 1898. The Minister laughed and said the passages
in question were certainly difficult to reconcile with the treaty of
alliance with Portugal since renewed, and that it was important for
him not to publish anything which was in too flagrant contradiction
with the latter. He appeared to understand our latest intentions
perfectly. He nevertheless still avoids expressing himself on them,
and again makes no reply to my suggestions thereon.

I should like once again to repeat that London wants to place no
obstacles in the way of our aspirations for colonial expansion and is
indeed for obvious reasons not displeased to see our energies seeking
outlets in remote parts of the world.

On the other hand, England does not want to be forced into a
position involving the confession of a manifest contradiction with
obligations assumed in other quarters. In order to meet my desire,
however, Sir E. Grey wanted to discuss the matter once again with
Harcourt. A solution may perhaps be found in uniting both
renderings.

LICHNOWSKY.

TO THE IMPERIAL CHANCELLOR VON BETHMANN-HOLLWEG.

LONDON, *18th July*, 1913.

As already reported Sir E. Grey has let me know that after
consulting with Mr. L. Harcourt he is ready to insert the new draft
proposed by us in the Introduction to the latest draft of the treaty
on the Portuguese Colonies. That would imply the combination of
the two wordings together, making the whole Introduction read as
follows :

' Having regard to the possibility that Portugal might require the financial assistance of one or more foreign Powers, and with the object of avoiding the international complications which might be caused by such a condition of affairs and of maintaining the integrity and independence of Portugal, and having regard to the existing special interests of Germany and Great Britain in their Colonies and Protectorates in East and West Africa adjoining Portuguese territory, the undersigned, duly invested with full powers by their Sovereigns, are agreed as follows ' :

I had proposed this solution in order to make it easier for the British Government to meet us, as I believed that the resulting formulation took full account of the wishes of both sides, and I think its acceptance affords new proof that London wants to meet our Colonial desires in every possible way, provided at the same time the forms are observed which are required by a sense of political decency and by consideration for existing prior obligations.

As regards publication I do not think that our desires will meet with serious difficulties.   In order not to prefer too many demands at once I had only brought up the change in the Introduction in my last discussion with Sir Edward Grey on the question.   Since then, however, I have been able to learn that they will be ready to postpone publication for some time longer provided the treaty is initialled now, and I imagine they will be willing to wait in any case till after the reassembly of Parliament, which will not be till the New Year. I would therefore like to ask Your Excellency to empower me to initial as soon as possible.   Meanwhile I will get into touch with the Foreign Office with a view to having a more exact draft of the wording prepared so as to coincide in both languages, but should like to observe now that it will perhaps be a good thing to use the present English draft as a basis as far as at all possible, as any change would necessarily lead to complications.

LICHNOWSKY.

To THE FOREIGN OFFICE.   LONDON, 28th July, 1913.

Sir E. Grey is agreed to postpone publication of the treaty pending a mutual decision.   Next winter was indicated as the earliest, not the latest date, without binding obligation for us.

Report follows shortly.

LICHNOWSKY.

To The Imperial Chancellor von Bethmann-Hollweg.

London, 31st *July*, 1913.

As already reported Sir E. Grey had declared to me his consent to the postponement of the signature and publication of our treaty on the Portuguese Colonies pending a mutual decision on the matter. He had also, as may be seen from my report, contemplated next winter not as the latest but as the earliest date, so that we are under no sort of binding obligation in this direction. In these circumstances it appears to me doubtful if it would be a good thing to insist further on the matter being determined by an exchange of notes. The Minister's ready assurance of his desire to regard our wishes and interests should be quite sufficient, apart from the fact that for the present no signature is required.

Sir Edward Grey sent me on the same day the enclosed English text drawn up at the Foreign Office, together with a letter of which I enclose a copy.

Meanwhile the German translation has undergone a thorough revision and has been exhaustively discussed with the competent specialist at the Foreign Office but without committing anybody. I have the honour to enclose herewith two copies of the improved German text, which the British Government would very probably be prepared to recognize officially. Lichnowsky.

To The Foreign Office. London, 13th *August*, 1913.

The Portuguese Colonial Treaty has just been initialled by Sir E. Grey and myself. I took occasion to mention once again that minor alterations of an exclusively verbal character might perhaps be necessary in the German translation, so as to get a more exact rendering. Lichnowsky.

Convention [1]

In view of the possibility that Portugal may require financial assistance from some foreign Power or Powers and in order to obviate the international complications which such a condition of things may produce and to preserve her integrity and independence and in view of the special interests of Great Britain and Germany in their

[1] I have here copied the original English text of the Convention, kindly placed at my disposal by the German Foreign Office. (Translator's Note.)

respective possessions and protectorates in East and West Africa contiguous to certain Portuguese dominions the undersigned, duly authorised by their respective Sovereigns, have agreed as follows :

ARTICLE I

(1) Whenever either the British or the German Government is of opinion that it is expedient to accede to a request for an advance of money to Portugal on the security of the customs revenues or other revenues of Mozambique or Angola, it shall communicate the fact to the other Government and the other Government shall have the right to advance a part of the total sum required.

(2) In the event of the other Government signifying its intention to exercise this right the two Governments shall consult as to the terms of the two loans and these loans shall be issued on the securities of the customs revenues of Mozambique and Angola, as nearly as possible simultaneously. The loans shall bear as nearly as possible the same proportion to each other as the amount of the customs revenues respectively assigned as their security.

(3) The loans shall be issued on terms as favourable to Portugal as the condition of the money market and the security of the loans permit and shall in other respects be subject as nearly as possible to similar conditions.

ARTICLE II

In the contingency contemplated in the preceding article the customs revenues of that portion of Mozambique lying south of a line starting from the mouth of the River Lukugu, running thence along that river to its confluence with the River Lugera, thence along that river to its source, thence along the meridian of that source to the sixteenth parallel of south latitude and thence along that parallel to the boundary of the British protectorate of Nyassaland, as also the customs revenues of the province of Angola lying to the east of the 20th meridian of east longitude and south of the Kassai River, shall be assigned to the British loan ; whilst the customs revenues of the remaining parts of the provinces of Mozambique and Angola (which latter includes the administrative district of the Congo which has its seat of government at Cabinda) shall be assigned to the German loan.

ARTICLE III

In the event of Great Britain or Germany sending delegates to take note of the collection of the revenues, which are the security for their respective loans, the Portuguese Government shall be asked to give such delegates right of inspection only, but no rights of administration, interference or control so long as there is no default in the payment of interest or sinking fund.

ARTICLE IV

In case of default in the payment of the interest or sinking fund of either loan, it shall be agreed with the Portuguese Government that they will hand over the administration of the various custom houses in the two provinces : those assigned for the German loan to Germany ; those assigned for the British loan to Great Britain.

ARTICLE V

(1) In the contingency contemplated in the preceding article all rights, whether British or German, acquired in the provinces affected, before the date of this convention, shall be fully safeguarded, provided that they are of a purely private character and do not convey either political rights, territorial jurisdiction or administrative powers.

(2) It is well understood that no influence will be used in the future, either by the British or the German Government to obtain fresh concessions except in those portions of the provinces of which the customs revenues would be assigned to their respective loans under the present convention.

ARTICLE VI

From the date of the conclusion of the present convention Great Britain will abstain from advancing any claim of whatsoever kind to the possession, occupation, or control of those portions of the Portuguese provinces in which the customs revenues would under the present convention be assigned to Germany or of the islands of São Thomé and Principe or to the exercise of political influence in those territories or islands, and Germany will in like manner abstain from advancing any claim of whatsoever kind to the possession, occupation or control of those portions of the Portuguese provinces in which the customs revenues would under the present convention be assigned to Great Britain, or of the Portuguese parts of the island of Timor or to the exercise of political influence in those territories or in that island.

ARTICLE VII

(1) In the event of either Government obtaining from the Portuguese Government a cession of territory or the concession of

special privileges not of an occasional, that is, minor and temporary, character, in those portions of the provinces of Mozambique or Angola of which the customs revenues would be assigned to it, such cessions of territory or concessions of privileges shall not become operative until analogous drafts, as nearly as possible of equal value, have been accorded to the other Government in those portions of the provinces of which the customs revenues would be assigned to it by the present convention.

(2) In case either Government applies for special privileges of an occasional, that is, minor or temporary, character in those portions of the Portuguese provinces of which the customs revenues would be assigned to it under the present convention, it shall immediately inform the other Government and, if these privileges are granted, and if the other Government should so desire, shall use its influence to obtain for the other Government similar special privileges of an occasional character and of equal value.

Article VIII

If in any part of the provinces of Mozambique or Angola the lives or property of British or German subjects, or the vital interests of the adjoining British or German dominions or protectorates, are endangered by local disturbances or by the action of the local authorities, and the Portuguese Government are not in a position to afford the necessary protection, or otherwise fail to do so, the British and German Governments after consulting together, and after a joint communication to the Portuguese Government, shall determine the nature, duration and scope of such measures as it may be deemed necessary to take for the protection of the interests endangered.

Article IX

If any of the Portuguese colonies in question, having become independent and having been recognized as such by the two high contracting parties, or if any part of such independent colony, should declare its annexation to the dominion of one of the two contracting Powers, the other contracting Power shall, for its part, be entitled, after previously informing the first Power, to annex those portions of such colony thus become independent, of which the customs revenues would be assigned to it under the present convention.

ARTICLE X

Great Britain and Germany, having regard to the interests of their respective possessions in East and West Africa contiguous to the Portuguese provinces of Angola and Mozambique, which would be materially affected by the intervention of any third Power in those provinces, agree jointly to oppose such intervention whether by way of loan to Portugal on the security of the revenues of the said provinces, or by way of acquisition of territory by grant, cession, purchase, lease or otherwise.

ARTICLE XI

In so far as Great Britain or Germany may hereafter influence or control the administration of Mozambique or Angola or any portion of those provinces, it is understood that the subjects and natives of the protectorates of one contracting party, together with their goods and ships and also the produce and the manufactures of its dominions, possessions, colonies and protectorates, shall, in such portions of the territories comprised in the present convention as may fall under the influence or control of the other contracting party, participate in all the prerogatives, exemptions, and privileges with regard to trade, commerce, taxation, and navigation which are there enjoyed by the subjects, and natives of the protectorates, of the other contracting party.

ARTICLE XII

The effect of the provisions of the present convention is shown generally on the annexed copy of Stanford's Map of Africa, 1911.

ARTICLE XIII

The present convention shall replace the convention, secret convention and secret note concluded and signed in London on the 30th August, 1898, which are hereby abrogated.

ARTICLE XIV

The present convention shall be ratified and the ratifications thereof shall be exchanged as soon as possible. The convention shall come into force immediately after the exchange of ratifications.

In witness whereof the undersigned, duly authorised, have signed the same and have affixed thereto their seals.

Done in duplicate at London, the   day of   1913.
London, 20th October, 1913.

THE GERMAN MINISTER AT LISBON, DR. ROSEN, TO THE IMPERIAL
CHANCELLOR VON BETHMANN-HOLLWEG.

LISBON, *9th November*, 1913.

The Anglo-German Treaty on the Portuguese colonies
initialled in London on 20th October, which Your Excellency has
communicated to me in strict confidence, is in its present (final) form
a document whose far-reaching importance and substantial advantages for the German Empire can be recognized at a glance by
anyone with any sort of political training. Nobody who looks back
on the frequently clouded relations between Germany and England
during the last twelve years and remembers the numerous disappointments we have experienced in our efforts to expand our
economic and political activity, can help being surprised that the
final result of the prolonged negotiations has turned out so favourably
for us. This impression is further confirmed and strengthened on
closer examination of the treaty and on comparing it with the treaty
of 1898. Such a comparison of the two treaties must naturally be
made in two directions, namely, the partition of the spheres of interest
and the possibility of realisation. The loss of the Portuguese half
of the island of Timor, the advantage of which to us was always
more than problematic anyway, and of the strip on the left bank of
the Zambesi is, in my view, more than liberally compensated for by
our gaining Central Angola and by England's renunciation of São
Thomé and Principe, which two islands form probably the most
important part of all Portugal's colonial possessions. What we
surrender in Africa, namely, the Zambesi territory, which is entirely
under British economic control, and a relatively small part of eastern
Angola, is almost negligible as compared with the fact that our
sphere of influence in Angola will form, with German South West
Africa, a compact colonial area extending over 20 degrees of latitude,
where good ports and fertile highlands suitable for colonisation
promise an exceedingly prosperous development for the future.

The advantages of the treaty as regards the possibility of its
realisation appear to me still greater than any gains from the distribution of territory. The treaty of 1898 was based entirely on
the assumption that Portugal was on the edge of an unavoidable
financial collapse and would be glad to pledge its colonial customs
revenues against a loan from Germany and England. This
assumption has proved false. Portugal has taken up no large loan

since. Financially speaking, she has, if with some difficulty, kept her head above water, and of late it even looks as though she has put an end to her deficits and balanced her budget. The timely recognition of this fact has led Your Excellency to insert clauses in the new treaty which give scope to our aims independently of Portugal's need for loans, so that we have no need to fear a second time that what we have gained by treaty will be lost to us in practice.

Last not least, the whole agreement between the German and British Governments displays such balance and adjustment on all sides and so admirably satisfies the needs and interests of both parties that they must both have the feeling of having done a good piece of business. There is no occasion to fear that, as in other agreements both of old and recent date, one party will be left with a sense of grievance. On the contrary it may confidently be expected that *the publication of the treaty will substantially contribute to a permanent improvement in Anglo-German relations.*

As far as can be observed from here there are no indications that other Powers, France for instance, contemplate taking up a hostile attitude towards the Anglo-German understanding. Owing to some indiscretions in the Press my colleagues are of course becoming more and more inquisitive, but as yet their manner does not give ground for supposing that their Governments are seriously disturbed, and I have no difficulty in turning away their quite discreetly expressed enquiries without unfriendliness.

As regards the party principally concerned, Portugal herself, the moment is relatively favourable for the publication of the treaty. The country is so occupied with party feuds and conspiracies at home that the danger threatening its colonial possessions has not yet aroused the excitement which might otherwise have been expected. Days occasionally pass without any article on the colonial question appearing in the Press, and the few articles that do appear strike a note of more or less calm resignation. They call upon the Government to give this important matter its full attention, but do so without bringing forward positive proposals for averting the danger. When the text of the treaty becomes known we must certainly reckon on public opinion displaying a greater degree of excitement. But in view of the violent conflicts which will shortly follow the opening of Parliament even this will hardly be so pronounced as would be the case in normal times. ROSEN.

To The Imperial Chancellor von Bethmann-Hollweg.

LONDON, 15*th December*, 1913.

During my visit to Sir Edward Grey to-day I among other things brought up the Portuguese secret treaty for discussion. I mentioned that according to certain information which had reached us it appeared to be the intention in London to publish the so-called Windsor Treaty at the same time as our treaty. We were unaware of the contents, but should it chance to contain a paragraph in which England pledged herself to maintain the integrity of Portugal's entire colonial possessions, then the publication of our treaty would not in any way achieve the desired object of demonstrating the existence of a good understanding between the two Governments in the field of colonial politics. On the contrary, public opinion in Germany would reproach the Imperial Government with allowing itself to get into a mess, and England with not acting straightforwardly towards us.

Sir Edward Grey replied that the new treaty did nothing more than reaffirm the old, which certainly did mention the protection of Portuguese possessions. He had been unwilling to comply with the Portuguese Government's repeated and urgent requests for the publication of the treaty till he was also in a position to publish our treaty. Before, however, approaching the Portuguese Government and informing it of the contents of our agreements he wanted to acquaint me with the whole material, so that we should be in a position to determine in advance our attitude to the question.

In these circumstances I have thought it best to refrain from further steps, as that would place us in the position of having to make our consent to publication dependent upon the contents of the Windsor Treaty.

LICHNOWSKY.

To The Imperial Chancellor von Bethmann-Hollweg.

LONDON, 7*th January*, 1914.

On my visit to Sir Edward Grey to-day I again took occasion to point out that the simultaneous publication of the German and the Portuguese secret treaties would be bound to make a most unfavourable impression on German public opinion and that the proposal therefore caused the gravest misgivings on our side.

Sir Edward again replied that the so-called Windsor Treaty only contained a confirmation of the older one and had been concluded as a result of pressure from the Portuguese, who had got wind of our secret treaty. He had always rejected the repeated desire of the Portuguese for the publication of their treaty on the ground that it could only be published simultaneously with ours.

I replied that it made some difference whether the guarantee referred to Portuguese possessions as they stood in 1661 or in 1899. The Minister was obviously surprised by this objection and said this idea was quite new to him, and that he would like to examine the treaties again from this point of view. On my enquiring whether he was in a position to let me see the last treaty, since its contents would very materially affect our attitude, he promised me an early reply. He has apparently forgotten the exact contents of the treaties themselves and wants to study them thoroughly again.

He also gave me to understand that the question of publication was by no means urgent for him either.

LICHNOWSKY.

To The Imperial Chancellor von Bethmann-Hollweg.

London, 27th January, 1914.

In the course of my visit to Sir Edward Grey to-day he brought up our secret agreement on the Portuguese colonies and said he was willing to inform me of the contents of the so-called Windsor Treaty in accordance with our desire. This last treaty with Portugal substantially endorsed all the previous ones, but referred especially to two earlier Articles, namely Article 1 of the London Treaty of 29th January, 1642, and the secret Article of the treaty of 28th April, 1660. Under the latter, to which Sir Edward drew my particular attention, England promises ' to defend and protect all conquests or colonies belonging to the Crown of Portugal against all its enemies as well future as present.' The Windsor Treaty contained no fresh additions, but the British Government had certainly pledged itself to protect Portugal's possessions at all times and up to their actual extent at any given moment.

Sir Edward declared that he fully appreciated our misgivings, and appeared to understand that the simultaneous publication of both treaties would produce an undesirable impression on our side. He had therefore, he said, considered the matter and thought a solution was to be found in only publishing to begin with the treaties of 1898 and 1899, that is, the former Anglo-German and the last Anglo-Portuguese ; the publication of our latest treaty would not follow till later.

This would take the edge off the matter, as present statesmen could not be made responsible for earlier treaties ; our latest treaty would then subsequently appear as a mere natural continuation and could not therefore occasion attack or misconstruction.

The Minister, while desiring to publish the two treaties above mentioned, that is, those of 1898 and 1899, at the earliest possible moment, will undoubtedly be willing to delay the announcement of our latest agreement till a time convenient to us. He asked me to convey his proposal for Your Excellency's consideration. This I promised to do and withheld my reply for the time being. Will you please therefore put me in a position to give Sir Edward an early answer. I should mention that the Windsor Treaty repeats verbally the two paragraphs referred to, so that they will be known to the public without special documentary research. Despite sundry misgivings, I think I ought to accept the proposal made on this side, as it creates some sort of an historical basis and takes the onus off the present. The British Government can, however, hardly be induced to renounce publication altogether, as it feels bound by promises made to the Portuguese.

LICHNOWSKY.

To THE FOREIGN OFFICE.   LONDON, *7th February*, 1914.
FOR SECRETARY OF STATE VON JAGOW.

Your letter to hand. It is quite out of the question that London would discuss the inclusion in the preamble of our latest treaty of a clause expressly invalidating the Windsor Treaty. There could therefore be no object in authorizing me to approach Sir Edward with such a proposal. As I have repeatedly explained, the desire here is to bring the century-old treaty of alliance with Portugal, which was merely renewed at Windsor, at least formally into harmony with our treaty. No British Minister would agree to conclude a treaty which, while neglecting this formality and thus involving an open violation of the sovereign rights of Portugal, aimed at the undisguised spoliation of a friendly Power who in the present case was an ally as well. To the best of my knowledge even the treaties concluded with regard to Morocco guaranteed the full sovereignty of the Sultan in the first instance. All the treaties concluded with England with regard to the Portuguese colonies are formally concerned, in the main, with the creation of mutual spheres of interest. Our real intentions are perfectly well known here, and both treaties acknowledge them by taking within their purview conditions which open up the possibility of circumventing the old basic principle of the Anglo-Portuguese treaties and occasioning violent encroachments on Portuguese sovereign rights. I cannot therefore understand how the German public, especially if the publication is accompanied by suitable reference to the prospects and possibilities entailed, could object to the continuance and renewal of old treaties in the expectation that we and England should come to an arrangement in time of peace for the conquest of the possessions of a friendly Power.

LICHNOWSKY.

THE SECRETARY OF STATE AT THE FOREIGN OFFICE TO THE AMBASSADOR AT LONDON, PRINCE LICHNOWSKY.

BERLIN, 26th February, 1914.

I would certainly not have proposed in my last letter to you that the English should be induced to disclaim the Windsor Treaty in the preamble to our treaty had I been able to foresee that the idea of having to approach Grey in this sense would cause you so much alarm. I was of course only thinking of an incidental remark to the effect that as things now were there remained nothing else to do but to cancel the Windsor Treaty, just as England herself by this treaty annulled our agreements of 1898. Such a remark made half in jest, half in earnest, might easily lead on to a further discussion of the whole question. For, as I have already written you, Grey's proposal for the simultaneous publication of the treaties of 1898 and 1899 provides no suitable solution of the problem. It would not exactly serve our purpose to force on the notice of public opinion here the fact that our agreements of 1898 were already rendered illusory by England in 1899. Grey has repeatedly said, I believe in public too, how important it is for him to free English policy from the odium of untrustworthiness which encumbers it. There is hardly any doubt that his tenacious adherence to the Entente and especially, too, the far-reaching obsequiousness which he has displayed towards France in the Morocco question and which was not necessitated by the agreements of 1904 were ascribable in no small degree to the fear lest he might hear the cry ' perfidious Albion ' once more ring through Europe. I think that if you expressed to him your anxiety as to the reaction which England's 1899 trick might have on public opinion it would not fail to make an impression. Grey is no doubt an exceptional man in political as well as in private life and requires very cautious and skilful handling. But that is precisely where you seem able to score. I would remind you, for instance, of the episode last spring when we wanted to effect certain additions to the preamble of our treaty. You were at that time very dissatisfied with us and, as I happen to know, gave free rein to your annoyance at the ' bureaucracy ' prevailing here and at our deficient sense of what was possible in our dealings with England. All the more relieved did we feel when you were able to report shortly afterwards that Grey had laughingly acknowledged the correctness of your arguments. The preamble was duly amended as we desired and the treaty was thereby substantially improved, as viewed from the standpoint of its probable reaction on German public opinion. About the same time you, on 2nd July, wrote me in a private letter which I have before me, that in the Baghdad railway and Portuguese questions we had got about as much as we ever could get. You urgently advised the conclusion of the treaties. Yet look at all you have gained since then by calm, tenacious adherence to our demands, without in the least damaging our relations with England ! Good relations, after all, are not an end in themselves but are only worth while when they produce positive results. British policy pursues a sober, consistent course dictated by British interests and totally devoid of all sentimentality. There is no reason at all why we should not employ the same system. No special argument is needed to show that the publication of our treaties on the Portuguese colonies is not in accordance with our interests when the advantages and disadvantages are compared. (!) There is certainly some advantage in our having less fear of the penetration of English capital into our sphere of influence when the respective spheres have been publicly announced. Against this, however, there is the grave disadvantage of the resistance to be expected from Portugal to the penetration of German capital into the parts of the Portuguese colonies assigned to us. After strong resistance, as you know, we finally gave way to British wishes and declared our readiness to publish. When we did that we certainly did not imagine that England would conceal from us such an important fact as the conclusion of the Windsor Treaty. I cannot absolve Grey from the reproach of not having behaved quite frankly towards us in this respect. It is of course no use wanting to call him to account for that. But neither have we any occasion to make matters easier for him by accepting his argument that the Windsor Treaty is nothing but the old treaties of alliance over again. That is not the case at all. The treaty of 1660 does not contain *one word* pledging the British Government to protect Portugal's possessions at all times and *in accordance with their actual extent at any given moment.* If this pledge is contained in the *Windsor Treaty* then this treaty must go beyond the terms of Article 1 of the London Treaty of 1642 and the secret Article of the Treaty of 1660. Yet it can hardly be assumed that in 1899 England would have had the grim irony to guarantee her Portuguese ally in the possession of any future colonies it might acquire ! But if the English view was that such a guarantee was already contained in the old treaties, what on earth was the need for the renewal of these treaties in 1899 ? The English thesis is quite untenable, even if it is possibly useless to go into discussions about it. When you are talking to Grey it is nevertheless desirable to adhere to our view so as to strengthen our position.

As regards the further treatment of the matter, delaying tactics are to our advantage seeing that our economic schemes in Angola and Nyassaland will probably take some considerable time to realise. Please, therefore, when the matter comes up again, begin by pressing Grey once more to renounce publication of the treaties altogether. If he refuses, as is to be expected, then tell him that the most you think you can possibly manage is to get us to agree to publication provided the publication of the Windsor Treaty is withheld. Tell him I have observed in this connection that there is no indication in any of the reports from Lisbon—and these have been communicated to the Embassy—that England has pledged herself to the Portuguese Government to publish the treaty. In any case it is the British Government's affair to determine how it will arrange the matter with Portugal. It is not our business to rack our brains over that. There is indeed nothing to prevent attention being simultaneously drawn to the old treaties of alliance. If Sir E. Grey thinks the Windsor Treaty contains nothing that was not already in the others, the publication of the Windsor Treaty is superfluous. It is absolutely sufficient to refer to the old agreements! It would of course be better if even this could be avoided, as the conclusion will again be drawn by people here that our agreements are after all pretty worthless, and that they merely exist on paper. *In view of your great influence with Grey* and of your perfect mastery of the English language, I can hardly imagine you would not finally succeed in persuading him. If he is really keen on good relations with us, he must surely be prepared for a sacrifice that is of no great consequence in view of England's position in Portugal, where she can achieve everything she wants.

So be a little more optimistic in judging our English friends. I am disposed to think you sometimes take too black a view of things. This applies, too, to your opinion that in case of war England will be certain to take the side of France. After all we have not built our fleet for nothing, and I am convinced that in the event of war England will very seriously reflect whether it is such a simple and harmless matter to play the part of guardian angel to France against us. (!)

Your Marine Attaché's tendencious dispatch writing, by the way, is most objectionable. Can you not keep a tighter rein on him? These eternal denunciations and incriminations of English policy are extraordinarily disturbing, particularly because *en haut lieu* it is always being used in argument against me. This latter remark is of course strictly confidential.

JAGOW.

To The Imperial Chancellor von Bethmann-Hollweg.

LONDON, *3rd March*, 1914.

As already briefly reported, I have succeeded in inducing Sir E. Grey not to proceed for the present with the publication of the secret treaties, either ours or the one with Portugal. I represented to the Minister that the so-called Windsor Treaty, even if it did nothing more than confirm the previous Anglo-Portuguese treaties, would nevertheless produce an unfavourable impression on German public opinion and might in any case diminish the satisfactory effect resulting from our agreements. It would therefore be a good thing to defer publication of both treaties or forgo it altogether, and at the very least to exclude the Windsor Treaty.

The Minister replied that he was being pressed by the Portuguese to publish the last-named treaty, but that he did not want to disregard our wishes as he was anxious to avoid anything that might be calculated to disturb good feeling among the German public. He had been actuated-by two reasons when he took up the revision of the treaty. In the first place, *at a time when the relations between the two countries had been less favourable than they were to-day, he had desired by publishing the treaty to prove to the world that we were able to agree concerning important common interests*, and thus help to improve our mutual relations. Secondly, it was important for him to eliminate the island of Timor from the treaty out of consideration for Australia.

Our relations had in the meanwhile materially improved, so that it was no longer necessary to publish the treaty in order to create good feeling. Our mutual spheres of interest were now defined, and we could, for instance, pursue our plans in the Benguela Railway question. Under these circumstances he, too, had no reason at the moment for proceeding with the publication.

I learn in strict confidence that the French have made strong representations here about the contents of our treaty, details of which have become known in Paris. Particular objection is raised there to the inclusion of São Thomé and Principe in the treaty, as these islands lie north of the equator and therefore belong to the French sphere of influence. Paris is altogether uneasy about the increasing intimacy of our relations with England, and it is no doubt partly out of consideration for French susceptibilities that Sir Edward is prepared not to publish for the moment. The impending Royal visit will thus have been a means of furthering our desires in this direction.

LICHNOWSKY.

TO THE SECRETARY OF STATE AT THE FOREIGN OFFICE, VON JAGOW.

LONDON, *7th March*, 1914.

As you know from my dispatches the Portuguese affair has been settled for the present on the lines you desired. It is therefore unnecessary for me to enter more closely into the details of your letter of the 26th ult., although I cannot entirely agree with all you say. Whether, indeed, we shall succeed in preventing publication altogether is a question to which it is as yet impossible to give a definite answer. Grey will at any rate refrain from bringing up the matter again in the immediate future, partly, as I have indicated, out of deference to French susceptibilities. Once, however, the Paris visit is over and he has succeeded in easing the minds of the French concerning our agreements, I think it not impossible that he will then return to the question of publication. And I do not see how, in the long run, we are to keep the contents of our agreements quiet after so much has been said about them in public and the Chancellor has mentioned them in the Reichstag. I incline, moreover, to the view *that the treaty attains far greater importance after than before publication.* For its terms pretty clearly indicate that it means in practice the partitioning of the Portuguese colonies, even though the integrity of Portugal's possessions is formally confirmed and spoliation is not directly avowed. It would also doubtless not be unimportant from the general political standpoint if such a treaty between ourselves and England came before the public, and this is precisely the reason why London appears not exactly anxious for publication *at this particular moment* out of regard for Paris. Moreover, I do not by any means take the view, as you know, that the so-called Windsor Treaty of 1899 had 'annulled' our agreements. Even before their renewal the Anglo-Portuguese treaties were fully valid, as every British Cabinet again and again emphasized on widely separate occasions. And the secret Article of the Treaty of 1660, as a glance at the documents will show you, does actually contain a promise to defend all possessions of the Portuguese Crown for the present and the future. We were quite aware of this treaty in 1899, and no one at that time thought of demanding that it should be declared invalid. Any such request would therefore certainly be regarded here as a bad joke. It is quite intelligible that the Portuguese, on getting wind of our first treaty, pressed for the resuscitation of their antiquated alliance on the initiative of Soveral, but in point of fact our 1898 agreements with England were made on the basis of precisely the same assumptions as those of 1912 and 1913, and our public cannot reasonably expect us to conclude with a friendly State agreements as to the property of a third State likewise friendly and in alliance moreover with the other contracting party, when these agreements *undisguisedly* announce the spoliation of this third State in time of peace.

We need not get excited about this now, however, for the matter is, at least for the present, settled in the way you desired, and I do not think Grey will revert to the question of publication so very soon.   It is certainly another matter whether we consider it advisable to proceed to the final signature of the treaty, which has as yet of course only been initialled.   I have not yet discussed this with Grey, as I did not know what you wanted.   In my view early signature would be desirable, because it would bar the way to subsequent alterations brought in, let us say, to satisfy complaints from France.   Not that I think Grey would afterwards mutilate a treaty which he had already as good as concluded.   That would be entirely contrary to his otherwise honourable and straightforward nature ; but you never can tell whether the Unionists may not come into power, and whether Lord Curzon or Lord Lansdowne or whoever else takes over the Foreign Office will take the same view as he. Certain hints which have reached me suggest that London might quite possibly desire the signature of the treaty prior to its publication.   I should like, however, provided you agree, to mention the question of signature incidentally to Grey, and in doing so to take the line that I am personally very anxious to bring our treaty to a final conclusion, so as to have a positive achievement to my credit in this special sphere.

It would make my task very much easier both in this and in everything else if, in view of the forthcoming Paris visit, you could use your influence to restrain our Press from unfriendly and schoolmasterly criticism both of the visit and of Franco-British relations generally.   As you know, Sir Edward Grey will be accompanying Their Majesties, since M. Pichon came here with M. Poincaré.   Otherwise Sir Arthur Nicholson would have gone.   Naturally Grey would be considerably upset if this circumstance were made the subject of offensive comment, after the style of the *Kölnische Zeitung's* latest article on Russia.   As I have reported over and over again, the British Government is anxious to live *on good terms with us no less than with France.*   The *rapprochement* with us has been greeted with lively satisfaction by most English politicians and particularly by the business world.   London does not, however, desire the improvement in our relations to take place at the expense of the Entente with France, and an estrangement with Paris would expose Sir Edward Grey to violent attacks from his friends as well as from the Opposition, where Mr. Balfour, Lord Lansdowne and Mr. Chamberlain, for instance, are strong adherents of co-operation with France.

I learn in strict confidence that official French circles are disturbed at the growing cordiality of our relations with England and at the influence we exercise here.   The Colonial agreement in particular, of which the essential details are apparently known in Paris, seems to have aroused displeasure there and to have led to strong representations being made to Sir Edward Grey.   He will therefore endeavour to pacify the French and flatter their vanity ; it is also important for him to retain his influence there, because the internal development of that country inspires him with no great confidence and the return to reaction in Russia causes him additional disquiet.   The less our Press relapses into the blustering tone for which we unfortunately have such a partiality, and the less it adopts arrogant or bellicose language towards France, the less will he be compelled to break away from us.   For we need have no doubt that if he is faced with the choice, he will decide for France, just as we, if we had to choose between Austria and Russia, would decide for the former. The maintenance of France intact is just as much a political necessity for England as that of Austria-Hungary for us, and she would therefore, as I should like again to emphasize, *under all circumstances take France under her wing in the event of a war between that country and ourselves.   To my extreme regret this fact is still held in doubt despite my repeated and thorough elucidation of this important point.* It is just because England desires peace and wants to avoid being involved in a war to prevent a change in the existing balance of power that abstention on our part from all demonstrations suggesting that we want to cause trouble is the condition of Grey's readiness to meet our wishes and to cultivate the friendship of Germany.   I take every suitable opportunity of repeating in London that we have absolutely no objection to Franco-British friendship, as British influence in Paris has always made for moderation and peace, thus affording us no ground for complaint at the intimacy between the two countries.   Our aims and interests in England would best be served if the German Press struck a similar note in connection with the forthcoming visit.

LICHNOWSKY.

To The Foreign Office.   London, 26th March, 1914.

In view of the development of affairs in Ireland due to the failure of the English officers to take action, the early resignation of the whole Cabinet is by no means outside the realm of possibilities.

In these circumstances I should like to suggest that the political situation makes the early signature of the Colonial treaty appear extremely desirable. The resignation of Sir E. Grey might very gravely endanger the existence of the treaty, which still remains simply initialled. The Baghdad negotiations may, however, still take some considerable time. As regards the publication of the Windsor Treaty it may be seen from my dispatches :

1. That Sir E. Grey has postponed publication of both treaties indefinitely and has never thought of publishing anything at all without our consent ; and

2. That he wants to publish both treaties together, not one of them alone, and that therefore so long as our treaty is unpublished the Windsor Treaty will likewise remain so. Should, however, our treaty be published later by mutual consent this must necessarily be accompanied by the simultaneous publication of the Windsor Treaty.   LICHNOWSKY.

To The Imperial Chancellor von Bethmann-Hollweg.

LONDON, 1st *April*, 1914.

I had an opportunity of speaking to Sir Edward Grey to-day before his departure to-morrow. He had really wanted to leave yesterday, as now is the right time for fishing and Parliament is also just about to adjourn for the Easter vacation, but the state of parliamentary business necessitated his remaining for a day or two. He will probably be back in London shortly after Easter.

I told him I had come to ask him whether he had any objection to proceeding now to the signature of our secret treaty which had as yet only been initialled. I should extremely regret if after all the toil and trouble on both sides the work, when so near completion, were left unfinished. The result so far afforded a moral, but no legal guarantee, and it appeared to me undesirable to postpone the matter and leave it exposed to the vicissitudes of politics. I put in a word to the effect that while we had agreed to defer the publication of the treaties for the time being, I nevertheless thought a way might be discovered in the future of solving the question in a manner satisfactory to both parties, should this question of publication form an obstacle.

Sir Edward Grey replied *that he could not sign the treaty except on condition of publication.* He had repeatedly stated in public that he had no intention of making any new secret agreements, and it was therefore impossible for him to conclude a secret treaty. He had learned not only from me, but in much stronger terms from the Secretary of State himself through Sir E. Goschen, the fatal effects which the announcement of the Windsor Treaty would have on German public opinion, and there was nothing he desired less than to becloud the relations between the two countries. He repeated what he had said at our last discussion, that his principal object in revising our treaty had been to improve our relations, which at that time had not reached the present agreeable degree of warmth. If, therefore, as he learned, German public opinion would take offence at the Windsor Treaty the whole object would fail. For reasons, however, that were well known it was impossible for him not to publish the Portuguese treaty if ours saw the light of day. If our treaty were signed, both treaties must be published and as far as possible concurrently. Besides, our *locus standi* was the treaty of 1898, which had turned out quite well as the Benguela Railway showed.

I replied that the treaty of 1898 was much less satisfactory for both parties than the latest agreements, and was urgently in need of revision on geographical and practical as well as on political grounds. It would therefore be extremely regrettable if all our laborious work came to nothing over the question of publication, and I thought I could say there was perhaps some prospect of our being able to approach this question again after the end of the Reichstag session despite all our fears as to the effect of the Windsor Treaty. I again took occasion to emphasize that in my view both parties were already morally, even though not legally, bound by the terms of the treaty on the strength of the initialling, and that it would therefore hardly be right to omit the coping-stone at the last moment. It was of course no easy matter for me to cover up in some measure our sudden change of direction after all that I had been obliged to say to him hitherto against the publication of the treaties ; but I could see how well founded was my fear that our refusal to publish and England's regard for French susceptibilities would bring the whole treaty to the ground. I thought it better to avoid for the present all proposals as to the form of publication and to wait till the British Government came forward with its own proposals, provided, that is, it can be moved at all to resume the abandoned negotiations.

Sir Edward confined himself to repeating with emphasis that *he fully appreciated our objections to publication, but that this, of course, meant the treaty could not be signed.* Otherwise he listened to my suggestions with his usual friendliness, but said he must discuss the matter with the Prime Minister ; for the present he could give me no definite answer. I finally emphasized once more my hope that we should come to an agreement as to the date of publication, as we on our side were not fundamentally opposed to publication but merely considered it inexpedient just for the present.

My general impression was that he is very unwilling to return to the subject of the treaty at all, as he has no doubt given assurances to the French and has apparently stated in the Cabinet that he has let the treaty drop owing partly to our resistance to publication, partly to the susceptibilities of the French. At any rate various members of the Government have spoken to me in this sense without, however, mentioning France.

LICHNOWSKY.

THE SECRETARY OF STATE AT THE FOREIGN OFFICE, VON JAGOW, TO THE AMBASSADOR AT LONDON, PRINCE LICHNOWSKY.

BERLIN, *4th March*, 1914.

Please let the question of signing the treaty rest for the present and do not in any case bring it up again on your own initiative just now. We take the view that an initialled treaty at least implies a moral obligation and that the old treaty of 1898 also affords us the possibility of looking after our interests in the Portuguese colonies.

Should Sir E. Grey come back to the matter, please take the general line that there can be no question of publication so long as the Reichstag is sitting. I do not think the responsibility for this can fall on me. As regards the publication of our agreements with England this, pending a positive issue of our expedition to Angola, would endanger the success of an enterprise on which an infinite amount of trouble has been expended and which would form the first step towards the realisation of our aims. We would therefore, as things are, prefer to let the matter stand as it is and to content ourselves with the initialled treaty.

I entirely agree with your view that Grey's attitude is determined to a very large extent by consideration for France. I wonder whether we could overcome the difficulties by letting it be known to the British Government that we should be ready to abandon São Thomé and Principe in return for compensation elsewhere. Perhaps you would cautiously feel your way in responsible quarters and then kindly let me know your opinion.   JAGOW.

THE SECRETARY OF STATE AT THE FOREIGN OFFICE, VON JAGOW, TO THE AMBASSADOR IN LONDON, PRINCE LICHNOWSKY.

BERLIN, *17th April*, 1914.

With reference to my note No. 554 of the 4th instant :

Sir E. Goschen told me to-day that he had succeeded in convincing Sir E. Grey that the publication of the Windsor Treaty was not feasible, and read to me a letter from the Minister confirming your reports.

I explained to the Ambassador that though, in order to meet Sir E. Grey's wishes, we had offered our consent to the publication of the Windsor and Angola Treaties, provided it was done at separate times, we nevertheless preferred that publication should be withheld altogether and regarded the initialled treaty as an *obligation morale*. I hoped the time would come to enable us as soon as we had gained a sufficient footing in our sphere of influence on Portuguese territory to propose publication ourselves.

I now regard the matter as definitely settled, so please take no further steps.
                    JAGOW.

TO THE IMPERIAL CHANCELLOR VON BETHMANN-HOLLWEG.

LONDON, *23rd May*, 1914.

Mr. Harcourt was our guest last evening and I took the opportunity of discussing the question of the Colonial treaty confidentially with him after dinner. I pointed out that we regarded the initialled document as morally binding both on ourselves and on the British Government and were therefore very unwilling to allow the result of two years' hard work to come to nothing, when it satisfied the interests of both parties far better than the situation it replaced. On the question of publication I thought an understanding might perhaps be achieved later.

Mr. Harcourt expressed in reply his extreme regret that our misgivings about the Windsor Treaty had hitherto delayed the settlement of the matter and *had created a state of uncertainty which could not possibly continue for any length of time.* British enterprise and capital were now in the dark as to where they were, for no one could tell them for certain which was the British and which the German sphere of influence. An initialled treaty was no better than none at all and could not be taken as a basis, nor would it be recognized by a new Government in case the present one fell. *There were therefore only two possible alternatives, either to return to the old treaty and to regard the new one as invalid, or else to publish the new one together with the Windsor Treaty. The present situation, however, could not be tolerated for long owing to the uncertainty attaching to it.*

On this I should like to observe that I too do not think we have any other choice but to publish or else to go back to the treaty of 1898. Your Excellency is aware that I am unable to share the view that the objections to the Windsor Treaty outweigh the advantages arising from the new treaty and from the impression which must be evoked by an Anglo-German understanding in this field.[1]

LICHNOWSKY.

THE IMPERIAL CHANCELLOR VON BETHMANN-HOLLWEG TO THE AMBASSADOR AT LONDON, PRINCE LICHNOWSKY.

BERLIN, 29th May, 1914.

From your dispatch of the 23rd instant I observe that, in conversation with Mr. Harcourt, you have on your own initiative

---

[1] In a private letter dated 26th May, to the Secretary of State, von Jagow, I sought to allay the fears entertained in Berlin as to the unfavourable reaction which the publication of the Windsor Treaty might produce on German public opinion. I said in the letter : ' I should like once more to suggest your considering whether it might not be possible, when the treaties have been published, to hold out to some of the screeching Pan-Germans that no new situation was created by the '99 treaty (Windsor), and that, having regard to the alliance between England and Portugal and to the dictates of elementary political decency, our treaty could not proclaim the partitioning of the colonies by acts of annexation. The Windsor Treaty (you could say) fitted perfectly into a framework constructed on these lines, while our treaty afforded a suitable lever for future developments which were not affected by the alliance. If this were accompanied by skilful inspiration of the Press and by comment to the effect that the integrity of the Portuguese Colonial Empire remained assured, the thing could be managed quite well and the general impression would surely be in our favour. The Reichstag session is over ; there is still the possibility of elections here in the summer, and no one can know what will happen later. I would therefore urgently advise that no time be lost. In such matters everything depends upon the sauce with which the dish is served up. I often think we go a little too far in our nervousness about public opinion. The British, after all, have the same interest as ourselves that one of the events foreseen in the treaty should arise and thus afford them the opportunity of intervention. They too want to extend and consolidate their sphere of influence.' (Author's Note.)

brought up the question of the publication of the Anglo-German colonial agreement. I regret this all the more because this step was contrary to your definite instructions. You were told to make no further move in the matter. Your action has also had the very undesirable effect of again compromising the satisfactory situation which had been created by the declarations made here on behalf of Sir E. Grey by Sir E. Goschen, a situation entirely adequate to the needs of the immediate future. (?) In any case there is nothing to indicate that you had any arguments with which to meet the representations of the British Colonial Minister, or that you pointed out to him the extremely painful and unfavourable impression which would necessarily be made here if the British Government should subsequently be disposed to adopt Mr. Harcourt's standpoint. If, as is to be feared, Sir E. Grey should reopen the matter with you, please tell him that the Imperial Government regards the question of publication as closed for the present and that you therefore have no instructions, and, without letting yourself be drawn into further discussions, request him, if need be, to convey to me through the medium of Sir E. Goschen any fresh suggestions or representations he may have to make.

BETHMANN-HOLLWEG.

NOTE BY THE MINISTER AT LISBON, DR. ROSEN.

BERLIN, 30th May, 1914.

The reasons for or against the signature and consequent publication of the Anglo-German agreement must be examined from two points of view, that of the effect on international politics and that of the echo which the publication would probably arouse in Germany.

Among the effects on the external side, the main question to be examined is whether, if the Windsor Treaty is published simultaneously, the Anglo-German agreement would still be realisable at all, that is, whether it is to be assumed that England would place obstacles in the way of a German policy of gaining a gradual foothold in the Portuguese colonies, or would support such a policy to the best of her ability. The Windsor Treaty guarantees Portugal's possessions, and therefore also her colonies. It is obvious that this treaty is in flagrant contradiction to the spirit and letter of the Anglo-German treaty concluded a year earlier and affords at the first glance an apparent proof of English perfidy. It would hardly be going too far to say that it nullifies the Anglo-German treaty. But if the new treaty annuls the old one so also does the present Anglo-German treaty annul the Windsor Treaty. It does actually annul that treaty on definite assumptions and in definite points. It is a restriction of the Windsor Treaty and of all similar treaties of alliance between England and Portugal in the past. That and that alone can be the sense of the Anglo-German treaty. Unless we started from this assumption it would be entirely meaningless to conclude such a treaty at all.

So much for the formal side. The question now further arises what would be the probable attitude of England if, after the signing of the treaty, one of the possibilities which it anticipates became ripe for realisation. Nothing could be more misleading than to draw conclusions as to the present from the circumstances that prevailed at the turn of the century. At that time the ill-feeling between England and Germany was at its height, while Portugal was far more dependent on her ally than now, owing to her King's friendship with King Edward and to the exceptional position which the Marquis de Soveral enjoyed in his relations with the British Court and Cabinet. England has not the same sentiments towards the Portuguese Republic that King Edward had for the Monarchy, nor does republican Portugal regard herself as the vassal of the British Empire to anything like the same extent as the Monarchy did in those days. And above all, public opinion in England to-day is by no means friendly towards the Portuguese colonial régime in Africa. The agitation of the Anti-Slavery and Aborigines Protection Society against the ' slavery ' practised by the Portuguese in São Thomé and Angola, the campaign of the Duchess of Bedford against the treatment of political prisoners by the Republic, and to a certain extent the anti-republican feeling created by the ex-King among the upper ranks of society in England, all these things have prepared the ground for an understanding with Germany and would ensure the publication and even the execution of the treaty being favourably received. But the British Government will undoubtedly follow the course which corresponds with public opinion in the country. The only question now is whether the Cabinet of St. James might be actuated by considerations of foreign policy in a possible conflict between Germany and Portugal to take the side of Portugal, the agreement notwithstanding. Of the Powers, that is to say, France and Spain, which are interested in south-western Europe and Africa, Spain is directly hostile to the Portuguese Republic and would be delighted at any events which seemed likely to undermine the Republican régime in Portugal. On the other hand, it is certain that France is unfavourably disposed towards any extension of German power and to any *rapprochement* between England and Germany. Meanwhile the British Government has already proved on several occasions that it is determined to stand by us against French objections to the agreement. If all these considerations are taken into account, there is no reason to fear that England would come to the protection of the Portuguese Colonial authorities against ourselves and for Portugal's sake risk an inevitable conflict with Germany.

We now come to the question as to what effect the ultimate publication of the agreement is likely to have on Portugal itself. The first effect would undoubtedly be to produce dismay. Portugal would consider herself betrayed and despoiled by her old ally. The feeling of alarm might possibly go so far as to shatter the Republican régime. In any case we must be prepared for a storm of indignation and expect this storm to be directed rather against Germany than against England, despite the latter's bad faith. This outburst, though perhaps violent, will certainly not be of long duration if the two great Powers face it with equanimity. It will doubtless be followed by a feeling of resignation to an inevitable fate. Some such feeling is already noticeable among broad circles of the politically minded. People will reflect that it will be better to allow free play to the aspirations of their two big colonial neighbours for economic expansion than to invite conflicts with them. Once the agreement is published such conflicts would be inevitable if concessions were refused. The Portuguese would make a reservation, more or less seriously intended, as to rights of sovereignty whenever a concession had to be granted, and would seek to pacify their own public opinion with the assurances thus obtained from both Governments. . . . The continuance of the present situation, on the other hand, would have an entirely different effect. A tendency is already noticeable in Portugal to give as many and as important concessions as possible to English firms in what is assumed to be the German sphere of influence, and to place enterprises already begun there on an ' international,' that is presumably a French financial basis. If such a plan succeeded, we should have achieved with our treaty the very opposite of what we were aiming at, and a large and promising market for our industry would have been lost instead of won. It should be remarked, moreover, that experience has shown that English enterprise fights shy of areas which are not English or subject to English influence.

Whilst these considerations leave scarcely any doubt that the prospects of realising the treaty would only be enhanced if it were signed and published, another important side of the question nevertheless remains to be studied, namely, the effect which publication, as far as can be foreseen, would have on public opinion in Germany. It must be admitted at once that the Windsor Treaty, which followed so closely on the agreement of 1898 and appeared to contradict it, can only be expected to produce an unfavourable impression. As already pointed out, it will be taken as proving the unreliability of British policy, which within a single year could conclude two mutually contradictory treaties. From this people will probably draw the inference that the present agreement will also prove valueless for us. Certain quarters might even reproach the Government with allowing itself to be imposed upon despite all the experiences that we have already had. One could go to still further lengths and fear lest the tender plant of Anglo-German understanding might perhaps be destroyed by a storm of indignation sweeping through the German Press. Such eventualities must naturally make it seem advisable rather to leave the agreement in its present half-finished state than expose it to the above-mentioned dangers by publication.

It would be foolish to underestimate these dangers, which have their roots deep down in our Parliamentary life. On the other hand, it would be just as big a mistake to attach more importance to them than they warrant. With the aid of suitable preparatory work among the political parties, and especially in Press circles, it would be possible to create an atmosphere favourable to a correct appreciation of the importance of the Agreement without necessarily having to reveal its contents prematurely. The most essential thing would be to show, in a series of newspaper articles, how very different the situation was fourteen years ago from what it is to-day. The events of those days are not yet too remote for the German newspaper reader to understand the difference. Close upon the heels of the agreement of 30th August, 1898, followed the threatened outbreak of war in South Africa, a war in which, of course, the feeling in Germany was profoundly hostile to Great Britain. The seizure of German mail steamers and various other incidents still further embittered the feeling between the two countries. The unfavourable progress of the Boer War compelled the British to have recourse to the services of their Portuguese allies. The war could not be brought to a victorious conclusion unless Portugal permitted and facilitated the transport of British troops from Lourenço Marques to the Northern Transvaal. This involved an obvious breach of neutrality, as a result of which Portugal required suitable guarantees by way of protection against attacks from those Powers which appeared at that time hostile to England. From the Portuguese point of view there was every possibility that matters would come to a conflict between Germany and England, in which case Germany might easily invade Mozambique or even Angola and occupy Portuguese territory. If you add to this the whole series of personal misunderstandings and unpleasantnesses on both sides of the North Sea, then the situation prevailing at that time at least explains, even if it does not justify, the conclusion of the Windsor Treaty.

It has required a decade and a half to overcome in some measure the evil effects of that period and to create the possibility of an understanding at all. *If we were now to continue our negative attitude towards the final conclusion of the agreement, we should destroy the favourable effect of the healing process which has been made possible by time and hastened by the constant efforts of the Imperial Government.* It might indeed be said that both parties must consider themselves morally bound by the initialling of the treaty, but I think it highly doubtful whether a British Government would regard a treaty as binding which its predecessor had only initialled. If the situation anticipated in the agreement arose and Germany proposed to England that joint representations be made to Portugal regarding some colonial incident and be followed up with pressure amounting to a kind of ultimatum, I think it more than questionable whether a British Cabinet, even if it had the best of intentions, would find it possible to accede to such a proposal or to substantiate and justify it before Parliament. It would be liable to an interpellation enquiring on the basis of what arrangement so unusual a diplomatic step was taken, and would be faced with the dilemma of either having to admit the existence of an agreement which it had withheld from the knowledge of Parliament, or else denying that there was any agreement and thus depriving itself of any basis for explaining the joint action of the two Governments. I therefore believe there is good foundation for my fears lest the present and still more, a future British Cabinet, would be bound to refuse a step of that kind which aimed at putting the agreement into effect prior to its signature. In that case the whole agreement would fall to the ground and become useless. The ill-feeling which would inevitably follow would be a far more serious danger to the improved relations so carefully fostered by us than the noise which a few irresponsible newspapers and Parliamentarians might possibly raise in the other event.

These objections might still be countered by the argument that after all the first agreement remained in force so long as the second one was incomplete. But this argument should be rejected with all possible emphasis. The whole case for not signing the new agreement is based on the assumption that the old one was annulled by the Windsor Treaty. And apart from that the division of the spheres of influence, especially in West Africa, is so different in the 1898 agreement that its application to the present situation would be bound to cause grave confusion, always provided, as I have already said, that the agreement is still applicable at all.

There is yet another consideration which, as well from the point of view of our public opinion as on other grounds, merits particular attention. German capital is being, and has already been, sunk in the various colonial enterprises to such an important extent that it would necessarily lead to substantial losses and to a justifiable feeling of depression in German financial circles if all the trouble and expense should one day prove to have been wasted. The further question would then arise as to what quarters or persons were responsible for these losses or even liable to make compensation. For there can scarcely be any doubt that the financial world was only encouraged to make the investments because it was led to assume that the conclusion of the treaty with England could be regarded as certain.

Much more important than the realisation of the agreement would appear to be the question of its signature in connection with the broad general outlines of our policy. *With this agreement Germany stands at a turning-point in her destiny.* The consensus of our experiences in all our overseas enterprises, and not only in the case of the Baghdad railway and in that of Morocco, has taught us that we cannot in the long run carry on a successful world policy without England or against her. And far beyond all that is the effect of the present issue on our future relations with England and on our position within the grouping of European Powers. Since we have several times, in 1901 and 1912 for instance, rejected offers of a closer understanding with England with the prospect of an ultimate alliance, there is no doubt that another display of aloofness on our part would bring about a feeling of profound and lasting disinclination towards us on the other side of the North Sea. England, who is being warmly wooed by the Entente Powers, would be unable to maintain her resistance if she were faced with a suspicious and unfriendly Germany. *Up to the present Sir Edward Grey, as is well known, has firmly held his ground against all the efforts of M. Paul Cambon, whenever he has expressed on behalf of his Government his extreme uneasiness about the Anglo-German understanding.* He likewise withstood the inducements which M. Sazonov offered him in April through his confidant, Prince Trubetzkoi, in the form of an alliance proposal accompanied by a naval convention. He was guided in his decision not only, of course, by the interests of Britain, but also by consideration for us. *If*, however, *we reject an understanding the British Cabinet gets a free hand, and a future Cabinet would consider itself still less than the present one bound by the uncompleted agreements with us.*

On the other hand, the advantages we should gain by the final conclusion of the agreement have every prospect of going far beyond its immediate objects. Various political imponderabilia come into consideration here on the analogy, for instance, of the results which accrued to the Entente Cordiale from the Franco-British agreement of 1904 on Egypt and Morocco. To take one thing only, the article in the agreement which provides for common action by Germany and England to exclude third parties from sharing in the solution of the Portuguese colonial question will automatically lead to closer co-operation between the two countries in other questions also, such as was displayed in so gratifying a manner in the handling of the Balkan crisis. It would, indeed, hardly be too optimistic to expect that the final conclusion and also the publication of all our agreements with England would, despite the Windsor Treaty, of which we were, after all, informed, go very far towards mitigating the political tension and open up for us an era of success, of which the effects at home would be seen in an increased confidence in the aims and methods of the Imperial Government. *The agreement with England is the best achievement of Imperial policy*—in so far as it has scope to be constructive and expansional—*since the great days of the foundation of the Empire.*

To The Imperial Chancellor von Bethmann-Hollweg.

London, *4th June,* 1914.

In reply to Your Excellency's note of the 29th ultimo I have the honour to report as follows :

The assumption that I raised the question of publication with Mr. Harcourt on my own initiative is based on an error. This question was, of course, bound to come up in the course of the conversation, which took place in an entirely free and easy atmosphere after dinner. As may be inferred from my dispatch, however, it was the question, not of the publication, but of the validity of the new agreement which I brought up with the Colonial Minister. From various indications I had gathered that, assuming the new agreement remains unsigned, both the Foreign Office and the Colonial Office regard the old treaty of 1898 as continuing to form the legal basis of our mutual relations in the Portuguese colonies, and that the new treaty is not considered morally binding here except in so far as Sir E. Grey feels a personal obligation not to refuse his signature in the event of our so desiring and accepting the well-known conditions.

I can hardly believe that Sir E. Goschen has made a statement in Berlin directly contradicting the above point of view ; at any rate there is nothing in the documentary material at my disposal which suggests anything of the kind. Sir E. Grey has always most scrupulously avoided broaching the question with me as to which of the two treaties was to be regarded henceforth as the basis of our mutual relations in matters of colonial policy. Sir W. Tyrrell, however, has left me without any further doubt that the new treaty is null and void, at any rate for the present. In my former discussions with Sir Edward he always confined himself merely to saying, ' then it is better to leave things as they are,' just as he appears to have done in the letter to Sir E. Goschen. What he intended to convey with these words was not difficult to discern, though he added nothing more definite. And since my last conversation with him, which was on 1st April and which I reported at the time, I have had no occasion to take any further steps officially.

Sir Edward Grey will probably continue to avoid expressing in clearer terms the view held here, namely, that the treaty which remains in force henceforth is the old one and not the new. For he would much prefer to let the whole matter rest, in order to escape from the embarrassment which the attitude of the French is causing him. He will probably, therefore, not broach the subject with me any more, if only because there has been no change in the situation since the conversation between Sir E. Goschen and the Secretary of State. If Sir E. Goschen, however, has said things which warrant the opposite view being taken, this may probably be ascribed to his slight acquaintance with the relevant circumstances.

I thought I was acting in the interest of my official duties when I pointed out incidentally in the course of conversation with the Colonial Minister that we still held to the material clauses of the new treaty ; at the same time I learned the views taken by responsible quarters as to the actual legal position. This discussion was therefore no infringement of my instructions to refrain from any further official step on the question of publication. On the contrary I should have thought that Your Excellency would be pleased if I succeeded in ascertaining for certain the real view of the British Government on this important question and in elucidating an error which appears to have gained currency.

I am, however, particularly surprised at being reproached with having again compromised by my conversation a satisfactory state of affairs which was entirely adequate to the needs of the immediate future. That would imply that the conversation had caused the Minister to change his attitude in a sense unfavourable to us, and not merely given him an opportunity of expressing his views. I was certainly unable to bring up counter-arguments, as these would only have been effective if I had been in a position to prove that the views of the British Government had undergone a change. But Your Excellency had given me no authority to do that and I could not reply to the Minister that the statements made by the Berlin Ambassador on behalf of Sir E. Grey directly contradicted his views.

In conclusion, I regret to have to point out that the instruction contained in the last sentence of the letter already referred to is one which I am unable to reconcile with my position here.

LICHNOWSKY.

To The Imperial Chancellor von Bethmann-Hollweg.

LONDON, 14*th July*, 1914.

During my last visit to Berlin Your Excellency had authorized me to inform Sir Edward Grey that we were now prepared to sign the agreement with Great Britain on the Portuguese colonies and to consent to the publication of the new treaty together with both the old ones, namely, the Anglo-German of 1898 and the Anglo-Portuguese of 1899.   The publication was, however, to be deferred till the late autumn, in order that our mission in southern Angola might have sufficient time to conclude its investigations there into questions of railway construction.

I scarcely need again to demonstrate the importance of our new treaty or to emphasise that it creates a permanent basis for the future extension of the colonial interests of both countries in Africa and removes sources of friction which might arise from their colonial policies.   In contrast to the old treaty, which took too little account of geographical dividing lines in Angola, it assigns to us a well-rounded area comprising the greater part of this Colony.   It gives us, moreover, the valuable islands of São Thomé and Principe, which were not mentioned in the old treaty at all, together with the section of the Benguela Railway which was previously in the British enclave.

I had taken the above occasion to report that the British Government attaches the greatest importance to the successful conclusion of the new treaty, partly owing to the deficiencies which the old one contained even from the British standpoint, and partly in view of the uncertainty which the present situation entails for economic enterprise.   I might add *that quite recently Mr. Asquith*, whilst I was visiting him in the country, *himself asked me what was really going to come of our treaty, and gave unequivocal expression to the hope that we should bring it to a definite conclusion*.

As against the fears entertained for a time by Your Excellency against the publication of the Windsor Treaty, I endeavoured to show that this treaty did nothing more than confirm the legal situation which has been established by treaty since the days of Charles II.   I ventured to observe that if, as I considered not unlikely, Pan-German or other quarters were really to adduce England's duplicity as proving the political ingenuousness of our Government there was a fairly easy answer to this reproach.   It could be said, namely, that Your Excellency had in the new treaty discovered a way of evading and even, under certain conditions, of rendering invalid the very stipulations which appeared to contradict the spirit of our agreements, yet without violating either the dictates of political decency or treaties which had been in existence for centuries. For whereas the old convention, entirely in the spirit of the Anglo-Portuguese treaty, makes its object the ' maintenance of the integrity and independence of Portugal,' and merely determines the conditions under which both parties may grant loans, the new treaty speaks of the special interests which the two countries have in the adjoining Colonies and Protectorates.   The greatest importance for estimating the significance of the new treaty might, moreover, be attached to Article VIII, which was worked out with Your Excellency's personal co-operation and which envisages the possibility of danger arising to the life and property of German or British nationals in the Portuguese Colonies and even to the vital interests of adjoining German or British possessions.   It is clear that the provisions of this Article permit of a very far reaching interpretation, as they anticipate that the Portuguese Government may not be in a position to afford the necessary protection, and leave it to the two contracting parties to agree on the requisite measures.   It is further clear that a lever is thereby created for carrying the treaty into effect such as was not contained in the old one.   It would be superfluous to make additional reference to the advantages of Article IX dealing with the secession of the whole or part of a Colony.

Far, therefore, from affording occasion for justifiable attacks on the Imperial Government, I thought I should find Your Excellency sharing my view that the new treaty can be represented as an important success on Your Excellency's part, and that not only because it marks a further step towards realising the aims of our colonial policy, but also because it forms a significant practical result of the *rapprochement* about which so much has been said.

Since I may assume that Your Excellency does not intend letting the patriotic work, when it is already ripe for completion, come to nothing on the strength of objections which can easily be answered, I venture to ask whether I may now have authority to approach Sir Edward Grey in accordance with my instructions mentioned at the beginning of this dispatch.

The date of publication could be settled by agreement afterwards. I think no time should be lost, because Sir Edward Grey will be leaving London in August at the close of the Parliamentary session, and I should like to bring the matter to a conclusion before I start my leave.

LICHNOWSKY.

NINTH SECTION

THE BAGHDAD RAILWAY [1]

TO THE SECRETARY OF STATE HERR VON JAGOW.

2nd June, 1913.

I am quite in accord with the statements contained in your letter of the 29th ult.   I too am of opinion that it would be extremely unwise for us to enter into conversations with either Cambon or Pichon concerning the partition of Asia Minor into spheres of interest ; on no account must we lead them to suppose that we would entertain the idea of dividing up Turkey's possessions at some later date.   That the French have designs on Syria is just as well known as that these designs are being opposed by England.   Kitchener's attempts to carry on from Egypt a campaign of English propaganda in Syria, to stimulate the already strong British sympathies prevailing in that country, were doubtless by no means welcome in Paris.   But from here, too, he was given to understand that the British Government was opposed to such plans and that it wished, as I have repeatedly observed, to work hand in hand with us for the maintenance of Turkey in Asia.

The disintegration of the latter would not accord with British wishes if only for the reason that Great Britain would not care to see us established as a Mediterranean Power and that it would be difficult for Great Britain, from geographical considerations alone, to pick out a suitable piece for herself.   Now that we have repeatedly emphasized the fact that we regard it as absolutely essential to maintain the integrity of the Turkish possessions in Asia Minor, it would make a most unfavourable impression if it got about that we had, behind England's back, entered into negotiations with France for the partition of Asia Minor.   In view of France's dependence on England, it is, as you yourself point out, hardly to be assumed that such conversations would remain a secret.   Grey is just on the eve

---

[1] Owing to the mass of material bearing on this question, considerable cuts have had to be made.   (Author's note.)

of coming to an arrangement with us about the Baghdad Railway question and is showing great readiness to meet our wishes. He would regard it as ' unfair ' if we at the same time were to carry on secret negotiations with France without his knowledge.

If we decide to enter into discussions with France, these discussions should be confined to matters of a general economic nature, such as the Baghdad railway and methods of financing it. Grey would like to see us come to some arrangement with Paris on this point and has said as much in conversation with Cambon. In any case, the present moment would undoubtedly be propitious, as the French, partly at England's suggestion and partly from fear lest we come to an understanding with England without them, seem not disinclined to come to some arrangement. But whatever you do, avoid at all costs having anything to do with matters that are allegedly to be negotiated behind England's back. We should undoubtedly fall in by adopting such a method, for it is quite clear that in Paris,—quite apart from the unreliability of the people in power there, as you yourself point out,—there are a number of people only waiting for an opportunity of again sowing distrust between us and the English. Intrigue is entirely foreign to Grey's nature, and he would therefore feel the more aggrieved should we resort to it.

P.S.—Your second letter just to hand. I have only told Grey that the French, in accordance with his wishes, seem to desire to come to an agreement with us about the Baghdad Railway and the questions of financing it. Grey is most anxious to see this plan carried out.

LICHNOWSKY.

To The Imperial Chancellor von Bethmann-Hollweg.

LONDON, 16th July, 1913.

Sir Edward Grey, I am confidentially informed, still clings to the idea of arriving at a satisfactory settlement of all the questions connected with the Baghdad Railway by means of a compromise brought about simultaneously between German and French interests. He has therefore in strict confidence taken steps to ascertain the French wishes with regard to the railway engineering works and concessions in Turkey in Asia and how far the direct exchange of ideas between the Germans and French interested in the question has progressed in Paris.

From what the French have told him, the Minister has apparently received the impression that French wishes are far-reaching and that they are partly in conflict with German aspirations, but that a compromise is perhaps possible. As the Minister is so bent upon the project of using the Baghdad Railway transaction to prevent the conflict of interests between France and Germany from becoming more acute, he is quite ready, should it fall in with the wishes of the Imperial Government, to take note of all our wishes and demands in Turkey in Asia in order to bring about a fair compromise in Paris, should the direct exchange of opinions hitherto carried on fail to achieve success.   LICHNOWSKY.

To The Imperial Chancellor von Bethmann-Hollweg.

LONDON, 4th February, 1914.

I learn in strictest confidence from a private source that M. Cambon has enquired of Sir Edward Grey whether England could postpone the conclusion of her negotiations with us concerning the Baghdad Railway and related questions until the French have concluded their parallel negotiations in Berlin, as otherwise France's position would be unfavourably affected. The British Foreign Office has in reply informed the French Embassy in writing that at least a provisional conclusion of the negotiations with Germany was necessary, in order to make it possible to complete the ratification of the treaties with Turkey that had already been several times postponed. It was impossible for England still further to delay the conclusion of a settlement with Germany out of consideration for the Franco-German negotiations.

Similarly M. Cambon's further enquiry as to what attitude England would adopt towards France's participating in the Mesopotamian River Navigation Company was answered in a negative sense.   LICHNOWSKY.

To The Imperial Chancellor von Bethmann-Hollweg.

LONDON, 7th May, 1914.

Hakki Pasha, whom I met by chance at the Foreign Office, asked me to spare him a few minutes for a short discussion at which the railway expert Muchtar Bey was also present. Hakki Pasha told me that Dshavid Bey found it impossible to get away from Constantinople at present owing to a press of work. According to reports he had received from that city, he himself had been chosen to conduct the negotiations in Berlin. From the communications he had received from Dshavid Bey and Muchtar Bey on the subject, he hoped, he said, to be able to arrive at a satisfactory result.

There was only one matter that was causing him anxiety and that was Russia. This Power had so definitely pledged itself to demanding a delegate for the *Dette publique* and there had been so much talk in the Press about this delegate's being Russia's main achievement at the termination of the Balkan crisis, that any retreat on the part of the Russian Cabinet or the abandonment of this demand seemed to him out of the question. As far as he was acquainted with the German standpoint, we made our consent to the appointment of a Russian delegate conditional on the appointment of a second German delegate and on an arrangement by which Germany, England and France should each preside in turn. According to his information, France was offering a good deal of resistance to the German wishes, whilst Russia, if no delegate were appointed, would certainly not agree to the customs duties being raised. Hakki Pasha concluded by expressing the opinion that so far as the customs tariff was concerned, this question threatened to interfere with the whole treaty, a treaty that had been built up at the cost of so much trouble.

Hakki Pasha intends to go to Berlin as soon as he has finished the present negotiations ; he hopes to be there in about a fortnight's time.

An agreement was come to yesterday in the matter of the demand put forward by the Smyrna-Aidin railway for guarantees for part of its lines in the event of the Italian Adalia line actually being built. Muchtar Bey is leaving to-day for Constantinople, in order to induce the Porte to expedite the acceptance of the compromise.

In the question of the English claims, no agreement has yet been come to. Hakki Pasha is offering to pay a lump sum in cash amounting to 50 per cent. of the total claims. The British Government is not inclined to accept this offer ; it would prefer that the individual claims should be submitted to a court of arbitration.

The British assent to the Turkish Petroleum Monopoly has once more been delayed by the discussion of certain technical questions concerning which I have reported elsewhere.   LICHNOWSKY.

TENTH SECTION

ASIA MINOR PROBLEMS

To The Secretary of State Herr von Jagow.

LONDON, 26th June, 1913.

I am confidentially informed that Sir Edward Grey will to-day tell President Poincaré that his Cabinet is not inclined to enter into any plan whatever for the partition of Asia Minor, and that England wishes to preserve the territorial integrity of the Turkish dominions in their present form. England reckons on our support in this question and also counts on our adopting the same standpoint. I have, as you know, in accordance with your views and those of the Chancellor, repeatedly explained to Sir Edward Grey that we wish to maintain the integrity of Turkey as long as the British Governmant acts in the same sense, but that should the other Powers put forward claims to the Turkish inheritance, we should then draw attention to our own interests and rights in that region.

Unfortunately Herr von Gwinner during his stay here seems to have made various statements which have given the impression that we are already thinking of broaching the subject of a partition of Asia Minor. These utterances have aroused some astonishment and caused uneasiness here. Various people—but not Sir Edward Grey—have since drawn my attention to this fact, and in order to prevent Sir Edward Grey in his conversation with French statesmen from backing up these French desires under the impression that our standpoint has changed, I have again declared that there has been no alteration in our views on this subject.

It is of great importance that the suspicion should not gain a footing here that we are lacking in the necessary sincerity in our dealings with the British Government. My position towards Sir Edward Grey would sensibly suffer should he conceive the idea that he could not depend on what I told him. I should therefore like to ask you to give Gwinner or any other persons who are in touch with London a hint to the effect that our attitude has in no wise changed and that it is therefore dangerous to foster views to the contrary.

Postscript (in my own handwriting): I shall try to prevent them from coming to us with proposals for a naval holiday, but you must prevent people in Berlin from talking and railing too much about the matter.
LICHNOWSKY.

To The Imperial Chancellor von Bethmann-Hollweg.

4th July, 1913.

I learn from a reliable source that Sir Edward Grey in the course of a political talk with M. Poincaré and M. Pichon specially emphasized the fact that he regarded the preservation of Turkey in Asia as one of the most important aims of his policy. He received from the French statesmen the assurance that France too would do everything in her power to support this policy. The British Minister led the conversation to a discussion of the best means of affording Turkey support, and expressed the view, as he had already done in Parliament, that a better administration of justice and sound finance were the two most important essentials. In connection with this topic he expressly declared that he could not consent to a war indemnity to the Balkan Powers.

According to words let fall by M. Pichon, Sir Edward Grey's pronounced opinion on this point seems to have been received with satisfaction by this French statesman. He himself, he said, in the interests of French capital was opposed to a war indemnity, but he had hitherto refrained from putting forward this view out of consideration for Russia's wishes. Sir Edward Grey's decided views on the subject would make it easier for him to deny his support to any Russian wishes that might seem excessive.

My impression is that Sir Edward Grey will remain firm on the war indemnity question, so that in this matter we may count on England's supporting the German standpoint.

LICHNOWSKY.

To The Imperial Chancellor von Bethmann-Hollweg.

LONDON, *21st February,* 1914.

Although from time to time reports appear in the Press according to which the Anglo-Italian negotiations concerning the plans for Italian expansion in the hinterland of Adalia are said to be making satisfactory progress, I learn from a reliable English source that there can be no question of any great progress, as the Italians have not yet been able to make up their minds to formulate clearly what they really want. It seems, my informant says, to be a question of the construction of a projected railway line from Adalia to Burdur. In the opinion of the general director of the Smyrna-

Aidin Railway, the construction of such a line, although technically possible, would present great difficulties and would be impossible of realisation without considerable guarantees.

The Turks have addressed a confidential enquiry to the British Railway Company above referred to asking whether the company would be inclined to undertake the construction of the line. The English are inclined to regard this as a Turkish dodge with the object of being able to say later on when the British company formulated its indubitable pre-emptive rights that the Smyrna-Aidin line had declined to undertake the construction. The building of an even moderately good harbour in Adalia would, according to the report of an Admiralty expert, cost not less than £2,500,000, while to make a really good job of it would entail a considerably larger outlay. The English are therefore inclined to think that the Adalia plan is not to be taken seriously, but that it has its origin in an endeavour to acquire rights which under certain circumstances might be utilised later on as a basis for establishing political claims in connection with a sphere of influence. The British Admiralty is of opinion that Makri is the only point on that coast at which a good harbour could be built at not too excessive a cost. It is therefore to be conjectured that Italy will try to get hold of this harbour in order if necessary to push forward from this point with a line to the hinterland at Burdur. This is, however, mere surmise. In the opinion of the two representatives of the interests of the Deutsche Bank who are here at present, a line from Adalia to Burdur would principally affect the Smyrna-Aidin Railway, although it would not be without influence upon our own interests, as considering the shortness of the line to the sea, a certain part of the trade of the lake area might be expected to be diverted southwards. The harm done to the traffic interests of the Smyrna-Aidin line would probably be by no means insignificant.

As the Italians have hitherto avoided getting into touch with me concerning their plans in Asia Minor, I restricted my efforts, when the matter came up for discussion, to giving the Foreign Office a declaration couched in general terms to the effect that we supported the Italian plans. Since then I have not returned to the question.

LICHNOWSKY.

ELEVENTH SECTION

THE LIMAN-SANDERS AFFAIR

To The Foreign Office.   London, 15th December, 1913.

Sir Edward Grey received me to-day and expressed his satisfaction at Your Excellency's speech [1] on German foreign policy. He was especially pleased, he said, with the passages in it that had reference to England ; the sentiments contained in them quite corresponded with his own.

In the course of a long conversation, during which I could not help noticing that the Minister was in excellent spirits, Sir Edward Grey referred to the matter of the German officers at Constantinople. The question seemed to have occupied him a good deal and he said he was glad to be able to talk the matter over with me. He had never before seen the Russian Government so excited over any question. In consequence of repeated and urgent representations made in London by St. Petersburg, he had declared his readiness to collect personal and confidential information in Constantinople with regard to the nature of the authority to be granted to the German officers in Turkey. The main point at issue was, he thought, whether the position bestowed upon General Liman corresponded to that formerly held by General von der Goltz or whether it was something entirely new. To him, personally, this was a matter of indifference. He could not but fear, however, that if the powers granted to the German officers now in Constantinople represented any considerable extension of their executive functions, Russia might demand compensations in Constantinople in the form of the transfer to her of a command in Armenia. Such a solution seemed to him to be fraught with danger, as it might mean the beginning of the end—the beginning of the partition of Turkey in Asia. He would do everything in his power to prevent things taking such a turn, but in view of the excitement in St. Petersburg he could not guarantee that his efforts would be crowned with success.

For the present, the Minister promised not to do more than collect the personal and confidential information referred to ; the

[1] In a speech on foreign policy delivered before the Reichstag on 9th December, 1913, Bethmann-Hollweg laid special stress upon the ' homogeneity of the ideas at the base of German and British policy with regard to Turkey's future development.' The Chancellor also emphasized ' the very satisfactory improvement now observable in Anglo-German relations.' (Author's Note.)

enquiries would be made separately and not *in corpore*. He would confer with me about the result of the enquiries before taking any further steps.

On my replying that the position occupied by the British Admiral, who was appointed to command the whole Turkish fleet, by far exceeded that of General Liman, the Minister answered that Admiral Limpus occupied exactly the same position as that held by his predecessors and that his appointment had not signified any change in the situation, whereas General von der Goltz had not really held a supreme command. In Russia, moreover, people were much less touchy with regard to the fleet than with regard to Constantinople. Had the German general been given command of the army corps at Adrianople, they would have been more easily pacified. Constantinople happened to be a most sensitive spot for Russia and the Anglo-Russian understanding had been based on the idea that Constantinople should remain Turkish and that no other Power should be given a predominant influence there. It was difficult for him, he said, to do anything that might shake the understanding that was so important for the two countries by lending indirect aid to another Power in its efforts to gain a decisive influence in that quarter.

I tried to make it clear to the Minister of how little actual importance the despatch of these officers to Turkey was for Germany and how improbable it was that a few officers could influence the course of foreign policy in Constantinople. We had, I said, given our consent merely on grounds of courtesy and out of regard for tradition. We had only handed in the names of a few officers to the Turkish Government, leaving all details to be arranged between the Government and the officers themselves. I could only think that the excitement that seemed to have been aroused in St. Petersburg was due to a certain nervousness felt by the Russian rulers as to what the Nationalist Russian Press would say.

This conversation was carried on, as I have already said, in a courteous and friendly tone and my impression was that the whole affair was very unpleasant for the Minister and that he does not quite know how he can get away from the pressing and excited representations of the St. Petersburg Cabinet without endangering his position at the Russian capital.

LICHNOWSKY.

To The Foreign Office.   London, *23rd December*, 1913.

Sir Edward Grey away, does not return before the holidays. I too think it better to wait until he comes to me with proposals and avoid giving the impression of brusqueness and ill-will by prematurely and indiscriminately turning down all projects, even those yet unformulated.   Otherwise he would be in a position to answer inconvenient suggestions from Russia by making our attitude solely responsible.

As the whole affair is exceedingly embarrassing for him, inasmuch as it seems calculated to disturb the harmony between the Powers, he will try to find a solution or, as an alternative, will probably try to let the dispute gradually fizzle out.   Count Benckendorff has gone to Naples for a fortnight.   Before leaving, he told me that he hoped that we should succeed here in finding a way out of the difficulty, as conversations between Berlin and St. Petersburg had been broken off.   What the solution might be he did not know. Czar Nicholas felt that he had suffered a personal affront and was in a very bad humour.

LICHNOWSKY.

To The Imperial Chancellor von Bethmann-Hollweg.

London, *7th January*, 1914.

Sir Edward Grey, who arrived here yesterday and is leaving again this evening not to return before the 19th, has just asked me to call again to discuss with him the question of the Military Mission to Constantinople.   He told me that the Russian Government was by no means pacified and was being urged moreover by public opinion to take further steps.   He, Sir Edward Grey, had done everything in his power to persuade St. Petersburg to moderation and would continue his efforts in this direction, especially as his impression was that we were striving to meet Russian wishes to some extent and to find a solution acceptable for all parties.   Should this not prove possible, he could not help fearing that Russia might act on her own initiative and demand compensations from Turkey.   Such a step would naturally have very undesirable consequences.

On my asking what measures he thought Russia might take, he answered that he thought it not impossible that she would demand that a Russian general should be appointed to the command in Armenia with the collaboration of a suitable number of Russian officers.   Nor was it unthinkable that Russia might under certain circumstances proceed to occupy Turkish territory in order to bring more pressure to bear on the Ottoman Government.   Constantinople was after all Russia's most sensitive spot and he did not think that people in St. Petersburg would be pacified unless we could find some way out.

I replied in accordance with the lines laid down in your note that I did not doubt that the Imperial Government would be quite ready to meet the Russian wishes to some extent, although I could by no means acknowledge the justification of the Russian standpoint ; this would however presuppose that no further official steps should be taken by the Entente at Constantinople.   It would be impossible to yield, or even to make the slightest concession, if formal pressure were brought to bear.

Sir Edward Grey again promised to take no steps for the present. He hoped, however, he said, that by his return on the 19th, an agreement between ourselves and Russia would have been reached.   By that time, too, Count Benckendorff would be back again ; it would otherwise be difficult to put the Russian Government off any longer and keep it quiet.

For the time being, then, the British Government seems not to wish to take any steps, but to continue a waiting policy.   Nor does the withdrawal of the British naval officers seem to be under consideration, as Sir Edward made no mention of such a contingency, confining himself to the remark that the Russians were always pointing out that it was misleading to compare the British Naval Mission with the German Military Mission, seeing that Turkey had an army but no fleet, a remark that I tried to parry by pointing to the recent purchase of the Rio de Janeiro.

I should like to sum up my impressions by saying that Sir Edward Grey who, for the rest, was quite calm and in the best of spirits when discussing the affair, would be loth to take part in any new steps.   He fears, however, that Russia's attitude may place him in an awkward position and that under certain circumstances he would not venture to leave the Russians in the lurch in this matter.

LICHNOWSKY.

TWELFTH SECTION

GERMAN-ENGLISH NAVAL POLICY

To The Imperial Chancellor von Bethmann-Hollweg.

LONDON, 8th February, 1913.

The statements made by the Secretary of State for the navy before the Budget Commission of the Reichstag and telegraphed here have caused the greatest sensation in the London Press and are made the subject of a leading article by almost all the more important papers.

According to the reports that have reached here, Grand Admiral von Tirpitz is said to have examined in detail the naval speech delivered by Mr. Churchill in March last year and to have expressed the opinion that a ratio of 10 : 16 would be acceptable between the German and the British battle fleets and that he, as head of the Imperial Admiralty, had no objection to urge against this proposal.

The Times welcomes this statement, on the ground that it is evidently prompted by friendly feeling towards England. At the same time the journal attaches no very great importance to Herr von Tirpitz' words. Mr. Churchill, it says, had made an offer to the effect that if Germany would agree not to increase her building programme, England would not increase hers. No binding acceptance of this offer can be seen in the utterances of Herr von Tirpitz, says the journal. Nor should his statement be interpreted to mean that Germany will now necessarily pursue a policy of limitation of armaments. As a matter of fact, neither England nor Germany can unconditionally and for ever bind their hands with regard to the development of their fleets. If Germany be really ready to come to an understanding within certain limits with regard to the question of the fleet, her resolve to do so would be welcomed in England. The growth of friendly relations between the two countries, which had been helped on in the past few months by a harmonious collaboration between their two Governments, ought to induce them to discuss the naval policy from now on without bitterness and without mutual suspicion.

The Liberal *Westminster Gazette* [1] emphasizes the fact that the

---

[1] The editor of the *Westminster Gazette*, Mr. Spender, was one of Sir Edward Grey's most intimate friends. It was therefore to be assumed that this expression of opinion on the naval question corresponded with the views of the Minister. (Author's Note.)

naval question can only be dealt with in connection with political questions. The fixing of the naval strength of the two countries, says the paper, will always depend on the general political relations existing between them.

Regarded from this standpoint, the main consideration must be to prevent the natural and healthy rivalry of two powerful commercial nations from giving rise to political friction. In order to achieve this, both sides must have a clear idea with regard to certain important principles. In the first place, it is to be remembered, says the *Westminster Gazette*, that England cannot restrict the overseas expansion of Germany without incurring Germany's hostility in Europe. It is therefore better for England if Germany distributes her interests and her power equally over the whole world, just as England has done, rather than have her whole fleet collected at one spot, confronting the Power that blocks her outlet. On the other hand it is better for Germany that England should be a sea-power with a small army and keep a free hand as far as possible in European politics, rather than that she should be driven by German naval armaments into becoming a Continental Power with a large army and Continental alliances. If Germany succeeds in wresting from England her supremacy at sea, the result will be that the English Channel will practically disappear and that England will be forced to enter into definite military and naval alliances with other Powers for the protection of her territory.

LICHNOWSKY.

TO THE IMPERIAL CHANCELLOR VON BETHMANN-HOLLWEG.

LONDON, 14*th March*, 1913.

Last evening Mr. Churchill, somewhat earlier than was expected in Parliament, had the Naval Budget for 1913-14 issued, together with an explanatory commentary. The budget provides for 5 battleships, 8 small cruisers and 16 destroyers—1 battleship more and 4 destroyers less than in last year's budget—and estimates an expenditure of £46,000,000, an increase of about £1,200,000 as compared with last year.

The preliminary estimate keeps within the limit that has generally been regarded as probable in political circles. The advocates of increased armaments, who sit for the most part on the Unionist benches, would have preferred to see six battleships asked for instead of five.   This wish finds frequent expression in the Press, in the *Times* among other papers.   In the Radical newspapers, the pacifists and enthusiasts for disarmament lament even this small increase of expenditure on marine armaments.   So far as one can judge from first impressions, both Parties are fairly satisfied with the Draft Bill, so that stormy debates on the question are scarcely to be expected.   In various quarters the amount of money set aside for aircraft is criticized as being too small.   Many members of Parliament consider it probable that there will be a supplementary estimate for this arm.

When one recalls the bitter Press campaign and the heated discussions concerning Anglo-German naval problems and the ratio of the one fleet to the other which formerly always accompanied the debates on the Naval Budget, the generally prevailing calm on this occasion, and the absence of any provocative references to the German naval armaments may be noted as an eloquent symptom of the present mood.   Various politicians have referred in conversation to the very striking difference in the attitude of the public on this occasion.   It is to be hoped that during the coming debates there will be no revival of the old anti-German feeling.

LICHNOWSKY.

To The Imperial Chancellor von Bethmann-Hollweg.

LONDON, *27th March*, 1913.

At yesterday's sitting of Parliament, the First Lord of the Admiralty, Mr. Winston Churchill, gave his annual detailed statement on the British naval programme.   The preliminary estimates of costs, he said, showed a considerable increase which was not attributable so much to the construction of dreadnoughts as to five other reasons.   The number of ships had been increased in consequence of the new German Navy Bill and with it there has been a corresponding increase of crews and pay.   In the second place he had to record a further increase in the size, speed, thickness of armour plates and costs of all types of ships.   In the third place, various new services such as oil-firing, aeronautics and improvements in wireless telegraphy demanded considerable funds.   In the fourth place the price of material and the rates of pay had again risen.   In the fifth place there were arrears of instalments on new ships built during the past two years to be met, sums that were still outstanding

owing to the fact that the dockyards had not completed their con-
tracts to time.   The estimates for this year would have been considerably higher, had the dockyards not been overburdened with
work.   It would therefore serve no purpose to demand large grants
from Parliament for ships that could not be built.   He had therefore
based his preliminary estimates not so much on what was necessary
to complete the naval programme as on the maximum output
possible in the dockyards.   If in the course of the year it should
prove possible to speed up the execution of the naval programme,
he would be obliged to lay supplementary estimates before Parliament.   As soon as there was any noticeable slackening in the
shipbuilding industry, the warship construction that was in arrears
would be immediately taken in hand.   This automatic increase had
the advantage of guaranteeing constant employment in the yards.
Mr. Churchill then went on to say that there was no prospect of
reducing the expenditure on the navy in the near future, unless the
sharp international rivalry came to an end.   Of all countries, England was probably best able to meet these demands, for in no other
country was so much wealth stored up.   Nor did England, like
Continental countries, need to maintain a large standing army.
Without raising the cost of living for the poorer classes, she could,
moreover, easily increase her taxation.   In spite of the fact that
England would have no difficulty in getting men and money, the
regrettable absurdity of what was happening in the whole world
must be clear even to the dullest.   A common effort to put a stop
to or at least to check this absurdity must be regarded as one of the
most important aims.   There was, fortunately, still a way open that
had no influence on the relative strengths of the fleets.   Why, he
asked, should we not, for one year at least, have an interval in the
construction of battleships ?   This was a question at which he had
hinted last year and which he now repeated.   This proposal he
said, involved no renunciation of any naval organisation or naval
increase that might have been planned—it ran counter to no Navy
Bill, it could give rise to no misunderstanding and would bring relief
to the finances of all countries.   This appeal was directed to all
countries, but to none more sincerely than to England's great neighbour on the other side of the North Sea.   The quiet and friendly
tone of the last German naval debates had made an agreeable
impression in England, but care should be taken not to read into
the German declarations a meaning they did not possess   Nor

should England try to fetter German naval policy to English wishes by interpreting in too literal a way the friendly speeches delivered in the Reichstag. One might, for example, argue that Admiral von Tirpitz had declared his acquiescence with an English superiority of 16 to 10 dreadnoughts and that as this ratio applied to the present number, Germany ought not to build any more vessels. This would perhaps be logical, but would be certain to do great harm, and if England were to try through diplomatic channels to induce Germany to build no ships this year, this would doubtless lead to a refusal and to mutual recriminations. England's naval policy with regard to Germany rested on three elements, strength, frankness and clearness. Both nations must have a free hand to develop their fleets as they thought necessary. Germany had for a long time past always fixed her programme for a number of years in advance. England had also gone over to this plan, so far as it was possible to declare in advance what influence would be exercised by the German programme on English building. In this way dangerous aspirations and anxieties were forestalled. Nothing had happened to make it advisable to alter the English programme which was based on the relative strengths of the fleets. As Germany for the next six years would be building two ships more, England found herself obliged to build four ships more for the same period. For each additional German ship, two additional English ships would be laid down, as well as other ships besides, should there be new developments in the Mediterranean. In addition to these came the ships that were built by the Colonies. The plan was to assemble these ships in a uniform squadron and to station them at Gibraltar. The Admiralty would get the Colonies to establish naval bases. These developments would not render impossible the naval holiday he had proposed. Such a proposal must naturally be limited to a definite year. For 1913 it was already too late, but if Germany cared to cancel her programme for 1914, or if this were too early, for 1915, she only needed to say the word. The naval building programmes of the other Powers would naturally also have to be considered, but this would probably not present any very considerable difficulty. It was not easy to overestimate the influence that a collaboration between Germany and England might have in the interest of the peace of the world. If a treaty were concluded against this senseless extravagance, and this treaty then proved able to exert a further influence on the nations themselves, such an event could only be welcomed with most genuine satisfaction. England was in an excellent position to make such proposals, for in the past few years she had shown that she could maintain her superiority against all comers.

Mr. Winston Churchill then went on to discuss a number of purely technical questions. In the course of his speech he also mentioned the projected armament of the bigger English passenger liners, a plan in which the Admiralty had been met halfway by the ship-owners. Great attention was also being bestowed on aeronautics and there was no ground for any anxiety.

Mr. Churchill spoke words of warmest praise concerning the development of the German fleet. How England would have to meet this challenge he had already explained last year. He welcomed Admiral von Tirpitz' statement that this ratio of 8 : 5 squadrons was acceptable to Germany. The ratio would also remain the same, if each squadron instead of eight contained only six or seven ships, and England was quite ready to come to an understanding on this basis. At the close of his speech Mr. Churchill remarked that Great Britain could not afford to let any other naval Power come so close to her that this Power might be able to exert an influence on English policy by means of naval pressure. Such a situation would doubtless lead to war. Nor was a superiority that did not suffice to ensure victory sufficiently large to maintain peace. Mr. Churchill in his statements was evidently striving as far as possible to be just towards all the conflicting opinions existing here in connection with the naval question. He was in a difficult position in so far as in the Left Wing of his own Party there is a strong inclination to limit naval armaments, while the Opposition for the most part energetically advocates an extensive building programme to be carried out as soon as possible. The proposal to have a naval holiday after coming to an understanding with Germany was meant for the Radical opponents of the building programme belonging to Churchill's own Party ; the proposal was merely made for show and will hardly be taken seriously by anyone here, least of all by Mr. Churchill himself. Mr. Churchill tried to meet the Opposition halfway by declaring that the British Government would in any case maintain her supremacy at sea should other Powers increase their naval armaments. By trying to satisfy both Parties in this manner, Mr. Churchill made a clever move. This is already clear from the attitude of to-day's Press, for although the journals of the Opposition have many faults to find with the speech, and think it dangerous, for example, that next year's building programme provides for only five instead of six battleships, the Unionist *Daily Mail* finds the statement made by the First Lord of the Admiralty satisfactory, while the Radical *Daily News*, on the other hand, expresses its approval that Mr. Churchill should in his speech have pronounced against the race for armaments.

The speech is hardly likely to lead to important or agitated debates such as in former times accompanied any discussion of the British preliminary estimates for the fleet. This can only be welcomed in the interests of the further development of our relations with England.   LICHNOWSKY.

To THE IMPERIAL CHANCELLOR VON BETHMANN-HOLLWEG.

LONDON, 1st *April*, 1913.

In yesterday's general debate on the preliminary naval estimates which, on the whole, went off very smoothly, Mr. Winston Churchill spoke a second time in order to defend this year's naval programme against the attacks made on it by the Opposition. He did not, however, add anything essentially new. He declared that his proposal for an interruption of naval shipbuilding for one year was meant quite seriously and that he had by no means been induced to put forward this suggestion by the fact that the British dockyards were overburdened with work. Mr. Winston Churchill then contradicted in detail the assertion made by Lord Charles Beresford to the effect that the British navy had not at its disposal a sufficiently large supply of men completely to man the ships. He tried in a lengthy statement to prove that for the next few years the superiority of the English over the German fleet would be maintained to the extent of fully 60 per cent.   LICHNOWSKY.

To THE IMPERIAL CHANCELLOR VON BETHMANN-HOLLWEG.

LONDON, 30th *April*, 1913.

Mr. Winston Churchill, whom I met at a dinner given in honour of Their Majesties at Lord Granard's, took the opportunity of speaking to me about the question of the fleets. He said he had meant the naval holiday to be taken quite seriously and he regarded

the idea as quite practicable. He would try, he said, to induce the
other naval Powers to support it. Armaments had gradually
become too large and too costly and no State could in the long run
stand the strain of this race in naval construction. A big modern
ironclad to-day cost £3,000,000. It would be better to expend the
money on more useful things. The German fleet, he said, was
the only obstacle to a really intimate understanding between
the two countries, for by the creation of our naval forces a kind
of second Alsace Lorraine had been called into being ; it was a
question that separated the two nations just as completely as the
two provinces he had mentioned prevented a real *rapprochement*
between Germany and France.

I told him that I refrained on principle from meddling with naval
questions, but that I had seen that despite the question of the fleets
it had been possible to arrive at friendly relations with Great Britain,
and that I had noticed with satisfaction that England was coming
more and more to understand that our fleet was not built to fight
against Great Britain. I said that Your Excellency had moreover
expressed your readiness to accept in a friendly spirit any British
suggestions and to look into them carefully, but I did not think
that the German people who saw in the fleet a national work and the
embodiment of a national idea would ever cease to demand that this
creation should be vigorously fostered.

The Minister quite saw my point, but again and again came back
to his idea of the naval holiday and discussed the whole matter with
me in a thoroughly pleasant and genial tone. He seems, however,
to attach very great importance, probably on technical and other
grounds, to having a pause in naval shipbuilding. In his general
attitude, however, I could not help noticing a certain distrust of our
foreign policy ; this I ascribed to his somewhat imaginative nature ;
at the same time, however, he did not conceal his genuine admiration
for our fleet. I believe I succeeded in quietening him a little and in
partly dissipating his misgivings. For at the close of our conversation he said that I must have perceived during my sojourn in England
that the English were not difficult people to deal with. As he is
very vain, and is bent, come what may, on playing a brilliant part,
it will be necessary for us to humour his vanity and to avoid doing
anything that might make him look ridiculous, even though the
actual result of his suggestions, as I anticipate, should not correspond
with what he hopes for from the plan put forward by him. I should

moreover not feel inclined to overestimate his influence on the Government's foreign policy. Sir Edward Grey and Mr. Asquith have the chief say in such matters, and I hardly think that Mr. Churchill's views have any great weight with them, from the mere fact that they regard him as impulsive and flighty.

LICHNOWSKY.

To The Imperial Chancellor von Bethmann-Hollweg.

LONDON, 23rd June, 1913.

Although I quite agree with the conclusions arrived at by our naval attaché here, at the end of his interesting report No. 461 of the 20th inst. concerning the naval holiday, and although I, like Captain von Mueller, think that it would not be advisable for us to accept Mr. Churchill's proposal in the event of his approaching us in the matter, I should nevertheless like to add a few remarks to Captain von Mueller's statement.

Ever since my appointment to the London post, I have tried to advocate the view that it is possible to pave the way for relations of confidence and friendship between ourselves and Great Britain, despite the Triple Entente and despite the naval question, provided we do not give people here reason to suspect that we are pursuing an expansionist policy inside Europe and that we entertain warlike intentions, especially towards France. In saying this, I start from the assumption that our Navy Bill will in all essentials retain its present form and that public opinion here will not be given cause for anxiety by any sudden and unforeseen new formations and new demands. Even without submitting our present building programme to any limitations, I am to-day still of opinion that the *rapprochement* that took place in the course of last winter without the sacrifice of any German interests whatever can be further strengthened and deepened. I also regard as a further basis for undisturbed political collaboration, a cautious reserve on our part with regard to all attempts to arrive at a so-called naval agreement between the two countries. Experience has already shown how difficult it is to find an unexceptionable formula satisfactory to both sides to serve as a basis for such an agreement—a formula which will not permit of various interpretations and which can be carried out without the suspicion of disingenuousness and insincerity arising on one side or the other. As Captain von Mueller has conclusively shown, the fleet destined by the British for ' world protection ' would not come into consideration for the ratio number, although it certainly would in case of war.

If Mr. Churchill now suddenly comes forward with his scheme for a naval holiday, that is, a limitation of armaments, it is to be assumed, unless we are inclined to place him on the same level as Mr. Carnegie, that he has chosen for this proposal a moment specially suited to British interests, and that he has been led to adopt this plan not exclusively by feelings of friendship for a Power against whose growing development the re-inforcements of the British fleet, despite occasional denials, are nevertheless mainly intended as a guard and counterpoise. The more favourably the scheme turned out for England, after taking all the different factors into account, the greater would be the merit of the British Naval Minister, and I for my part can only urge a reproach against a statesman when he fails properly to perceive the interests of his own country or when he is too simple in forming judgments as to the intentions of his foreign colleagues. The reproach of dishonesty would, however, certainly be merited if it were proved that Mr. Churchill had been deliberately untruthful in the data he had given us.

England's geographical position with regard to us and the favourable view general here concerning the efficiency of our naval forces make it comprehensible that a British Minister should harbour the wish to make a breach in our Navy Bill. The bigger and stronger our fleet is, the more irksome will the British Government feel the duty of constantly holding in readiness a force whose mere existence suffices to make its political influence felt, no matter what circumstances may arise.

On the above grounds I should consider it regrettable if the naval policy of Great Britain were judged by us *ab irato* and Mr. Churchill's action give rise to bad feeling. Rather would I consider it in the interest of the undisturbed further development of a *rapprochement* that is of such extreme political importance for us to give a friendly but evasive answer to any such suggestion, putting forward, perhaps, technical and economic difficulties. Or perhaps Mr. Churchill's recent statement with regard to speeding up the construction of the three ships to be built this year might be utilised.

For the rest, I am also in a position, should Your Excellency wish it, to find an opportunity of approaching Sir Edward Grey confidentially or of getting some third person to give him a hint that we should prefer that Mr. Churchill should not again come forward with his suggestion for a naval holiday.

LICHNOWSKY.

To The Imperial Chancellor von Bethmann-Hollweg.

LONDON, 18th July, 1913.

In his speech delivered yesterday in the House of Commons, in connection with the debate on the preliminary naval estimates, Mr. Winston Churchill declared that he had, in March, gone into the whole situation, and especially into the Anglo-German ratio, so thoroughly that there was no necessity for him at present to add anything further to his remarks on the subject of ship construction. As regards the distribution of naval forces in the Mediterranean, there was up to the present no change to be reported in the building programmes of the Mediterranean Powers. There was no doubt that both in Austria and in Italy new programmes were being discussed, but it was not a question of facts so much as of intentions and rumours. He knew of nothing at present that would necessitate an extension of the British building programme, nor did he believe that any change that would have to be provided for in the British building programme of 1914-15 was to be expected this autumn in the relative strengths of the naval forces in the Mediterranean.

Since his programme speech in March there had been one occurrence of some importance for the British building programme—the Senate at Ottawa had declined to pass the Canadian Shipbuilding Bill. It would, however, be quite wrong to assume that this meant that Canada's wish to take an active part in its own defence and in the defence of the Empire was a thing of the past. Utterances made by leaders of the Government and of the Opposition parties clearly showed that nobody had a right to suppose that England would have to bear the burden of future armaments alone and without Canada's support.

The British Government had therefore resolved on a merely temporary measure. The gap created by the Canadian ships dropping out was not to be filled by increasing the number of new ships planned, but by speeding up the building of the ships that were already included in the programme. The building of these ships, which would otherwise not have been laid down till the end of the year, had therefore already been commenced, and if everything went according to programme, these ships ought to be ready in the

third quarter of 1915.   In the absence of new Italian or Austrian
ships, the relative strengths in the Mediterranean, and in the whole
world, which he had declared necessary in March would be fully
maintained.   The speeding up of the new ships would, he confessed,
be only a temporary makeshift, but the result would be that for
seven or eight months, at the end of 1915 and the beginning of 1916,
the same conditions would be reached as would have been achieved
had the Canadian Naval Bill been passed.   By next year, he said,
the situation in Canada would probably have cleared and he would
be better able to decide whether a further acceleration in the building
of next year's ships would be necessary or whether an extension of
the British building programme would suffice.

At the close of his speech the Minister pointed out that the coming
months would see the biggest deliveries of warships to the Admiralty
that had ever taken place in the history of the British fleet.   During
the next nine months there would be delivered on an average one
torpedo boat per week—not to mention numerous submarines—for
the next twelve months on an average one light cruiser every thirty
days, and for the next eighteen months on an average one super-
dreadnought every forty-five days.

LICHNOWSKY.

To The Imperial Chancellor von Bethmann-Hollweg.

London, 18th December, 1913.

The resistance of the Radical Wing of the Government party
to the increased British naval expenditure is beginning to cause the
Government serious difficulties.

Yesterday delegates representing a large number of Liberal
members of Parliament waited on the Prime Minister to express to
him the dissatisfaction prevailing in certain circles of the Liberal
party with regard to the prospective increase in the Naval Budget.

An official statement published last night concerning the interview
says that the delegation laid stress upon the necessity for limiting
naval armaments, pointing out the growing uneasiness felt in the
country with regard to the steadily mounting expenditure under
this head.   Mr. Asquith answered that he could well understand the
anxiety of the Liberal members and that the matter was receiving
the constant and earnest attention of the Government.

It will probably not be easy for the Government to reconcile the wishes of the Radicals with Mr. Winston Churchill's plans. One may certainly anticipate that Mr. Churchill, who is more and more becoming the *enfant terrible* of the Government, will not surrender so easily, especially in view of his added prestige as First Lord of the Admiralty. His intimate and much commented on friendship with Mr. Austen Chamberlain, and his readiness to make compromises in the Irish question—which has already more than once brought him the censure of the Liberal Press, show that Mr. Churchill is not afraid to go his own way. There is no lack of voices that go so far as to suggest the possibility of his returning to the Unionist camp and that prophesy a big future for him there.

LICHNOWSKY.

To The Imperial Chancellor von Bethmann-Hollweg.

LONDON, 2nd January, 1914.

Mr. Lloyd George has quite unexpectedly disturbed the holiday truce in home politics by issuing from his Christmas retirement in Wales a manifesto in the form of a conversation with an acquaintance, published in a prominent place in the *Daily Chronicle*.

The Minister stressed the necessity of lightening the immense burden of taxation and expressed the opinion that this could only be done by limiting the excessive expenditure on armaments. No country had ever derived any benefit from increasing its military and naval forces, but all, he thought, had probably at one time or another felt the disadvantages of such a policy.

The present moment was, he said, the most favourable that had offered for the past twenty years for a reduction of the expenditure on armaments.

In the first place, the relations between England and Germany were infinitely more amicable than they had been for many years. Both countries appeared at last to have realised that they had nothing to gain but everything to lose by bickering, while by returning to the old friendly relations which had prevailed for centuries between them, they had nothing to lose and everything to gain. The Agadir incident had, at a propitious moment, made clear to both countries what dangers might arise from an artificially created atmosphere of distrust.

The Continental Powers were, moreover, directing their attention more and more to strengthening their land forces. Germany had in the last two years had to learn by experience the well-known fact that a country could not devote itself to the development of one branch of its defence forces without the other branch having to suffer. The army was for Germany, situated as she was in the midst of strongly armed rivals, a life and death question. The demands made on Germany by the dislocation of her land forces could not but drive every thought of a struggle for naval supremacy out of the heads of German statesmen. Under these circumstances England might well content herself with maintaining her present superiority without making feverish efforts to increase it.

The possibility of any interruption in the friendly relations between England and France seemed out of the question, said the Minister, and far from wishing any weakening of the Entente, he advocated strengthening the bonds that bind the two countries together.

In conclusion Mr. Lloyd George said that he thought the present moment propitious for a limitation of expenditure on armaments because throughout Christendom, and especially in Western Europe, there was evidence of increasing impatience of military burdens. If Liberalism failed to seize the opportunity offered her, she would be acting disloyally to her noblest traditions.

This unexpected appearance on the scene of Lloyd George, whose anti-military tendencies are in keeping with his other democratic views, will help considerably to widen the split that has arisen among the followers of the Government over the question of armaments. It will bring the Radical Wing, led by the Chancellor of the Exchequer, into even more marked opposition to Mr. Winston Churchill and his followers. The Cabinet had, as I learn in strict confidence, postponed until after the holidays the decision as to the amount of money to be granted for the naval estimates. That the Radical Left has resolved, come what may, to put a stop to the heavy expenditure of the Minister for the Navy is also proved by a letter published in several papers yesterday by Sir John Brunner, the Chairman of the National Liberal Federation. This well-known protagonist of an Anglo-German *rapprochement*, a Swiss by birth, in this letter summons the Liberal associations throughout the country to formulate before the end of the month a declaration in favour of a reduction of British outlay on armaments, so that the Government, before the Naval and Army estimates are finally fixed, may receive fresh evidence as to the real wishes of the party.

Lloyd George's manifesto and Sir John Brunner's letter find a joyous echo in the Liberal Press.   Several papers dwell with especial satisfaction on the change that has taken place in Anglo-German relations.

The tone of the articles in question makes it seem probable that the Government will be forced to take into consideration the mood of the Radical Left in regard to its naval policy.

LICHNOWSKY.

To THE IMPERIAL CHANCELLOR VON BETHMANN-HOLLWEG.

LONDON, 18th March, 1914.

The First Lord of the Admiralty at yesterday's sitting of Parliament made a detailed statement in explanation of the Government's building programme which was presented to the House a few days ago.

The total amount of the estimated expenditure is £51,550,000 sterling.   The Naval Budget thus shows an increase of £2,740,700 sterling as compared with last year's figures.

In the first part of his speech Mr. Winston Churchill dealt in detail with the standards of establishment which the Government had accepted as a basis for the naval estimates.   In view of the mass of material presented by the Minister, it will hardly be necessary for me to go into this part of his speech.   I will only state that Mr. Churchill laid stress upon the fact that England and Germany in drawing up their building programme had observed a wise moderation.   He mentioned that Grand Admiral von Tirpitz had recently expressed a similar opinion in the Reichstag.   It would have been possible, said Mr. Churchill, to have the new English ships finished earlier than was at present provided for, but the Government had decided on a much slower rate of building in consideration of the fact that the development of the German fleet organisation had not been as rapid as he had two years ago anticipated.

In the second part of his speech Mr. Churchill dealt with the various political questions which had influenced the new building programme.   He especially dwelt upon the fact that the Government would continue to adhere to the principle that the British fleet, so far as capital ships were concerned, must have a superiority of 60 per cent. over the next strongest maritime Power.   This principle was naturally by no means binding and did not imply an obligation of any kind towards foreign countries.   As to the question whether the ships placed at the disposal of the Empire by the Dominions should or should not be counted in as affecting this 60 per cent. standard, the Government did not intend to decide the point on theoretical lines. The Government would continue to be guided solely by practical considerations in the execution of its building programme. An English naval programme had two years ago been based on considerations connected with the German plans of construction. In the meantime the *New Zealand* had become available for service in home waters. The *Malaya* had been presented to the British Government and there had been some talk of Canada's also contributing towards the increase of the Imperial fleet. The British building programme had not been modified by these facts, as the Government after mature consideration had come to the conclusion that there was no need for any such change.

Britain's position in the Mediterranean deserved special consideration, said Mr. Churchill. In 1912 the British Cabinet had come to the conclusion that British interests in the Mediterranean were not adequately protected by the cruiser squadron hitherto stationed there. It had therefore been resolved to place a squadron of capital ships in commission for the Mediterranean at latest by the end of 1915. This measure had been decided upon mainly because the Government considered it urgently necessary that England should, quite independently, provide for the protection of her important interests in the Mediterranean and that she should for the protection of these interests on no account enter into obligations of an unusual character. The Admiralty had provided for the commissioning of an adequate squadron. As the Canadian Aid Bill had not been passed, the British Government had in the past year laid down three of the ships belonging to the 1913-1914 programme eight or nine months earlier than was originally intended. As the acceptance of the Canadian Aid Bill was not to be anticipated this year either, the British authorities would again have recourse to the device employed last year, though on a smaller scale, and again commence building two ships of the 1914 programme as early as possible. Should Canada not take part next year either, the Admiralty would have to make up for this by speeding up the construction of a ship. There was, however, a probability that Canada would change the attitude she had hitherto observed with regard to the fleet question. Canada had, he said, such important and manifold interests to safeguard that she ought, at least in part, to adopt measures for her adequate maritime defence. If Canada were some time or other annexed by the United States, she would doubtless contribute her share to the maintenance of the American name ; if Canada were an independent State, she would surely not lag behind the States of South America in granting means for her defence.

Later on in his speech Mr. Churchill dealt with the British position in the Pacific. Australia and New Zealand, he said, were profoundly interested in Britain's maintaining her supremacy at sea. No European Power could think of conquering Australia and New Zealand until the British fleet had been destroyed. The position of superiority held by the British fleet in home waters indirectly afforded these two Dominions protection against Japan as well. With the help of her fleet, England could effectually prevent any attack of a European Power on Japan. Japan therefore derived great benefit from her alliance with Great Britain and had by renewing the treaty shown how highly she valued these advantages. The Anglo-Japanese alliance was therefore a guarantee of the security of the British possessions in the Pacific and this alliance again was clearly based on the maintenance of British maritime supremacy.

Mr. Churchill afterwards explained how the British Dominions could best participate in naval armaments. New Zealand, he said, had done very wisely in placing a capital ship at the disposal of the Mother Country for service in home waters, for the political situation in the Pacific would be decided in European waters. A New Zealand ship in British home waters could very effectively play a part in such a struggle, whereas in Australian waters it would be thrown away. On the other hand, it was quite natural that the Dominions should desire to have their ships, of which they were very proud, under their own control. The wish to pursue a naval policy built up on strategic principles and at the same time to satisfy the feelings of the Dominions had led to the suggestion that an Empire squadron should be created which should in regular sequence visit the different Dominions. For the execution of this plan it was necessary that docks and repairing workshops should be established in Canadian, Australian and South African waters, so as to render it possible for the Empire squadron to make a prolonged stay there. Local defence flotillas would also have to be called into being in the various Dominions, and these would have to carry out manoeuvres in conjunction with the Empire squadron when the latter visited those waters. In the third place, the Dominions would also station small cruisers in their home waters for the defence of trade. If, then, at the same time, the Dominions gave capital ships for service with the Empire squadron, the interest of the Dominions in the fleet would be developed and at the same time a step would be taken towards the creation of a uniform force which would benefit all the Dominions.

At the close of his speech Mr. Churchill emphasised the fact that the maintenance of England's superiority at sea was a life and death question for the nation. In other countries the navy had far less important tasks to fulfil than was the case in England. The British fleet had not only to undertake almost exclusively the defence of the country, but had also to protect the commerce of the Mother Country, spread as it was over the whole globe, as the Mother Country was unable to supply its population with foodstuffs grown within its own borders. Only by possessing a strong fleet was England able to enjoy undisturbed possession of her overseas colonies, to have a voice in the regulation of international affairs and effectively to contribute towards the maintenance of peace.

To The Secretary of State for Foreign Affairs
    Herr von Jagow.

LONDON, 10th *May*, 1914.

I cordially agree with what you write about the visit of the fleet. But please no *coups de théâtre*, for that sort of thing is thoroughly distasteful to the English. We are rather inclined to overdo things and this would be dangerous. People here don't want any fraternising that might give offence in Paris, while, as we have just seen, the English will avoid anything that might be taken exception to in Germany.

To judge by what I hear, Churchill now seems inclined to make one of the party, and will probably come on board his yacht, accompanied by a few Sea Lords and his beautiful and charming wife.[1]

---

[1] In my reports there is no mention of a possible visit of Sir Edward Grey at Kiel ; on the other hand in a private letter to the Secretary of State, Herr von Jagow, dated 26th May, I again referred to Churchill's visit, and also to the reports current in London concerning a new German Navy Bill that was projected : ' It is said here that Churchill will not be going to Kiel with the others. He recently dined with us, together with his wife and mother, but made no mention of the affair to me. I took good care not to broach the subject to him. I only said to his mother, who was sitting next me at table, and who gave me a hint that he would probably not be going to Kiel, that we naturally had not invited him, but that should he decide to come, he might be sure of a cordial reception. He has of late been very friendly to me and is

Provided that too much foolish talk is not indulged in and that we are tactful and keep within bounds, the affair ought not to turn out so badly. Churchill is an exceedingly crafty fox and is sure to try to spring some proposal or other on us. I hope you will stay at Kiel throughout the visit and that you will succeed in answering him evasively or in getting the matter shelved. In other respects Churchill is quite pleasant and without doubt a personality. As a politician he is somewhat fantastic and unreliable. He is much franker to me now than he used to be. I think he has overcome his distrust of us, a distrust that until a short time ago characterized most of the present politicians. They like Bethmann, you and me, and they have calmed down. France was, and still is, the sensitive spot, her preservation being regarded here as an axiom ; I warn you above all against any measures that might be interpreted as a challenge to the French. Such a thing would at once cause a complete revulsion of feeling !

Our relations with England are as good as they possibly can be. To ask more would be both unwise and futile. After all, there is nothing in which they are not ready to meet us halfway.

I greatly regret our refusal to publish the Colonial Treaty and should like to propose that we return to the subject before long. I am afraid that otherwise the whole business will fall through. The impression made on the public by such a treaty would certainly be a good one. The Treaty of Windsor can, of course, be served up with the necessary sauce.

less reticent and reserved than formerly. Should he go to Kiel after all, I cannot imagine that it will do any harm, unless we start discussing unnecessary stuff with him. I could perhaps give him to understand that it would be better for him not to refer to the naval holiday or other nonsense of that kind. What seems to me far more dangerous would be if the Battenberger were to be of the party, not only on account of his friendship with Prince Heinrich but also because he, as a German and as a naval man, might learn more than was desirable. I should have no serious objection to Churchill's being present, should he announce his intention of coming, provided the affair did not end in pique or in gush. Neither contingency is, I confess, altogether impossible. . . . There was, by the way, quite recently some anxiety at the Foreign Office about an alleged Supplement to the German Navy Bill. Tyrrell, who is in Grey's confidence, had a talk with me shortly afterwards. I replied that I could assure him that our naval armaments would not go beyond the limits set down in the Navy Bill and that there could be no question of our over-stepping these limits. Our naval attaché confirms my view on this point and assures me that Tirpitz too has no intention of going beyond the Navy Bill. Anything provided for in the Navy Bill, anything in fact that does not represent some new additional item, will be accepted calmly here. We must stick to that. New demands in the form of a Supplementary Bill would, however, produce restiveness and bad feeling among those in authority here and would be likely to undo all that we have latterly achieved.' (Author's Note.)

I should like to speak a word of warning, too, against carping and wrangling *à la* Zanzibar. By such methods nothing is achieved. They merely serve to create ill-feeling ; besides, the interpretation of the term ' protectorate ' in Africa is from a Constitutional stand-point extremely elastic. Especially in consideration of our own intentions for the future, it is important to keep the English in a good humour and not to take such treaties too literally.

They give me to understand here, that they would rather His Majesty did not come to England this year. The position in home politics and the impending elections make, it must be confessed, a good excuse. People here wish to be left in peace as much as possible, both in Court matters and in politics, and to co-operate with us on this basis. The later he comes the better. George finds him somewhat overwhelming too.

LICHNOWSKY.

THIRTEENTH SECTION
ENGLAND IN A EUROPEAN WAR

To The Imperial Chancellor von Bethmann-Hollweg.

LONDON, 3rd December, 1912.

Lord Haldane called on me to-day and discussed the political situation with me. During our long conversation he repeatedly dwelt on the necessity of arriving at some compromise between the conflicting interests in the Balkan crisis, as no one could foresee the possible consequences of warlike complications into which one or more of the great Powers might be drawn. England was unre-servedly in favour of peace ; nobody in this country wanted war, he said, if on economic grounds alone. But in the case of a general European mix-up, such as might easily arise should Austria invade Serbia, should Serbia refuse to yield to persuasion and evacuate the Adriatic coast occupied by her, it was scarcely possible that Great Britain could look on as an idle spectator.

I replied that I would not put the question to him whether that was equivalent to saying that England would in that case take up arms against us. He replied that that was certainly not a necessary, though it might be a possible, consequence of a war, between the two Continental groups. The roots of English policy, he said, lay in the opinion that was generally held that the equilibrium of the two groups should be more or less maintained. Under no circumstances, therefore, could England tolerate the overthrow of the French, a result that he, as a great admirer of our army and of our military arrangements, anticipated with some certainty. England could not afford after a French defeat to face a homogeneous Continental group under the leadership of a single Power, nor did she intend to do so.

Should Germany therefore be drawn into the quarrel by Austria and thus come to blows with France, currents would arise in England which no Government could withstand and the consequences of which were quite incalculable. The theory of the balance of power of the two groups formed, he said, an axiom for England's foreign policy and had led to her *rapprochement* with France and Russia. He could assure me that people in England were anxious for the best possible relations with Germany and the reception given for example to the statements of Your Excellency and to Herr von Kiderlen's speech in the Reichstag, as well as to my recent speech at the Royal Society's banquet, must convince me of the correctness of this view. Nor would anyone in this country wish to make war as long as there were no European complications. The results of a European war were, he said, quite incalculable, and if such a war took place, he could not guarantee anything at all.

Lord Haldane in the course of his remarks referred to the policy of Sir Edward Grey and to the proposal he had made. Everyone knows that Lord Haldane and the Foreign Secretary are intimate friends and that Sir Edward often stays with him for months at a time. He told me that Sir Edward was doing his utmost to act as mediator and carefully avoided appearing as a partisan of the Entente group in this crisis. Lord Haldane is of opinion that the suggested preliminary conference will force the Russians and the Austrians to come forward with tangible proposals, a thing they have not yet done. He suggests London as the most suitable place for such a conference. In the meanwhile, however, everything should be avoided that might tend to a sharp sundering of the two groups or, as he puts it, that might tend to ' harden the groups.' The groups must rather as far as possible be allowed to become ' gelatinous.'

LICHNOWSKY.

To The Imperial Chancellor von Bethmann-Hollweg.

London, 25th March, 1913.

As already reported Lord Hugh Cecil in the debate on the speech from the Throne recently asked the Prime Minister whether there were any secret agreements between England and any other Power which would force Great Britain to take part in a Continental war. The Prime Minister replied with a formal declaration that no such agreements existed.

Yesterday Mr. King asked Mr. Asquith in the House of Commons whether England's foreign policy was at present bound by treaties, agreements or obligations of any kind in consequence of which British military forces would be obliged under certain conditions to take part in military operations on the Continent. Mr. Asquith answered that there were no obligations of any sort which would bind England to co-operate in any war, in other words, if war broke out between European Powers, there were no unpublished treaties in existence which could hamper the freedom of the Government or the Parliament in coming to a decision as to whether or not Great Britain should take part in a war. The use that would be made of naval or military forces in the event of the Government and Parliament resolving to take part in a war could, however, for obvious reasons, not be made the subject of a public declaration in advance.

To-day's *Times* discusses the above utterance of the Prime Minister in a form that clearly shows that the journal is reproducing the views of people in authority here with regard to England's position in a European war. The statements contained in the *Times* coincide with the views that I have repeatedly had the honour to communicate with regard to this question, and they are deserving of special attention as they give an exact picture of the guiding principles of foreign policy. The *Times* says that England is as firmly resolved as ever to maintain the balance of power in Europe, this being of vital interest for Great Britain. Any serious attack made with the object of destroying the balance of power would certainly meet with the opposition not only of British diplomacy, but if necessary of British arms, and this not as a consequence of diplomatic obligations but essentially as an act of self-defence. In the last few years there had been more than one occasion, says the paper, referring apparently to Agadir, when such a state of things seemed to threaten. In every such contingency, Great Britain has resolutely placed herself on the side of the threatened Powers. Should circumstances again arise that might menace the balance of power in Europe, Great Britain's attitude would be the same. She is a permanent member of the group to which she belongs, since this is a *sine quâ non* of the balance of power in the two groups which her vital interests demand. The paper concludes by saying that it does not believe that this basis of British policy can possibly give rise to misunderstandings either in England or elsewhere.   LICHNOWSKY.

TO THE FOREIGN OFFICE.   LONDON, *6th August*, 1913.

   According to to-day's *Times* Lord Haldane yesterday made the following statement : We have no alliances. I admit, however, that one dare not ignore the groups that are forming, especially in making forecasts for the future. Our relations with the countries belonging to the other group are of the most friendly nature. I hope they may remain so. I believe that within the groups themselves there is an inclination to enter into closer relations.

   From this one may deduce that Lord Haldane meant that the differences between the individual groups were gradually disappearing. In saying this he no doubt was alluding to the improved Anglo-German relations. His declaration that England had no alliances is in complete accord with the declarations of the Prime Minister on the same question made in the House of Commons on 10th March of this year. As I have repeatedly stated, England has no need of any definite contractual relationship with France, as she will, even without a pact, under all circumstances protect the French should we attack them. On the other hand, she will in the same way endeavour to check any inclination on the part of the French to indulge in a war of revenge.

   As regards Mr. Asquith's speech on the question of a tunnel under the Channel, he confined himself to discussing the new factors that have recently influenced experts in revising the former negative attitude of the British Government. The most important of these new factors, he said, was the ' establishment of our friendship with France on a solid and, as I believe, unshakable foundation.'

   Neither in these statements nor in the utterances of the Lord Chancellor can I see any reference to any kind of agreement, especially as the Minister immediately afterwards remarked that Lord Wolseley's opposition to the tunnel was based in part on the theoretical possibility of a French attack, but that this danger had completely vanished as a result of the excellent and cordial relations that had existed between England and France ever since the conclusion of the agreement of 1904, that is to say, for nearly ten years.

LICHNOWSKY.

TO THE IMPERIAL CHANCELLOR VON BETHMANN-HOLLWEG.

LONDON, 19*th February*, 1914.

The report of our naval attaché here, discussing whether there is in existence an agreement between England and France, to take effect in the event of a war undertaken in common against Germany and the Triple Alliance, the said agreement referring to assistance to be rendered to each other by the two fleets, touches the sphere of politics in so far as Captain von Mueller mentions the apparent contradiction between the alleged agreements supposed to have been come to between the naval and military authorities on both sides and the well-known formal declarations of the British Government. Without wishing to go into the question as to whether it is probable that in view of the possible collaboration of the two fleets, a plan has been agreed upon, I should like to point out that even should such a plan have been agreed, I should regard such an agreement as compatible with the official declarations of the British Government, for in the case of such an agreement we are concerned principally with the question of whether any obligation has been undertaken by England to come to the help of her French friends in case of a war with Germany. That such an obligation does not exist in the form of a treaty is to my mind beyond all doubt It is foreign to the British character, and especially to the nature of the men at present in power, deliberately to make a public statement that is untrue. It is moreover foreign to the disposition of the present Government to burden itself with new secret treaties, especially in a question of such importance for the future of the country. Nor is there any logical necessity for England to bind herself by treaty to lend assistance, seeing that France is well aware that no British Government, as I have repeatedly pointed out, could permit France to be humiliated a second time and her territory diminished. The French know, moreover, that England, in order to maintain some sort of equilibrium of groups on the Continent, will under all circumstances hold a protecting hand over France. On the other hand, the English know perfectly well that the French would use any favourable opportunity to reconquer Alsace-Lorraine with or without a written treaty, but without the support of Russia they would never venture into a war with us. It is thus obvious that neither the French nor the English feel the need of a treaty. For us it can be a matter of indifference whether such a treaty exists or not, as in the case of a war with France we should, in either contingency, have to reckon with the fact that the British fleet will protect France. As, however, the maintenance of peace and of the *status quo* in Europe coincides with British interests, and as England for this if for no other reason will seek to prevent a Continental war out of fear lest she herself be drawn into it, the question of whether an arrangement exists between the two Admiralties, defining their activities in the case of their having to collaborate, is one of mere theoretical importance. It would, at any rate, be very remarkable if no such exchange of ideas had yet taken place.

LICHNOWSKY.

FOURTEENTH SECTION

THE GERMAN DEFENCE BILL

To THE IMPERIAL CHANCELLOR VON BETHMANN-HOLLWEG.

LONDON, 5*th June*, 1913.

The violent controversy now going on in France about the re-introduction of the three years' military service system has brought in its train a fierce anti-German agitation. Here in England these occurrences are being followed with closest interest. Both the *Daily News and Leader* and the *Westminster Gazette* to-day publish leading articles dealing with this topic. Both papers declare that the bringing in of the French Bill is due to Russian instigation, and that this line of action had already been decided on before the German Army Bill was brought in. At the close of its article the *Westminster Gazette* points out that the majority of the French nation is in favour of peace and that in France, as in England, most people see that a temporary victory would not mean a permanent success. The French know very well, too, says the paper, that their neighbours are peacefully disposed and that France in a war of aggression could not reckon on getting assistance. LICHNOWSKY.

To The Imperial Chancellor von Bethmann-Hollweg.

LONDON, *27th December*, 1913.

In a confidential conversation with a member of the Press, M. Caillaux stated that people had quite unjustly represented him as an enemy of England's and as an opponent of a cordial understanding between England and France. His views on the interpretation that ought to be put on the Entente differed somewhat, he confessed, from those of his predecessors in office, but his views were at least shared by the President of the Republic. The Entente had looked too much like a *tutelle*. France must be allowed complete liberty of action and be in a position to arrange her policy primarily to suit her own interests. Sir Francis Bertie, the British Ambassador, was continually meddling in questions of France's internal policy. This could not be tolerated. Should this sort of thing again occur, he would complain to Sir Edward Grey.

Passing over to the question of official appointments, M. Caillaux in answer to a question put by the journalist said that it certainly was intended to recall M. Cambon from London, but it was necessary in the case of a man of M. Cambon's eminence and past achievements to show a certain amount of consideration. One could not turn him out at a moment's notice. M. Caillaux thought that a suitable successor might be found in M. Jusserand or M. Barrère. The latter spoke excellent English and had many friends in England. The reports concerning the appointment of M. de Margerie to St. Petersburg were to be accepted with caution. He himself thought that General Lyautey would be a good man for Russia.

These utterances of the French Minister of Finance appear to bear the stamp of genuineness and show that his dislike of the British Ambassador at Paris is still as strong as ever. The unpopularity of M. Caillaux in English Government circles and in the British Press is not, as the German Press often assumes, due so much to his attempt to get rid of the Morocco question by means of the Congo Treaty with Germany as to his various collisions with Sir Francis Bertie which came to a head when Caillaux declared that he ' didn't care a hang ' for the Entente cordiale, an expression that induced the British Ambassador to lodge a complaint with the President. Sir Francis Bertie, both in his official reports and in his intercourse with the Paris correspondents of the big English newspapers, has since that time been untiring in his efforts to paint M. Caillaux as black as possible. The British Ambassador has, it is clear, made M. Caillaux's wish to remove M. Paul Cambon from London the subject of his official dispatches, for Mr. Asquith a few days ago told an acquaintance that there were people in Paris who would like to see M. Cambon ousted from his post, but M. Cambon was an important man, one who could not be dismissed without due consideration, and the Caillaux Ministry would probably be much too shortlived for the realisation of its plans in this direction.   LICHNOWSKY.

FIFTEENTH SECTION

RUSSO-GERMAN RELATIONS.

TO THE IMPERIAL CHANCELLOR VON BETHMANN-HOLLWEG.

LONDON, 10*th March*, 1914.

To-day's leading article in the *Times* headed ' What does it mean ? ' deals with the Press campaign that has recently been started in the German Press against Russia. This article may be regarded as giving a good picture of the mood produced in England by these newspaper attacks. No one knows exactly how to explain the bellicose note struck against the Triple Entente and especially against Russia. At any rate, a certain uneasiness is felt at the enigmatic tone adopted by the German Press. The conclusion arrived at by the *Times* is very significant and I can only express my complete agreement with this journal when it says that if there were anything specially calculated to draw closer the bonds of the Triple Entente and help the French to get their three years' service, no more effective means could be devised than the kind of article that is being permitted to appear at the present time in the German Press. I might for my part add that if our leading newspapers continue to write in the bullying tone that they have fallen into of late, everything that has been achieved in the direction of an improvement in Anglo-German relations will very soon again be scattered to the winds, and that no personal influence of any kind whatever will then be able to prevent British statesmen from becoming closer friends than ever with France and Russia. Distrust of our foreign policy and distrust of the sincerity of our will for peace cannot but once more lead to an alienation of the two peoples.

LICHNOWSKY.

To The Imperial Chancellor von Bethmann-Hollweg.

London, 10*th March*, 1914.

In the course of a lengthy confidential conversation with Sir Edward Grey, the German Press campaign at present being waged by some of our newspapers against Russia came up for discussion. I mentioned that as far as I knew official relations between the two Governments were of a thoroughly friendly nature and that since the question of the Military Mission had been settled nothing had occurred to give rise to ill-feeling. I therefore surmised that no exaggerated importance was to be attached to the utterances of individual organs of German public opinion, and that our Press was perhaps infected with a touch of the nervousness to which the Austrians were so prone when commenting upon Russian affairs. It was natural enough, I said, that the strong Russian armaments and the increase in the number of troops on the western frontier had caused uneasiness and were interpreted as omens of unfriendly intentions. Sir Edward told me that neither from the reports of the Ambassador nor from those of the military attaché nor indeed from information received from any other source, had he got the impression that there was any change in Russia's attitude towards us and least of all that any hostile intentions were being fostered by her. He could therefore see not the faintest cause to justify the apprehensions alluded to. The increase in the numbers of the Russian troops were a sequel to the increase in population and there were no threatening intentions of any kind behind this increase. Should the utterances referred to not be in agreement with German official opinion, the Foreign Office would doubtless find an opportunity in the debate on the estimates to define the position of the Government.

The whole conversation was carried on between us in an easy and friendly tone and I think I succeeded to some extent in removing the painful impression made by the utterances in question.

Lichnowsky.

Sixteenth Section

THE RUSSO-ENGLISH NAVAL CONVENTION AND THE
ENTENTE PREVIOUS TO THE WORLD WAR.

To The Imperial Chancellor von Bethmann-Hollweg.

London, 17th April, 1914.

A British journalist to-day visited Sir W. Tyrrell to ask him
for some general outlines for the guidance of the British Press
during the forthcoming visit of the King and Queen to Paris.
According to the strictly confidential report given me by my informant, Sir Edward Grey's private secretary had expressed himself
somewhat to the following effect :

The Entente with France had arisen out of the agreement of the
year 1904 and the political events that followed. Sir Edward Grey
had frequently discussed the scope and significance of that relationship in public speeches. These speeches should be used by the
Press as a basis. The newspapers should as far as possible avoid any
mention of third Powers in discussing Their Majesties' visit to
Paris ; above all there should be no allusions that could be interpreted to signify that the Entente or the visit to Paris had a point
directed against any other Power whatever. This was in no wise
the case. The Entente by no means prevented England from
entering into friendly relations with states outside it. France had
officially never given it to be understood that she wished to have a
written treaty with England. There were, however, signs that
French military circles considered a military convention desirable.
Such a thing, however, was probably out of the question, as a military
convention always included a political tie of one kind or another.
Most Continental critics quite forgot that Great Britain no longer
had the sole voice in military and naval questions, but that the whole
British Empire shared the responsibility, and that the British Cabinet
must therefore in the widest sense take into account the wishes and
needs of the Dominions. The *Times* had in the last few days felici-
tously expressed this standpoint in a leading article which might
be utilised by other papers. The letter from the French Professor
Lavisse, published in the *Times*, contained absolutely mistaken
conceptions concerning the nature of the Entente. These were the
views of a French Chauvinist and fortunately did not represent
those of really authoritative circles in France.   Lichnowsky.

To The Imperial Chancellor von Bethmann-Hollweg.

London, 18th April, 1914.

In a letter published in the *Times* of the 16th April, the well-known French historian, M. Ernst Lavisse, has expressed his views at considerable length on the significance, effects and aims of the Anglo-French Entente. While laying stress on the peaceful objects of the Entente, M. Lavisse at the same time emphasises the desirability of strengthening the friendly relations between England and France. In cautious language he criticises England's lukewarmness and refers to the heavy sacrifices that France is called upon to make in military directions and asks whether the time has not come for England to develop her land forces. He compares the military preparedness of the Triple Alliance with that of the Triple Entente in case of war and expresses the conviction that the British and French military and naval authorities are in touch and that they have fixed their plans in common, but expresses doubt as to whether England has similar connections with Russia. In a carefully written leading article, the *Times* of the same issue discusses the professor's criticisms.

England, says the article, likewise recognises the dangers threatening the Entente Powers, but does not regard these dangers as so imminent or so inevitable. An unjustified attack on France will always find England on the side of her friend.

The paper declines to discuss the question of England's military preparedness and diplomatic attitude on the ground that these questions must be reserved for discussion between the two Governments. At the same time the journal defends England against the reproach of lukewarmness and expresses the conviction that England would in a just cause fight as courageously as history shows she has done in the past.

Naturally, says the article, the British nation must first be convinced of the justification and necessity of such a struggle. It would never give its approval to a preventive or an aggressive war. It feels no hatred towards any other nation and has no wish to wrong another nation. The British Empire could, moreover, only act as a whole, that is to say, with the express consent and support of its overseas Dominions, Dominions which could only be moved to entertain the idea of war by the conviction that wrong had been done. The Dominions supported the policy of the Entente because it served the cause of peace, but if the roots of the Entente were to be strengthened, it would have to remain true to the principles on which it was founded.

M. Lavisse's letter and the article in the *Times* have, both in England and abroad, given rise to comment in the Press. This comment again shows, as was to be expected, that English public opinion is most strongly opposed to any suggestion of giving to the Entente the character of an alliance.

In a leading article the *Daily News* to-day sharply protests against the efforts that are being made in certain quarters in France to exploit the King's visit for Chauvinistic and anti-German intrigues that are intended to serve party aims. The Radical journal declares in opposition to M. Lavisse's statements concerning the military co-operation of the Entente Powers that British public opinion will tolerate no such thing as a military and naval alliance with France, while the mere suggestion of such an alliance with Russia would raise a storm of indignation that would sweep away the Government guilty of such a conception. The Entente is in England's eyes not an alliance ; it is not directed against Germany and has no wish to be exclusive. No reasonable man in England, says the paper, has any desire to encourage the French hotheads who are unwilling to let the quarrel with Germany die down.

Manifestoes like those of M. Lavisse and similar writers in the French Press which reveal France's intention of trying to bring friendly pressure to bear on England to induce her to strengthen her armies and to enter into a more binding contract are under present circumstances bound to meet with a rebuff in England. It is a piece of sheer tactlessness to renew such attempts on the very eve of the King's visit, says the paper.

I am confidentially informed that M. Lavisse's letter has displeased the British Government. The French Embassy in London too is anything but edified at this rather disagreeable prelude to the King's visit to the French capital.

LICHNOWSKY.

To The Imperial Chancellor von Bethmann-Hollweg.

LONDON, *20th April*, 1914.

The Radical Left in England continues to protest angrily against Professor Lavisse's views on the nature of the Anglo-French relationship as revealed in his letter to the *Times*. The *Nation*, which reflects the views of these circles, denounces, although in a tone somewhat less brusque than that used by the *Daily News*, any attempt to give the understanding with France the character of a military alliance.

Mr Garvin who all along has been among the warmest supporters of the Entente, publishes in the *Observer* an article that is conspicuous for its moderation and which may be regarded as fresh proof of the admirable discipline observed by the British Press at important moments. This journalist, who is generally known for his vehemence, points out that England and France are this week about to renew their friendship. After a short review of the effects that the understanding between England and France has already had on European politics, in which he emphasises the improvement of the position in Egypt and the better feeling between the French and English in Canada, he insists that the existing friendship between the two countries prevents neither of them from seeking closer friendly relations with third countries. Far above all political results of the Entente, however, must be placed the cultural results, results which have made it possible for each nation to be permeated and stimulated by the spirit of the other.

Professor Lavisse's letter was, as I am confidentially informed, planned beforehand and carefully worked out by a group of French politicians who expected great results from it. Extracts from it found their way some four weeks before its publication into the hands of British journalists. I learn from various sources that the letter has met with an unfavourable reception in official circles here. Sir W. Tyrrell told a reliable informant of mine that it was not at all in keeping with the nature of friendship publicly to discuss before a visit the advantages which the two friends might reap from their relationship. Once friends began to reckon up beforehand what advantages their good relations would bring them, it was an sign that their friendship was in a bad way.   LICHNOWSKY.

To The Imperial Chancellor von Bethmann-Hollweg.

LONDON, *22nd April*, 1914.

In the past few days almost all the leading London papers have published lengthy articles concerning the significance of the visit of His Majesty the King to Paris.

The tone of the articles is, as the occasion demands, for the most part a cordial one. Emphasis is laid on the fact that the friendly relations between the two countries during the ten years of the Entente have brought the English and French nations closer together, so that their political collaboration is no longer based merely on the will of the two Cabinets but on that of the two peoples. The splendour of the preparations Paris has made for the reception of the King and Queen finds warm words of appreciation.

In summing up the results of the Anglo-French Entente policy it is pointed out that it has above all helped to preserve the peace of Europe and that its principal function is to continue to do so.

Professor Lavisse's letter to the *Times* and similar expressions of opinion published in the French Press have on the other hand served to put the British Press on its guard, as is to be seen in certain somewhat cool comments.

The idea of converting the Entente into a formal alliance fails to find support in the leading newspapers of either Party, and is politely but firmly rejected wherever mentioned. In clear terms it is declared that England is neither able nor willing to give her support to any aggressive policy on the part of her French friends. On the other hand, support is promised to France in the event of her having to defend herself against an unjustified attack. The maintenance of the balance of power and of the *status quo* on the Continent appears afresh as the main objective of England's continental policy. No secret is made of England's disinclination to be drawn into Continental squabbles.

Many papers emphasise the fact that the Entente has no hostile intentions towards any other Power, that it is not at all exclusive and leaves its members free to enter into closer relations with third Powers.

The general impression given by these articles in the Press is one of friendly cordiality mingled with a certain reserve. Of actual enthusiasm there is not the faintest trace.

I should like especially to draw attention to the noteworthy utterances of the *Westminster Gazette*, a paper that is closely associated with the Government.

The journal regrets the misunderstandings with Germany that had arisen at an earlier period on account of the friendly relations between France and Germany, and points out that the English sponsors of the Entente had never conceived it as a leap into the

arena of European politics, any more than they did to-day.   More
recently occasion had arisen to show that Anglo-French friendship
was quite compatible with a friendly attitude towards Germany
on the part of England.   England, says the paper, will be doing
its friends and neighbours the greatest service by making it perfectly
clear that her power and influence will be employed to prevent
attacks and to frustrate any policy of aggression no matter from
what side such aggression may come.

LICHNOWSKY.

TO THE IMPERIAL CHANCELLOR VON BETHMANN-HOLLWEG.

LONDON, 27th April, 1914.

After a short week-end following on the Paris visit, Sir
Edward Grey returned early this morning to London and intends
to go away again on Thursday for a few days' fishing.   The crisis
here and his stay in Paris have somewhat interfered with his sport.

This morning he sent word that he would like to see me.

He was obviously anxious to talk to me about Paris and the
impressions he had received there, in order to prevent the impression
being formed that his wish to remain in friendly touch with us had
in any way suffered from contact with French influences.   With
his usual geniality he told me about his experiences, about the
tremendous cordiality of the reception and the model behaviour
of the crowds, whose enthusiasm had surpassed all expectations.
Their Majesties had been deeply touched by the homage paid them
and the delightful gaiety of the Parisians left a most pleasant
memory behind.

Concerning the actual business transacted, he said that in the
first place the Greek Note had been discussed, and that he had found
the greatest readiness to fall in with our proposals.   For the rest,
he had found the French as far as politics were concerned in a calm
and thoroughly pacifist mood and without any Chauvinist leanings.
This state of things had proved very helpful for his work at Paris.

He seemed to be more than satisfied with the result of his Paris
visit, but the state of internal affairs there pleased him less.   In
view of the increasing difficulties he thinks it unlikely that the new
elections can be deferred till next year ;   the dissolution of the
French Chamber was, he thought, to be expected at no very distant
date.

LICHNOWSKY.

To The Imperial Chancellor von Bethmann-Hollweg.

London, *29th April,* 1914.

In the House of Commons yesterday Sir Edward Grey was asked whether he was aware that a demand had recently been made that the three Entente Powers should co-operate more closely in military matters in view of possible future collaboration on the Continent and whether the policy of England was still based upon the principle of keeping free of all obligations to take part in military operations on the Continent.

Sir Edward Grey answered the first part of the question in the negative. For the second part, he referred the questioner to a declaration made by the Prime Minister on the 24th March, 1913, which he described as still holding good.   Lichnowsky.

To The Imperial Chancellor von Bethmann-Hollweg.

London, *1st May,* 1914.

I learn from a reliable source that the conference between Sir Edward Grey and M. Doumergue has proved thoroughly satisfactory to the former. Any deepening of the present Entente which as I have repeatedly pointed out consists in the main in a British assurance to protect the French in the event of their being attacked was, according to this information, not even suggested, and there was no mention whatever made of concluding an actual alliance. M. Doumergue, who made an excellent impression on the British visitors, is said to have confined himself to giving an emphatic assurance that France was thoroughly opposed to any sort of adventures in foreign policy and wished to devote herself entirely to her internal development.

M. Clemenceau, too, expressed himself in a similar sense. He is said to have told the British Minister that he was now quite reconciled to the Entente, as he expected England to act as a mediator between France and Germany with the object of bringing about a relation of mutual trust that would render possible a limitation of armaments.

M. Isvolsky is represented here as the originator of the agitation in favour of an alliance. It is said that he is inordinately vain and that he would fain play a prominent part.

All in all, the Government here is quite pleased with the present Paris Cabinet, and hopes that it may long remain in power.

Lichnowsky.

To The Imperial Chancellor von Bethmann-Hollweg.

London, 18*th May*, 1914.

Both Mr. Asquith and Sir Edward Grey have repeatedly declared, as they did again on the 25th and 28th of last month, that there are in existence no secret treaties or agreements that bind the British Government to take part in any European war that might break out, or to take sides with one or other party. The Entente which arose from the need for some kind of association of the Powers concerned as a counterpoise to the group of Powers forming the Triple Alliance, came into existence at a moment when France felt herself threatened by us in the Morocco crisis and in need of a support of some kind ; it has accordingly never condensed into a formal alliance implying definite engagements and agreements on both sides. Nor has the recent visit of the King to Paris made any difference in the nature of the relationship. The question of a real alliance did not come up for discussion.

If I have nevertheless repeatedly and emphatically expressed my conviction that England in the case of a war between us and France, and especially in the event of an attack on the part of Germany on her western neighbour, would hold a protecting hand over her French friend, this view is doubtless quite compatible with the repeated declarations of British Ministers to the effect that there are between the two countries no formal agreements which lay any obligations whatever upon the British Government. The basis of British foreign policy, as far as European Powers are concerned, is so well known and so transparent that there can be no possible doubt as to its nature. It is based first and foremost on the principle of the equilibrium of the two groups. The hegemony of an individual Power in Europe is just as little in accordance with British interests as is the preponderance of one or other of the groups. The growing strength of our Fleet, although not the primary cause of the British need to support the Franco-Russian group, nevertheless stimulated this need, as this increase in naval power had brought about a shifting of the power ratio on the Continent to our advantage and to the disadvantage of the Franco-Russian group. Other factors such as the decline in the French birth rate and the defeat of Russia in the Far East had also contributed to the same phenomenon. As most questions, in politics as elsewhere, have always more than one side to them, the development of our sea-power has doubtless not only fostered in England the wish to live at peace with us but also stimulated her to recognize the fact that it is in her interest to support the group opposed to us. It is therefore quite evident that any further weakening of France, and especially a defeat on the battlefield, which would relieve us of the necessity for such large armaments on land, would render still greater sums available for naval expansion, a development that would not be in the interests of Great Britain.

Soon after my arrival in London, at a time when the development of the Balkan War made the danger of an European war seem not improbable, Lord Haldane called on me, as I reported on the 3rd December, 1912 (cf. p. 348) and drew my attention to the consequences that might ensue for England from a European war. England, he said, would then find herself compelled to protect France, and this despite the fact that there was in England a fervent wish to remain permanently on friendly terms with us. I have not the faintest doubt that he was acting on behalf of Sir Edward Grey and in agreement with him, and that the purpose of his visit was to warn us against entering upon a war with Russia and France for the sake of Austria. The same warning, although perhaps in somewhat vaguer terms, was uttered in the summer of 1911 by Mr. Lloyd George when our appearance at Agadir had given rise to the suspicion that we were seeking a quarrel with France, and after Sir Edward Grey had for several weeks in vain waited for us to enlighten him on the subject.

From Sir Edward Grey, too, during the first few months of my stay in London, at a time when the Balkan War was still going on, I repeatedly received hints to the effect that England could not remain an idle onlooker in a European war. His remarks, although they were only gentle hints, could not possibly be misunderstood, and on each occasion I was able to observe how anxious he was not only to prevent the European situation from becoming acute but also to check all signs of Chauvinism among the French in order that he might avoid being compelled to intervene in favour of France.

It would have been very strange if this state of affairs had escaped the attention of such an astute diplomat as M. Cambon, and if no exchange of opinion had ever taken place between him and Sir Edward Grey on such important questions. On the contrary, I am convinced that my French colleague knows just as well as I do that people here are just as determined not to permit a war of revenge as they are to prevent a repetition of the events of 1870-1871. In a case where the relations are so clear, there is no need for formal pledges or written treaties ; and Sir Edward Grey probably took good care not to formulate in definite terms the nature of the protection to be given, for under certain circumstances mere diplomatic mediation will suffice. Military assistance is not absolutely necessary and therefore need not be made the subject of a definite assurance. Even without any formal pledge, the French know perfectly well that should they be attacked by Germany they can reckon on British support. That suffices.

After the King's return from Paris, I had an opportunity of discussing the visit and its results with a well-informed person. On his assuring me that everything had remained unchanged and that no agreements had been entered into, I commented, ' Protection in case of aggression ? ' He nodded assent.   LICHNOWSKY.

To THE IMPERIAL CHANCELLOR VON BETHMANN-HOLLWEG.

LONDON, 29th May, 1914.

In a leading article, probably from the pen of Professor Henry Spenser Wilkinson, the well-known professor of military history, the Morning Post to-day publishes some rather sharp comments on the recent utterances of Professor Schiemann on Anglo-Russian relations.

The paper speaks of an attempt to clap a pistol at England's head and compares Schiemann's suggestion with the ruthless political methods employed by Bismarck against the German States and, later, against Russia.

There is to-day, the article goes on to remark, great readiness in England in her political dealings with Germany to bury the past and begin afresh on a basis of candid frankness. Such presumptuous utterances as those of Professor Schiemann can only make it more difficult to attain this object.

Whether England is for or against Germany, says the paper, depends entirely on Germany's own behaviour. A German attack on France will naturally find England on the side of France. On the other hand, no one in England believes that France should be encouraged to attack Germany. The instinct of self-preservation does not demand that England in the event of such an attack should lend France support.

The article in the *Kreuz Zeitung* has produced an unpleasant impression on wide circles here and has probably done far more harm than good.   LICHNOWSKY.

TO THE IMPERIAL CHANCELLOR VON BETHMANN-HOLLWEG.

LONDON, *12th June*, 1914.

In the House of Commons yesterday a question was put from the Ministerial benches asking the Government whether Great Britain and Russia had recently concluded a naval agreement and whether negotiations for the conclusion of some such pact had recently taken place or were at present going on.

In his reply, Sir Edward Grey referred to similar enquiries put to the Government last year. The Prime Minister had then answered, said Sir Edward, that there were in existence no un-published agreements that would restrict or hamper the free decision of either Government or Parliament as to whether Great Britain would or would not take part in a war in the event of hostilities breaking out between European Powers. This answer described the position to-day as accurately as it had described that of a year ago. Since then no agreement with any Power had been concluded that would make the Prime Minister's declaration on that occasion less to the point to-day. No such negotiations were in progress and, as far as he could judge, it was improbable that such negotiations would be entered into. If, however, any agreement should be concluded that made it necessary to modify or withdraw the above-mentioned declaration made by the Prime Minister last year, such withdrawal or modification ought, in his opinion, first to be laid before Parliament, and this course would no doubt be followed.

Most of the London newspapers to-day refrain from any comment on the Minister's statement.

Only the two Radical papers, the *Daily News* and the *Manchester Guardian*, devote a short leading article to the matter. The former expresses satisfaction at Sir Edward Grey's statement and says that it is clear enough to dispel all doubts on the subject. England is not in tow of any other country. She is not the vassal of Russia nor the ally of France nor the enemy of Germany. The Minister's statement, the paper concludes, is a wholesome lesson for those English journalists who would fain make out that there is a Triple Entente built on similar lines to the Triple Alliance.

                                                    LICHNOWSKY.

SEVENTEENTH SECTION

ON THE EVE OF THE CATASTROPHE

To The Imperial Chancellor von Bethmann-Hollweg.

LONDON, 24*th June*, 1914.

During my visit to Sir Edward Grey to-day I took the opportunity to express to him Your Excellency's thanks for the frank and
honest statement he had made in the House of Commons, disavowing
the rumours of an alleged Anglo-Russian naval convention. I also
told him that Your Excellency welcomed the explanation so much the
more gladly as it would help in no small degree to dispel the fears
entertained of late by wide circles of the German public with regard
to our foreign relations. I remarked that it was mainly Russia that
was supplying food for this uneasiness, and that was responsible
for the resultant efforts on our part for a further increase of our
armaments. I told him that in this connection I could point
particularly to the article in the *Novoye Vremya* which had made an
unpleasant impression in Germany. In view of the possibility
that a new war in the Balkans might break out, and that Russia
might then decide on a somewhat more active foreign policy, it
seemed to us to be of the greatest importance that the intimate
contact which had existed between Great Britain and Germany
during the last crisis should be maintained in all future occurrences,
in order that we might successfully encounter any warlike policy
on the basis of a common understanding. I also called the attention
of the Minister to the fact that only by maintaining the German-
British intimacy,—coupled with our conviction that he too would
in future endeavour by virtue of his far-reaching influence at Paris
and St. Petersburg to oppose all adventurous impulses,—would it
be possible for the Imperial Government to check the armament
fever that periodically got the upper hand in our country and to
keep the existing defence programme within the prescribed limits.
In my conversation with the Minister I purposely refrained from
going into our Navy Bill as I have never since my arrival in London
touched on this delicate subject, and as he too has hitherto carefully
abstained from discussing this matter with me.

The Minister took cognisance of my remarks with evident satisfaction, and stated that he too was endeavouring to continue to go
hand in hand with us and to remain in close touch with us in all

questions that might come up.   With this end in view he had, he said, just discussed with me the present Eastern situation in the belief that this was the way best adapted for the attainment of our mutual aims.   So far as Russia was concerned, he had not the slightest reason to doubt the pacific intentions of the Russian Government.   He did not need to assure me at this time of day that Count Benckendorff was pursuing no anti-German policy here. Czar Nicholas and M. Sazonov invariably expressed themselves towards Sir George Buchanan in the most peaceful sense.   It could, however, not be denied that M. Sazonov was anxious that the Triple Entente should come more energetically to the front as a counterpoise to the firmly cemented block of the Triple Alliance.   But so far as the article in the *Novoye Vremya* was concerned, to which I had referred, the Minister said that he knew nothing whatever about it. He added smilingly that he had only last evening seen in the journal mentioned a violent attack on Great Britain on account of the Persian oil agreement.   And so far as France was concerned he had learned from a reliable source that the French had not the slightest inclination for a war and he was strengthened in this conviction by American and other foreign reports.

There existed, so Sir Edward told me, no agreements between Great Britain and other members of the Entente that had not been made public.   He could repeat to me what he had stated in Parliament on this point and he was glad, he said, to be able to add that nothing would ever occur with his consent to give the Entente an anti-German direction.   He also believed that in our country a more satisfied view of this question had of late begun to make headway.   He wished, however, to be quite frank with me and did not want me to be led into any misapprehension ;   he would therefore like to take this opportunity to tell me that in spite of the facts mentioned above his relations with the other two comrades of the Entente continued to be very intimate and that they had lost nothing of their former cordiality.   He was permanently in close touch with the Governments concerned in all important matters.

I thanked the Minister for his confidential explanations, which he had made to me in an agreeable and friendly manner.   I told him that we had no ground to take exception to this state of affairs as long as he made his powerful influence felt in favour of peace and moderation.

LICHNOWSKY.

To The Imperial Chancellor von Bethmann-Hollweg.

London, *6th July*, 1914.

I visited Sir Edward Grey this afternoon and took occasion to discuss with him in a confidential tone the whole European situation.

I thought it necessary first of all to call his attention to the fact that as a result of the murder of the heir to the throne, the relations between Austria-Hungary and Serbia had become so acute as to cause a certain amount of anxiety. No one could blame the Austrian Government for refusing to let this new challenge go unexpiated or for demanding satisfaction from the Serbian Government, in view of the support which the conspirators had been proved to have received from Belgrade. I did not know, I said, whether this would be done or what form it would take, but I believed that it would be advisable even at this juncture to be prepared for the possibility of acuter tension between Vienna and Belgrade, so that he, Sir Edward, might be in a position betimes to bring his influence to bear in St. Petersburg and induce Russia to persuade Serbia to show a spirit of compliance with the Austrian demands.

Sir Edward did not appear to have received any news as yet on this matter. He did not fail, however, to recognise the danger with which the situation might be fraught and he seemed to understand that it would be difficult for any leading Austro-Hungarian states-man to refrain for long from taking energetic measures. He promised me that he would keep in touch with us in this matter too, but did not for the present commit himself to any definite expression of opinion.

I then mentioned in connection with our last conversation that Russia's immense armaments, coupled with certain other indications, such as the construction of strategic railways, had not failed, to judge by my own personal impressions gained on my last visit to Berlin, to give rise to a certain feeling of uneasiness there. Russia's mood towards us and Austria-Hungary was undoubtedly not a friendly one. These facts when taken together with the Bosnian crime had created in Germany a somewhat pessimistic view of the foreign situation. But as we felt convinced that our policy was in accord with that of Great Britain in our common desire to maintain peace and to bring the two groups of Powers closer together, I believed that I could serve the ends of both sides by discussing the matter with him.

Sir Edward repeated to me much the same as he had told me a short time before, viz. that there were no symptoms in St. Petersburg, as far as he knew, that pointed to any anti-German feeling. Still less did he believe in any warlike intentions on the part of Russia, but he would again give the matter his attention and would return to it and discuss it with me later on, as he too was anxious to remain in touch with us in all questions of foreign policy.

In conclusion I remarked that, as I wished to be quite open with him, and as I deemed it important that he should be accurately informed concerning our views and sentiments, he must permit me to touch confidentially on a somewhat delicate topic. We knew from his statements, I said, that there were no secret agreements of a political nature in existence between England and Russia. We had, of course, not the slightest occasion to doubt the correctness of his words and we therefore regretted it the more that rumours were always cropping up to the effect that there was a naval understanding the object of which was co-operation between Great Britian and Russia against Germany in case of war. I was not in a position to investigate the correctness of these reports, but I could well imagine that any discussions that might have taken place between the naval authorities on either side might not fall within the category of political agreements or binding treaties and that such discussions might therefore be quite in keeping with his statements. In this case, I regarded it as my duty to draw his attention to the fact that such conversational arrangements could not but help to strengthen the nationalist current that existed beyond doubt in Russia, and on the other hand would foster the desire felt by us for increased armaments and make it more difficult for the German Government to curb the demands already known to him and keep them within the limits fixed by law for naval and military expenditure.

Sir Edward, without going into the question of a naval agreement upon which I had touched, replied that he had already told me a short time before that there was no new or secret understanding, but that the relations between England and the other nations of the Entente nevertheless bore a very intimate character. From his reserve and from his remark that he would return to the discussion of the matter with me later, I was able to gather that he wants to think the matter well over before giving a definite reply to the question I had broached. In any case, he did not definitely deny that the two navies had got into touch for the contingency of a war in which they might both be engaged. He again emphasised, however, on this occasion that it was his endeavour to bring the two groups closer together and thus prevent European complications and render easier an understanding on all questions that might arise.

The Minister was obviously impressed by what I told him and thanked me for the frankness of my statements which had been made quite in the tone of our usual pleasant and friendly talks.

LICHNOWSKY.

TO THE IMPERIAL CHANCELLOR VON BETHMANN-HOLLWEG.

LONDON, 9th July, 1914.

Sir Edward Grey asked me to call on him to-day. He began by communicating to me the notes he had made on the conversation [1] we had had shortly before my visit to Berlin and Kiel. He said that he had to-day nothing to add to his statement on that occasion and could only repeat that there was no such thing as secret agreements between Great Britain on the one hand and France and Russia on the other which imposed obligations on Great Britain in the case of a European war. England wished to preserve an absolutely free hand, so that in the event of Continental complications she might be able to act according to her own judgment. The Government had to a certain extent pledged itself to Parliament not to enter into any secret obligations. Under no circumstances would the British Government be found on the side of the aggressor in any Continental complications that might arise.

As, however, he did not wish to give me a false impression—' as I do not want to mislead you '—he at once added that England's relations with the Powers mentioned had lost nothing of their earlier intimacy. Even though there were no such thing as agreements which imposed obligations of any kind whatever, he did not wish to deny that from time to time ' conversations ' had taken place between the naval or military authorities on the two sides, the first of these conversations as early as the year 1906, and then during the Morocco crisis when people here believed, as he laughingly added, that Germany intended to attack the French. But these conversations, too, about which he had known nothing very definite at the time, had like the others had absolutely no aggressive aim, as English policy then as now had been directed towards the maintenance of

---

[1] See dispatch dated 24th June, 1914, p. 368. (Tr.)

peace and would find itself in a very painful situation if a European war broke out.

I repeated to the Minister much the same as I had recently told him and then gave him to understand that it would be desirable that such military conversations should be limited to a minimum, as otherwise they might easily lead to unwished-for consequences.

Since our last conversation, Sir Edward added, he had informed himself very thoroughly concerning the feeling that existed towards Germany in Russia and had found no reason to take a disquieting view ; he seemed to be ready, moreover, in the event of our wishing it, to use his influence in some form or other to get Russia to modify her attitude. He had also been endeavouring to persuade the Russian Government even at the present juncture to adopt a calm view and a conciliatory attitude towards Austria should the Vienna Cabinet feel obliged in consequence of the Serajevo murder to take up a stern attitude towards Serbia. Much would, of course, depend, Sir Edward Grey thought, on the nature of any measures that might be contemplated and whether these measures were such as to arouse Slav feeling in a manner that might make it impossible for M. Sazonov to remain passive.

On the whole the Minister was quite optimistic and declared in cheerful tones that he saw no reason for taking a gloomy view of the situation.

LICHNOWSKY.

THE SECRETARY OF STATE FOR FOREIGN AFFAIRS TO THE
    AMBASSADOR AT LONDON.

BERLIN, 12th July, 1914.

The investigation of the crime committed at Serajevo shows more and more clearly that the people who are morally responsible for the murder are to be found in political and military circles at Belgrade. There is a possibility that Austria may consequently resolve on serious action against Serbia and that this may lead to general complications. We desire under all circumstances a localization of the conflict.[1] To attain this end it is necessary that public

[1] In the text of Radowitz, the recording Counsellor of the German Foreign Office, the passage ' a possibility ... conflict ' originally ran : ' Austria seems determined not to let this opportunity for a reckoning with Serbia pass. We are sympathetic with this point of view but desire that any possible war may remain localized.' The alteration was made by Zimmermann. (Tr.)

opinion in Europe shall make it possible for the various Governments to look on without taking sides at the settlement of the differences between Austria and Serbia. It is therefore necessary that in the British Press, too, there should be created at the present juncture a mood which sees in the murder of the Archduke as it did in the earlier murder of the King and Queen of Serbia the outcome of a political criminal code representing a morality which is incompatible with the civilised conscience of Europe and which makes it appear comprehensible that the neighbouring monarchy must defend itself against this permanent menace on the part of Serbia. Please do your best to influence the British Press along these lines, being careful, however, at the same time to avoid anything that might give the impression that we were inciting the Austrians to war.

JAGOW.

TO THE FOREIGN OFFICE. LONDON, 14th July, 1914.

I have already attempted confidentially and cautiously in the manner suggested to get into touch with public opinion, but in view of the well-known independence of the Press here, I do not promise myself much success as the result of that sort of influence. To brand the whole Serbian people as a nation of rascals and murderers and thus deprive it of the sympathies of civilized Europe, as the *Lokal-anzeiger* is trying to do, is a somewhat difficult task. Still more difficult will it prove to put the Serbs on the same level as the Arabs of Egypt and Morocco or the Indians of Mexico, as an official personage does in an interview with the Vienna correspondent of the *Daily Telegraph*. Rather is it to be assumed that directly Austria adopts violent measures the sympathies of people here will instantly and decidedly turn in favour of the Serbs, and that the assassination of the Archduke, who on account of his clerical leanings is already not very popular in this country, will be regarded as a mere pretext that is being utilized in order to injure an inconvenient neighbour. British sympathies, especially those of the Liberal Party, have in Europe mostly favoured the principle of nationality ; in the struggle of the Italians against the Austrian, Papal or Bourbon domination, British sympathies went with the Italians, just as in the various Balkan crises they have usually gone with the Slavs. Both during the annexation crisis and last winter when the various problems became acute, British public opinion was inclined to take sides with Serbia and Montenegro, and it would have been very difficult at that time to get the British to consent to energetic measures against King Nicholas.

However ready people here may be to understand the relentless punishment of the murderers according to the penal code, just as little will public opinion approve of the affair being transferred to the political sphere or of its being made a pretext for military measures against a 'nation of criminals.' In such an event the present Cabinet, already weakened by the crisis in home affairs, would hardly be strong enough to support a policy running counter both to the ethical sense of the nation and to the tastes of the Liberal Party.   LICHNOWSKY.

To The Foreign Office.   London, 15th *July*, 1914.

I have already attempted, not only by repeated conferences with Sir Edward Grey, concerning which I have already sent in reports, but also by cautiously getting into touch with the Press here, to prepare the ground for a favourable judgment concerning any more serious measures that may prove necessary to be taken by Austria against Serbia. Sir Edward Grey said that everything would depend on what kind of intervention was contemplated by Austria and that under no circumstances ought Serbia to be expected to forfeit a part of her territory. He has also, as has been reported, been striving to influence St. Petersburg in favour of Austria's claims. Should, however, violent excitement arise in Russia in consequence of Austria's military measures, he would be quite unable to put a curb on Russian policy and, in view of the feeling of dissatisfaction which at present prevails in Russia against England, concerning which Count Pourtalès has informed us, he will, he says, have to humour Russian sensibilities. In any case the Minister will, I feel certain, do his utmost to hold Russia back should a conflict between Austria and Serbia break out. I do not believe, however, that he is in a position to speak as decisive a word in St. Petersburg as he is in Paris.

As regards public opinion in this country, I must, I regret to say, abide by the statements in my telegram and must urgently warn you not to be misled. In spite of the bombs of the Mazzinists, who in the pursuit of their political aims were as little squeamish as were the members of the Ochrana, and who, as is well known, did not scruple to attempt the lives of sovereigns, British public opinion sided with the Italian movement for unity and Garibaldi was fêted here with extravagant enthusiasm. Austria in those days was just as unsuccessful in dealing a deathblow at the Italian nationalist movement as she is to-day in gaining sympathy here, and I doubt whether the Serbs can be induced to renounce their activities on behalf of the realization of their national ideals and hopes outside their official frontiers by threats to employ main force. LICHNOWSKY.

To The Foreign Office. LONDON, 16th July, 1914.

To-day's *Times* publishes a leader dealing with Austria and Serbia. The journal sharply condemns the provocative attitude of the Belgrade Press which, it says, is alienating the sympathies of the civilized world. The paper expects a ready compliance on the part of the Serbian Government with the demands for a thorough investigation of the crime, and for guarantees against further support of the revolutionary movement. At the same time the journal warns the Austrians against pursuing a policy such as that demanded by the military periodicals, a policy by which Austria has everything to lose and nothing to gain. The Yugoslav question, the most difficult of all Austro-Hungarian problems can, says the paper, never be solved by violence or threats. Any attempt in this direction will be much more likely to jeopardize the peace of Europe. Austria's own history ought to teach the Monarchy to what it would lead if the policy of calm self-control were abandoned.

I repeat my opinion that if military measures are taken against Serbia, public opinion will unanimously turn against Austria-Hungary. LICHNOWSKY.

To The Imperial Chancellor von Bethmann-Hollweg.

LONDON, 16th July, 1914.

From Count Berchtold's standpoint, it is quite comprehensible that he should conceive of making use of the present comparatively favourable opportunity of restoring, by means of a passage at arms with Serbia, his own reputation as a statesman, a reputation that was seriously shaken by the Peace of Bucharest, and of re-establishing Austria's influence in the Balkans, impaired as that influence had been by the desertion of Rumania. The leading military authorities in Austria have, as is well known, for some time past been urging that the Monarchy should strengthen its prestige by means of a war.   At one moment it was Italy whose irredentist movement was to be crushed, at another it was Serbia that was to be forced to renounce her claims and compelled to better manners by feats of war *à la* Prince Eugène.   Let me repeat that I quite understand this way of looking at things on the part of the Austrian statesmen and had I been in their position I might perhaps have exploited the Serbian disturbances even earlier to solve the Yugoslav problem in a Hapsburgian sense.

The primary assumption for the carrying out of such a policy must necessarily be a clear programme based upon the recognition of the fact that the present condition of national and international law within the Serbo-Croat family of nations cannot be looked upon as containing any elements of permanence.   For these anomalous legal conditions allot to the Austrian State one part of this family of nations, which is split up by differences of religion but not by differences of race, a second part they allot to the State of Hungary, a third to the Dual Monarchy as a whole and a fourth and a fifth part to independent kingdoms.   For the endeavour to maintain the sacred *status quo*, come what may, on mere grounds of convenience has often, as it recently did at the time of the last Balkan crisis, led to the complete collapse of the political house of cards built up on these foundations.

Now I doubt, first of all, whether any broad plan such as alone would offer a basis for a permanent settlement of the South Slav question,—I mean a Threefold Monarchy with the inclusion of Serbia,—has been thought out at Vienna.   From my personal knowledge of conditions prevailing in those parts, I doubt very much whether Austria is in a position to introduce a constitutional transformation of this description in the Monarchy.   For the first thing necessary would be to overcome the opposition of Hungary, which would oppose to the uttermost the cession of Croatia and Fiume. To carry such a programme into effect Vienna also lacks a man of sufficiently strong personality.   In the Austrian capital all they do, as a general rule, is to try to satisfy the needs of the moment, and they are happy when the many political difficulties, which are always cropping up as a result of the heterogeneousness of the Empire, have been temporarily removed, so that there is a prospect of being able to muddle along for another few months.

The infliction of military punishment on Serbia should therefore never have the purpose, as it could never achieve the result, of satisfactorily solving the extremely difficult Jugoslav problem, but at best could only result in once more bringing into the foreground the Eastern question, a question which had been settled with so much trouble at the Ambassadors' Conference in London, merely in order to afford Austria some sort of moral satisfaction.

Whether Russia and Rumania would stand idly by and leave Austria a free hand, Your Excellency is better in a position to judge than I. From the impression I have received here, and especially from the confidential talks I have had with Sir Edward Grey, I believe that I was quite right in the views that I expressed on my recent visit to Berlin concerning Russia's intentions towards us. Sir Edward Grey assures me that no one in Russia dreams for a moment of going to war with us. My cousin, Count Benckendorff, tells me much the same thing. A certain anti-German feeling regularly crops up from time to time in Russia, but is to be regarded as a mere ebullition of Slav temperament. Against this tendency there is always a strong pro-German party in existence. Neither the Czar nor any of the people who count are anti-German, and since the days when the Liman question was settled there has been no bad feeling that any one could take at all seriously. Count Benckendorff frankly admitted, on the other hand, that there exists in Russia a strong anti-Austrian sentiment; but no one in Russia, he says, dreams of trying to annex any part of Austria, such as Galicia, for example, by conquest

Whether in view of Russian feeling on this subject, it would be possible to persuade the Russian Government to remain a passive spectator of the Austro-Serbian passage at arms, I cannot judge. But what I do feel that I can say with certainty is that if there is a war it will be impossible to influence public opinion here against Serbia, even by summoning up the bloody shades of Draga and her paramour, whose removal has long since been forgotten by the British public, and thus belongs among those historic events with which so far as the history of non-British countries is concerned, people here are in general less familiar than is, say, the average third form schoolboy in our country.

[Now I am far from advocating the sacrifice of either our alliance or our ally. I consider the alliance, which has won its way into the sentimental life of both nations, as necessary, and this if only out

of regard for the many Germans living in Austria as the natural form
of their attachment to us.]   The question is whether it is wise for us
to support our ally in a policy or to guarantee a policy, which I look
upon as adventurous, since it will lead neither to a radical solution of
the problem nor to the annihilation of the Greater Serbia movement.
If the Austrian police and the Bosnian territorial authorities thought
good to let the Heir to the Throne run the gauntlet of an ' avenue of
bomb-throwers,' I fail to see in that fact any sufficient reason why we
should risk the life of the celebrated Pomeranian grenadier for the
sake of Austria's Pandour policy,[1] merely in order to strengthen
Austria's self-assertivemess, which then, as the Aehrenthal epoch
showed after the Bosnian crisis, regards it as its supreme function
to shake off the tutelage of Berlin as far as possible.

If, however, we really allow our policy to be decided by the consideration that as soon as the Greater Serbia movement has received
its deathblow, ' happy Austria,' relieved of this anxiety, will show
herself grateful to us for the assistance we have rendered, I cannot
refrain from asking whether the national movement in Hungary was
stamped out after the Hungarian rebellion had been crushed with
the help of Czar Nicholas and the manifold requisitioning of the
gallows after the subjugation of the Hungarians at Vilagos under
the direction of the Imperial General Haynau, and whether the rescue
of Austria by the Czar really laid the foundation of a cordial and
trustful relationship between the two Empires.

LICHNOWSKY.

THE SECRETARY OF STATE FOR FOREIGN AFFAIRS, HERR VON JAGOW,
   TO THE AMBASSADOR AT LONDON, PRINCE LICHNOWSKY.

DEAR LICHNOWSKY,   BERLIN, 18*th July*, 1914.
      Your verdict on our policy, as contained in your Serbian
report, is always appreciated by me, and I am sure that the Chancellor feels the same way about it.   Nor do I hesitate to acknowledge
the justification of many of your remarks.   But after all, we have
an alliance with Austria : *hic Rhodus, hic salta.*   It is also arguable
whether we are likely to find an alliance with that crumbling con-
stellation of States on the Danube a good investment ; but I say
with the poet—I think it was Busch—' If you no longer like your

---

[1] The Pandours were a Hungarian regiment recruited from wild Croatian
mountaineers, once notorious as marauders. Cf. ' Her whiskered Pandours
and her fierce Hussars ' (Campbell). (Tr.).

company, try to find other, if other there be.' And unfortunately
we have not yet been able to arrive at a relationship with England
that promises full success, nor could we, after all that has passed,
expect to do so—indeed who knows whether we ever shall.

Austria, as a result of her lack of energy, has lost more and more
of her prestige and has already almost ceased to count as a Great
Power in the full sense of the word. The Balkan crisis has still
further weakened her position. Our Triple Alliance group has also
been decidedly weakened by Austria's falling behind as a Power.

Austria no longer intends to put up with Serbia's subterranean
activities ; nor will she any longer brook the persistent provocative
demeanour of her small neighbour at Belgrade—witness the language
of the Serbian Press and of M. Pashich. She fully realizes that she
has neglected many opportunities and that she can now act, whereas
in a few years she will perhaps no longer be able to do so. Austria
is determined to settle her accounts with Serbia and has informed us
of this fact. Throughout the Balkan crisis we mediated successfully
in the sense of peace without forcing Austria to passivity at critical
moments. That we are nevertheless accused—quite unjustly—by
many people in Austria of manipulating her affairs for our own
future advantage is a matter of indifference to me. Nor have we at
the present juncture driven Austria to her decision (?). But we
neither can nor dare stay her hand. If we were to do so, Austria
might rightly reproach us (and we ourselves might do the same) with
having robbed her of her last possible chance of political rehabilitation. This would only serve to hasten the process of her wasting
away and of her internal disintegration. Her prestige in the Balkans
would be gone for ever. That an absolute consolidation of the
Russian hegemony in the Balkans would indirectly be inadmissible
for us too you will perhaps grant me (?). The maintenance of
Austria and, moreover, of as strong an Austria as possible, is essential
for us both for internal and external reasons. I am quite ready to
admit that Austria cannot hope to be maintained for ever. But in
the meantime perhaps we may discover other combinations.

We must do our best to localize the conflict between Austria and
Serbia. Whether this can be achieved depends in the first place on
Russia and in the second place on the moderating influence exercised
by her brethren of the Entente. *The more resolute Austria shows
herself and the more energetically we support her, the sooner will Russia
stop her outcry. To be sure, they will make a great to-do in St. Peters-*

burg, but when all is said and done, Russia is at present not ready for war.   Nor will either France or England wish for a war at present. In a few years Russia, in the opinion of competent judges, will be ready to fight.   Then she will crush us by the number of her soldiers. By then she will have built her Baltic Fleet and her strategic railways. Our group will in the meantime grow weaker and weaker.   In Russia they probably know this, and for this reason Russia definitely wants peace for a few years longer.   I am quite ready to believe your cousin Benckendorff that Russia is at present not anxious for a war with us.   Sazonov, too, gives the same assurance, but the Government in Russia which to-day is still pacific and half-pro-German, is growing weaker and weaker, the mood of Slavdom more and more anti-German.   How Russia would treat us in principle is shown by what happened last autumn.   During the Balkan crisis, she could not thank us enough for our quietening influence.   Hardly was the acute crisis over than she began to be unfriendly—about Liman, etc.   *If a localization of the conflict cannot be achieved and Russia attacks Austria, the* casus foederis *will come into force*, in that case *we cannot sacrifice Austria.*   We should then stand in a kind of isolation which could hardly be described as proud.   I do not desire a preventive war, but *if we are called upon to fight, we must not funk it.*

I hope and believe even now that the conflict can be localized. England's attitude will be of great importance in this matter.   I am absolutely convinced that public opinion there will not be exactly enthusiastic over Austria's line of action and I admit the correctness of all your arguments on this point.   But we must do everything possible to prevent British opinion from becoming too enthusiastic for Serbia, for it is a long way from both sympathy and antipathy to the starting of a world conflagration.   Sir Edward Grey is always talking about the balance of power which results from the existence of the two groups of Powers.   It must, therefore, be perfectly plain to him that this balance of power would be shattered should Austria be left by us and be smashed to pieces by Russia, and that the balance of power would be made to totter rather badly by a world conflagration.   He must, therefore, if he is logical and honest, stand by us and help us to localize the conflict.   But *satis superque.*   It is now 1 a.m.   Although these arguments concerning our policy may perhaps not have convinced you, I know that you will give this policy your support.

With best greetings, Yours very sincerely,   JAGOW.

19th July.

Have just received your letter of the 17th. In the main it is answered by the above. Leave of absence is for the present a *cura posterior* ; shall write you later concerning the Colonial Treaty.

J.

To The Imperial Chancellor von Bethmann-Hollweg.

London, *17th July*, 1914.

To-day's *Westminster Gazette* publishes the enclosed leading article on the European situation. It is noteworthy on account of its calm and objective discussion of the Austro-Serbian quarrel. In view of the friendly relations existing between the editor, Mr. Spender, and Sir Edward Grey, it is not difficult to guess that the views of the Minister have not been without influence on his arguments and that my repeated conversations with him have contributed *to getting this recognition of Austria's right to satisfaction*. But even this voice, which is friendly to the Government, expresses the definite expectation that the *ultima ratio* will be avoided.

Lichnowsky.

London, *20th July*, 1914.

To the Foreign Office.

Count Benckendorff, with whom I spent the week-end yesterday at Lord Lansdowne's, told me that he could assure me that the views he had recently communicated to me concerning our relations with Russia quite corresponded with M. Sazonov's ideas. It was even felt to be an inconvenience, he said, that M. Poincaré should pay his visit at this particular juncture, but one could not very well give him a hint to stay away. In Russia nobody thought of war, the armaments were purely a consequence of all the rest and of the improved finances. It was therefore much to be regretted that ill-feeling that was totally unjustified and probably was based merely on gossip and false reports could arise. A frank interchange of opinion would probably prove the quickest way to the goal. The excitement in Belgrade was, he said, being damped down as far as possible.

Lichnowsky.

LONDON, *20th July*, 1914.

TO THE FOREIGN OFFICE.

From the statements made to me to-day by Sir Edward Grey during my visit to him, I gather that he still regards the Austro-Serbian quarrel optimistically, and that he still believes that a peaceful solution will be found. He said he had received no information that would point to the contrary. I took this opportunity once more to assure him that I was convinced that Count Berchtold, after a minute examination of all that had happened and with the help of convincing evidence, would feel compelled to demand satisfaction from Serbia and a guarantee for the future, and that I hoped that Russia and England would succeed in influencing Serbia to fulfil these justified demands. He replied that everything depended upon what form of satisfaction would be demanded and whether this were done with moderation, and especially, too, whether the accusations brought against Serbia could be made on the basis of demonstrable proofs. In this manner he hoped, he said, that the dispute might be settled and restricted within certain limits, for the thought of a war between the Great Powers of Europe must under all circumstances be rejected.

The Minister has, moreover, had Vienna informed that the recent article in the *Westminster Gazette*, about which I sent in a report, had not been prompted by him, as he had learned that people in Vienna were interpreting the article as an encouragement to begin the attack.

LICHNOWSKY.

LONDON, *22nd July*, 1914.

TO THE FOREIGN OFFICE.

Sir Edward Grey will, as I learn in confidence, to-morrow inform Count Mensdorff that the British Government will strive to use its influence to persuade the Serbian Government to accept the Austro-Hungarian demands, provided the latter are moderate and are compatible with the independence of the Serbian State.

LICHNOWSKY.

THE SECRETARY OF STATE FOR FOREIGN AFFAIRS TO THE KAISER.

BERLIN, *23rd July*, 1914.

Your Majesty's Ambassador in London telegraphs :

' Sir Edward Grey, as I am confidentially informed, will to-morrow tell Count Mensdorff that the British Government will strive to use its influence to persuade the Serbian Government to accept the Austro-Hungarian demands, provided the latter are *moderate and that they are compatible with the independence of the Serbian State*. He believes, too, that Sazonov will use his influence in Belgrade in a similar sense. But the condition preliminary to this attitude is, he says, that no unproven accusations *à la* Friedjung be brought forward by Vienna and that the Austro-Hungarian Government should be in a position unambiguously to state the connection between the Serajevo murder and Belgrade political circles. Everything depends upon the form given to the Note in Vienna and on the results of the investigations hitherto conducted. It is impossible, however, to make representations in Belgrade on the basis of *frivolous* statements. I am in the meanwhile endeavouring to influence matters here so that in consideration of Austria's justifiable demands for satisfaction and for the cessation once for all of the constant irritations, they may advocate the unconditional acceptance of the Austrian demands, even if these demands should fail fully to take into consideration *Serbia's national dignity*. In doing this, I find that people are expecting that our influence in Vienna has succeeded in suppressing demands that are impossible of fulfilment. People here count definitely upon our not identifying ourselves with demands which manifestly aim at bringing about war and upon our not supporting any policy which uses the Serajevo murder as a pretext for the achievement of Austria's wishes in the Balkans and for the

It's not for him to decide as to this; that's the business of His Majesty the Emperor Franz Joseph!

That's their affair!

What does he mean by frivolous? How can Grey use such a word with reference to that old and venerable monarch!

There is no such thing!

Why should I do this! It's no business of mine what is meant by impossible of fulfilment. The rascals have carried on agitation coupled with murder and must get a good dressing down.

That's a monstrous piece of British impudence. It's not my task to prescribe à la Grey to His Majesty the Emperor what steps he is to take to preserve his honour!

Right! Grey must be told this quite seriously and plainly!

So that he may see that I am not to be played with. Grey makes the mistake of putting Serbia on a level with Austria and the other great Powers! That is monstrous. Serbia is a band of robbers that must be arrested for its crimes! I will not meddle with anything that the Emperor alone is competent to deal with. I have been expecting this telegram and it does not surprise me! Real British reasoning and condescending way of giving orders which, I insist, must be turned down!

WILHELM, I.R.

annihilation of the Peace of Bucharest. Sir Edward Grey has to-day again sent word to me to say that he is endeavouring to use his influence in St. Petersburg in the sense of the Austrian standpoint. It has, however, made an unpleasant impression here that Count Berchtold has hitherto ostentatiously avoided discussing the Serbian question with Sir Maurice de Bunsen.'

To guide him in his utterances, Your Majesty's Ambassador in London has received instructions [1] to the effect that we do not know the Austrian demands, but that we regard them as an internal question of Austria-Hungary's in which we have no right to interfere.

Most humbly and obediently,

JAGOW.

[1] On the same day, 23rd July, 1914, von Jagow sent the telegram quoted below to the German Ambassadors at London and Paris. In the message sent to London, but not in that sent to Paris, occurs the sentence, ' We are not acquainted with the Austrian demands.' This was added by von Jagow to von Stumm's original draft. (Tr.)

THE SECRETARY OF STATE FOR FOREIGN AFFAIRS TO THE AMBASSADOR AT LONDON.

BERLIN, 23rd July, 1914.

We are not acquainted with the Austrian demands.

We regard the settlement of the Austro-Serbian dispute as an internal matter to be fought out exclusively between the two participants, and as one on which we have no right to exercise an influence ; we have therefore exerted no influence whatever on the Vienna Cabinet.

Your Serene Highness will therefore not undertake to carry out the directions sent to London yesterday evening until after the wording of the Austrian Note to the Serbian Government has been made public through the Press. Otherwise the impression might arise that we had been acquainted with the Note in advance.

JAGOW.

To The Foreign Office. London, *23rd July*, 1914.

My Italian colleague told me in the course of a lengthy and confidential conversation that it would be extremely difficult for any Italian Government to come before the country and advocate Italy's participation in a war the aim of which might be the conquest or Austrianisation of Serbia. Italy was carrying on an active trade with Serbia and had not the slightest interest in seeing this trade ruined by Austria. The war would thus run directly counter to Italian interests and was therefore only to be waged if Austria promised adequate advantages in return.

I should like to ask that these statements be treated as strictly confidential.

Lichnowsky.

To The Foreign Office. London, *23rd July*, 1914.

The former Rumanian Minister, M. Take Jonescu, at present staying here, and with whom I became acquainted while I was at the Legation at Bucharest, tells me that M. Sazonov on the occasion of his recent visit gave King Carol the most explicit assurances of Russia's desire for peace. The Russian Minister had also refrained from any suggestion of a closer understanding with Rumania. M. Sazonov had, however, in definite language stated that Russia would not tolerate an attack on Serbia by Austria. M. Take Jonescu expresses the opinion that in the event of Austria's invading Serbian territory, Russia will find herself compelled to intervene with her armies, even at the risk of a defeat. From utterances made by the Ambassador Margrave Pallavicini who a short time ago, just before the Serajevo crime, paid a visit to Bucharest, the Rumanian statesman says that he gathered that Austria, even previous to the assassination, wanted war and had only been waiting for a suitable opportunity to rehabilitate her prestige in the Balkans, which had been forfeited through Count Berchtold's policy. He, too, regards the situation as extremely grave, and gave me to understand that Rumania, in a new Balkan war, could not remain disinterested, and that she wished to see the Treaty of Bucharest kept in force.

M. Take Jonescu characterized the relations of his country with Austria as bad ; the Russian visit had therefore come at an awkward moment for King Carol, but he had not been able to refuse to receive M. Sazonov.

Up to a fortnight ago Rumania had been ready, he said, to send a large force to Albania in the event of each of the Great Powers being willing to send even a mere hundred men in addition. Whether this willingness still existed, he could not tell me. He did not believe that the insurrection movement in Albania was being fostered by Serbians or Greeks, but rather that it had originated among the Young Turks, who imagined that if there were new complications, some fragment or other might fall to their share. Serbia, he said, was well aware that she would not be allowed into Northern Albania, and she preferred to see the country under Prince Wilhelm rather than have it occupied by an Austro-Italian force.

LICHNOWSKY.

TO THE FOREIGN OFFICE.   LONDON, 24th July, 1914.

Count Benckendorff has been to see me. He tells me in strict confidence that he thinks it scarcely possible to advise the Serbian Government to accept conditions of that description, unless Serbia is to sink to the level of a vassal of Austria's. He does not think that Russia is in a position to give such advice. It would be tantamount to handing the Serbs unconditionally over to Austria. Public opinion in Russia would not tolerate this. Only a Government that wanted war would write such a Note; that was not the tone of peace. Up to the present Sir Edward Grey had not spoken with him.

LICHNOWSKY.

TO THE FOREIGN OFFICE.   LONDON, 24th July, 1914.

Sir Edward Grey has just sent for me. The Minister was obviously deeply affected by the Austrian Note, which in his opinion went beyond anything of the kind he had ever seen. He said that he had so far received no information from St. Petersburg and therefore did not know how they felt there about the matter. He is very doubtful whether it will prove possible for the Russian Government to recommend the Serbian Government to accept the Austrian demands unconditionally. A State that accepted such

This is devoutly to be wished. It is not a nation in the European sense, but a band of robbers!

conditions would, strictly speaking, cease to count as an independent State. It was difficult for him, Sir Edward Grey, to give St. Petersburg any advice whatever at the present moment. He could only hope that a mild and calm view of the situation might gain ground there. As long as it was a question of a localized conflict between Austria and Serbia—as Your Excellency emphasizes in dispatch 1055,[1] which I utilized in my conversations with Sir Edward Grey, he, Sir Edward Grey, was not concerned in the matter ; the question would, however, assume another aspect if public opinion in Russia compelled the Government to take steps against Austria.

Right.

[1] The following circular dispatch from the Imperial Chancellor, signed by von Jagow, was sent to the Ambassador at St. Petersburg on 21st July, and to Paris and London on 22nd July. The last paragraph, ' Your Excellency will furthermore ' down to ' blind to the fact,' went only to St. Petersburg and was omitted from the German White Book of May 1915, where the dispatch is dated 23rd July. (See K.D. 100, note.) (Translator's note.)

THE IMPERIAL CHANCELLOR TO THE AMBASSADORS AT
ST. PETERSBURG AND LONDON

BERLIN, *21st July*, 1914.

The published statements of the Austro-Hungarian Government relating to the circumstances under which the assassination of the heir to the Austrian throne and of his wife took place, fully reveal the goal which the Greater-Serbia propaganda has been aiming at and the means of which it availed itself for the attainment of its ends. The facts that have been made public must also remove the last doubt that the centre of the activities that were to result in the separation of the Southern Slav provinces from the Austro-Hungarian Monarchy and in their union with the Kingdom of Serbia, is to be found in Belgrade, and were developed there at least with the connivance of members of the Government and of the Army.

The Serbian mischief-making extends back over a long term of years. The Greater-Serbia Chauvinism made its appearance in particularly marked form during the Bosnian crisis. It was only the extreme moderation and self-command of the Austro-Hungarian Government and the energetic intervention of the great Powers that prevented the provocations to which Austria-Hungary was at that time exposed by Serbia leading to war. The Serbian Government has not made good the assurances of future good conduct which Serbia gave at that time. The Greater-Serbia propaganda has since been continually increasing in extent and intensity under the very eyes of official Serbia, and, at least, with its tacit consent. It is to the account of that propaganda that the latest outrage, the threads of which lead to Belgrade, can be charged. It has become unmistakably evident that it would no longer be compatible either with the dignity or with the self-preservation of the Austro-Hungarian Monarchy to look on inactive any longer at the intrigues being carried on on the other side of the border—intrigues by which the security and integrity of its dominions are permanently menaced. In such a state of affairs neither the procedure nor the demands of the Austro-Hungarian Government can be

Right, for they aren't!
Right.

In reply to my remark that one could not measure the Balkan peoples by the same standard as the *civilised nations* of Europe—as was demonstrated by their barbaric methods of warfare—and that one had therefore to use a different tone towards them than towards the British and the Germans, the Minister said that although he might perhaps share this view, he did not believe

Then the Russians themselves are not any better.
Which will certainly happen.
He forgets Italy.

that it would be shared in Russia. The danger of a European war would become imminent should Austria *invade Serbian territory*. The results of such a war between *four* nations, and he especially stressed the ' four,' meaning thereby Russia, Austria-Hungary, Germany and France, were absolutely incalculable. However the affair might end, one thing was certain and that was that there would be total exhaustion and impoverishment, that industry and trade would be

regarded as otherwise than moderate and proper. Nevertheless the attitude adopted of late by both the public opinion and the Government of Serbia, does not exclude the fear that the Serbian Government may refuse to satisfy these demands and that it is allowing itself to be driven into a provocatory attitude towards Austria-Hungary. In such a case there would remain for the Austro-Hungarian Government, unless it wished to dispense for ever with its standing as a great Power, no alternative but to enforce its demands upon the Serbian Government by strong pressure and if necessary by the adoption of military measures, measures in which the choice of means must be left to the Austro-Hungarian Government.

I have the honour of requesting Your Excellency to communicate these arguments to the Russian Minister of Foreign Affairs and in so doing particularly to emphasize the view that the problem under discussion is one which it is solely for Austria-Hungary and Serbia to solve, and one which it should be the earnest endeavour of the Powers to confine to the two immediate participants. We urgently desire the localisation of the conflict, as any intervention on the part of another Power would, as a result of the various alliance obligations, bring about incalculable consequences.

Your Excellency will, furthermore, call M. Sazonov's attention to the serious consequences which might ensue for the monarchical idea, if, setting aside for the moment any possible national prejudices or political points of view, the monarchical Powers should not, in the case suggested above, stand solidly by the side of Austria-Hungary, inasmuch as it is a question of dealing the deathblow to the political radicalism now dominant in Serbia, a radicalism which does not hesitate to make even members of the families of its own rulers the victims of its criminal tendencies. Russia is quite as much interested in such a task as is Germany. I venture to hope that M. Sazonov will not shut his eyes to this fact.

I shall await with interest a telegraphic report of your conference at your earliest convenience.

BETHMANN-HOLLWEG.

ruined and capital destroyed. Revolutionary movements such as those of the year 1848 would follow as a consequence of the languishing of industrial life. Besides the tone of the Note, Sir Edward Grey deeply deplores the brief time limit which makes war almost inevitable, he thinks. He told me that he would be prepared to join with *Useless.* us in asking for a prolongation of the time limit at Vienna, as *a way out might then perhaps be found.* He requested me to forward this proposal to Your Excellency. He furthermore suggested that in the event of a dangerous tension between Russia and Austria, the four nations not immediately concerned, England, Germany, France and Italy, should undertake to mediate between Russia and Austria. This proposal, too, he requested me to submit to Your Excellency.

This is superfluous as Austria has already made matters plain to Russia and Grey has nothing else to propose. I will not join in it unless Austria expressly asks me to, which is not likely. In vital questions and those of honour one does not consult other people.

The Minister is obviously trying to do everything to avoid European complications and could not conceal his lively regret at the provocative tone of the Austrian Note and at the brief time limit.

I am informed from another quarter in the British Foreign Office that there is reason for assuming that Austria greatly underestimates Serbia's power of resistance. In any case, it will be a long and bitter struggle and one that will greatly weaken Austria and in which she will *Nonsense.* *bleed to death.* I am also told that the attitude of *It may bring England Persia.* Rumania is more than uncertain and that in Bucharest they have declared that they would be against anybody who attacked. LICHNOWSKY.

To The Secretary of State for Foreign Affairs.

                                        LONDON, *23rd July*, 1914.

DEAR JAGOW,

Many thanks for your letter of the 18th, which, however, was not able, I am sorry to say, altogether to convince me.

We have, I admit, an alliance with Austria and I should like to repeat at the very start, that I think this alliance useful, although it perhaps no longer altogether corresponds to the assumptions under which Bismarck concluded it. Bismarck was under the impression that there was a danger of a war of *revanche*, undertaken with the help of Russia. This danger no longer exists for us in the same degree as it did at that time. Russia's sphere of interest has shifted eastward. New territories are continually being opened up in those regions for the expansion of Russian power and new questions are continually cropping up to occupy Russia's attention there. I do not believe that Russia will attack us. It seems to me quite clear that France will only remain the vassal of Russia and that England will continue to shut an eye to the Russian advance in Asia only so long as the attention of both of them is concentrated mainly on us. What interest could Russia possibly have in making war ?—As far back as I can recollect, that is to say, as long as I have been in touch with diplomacy, and that is now nearly thirty years, people have always been saying that Russia was not ready but that she would be ready in a few years and that the General Staff was beginning to feel anxious. And when the year came round, Russia was still not ready. And so it will probably go on to the end of the chapter. In the same way I have repeatedly heard people discussing the question of the so-called prophylactic or preventive war. Even Bismarck was very sceptical with regard to this idea and told Waldersee and other generals who would fain have explained to him the necessity of a preventive war, that he could not be convinced without proofs, and proofs were things no one could offer him. Nor do I believe to-day that we shall have to wage war with Russia, if our policy is skilfully conducted ; least of all do I believe that a preventive war would achieve any result. It could at best turn a second neighbour into an implacable enemy.

But I do not wish to be taken to mean that I am in favour of our sacrificing Austria or the Austrian alliance for the sake of a friendship with Russia or even with England. [Nothing is further from my mind.] The maintenance of Austria is of the greatest importance for us ; in such an alliance we must, however, be the leading partner, not the led. The alliance was after all conceived as a mutual insurance against damage by political storms, and not as a fusion into a single political firm with everything in common. We are I confess, bound to protect Austria, but it is not to our interest to support her in an aggressive policy in the Balkans, a policy in which we have everything to lose and nothing whatever to gain. What advantages do you imagine will accrue to us from a strengthening of Austria's prestige in the Balkans and elsewhere ? Austria's value as an ally depends chiefly on her military efficiency and not on her prestige abroad, German's standing among the Powers is sufficiently high to serve as a guarantee for the influence of the Triple Alliance Group, and this despite Count Berchtold's diplomatic defeats. What would you say if England or Russia were to encourage the French to try to revive their very sensibly sunken prestige by adopting an aggressive and dangerous foreign policy ? It is just the comparative weakness of France and her fear of us that make her nestle up to England and Russia and show herself so accommodating. It is much the same thing with Austria ; I will not go so far as to say that a weakened Austria but that a frightened and timorous Austria is a convenient ally for us ; the ebbing of Austrian influence in the Balkans has hitherto proved highly advantageous for our economic interests in that region. From an economic standpoint, Austria and Germany are rivals in the Balkans, and as a leading Vienna financier recently complained to me, German trade is more and more coming to occupy the position formerly possessed by the Austrians.

Whether folk in Vienna accuse us of manipulations to this end or not is a matter of complete indifference, since they are sure to abuse us in those quarters whatever happens ; and as for our famous Nibelungen loyalty, we only get laughed at for it after our exploits. I am just as little a believer in the early break up of Austria as I am in the possibility of her being able to overcome her internal difficulties by the adoption of an aggressive foreign policy. The national feeling of the Yugoslavs and their urge towards union cannot be destroyed by a war but will only break out the more violently. By aggressive action on the part of Austria, however, the Balkan States will but be thrown the more into the arms of Russian hegemony, while they would otherwise, as is shown by the examples of Rumania and Bulgaria, have an inclination to stand on their own feet.

As for the ' localization of the conflict,' you will surely admit that such a thing, if it should come to a passage at arms with Serbia, belongs in the category of pious wishes. It seems to me, therefore, that everything depends on the Austrian demands being so formulated that, with a certain amount of pressure from St. Petersburg

and London on Belgrade, they may be acceptable. I think that
they should not be so formulated that they must necessarily lead
to a war. [Ad majorem illustrissimi comitis de Berchtold gloriam.]

LICHNOWSKY.

To THE FOREIGN OFFICE. LONDON, 25th July, 1914.

Shall express myself accordingly. Here, too, the view is
general that, to say the least, we share Austria's moral responsibility,
as without our encouragement such a Note would have been unthinkable. Count Mensdorff is able to report corresponding utterances
on the part both of His Majesty the Kaiser and King and of the
Chancellor. The general impression here is nothing short of
annihilating ; unless we participate in the mediatory action, all
confidence in us and in our peaceful intentions will be shattered here
for good and all.

LICHNOWSKY.

To THE FOREIGN OFFICE. LONDON, 25th July, 1914.

Would urgently advise not to refuse Sir Edward Grey's
proposal with regard to extension of time limit, as otherwise we shall
be reproached here with not having left nothing untried for the
maintenance of peace. An attitude of refusal might greatly influence
England's future conduct. To-day's *Morning Post,* a leading Conservative paper, already says at the end of an article condemning
Austria's action that the Note is a challenge to the Triple Entente
and that its purpose is to force England to decide whether she wishes
in future to take a hand in European politics. Despite the domestic
quarrels which have been agitating the British nation, the whole
people will stand united behind the Government and uphold whatever
line of action it may decide upon.

LICHNOWSKY.

To THE FOREIGN OFFICE. LONDON, 25th July, 1914.

PRIVATE FOR SECRETARY OF STATE VON JAGOW.

I should like to call your attention once more to the importance of Grey's proposal of a mediation by the Four Powers between
Austria and Russia. I see in this proposal the only possibility of
avoiding a World War, a war in which we should stake everything
and in which there is nothing to gain. If we decline, Grey, too, will

make no further move.   As long as we have not mobilized, mediation and a settlement of the quarrel on terms acceptable to Austria
is still possible.   Our refusal, on the other hand, would have a very
upsetting effect here, and I do not think that England could possibly
remain disinterested should France be drawn in.   I once more
urgently advise the acceptance of the English proposal and that this
be announced in Vienna and St. Peterrsbug.   LICHNOWSKY.

To THE FOREIGN OFFICE.   LONDON, 25th July, 1914.

Have just seen Sir Edward Grey and have spoken as suggested in Telegram 169.[1]   The Minister noted my explanations with
a full understanding for our standpoint.   Without any irritation or
ill-feeling and with great calm he discussed with me once more the
general situation and seemed to be more hopeful than he was yesterday, as Count Mensdorff had informed him on behalf of his Government that Austria, should her demands be refused, did not intend
to cross the Serbian frontier at once, but only to mobilize.   Sir
Edward Grey is still without information from St. Petersburg
concerning the decisions come to there, but feels certain that the
Austrian mobilisation will be followed by that of Russia.   In his
view, the moment will then have come to inaugurate, in association
with Germany, France and Italy, mediatory action between Austria
and Russia.   Without our co-operation, he said, all attempts at
mediation would be hopeless, and he could not approach Russia
and Austria alone.   He did not yet know whether France would
join in.   He had spoken to M. Cambon, but had so far received no
reply, and in the course of conversation he had told M. Cambon
that he had made the same proposal to me.   Sir Edward Grey
counts definitely on France's assent, although he does not know how
far France is already committed to St. Petersburg.

The Minister makes a sharp distinction, as he again told me,

[1] The following is the telegram referred to (see K.D. 153).   It was sent by
Herr Zimmermann, the German Under-Secretary of State for Foreign Affairs,
simultaneously on 24th July, 1914, to the Ambassadors at London, Paris
and St. Petersburg : ‘ In British diplomatic circles the opinion is general that
we prompted Austria-Hungary to send a sharp Note to Serbia and had a hand
in its composition.   Rumour seems to emanate from Cambon.   Kindly
refute it there if necessary.   We exercised no influence of any kind on the
contents of the Note and had as little opportunity as any other Power of taking
up any attitude to it before its publication.   That we are unable to counsel
Vienna to retract, now that Austria-Hungary has determined on strong
speech on her own initiative, goes withour saying.   Austria-Hungary's prestige,
both at home and abroad, would be completely lost in case of retraction.
(Translator's Note.)

between the Austro-Serbian quarrel and that between Austria and Russia. He did not wish to meddle in the former, as it was no concern of his. The Austro-Russian quarrel, however, might, he said, possibly mean the world war which last year we had all tried to prevent by means of the ambassadorial conferences. European complications, however, were not a matter of indifference to Great Britain either, although she was *in no way committed by any sort of binding agreements.*

He wanted therefore to go hand in hand with us as hitherto, to the end that peace might be maintained in Europe, and he hoped that by our joint mediation, with which France and Italy would doubtless associate themselves, an Austro-Russian war might be averted.

As far as the Austrian Note was concerned, he said, he fully recognized the justice of Austria's demands for satisfaction, as well as her desire for the punishment of all persons connected with the murder ; he refrained from discussing the details of the Note, but seemed to hope that through our mediation an agreement might be reached in this matter also.

I regard it as my duty to point out to Your Excellency that the British Government will, I am convinced, strive to maintain as friendly and impartial an attitude as possible towards us, so long as it believes in our sincere desire for peace and in our endeavour to go hand in hand with England in trying to ward off the threatening European storm. The rejection of his proposal to mediate between Austria and Russia or a brusque attitude that might justify the assumption that we were desirous of a war with Russia would probably have the result of driving England unconditionally to side with France and Russia.   LICHNOWSKY.

TO THE FOREIGN OFFICE.   LONDON, *25th July*, 1914.
         Have just received the following letter from Sir Edward Grey in his own handwriting : " I enclose a forecast that I have just received of the Serbian reply. It seems to me that it ought to produce a favourable impression at Vienna, but it is difficult for anybody but an ally to suggest to the Austrian Government what view they should take of it.

I hope that if the Serbian reply, when received at Vienna, corresponds to this forecast, the German Government may feel able to influence the Austrian Government to take a favourable view of it."
                              LICHNOWSKY.

To The Foreign Office.   London, *25th July*, 1914.

Supplement to Telegram No. 156.—Enclosed in Sir Edward Grey's letter: Telegram from Mr. Crackanthorpe, Belgrade, 25th July, 1914. ' Council of Ministers is now drawing up reply to Austrian Note. I am informed by Under-Secretary of State for Foreign Affairs that it will be drawn up in most conciliatory terms and will, in as large a measure as possible, meet Austrian demands. Under-Secretary gave me a brief summary of projected reply in advance. Consent of Serbian Government is given in it to the publication of declaration in *Official Gazette* and they accept the ten points with reserves. They consent to the dismissal and prosecuting of those officers who can be clearly proved to be guilty, and they have already arrested officer mentioned in the Austrian Note. They agree to suppress *Narodna Odbrana*.[1] They declare themselves ready to agree to mixed commission of enquiry provided that it can be proved that it is in accordance with international usage that such a commission should be appointed.

Lichnowsky.

The Imperial Chancellor von Bethmann-Hollweg to the Ambassador at London, Prince Lichnowsky.

Berlin, *26th July*, 1914.

Austria has officially declared to Russia that she wishes to make no territorial acquisitions in Serbia and that for her part she does not wish to interfere with the stability of the kingdom, but only to bring about peace and order. According to news that has reached here from a reliable source, although it must be confessed, it has not yet been corroborated, the calling up of several years' drafts of reservists in Russia is impending, which would be synonymous with a mobilization against us. Should this information prove correct, we should against our wish be compelled to take counter-measures. We are still endeavouring to localize the conflict and maintain European peace. We therefore request Sir Edward Grey to use his influence in this sense.

Bethmann-Hollweg.

[1] Narodna Odbrana = (Society for) National Defence. For full account of this Serbian Nationalist Association see Professor Seton Watson's *Sarajevo*, pp. 118 and 138. (Tr.)

To THE FOREIGN OFFICE.   LONDON, 26th July, 1914.

Prince Henry requests me to report to Your Excellency that His Majesty the King has expressed to him his keen desire that Britain and Germany acting together, with the assistance of France and Italy, may in the interest of peace succeed in keeping the exceedingly grave situation in hand.

LICHNOWSKY.

To THE FOREIGN OFFICE.   LONDON, 26th July, 1914.

To-day, Sunday, no one at Foreign Office to speak to.   Can therefore not carry out instructions till to-morrow.   Doubt whether Sir E. Grey is in a position to influence Russia in sense suggested, as since publication Austrian demands here, no one any longer believes in possibility of localizing conflict.   No one has ever doubted that from this sort of procedure on part of Austria world war must result.   Consider moment come to inaugurate mediation along lines suggested by Sir Edward Grey, which it is true would presuppose Austria's willingness to renounce further laurels.

LICHNOWSKY.

To THE FOREIGN OFFICE.   LONDON, 26th July, 1914.

Have just had a conversation with Sir A. Nicholson and Sir W. Tyrrell.   According to information to hand here, a general calling up of the Russian reservists is not contemplated, but only a partial mobilisation remote from our frontiers.   Both gentlemen see in Sir Edward Grey's proposal to hold a conference à quatre here the only possibility of avoiding a general war, and hope that by this means it will prove possible to get full satisfaction for Austria, as Serbia will be more inclined to yield to the pressure of the Powers and submit to their united will than to the threats of Austria.   As a preliminary condition, however, it is absolutely indispensable for the success of the conference and for the maintenance of peace that there shall be a cessation of all military movements.   Once the Serbian frontier were crossed, all hope would be lost, for no Russian Government would be able to put up with this, but would, unless they wanted to see their prestige in the Balkans forfeited for ever, be forced to advance against Austria.   Sir W. Tyrrell, who saw Sir Edward Grey last evening and is accurately informed as to his views, repeatedly and emphatically pointed out to me the immense importance of Serbia's territory remaining unviolated until the conference question has been settled, as otherwise all efforts would prove vain and a world war would be inevitable.   The localization of the conflict, as hoped for in Berlin, was quite visionary, and ought to be eliminated from practical politics.   Should we two,—His Majesty the Kaiser or his Government and representatives together with Sir Edward Grey,—succeed in preserving the peace of Europe, Anglo-German relations would for many a day to come be placed on a firm foundation.   Should we not succeed, everything would be uncertain.

I should like to utter an urgent warning against continuing to believe in the possibility of localizing the conflict.   I beg that our policy may be guided simply and solely by the need to spare the German people a struggle in which it has nothing to gain and everything to lose.

Sir Edward Grey returns this evening.

LICHNOWSKY.

To The Foreign Office.   LONDON, 26th July, 1914.

As I am confidentially informed at the Foreign Office, feeling in Italy, according to information received here, is so strongly opposed to any participation in the war that the Government would not dare actively to intervene.   The news that has been spread abroad from Vienna to the effect that Italy has given her consent and has made promises that are in accord with the alliance, is said not to correspond with the facts.[1]

LICHNOWSKY.

To The Foreign Office.   LONDON, 27th July, 1914.

I have just been to see Sir Edward Grey, who requested me to inform Your Excellency as follows :

The Serbian chargé d'affaires had, he said, just transmitted to him the text of the Serbian reply to the Austrian Note.   This reply made it clear that Serbia had acceded to the demands made by Austria to an extent that he would never have believed possible ; except on one point, viz. the participation of Austrian officials in the judicial enquiry, Serbia had actually expressed acquiescence in

[1] Marginal note by Zimmermann   What business of the Ambassador's is Italy ? '   (Translator's Note.)

all the demands made.   It was clear that Serbia's compliance was to be attributed solely to pressure brought to bear by St. Petersburg.

Should Austria not be satisfied with this reply, or should this reply not be regarded at Vienna as a basis for peaceful negotiations, or should Austria even proceed to the occupation of Belgrade, which was quite at her mercy, it would be quite clear that Austria was only seeking a pretext to crush Serbia.   This would mean that Russia and Russian influence in the Balkans were to be struck at through Serbia.   It was plain that Russia could not look on with indifference while this was taking place, and that she could not but interpret such action as a direct challenge.   The result would be the most terrible war that Europe had ever seen, and no one could tell whither such a war might lead.

Germany had repeatedly, even as recently as yesterday, said Sir Edward Grey, turned to him with the request that he should make representations at St. Petersburg recommending moderation.   He had invariably and willingly complied with such requests and during the last crisis had brought down Russia's reproaches on himself for siding too much with Germany and too little with Russia.   He was now turning to us, he said, with the request that we should use our influence in Vienna to get them either to regard the reply from Belgrade as adequate or as a basis for conferences.   He was convinced that it lay in our hands to settle the affair by means of appropriate representations and he would regard it, he said, as a good omen for the future if we two should a second time succeed, by using our influence upon our respective allies, in ensuring the peace of Europe.

I found the Minister in a depressed mood for the first time.   He spoke in a very grave tone and seemed to expect us without fail to use our influence successfully to settle the matter.   He is also going to make a statement in the House of Commons to-day in which he will express his point of view.   In any case I am convinced that should it now come to war after all, we shall no longer be able to count on English sympathy or the support of Great Britain, as people here will see in Austria's procedure every sign of evil intent. Everybody here is convinced, too, and I hear the same thing from my colleagues, that the key to the situation is to be found in Berlin, and that if peace is earnestly desired there, it will be possible to restrain Austria from, as Sir Edward Grey puts it, pursuing a foolhardy policy.   LICHNOWSKY.

To The Foreign Office.   London, *27th July*, 1914.

Supplementing my telegram of to-day's date I should like to emphasize the fact that our entire future relations with England depend upon the success of this step of Sir Edward Grey's. If at this significant moment, a moment in which, despite all internal differences, the whole British nation undoubtedly stands behind the Minister, he should succeed in preventing the situation from becoming still more acute, I guarantee that our relations with Great Britain will for many a day to come bear the same confidential and intimate character that has distinguished them for the past eighteen months. The British Government, no matter whether Liberal or Conservative, sees in the maintenance of European peace on the basis of the balance of power between the two groups its most vital interest.[1] The British Government is convinced that it lies entirely with us whether Austria shall jeopardize European peace by stubbornly pursuing a policy of prestige. Any signs of compliance on the part of Austria would therefore be interpreted by Great Britain as a proof of our sincere wish to unite with her in preventing a European war and would be looked upon as consolidating our friendship with England and our desire for peace.

Should we, on the other hand, regard our sympathies for Austria and the exact observance of our treaty obligations as being of so much importance that all other considerations have to yield to them, and that we subordinate even the most important point in our foreign policy—our relations with England—to the special interests of our ally, I believe that it will never again be possible to reknit the ties which of late have bound us together.

The impression is gaining ground here, as I clearly perceived in my interview with Sir Edward Grey, that the whole Serbian question is fast developing into a trial of strength between the Triple Alliance and the Triple Entente. Should therefore Austria's intention to make use of the present opportunity to ' crush Serbia,' as Sir Edward Grey put it, become more and more apparent, England will—of this I am convinced—place herself unconditionally on the side of France and Russia, in order to show that she is not willing to permit a moral and still less a military defeat of her group. If under these circumstances it should come to war, we shall have England against us. For the conviction that in view of the far-reaching compliance

[1] Annotation by Zimmermann : ' Where will the balance of power be, if Austria gives in ! ' (See K.D. 265, footnote.) (Tr.)

shown by the Serbian Government war might have been avoided, will be of decisive significance for the attitude of the British Government.

LICHNOWSKY.

To The Foreign Office.   LONDON, 27th July, 1914.

The Minister, it is true, draws a sharp line of distinction between the Austro-Serbian and the Austro-Russian dispute. As long as it remained an Austro-Serbian quarrel, he had held aloof. But now he finds himself compelled to intervene, since the affair threatens to develop into an Austro-Russian and consequently a European conflict. The Austro-Russian can accordingly not be separated from the Austro-Serbian dispute, as the former is based upon the latter. This was the purport of the Minister's statements to me. An understanding between Austria and Russia depends upon a settlement of the Austro-Serbian quarrel. Without such a settlement, every attempt at mediation appears entirely hopeless, according to opinion here. How am I to argue in favour of localization of the conflict, if nobody here has the slightest doubt that Austria's action has involved important Russian interests and that Russia will find herself compelled to intervene, despite her own wish to the contrary, in the event of our failing to bring pressure to bear on Austria? With such arguments I should only excite laughter and a shrug of the shoulders.

If an understanding between Vienna and St. Petersburg could be achieved on the basis of the Austrian Note and without having recourse to military measures against Serbia, everything would be attained that Sir Edward Grey is striving for. What he would fain avoid is any military action on the part of Austria against Serbia, because he fears from such action a rupture of European peace.

He to-day confirmed to me moreover the fact that the Russian reserves are not being called up.

LICHNOWSKY.

To The Foreign Office.   LONDON, 28th July, 1914.

The members of the Austrian Embassy here, including Count Mensdorff, have in their talks with members of this Embassy and with myself never made the slightest attempt to conceal the fact that Austria's sole concern was to overthrow Serbia and that the

Note was intentionally so drafted that it would have to be rejected. When on Saturday evening, the report was published here by the *Central News* that Serbia had given way, the gentlemen above referred to were positively stunned. Count Mensdorff told me only yesterday in confidence that in Vienna they were absolutely determined to have war, as Serbia was to be ' flattened out.' The same gentlemen also told me that Austria intended to present parts of Serbia to Bulgaria (and presumably also to Albania).[1] But I would earnestly request you not to refer to these statements in Vienna, as I do not want to risk my amicable relations with Count Mensdorff. Whether these gentlemen expressed themselves in similar terms in conversation with other persons I do not know, but the assumption would not be unjustifiable that it is not merely a question of such harmless pedagogical admonitions as those to which the lack of vigilance on the part of the Polish chatterbox Bilinski gave rise.

I have always energetically upheld the Austrian standpoint here and have explained to Sir Edward Grey and Sir W. Tyrrell that the instinct of self-preservation alone must necessarily prompt Berchtold to adopt an energetic line of action, as both he and Austria would otherwise get themselves into an impossible position. Both the English statesmen recognized this and I am of opinion that the objective attitude hitherto observable in the British Government is ascribable in no small measure to the mutual confidence we have in each other.   LICHNOWSKY.

To THE FOREIGN OFFICE.   LONDON, *29th July*, 1914.

During my visit to the Foreign Office to-day I had a short conversation with Sir W. Tyrrell who, next to Sir Edward Grey [and in consideration of the small importance of Sir A. Nicolson], is to-day the most influential and best informed official there. He again gave me to understand that, according to information received there, the Triple Alliance would not stand the ordeal of a world war. He knew, he said, that Italy would not take part in any

[1] Marginal note by Bethmann-Hollweg dated 28th July : ' This duplicity of Austria's is intolerable. They refuse to give us information as to their programme, state expressly that Count Hoyos' statements, which discussed a partition of Serbia, were a purely personal expression : at Petersburg they are lambs with not a wicked thought in their hearts and in London their Embassy talks of giving away portions of Serbian territory to Bulgaria and Albania' (see K.D. 301, note.) (Tr.)

world war that broke out on account of Serbia, and we ought not to allow ourselves to be deceived by official reports to the contrary. I imagine that this view is based on reports sent in by Sir Rennell Rodd, and I did not get the impression that Sir W. Tyrrell had invented the statement in order to frighten us.   LICHNOWSKY.

To THE FOREIGN OFFICE.   LONDON, 29*th July*, 1914.

    I have just had a talk with Sir Edward Grey who takes an extremely serious view of the situation. A telegram received here yesterday from Sir Maurice de Bunsen, according to which Count Berchtold absolutely declined Sazonov's proposal to empower Count Szapary to confer with him on the Austro-Serbian quarrel, has made a most unpleasant impression on him. The Minister to-day still regards a direct exchange of ideas between Vienna and St. Petersburg as the most feasible way. He asked me, however, what would happen if, as the Vienna telegram seemed to indicate, the conference were to break down. Would we then be in a position to make any sort of proposal? He had, he said, suggested a conference of the Ambassadors here, but this suggestion had not appeared feasible to us ; we had, however, accepted the suggestion of a mediation *à quatre*, and he would be glad if we could now put forward any proposal. I said that we regarded the Austro-Serbian quarrel as an affair in which we did not wish to meddle and that we could not expect Austria to submit to any humiliation. Austria, I said, was only doing what she was obliged to do, in order to ensure peace and order on her frontiers. This was at the same time also in the interests of the peace of Europe. Nor had Austria any territorial acquisitions in mind, but merely the restoration of tolerable conditions.

He replied that he fully comprehended that Austria must not be humiliated, there could be no question of that. He hoped, he said, that some way out might be found which would make it possible for Austria to receive full satisfaction, without expecting Russia to remain a passive spectator until Austria had gone to the bitter end of her military undertakings. This would be equivalent to humiliating Russia in a way that Russia could not possibly tolerate.

I replied [that as a matter of fact Serbia did not concern Russia at all and] that Russia had all the less cause to interfere in this frontier dispute between two neighbours, seeing that Austria had no intention of annexing Serbia.

He replied that even without annexation a form was thinkable by which Serbia could be transformed into a vassal state of Austria's. Russia could not and would not look on quietly while this happened. Russia's status among the Christians of the Orthodox Greek Church was at stake. Sir Edward Grey threw out the suggestion whether it might not be possible to bring about an understanding with regard to the extent of Austria's military operations and with regard to the demands of the Monarchy.

From what the Minister said to-day I again gathered that they are firmly convinced here, as I have repeatedly had the honour to report to Your Excellency, that unless Austria is willing to enter into a discussion of the Serbian question, a world war is inevitable.

Sir Edward Grey, half jestingly, remarked in this connection that one could never tell what houses would remain unscathed in such a conflagration ; even little Holland was already arming.

The Minister was obviously pleased when I told him that Your Excellency had been striving not without success to mediate between Vienna and St. Petersburg, and he declared that he would be ready to take part in any project that promised success.

I again begged the Minister to warn St. Petersburg against precipitate resolutions, and I especially urged him to prevent a general mobilisation there which would also affect our frontier. It was, I said, impossible to predict what the consequences might be. The Minister again promised me that he would use his influence in this direction and try to get them to keep as cool as possible.

In conclusion the Minister informed me that the Serbian chargé d'affaires in Rome had declared to the Marquis di San Giuliano that provided clear explanations were given beforehand as to the mode in which Austrian agents were to participate, Serbia would be inclined to swallow even Articles 5 and 6 of the Austrian Note, which would mean that she accepted all the demands. As it could not be assumed that Austria would enter into direct negotiations with Serbia, the matter might be submitted to Serbia through the mediation of the Great Powers in the form of advice. The Marquis di San Giuliano is of opinion that an understanding may be arrived at on this basis. Above all, however, the Minister desires that a conference be arranged with the least possible delay. Sir Edward Grey has referred Marquis di San Giuliano to the Vienna and Berlin Cabinets, not being himself in a position, he said, to arrange a conference without their consent.

Finally the Minister communicated to me a telegram from Sir George Buchanan according to which the Russian Ministry of Foreign Affairs is said to have informed the representatives of the Foreign Press that as negotiations between Vienna and St. Petersburg had produced no result, Russia found herself obliged to regard the violation of Serbian territory by Austrian troops as a *casus belli*.

LICHNOWSKY.

[TO THE FOREIGN OFFICE.]   LONDON, 29*th July*, 1914.

I hear from journalistic circles that an arrangement has been reached between England and Italy according to which Italy has promised in case of a European war to undertake nothing against England and *vice versa*.[1]

LICHNOWSKY.

TO THE FOREIGN OFFICE.   LONDON, 29*th July*, 1914.

The worst and most scandalous piece of English Pharisaism I've ever seen. I will never enter into a naval convention with such scoundrels.

At Sir Edward Grey's request, I have just been to see him again. The Minister was quite calm but very grave, and received me with the words that the situation was growing more and more acute. Sazonov, he said, had stated that now that war had been declared,[2] he was no longer in a position to negotiate direct with Austria *and had requested them here again to take up mediatory efforts*. The Russian Government regards a temporary cessation of hostilities as a necessary preliminary for such mediation.

That sets me out of the running

Sir Edward Grey repeated the suggestion already reported that we should take part in a mediation *à quatre*, such as we had already accepted on principle. It seemed to him personally, he said, that a suitable basis for mediation would be given, if Austria, say, after the occupation of Belgrade or other places, would proclaim her conditions.

Good.

We have been trying to accomplish this for days, in vain.

Should Your Excellency, however, undertake mediation, as I was able early this morning to

---

[1] This report was categorically denied on 30th July, 1914, by the Marquis di San Giuliano, who assured the German Ambassador at Rome that it was ' a fiction devoid of any foundation.' (See K.D. 458.) (Translator's Note.)

[2] By Austria on Serbia on 28th July, 1914. (Tr.)

Instead of media-tion, a serious word to St. Petersburg and Paris to the effect that England would not help them would quieten the situation at once.

tell the Minister was not improbable, that would, of course, be just as satisfactory to him. But *mediation* seemed to him, he said, to be now urgently necessary if *a European catastrophe was to be avoided.*

Sir Edward Grey then told me that he had a friendly and private communication to make to me, namely, that he did not wish that our cordial personal relations and our intimate exchange of ideas on all political questions should lead me astray, *as he did not wish later to be reproached with*

Aha! The com-mon cheat!

This means we are to leave Austria in the lurch, as if we were common as dirt and Mephisto-phelian! Thor-oughly English however.

Already made up!

This means that they will attack us!

insincerity. The British Government, he said, desired now as heretofore to foster the friendship that had hitherto prevailed between the two countries, and as *long as the conflict was confined to Austria and Russia, it could stand aside, but if we and France were drawn in*, the situation would at once be altered and it was possible that the British Government would then be forced to make up its mind quickly. In such an event *it would not be practicable to stand aside and wait for any length of time.* 'If war breaks out, it will be the greatest catastrophe that the world has ever seen.' It was far from his thoughts, he said, to wish to express any kind of threat, he only wanted to save me disappointments and *himself*

He has shown insin-cerity all these years all the same, down to this latest utter-ance of his.

So have we!

from the reproach of insincerity, and had therefore chosen the form of a private communication. Sir Edward Grey added that the *Government* had of course *to reckon with public opinion* ; up to the present British public opinion had on the whole been in Austria's favour, as people recognized that Austria could justly demand a certain amount of satisfaction ; now, however, in consequence of Austria's obstinacy, public opinion was beginning to veer round completely.

If it wants to it can turn and direct public opinion, as the Press obeys it unconditionally.

My Italian colleague who has just left me was told by Sir Edward Grey that he thought that if the proposal for mediation were accepted, he could get Austria every possible satisfaction and that a humiliating retreat on the part of Austria was no longer in question, as the Serbians would, whatever happened, be chastised and would, with Russia's consent, be compelled to subordinate themselves to Austria's wishes. Austria could, therefore, without having recourse to a war that jeopardised the peace of Europe, obtain guarantees for the future.   LICHNOWSKY.

England reveals herself in her true colours at a moment when she thinks that we are caught in the toils and, so to speak, disposed of. That common crew of shopkeepers has tried to trick us with dinners and speeches. The boldest deception, the words of the King to Henry, for me. 'We shall remain neutral and try to keep out of this as long as possible.' Grey proves the King a liar and his words to Lichnowsky are the outcome of an evil conscience, because he feels that he has deceived us. At that, it is as a matter of fact a threat, combined with a bluff, in order to separate us from Austria and to prevent us from mobilizing and to shift the responsibility for the war.
He knows perfectly well that if he were to say one single serious sharp and warning word at Paris and St. Petersburg and were to warn them to remain neutral, both would become quiet at once. But he takes care not to speak the word and threatens us instead. Common cur. England alone bears the responsibility for peace and war, not we any longer. That must also be made clear to the world. W.

K.D. 418.[1]

[TO THE FOREIGN OFFICE.]   LONDON, 30*th July*, 1914.

Notified Sir Edward Grey at once by letter. Consider Berlin as more appropriate than London for mediation of an agreement between Vienna and St. Petersburg, as Sir Edward is less acquainted with the whole question and also possesses less influence at Vienna and as I foresee long and wearisome transactions here, especially in event of an Ambassadorial Conference taking place. Count Mensdorff is also too timid and is lacking both in influence at Vienna and in personal initiative. For these reasons Grey's suggestions should serve as a basis.   LICHNOWSKY.

TO THE FOREIGN OFFICE.   LONDON, 30*th July*, 1914.

Have just been talking with Sir Edward Grey. He says he can assure me that the French are using their whole influence in

---

[1] K.D. 418 was in answer to the following telegram from the Imperial Chancellor to the Ambassador at London:

BERLIN, 30*th July*, 1914.

Kindly thank Sir Edward Grey for his frank explanation and tell him that we are continuing to mediate in Vienna and are urgently advising the acceptance of his proposal.   BETHMANN-HOLLWEG.

St. Petersburg towards a peaceful termination. Also, according to reports received here, only men on leave near the German frontier have been called up. Actual preparations for war such as the calling to the colours of the reservists have not taken place. He will, moreover, be having a talk with Cambon this afternoon, and has asked me to come and see him again that he may tell me the result.

As regards the Russian preparations for war, he will try through Count Benckendorff to take steps to-day in the sense we desired.

The Minister confidently hopes that Your Excellency's efforts at mediation will succeed in bringing about an understanding ; he will also bring his influence to bear in St. Petersburg in support of his proposal. He told an intimate friend this morning that if the Anglo-German co-operation should succeed this time in preserving peace, he believed that our relations would be placed on a firm basis for all time and that he would be enabled in future to prevent the recurrence of similar crises by exerting suitable influence on his associates.

LICHNOWSKY.

[TO THE FOREIGN OFFICE.]   30th July, 1914.

Sir Edward Grey has just told me that the British Fleet has just sailed along the east coast into Scottish harbours, and that no mobilization preparations preliminary to an announcement of ' strained relations ' by the Foreign Office had yet been carried out.

As long as we did not mobilize, he said, the French would not do so either, nor would England. Cambon had assured him that the French were not doing any more than we were ; simply certain precautionary measures were being taken.

LICHNOWSKY.

TO THE FOREIGN OFFICE.   LONDON, 30th July, 1914.

Sir Edward Grey has just shown me a telegram to Sir George Buchanan, in which he instructs him to support our suggestion to enter into conferences concerning an understanding, if Austria agrees to cease hostilities after occupying certain places on the frontier. At my suggestion no reference whatever is any longer made to the Austrian ultimatum, but only to the negotiations concerning the burdens and obligations to be laid on Serbia. The reply of M. Sazonov to Count Pourtalès concerning the alteration of the ultimatum, transmitted here through Count Benckendorff, I described to the Minister as unacceptable. I therefore regarded it as more practicable to omit all mention of the word ultimatum.

The Minister was quite calm and appeared not yet to have given up all hope. LICHNOWSKY.

To THE FOREIGN OFFICE. 30*th July*, 1914.

In my view and in that of people here, the only peaceful solution is that we should get Count Berchtold to declare that in the interests of European peace and out of regard for the wishes of his allies, he is ready, not only to regard the successes already attained as sufficient for the present, but also to suspend all military operations for the time being and through our mediation to enter into conversations with M. Sazonov with regard to the conditions to be imposed on Serbia, provided that the Russian Government ceases further warlike operations on the Austrian frontier. I have spoken in this sense with my Austro-Hungarian colleagues as well. LICHNOWSKY.

To THE FOREIGN OFFICE. LONDON, 30*th July*, 1914.

Sir Edward Grey and Mr. Asquith made statements in the Lower House to-day in which they emphasized the extreme gravity of the situation. The former announced that England now as heretofore was pursuing the one great goal, the preservation of peace. Asquith dropped the Amendment Bill from the agenda, as Party strife was out of place at the present time and as England, although not herself directly interested, ought to show a united front. He hoped that the patriotism of all parties would contribute if not to prevent the threatening catastrophe, at least to confine it within limits. LICHNOWSKY.

To THE FOREIGN OFFICE. LONDON, 30*th July*, 1914.

Telegram from Sir E. Grey *to* Sir G. Buchanan, St. Petersburg.

' The German Ambassador informs me that the German Government would endeavour to influence Austria, after taking Belgrade and Serbian territory in region of frontier, to promise not

to advance further, while Powers endeavoured to arrange that
Serbia should give satisfaction sufficient to pacify Austria. Territory occupied would, of course, be evacuated when Austria was
satisfied. I suggested this yesterday as a possible relief to the
situation and if it can be obtained I would earnestly hope that it
might be agreed to suspend further military preparations on all
sides.

The Russian Ambassador has told me of conditions laid down by
Sazonov, as quoted in your telegram 155 and fears no modification is possible ; but if Austrian advance were stopped after
occupation of Belgrade, I think the Russian Minister for Foreign
Affairs formula might be changed to read that the Powers would
examine how Serbia could fully satisfy Austria without impairing
Serbian rights or independence.

If Austria, having occupied Belgrade and neighbouring Serbian
territory, declares herself ready in the interest of European peace to
cease her advance and to discuss how a complete settlement can be
arrived at, I hope that Russia would also consent to discussion and
suspension of further military preparations provided that other
Powers did the same.'   LICHNOWSKY.

To The Foreign Office.   London, 31st *July*, 1914.
        Would not a telegram from the Kaiser to the Czar in which
His Majesty might propose in the interest of European peace that
the Russian military preparations should be suspended, provided
that Austria suspends operations against Serbia, and that Your
Excellency should act as mediator in finding a solution for the
Serbian question prove a feasible course ?

With regard to the conditions laid before Count Pourtalès by
Sazonov, it might perhaps be said that the first of them had already
been fulfilled, inasmuch as Count Berchtold is ready to enter into
an exchange of ideas with him through Your Excellency and that
with regard to the ultimatum, he was ready to take into consideration
and discuss other guarantees as well.   LICHNOWSKY.

[To The Foreign Office.]   London, 31*st July*, 1914.
        Sir Edward Grey has just informed me that he was wrong in
what he told me yesterday, there being no intermediate stage

between that in which the Fleet finds itself to-day and its mobilization, the naval preparations having all been made already. He did not want to feel that he had told me anything that might in any way mislead me.

To-day for the first time I have the impression that the improved relations with Germany of late years, and perhaps also some friendly feeling for Germany in the Cabinet, make it appear possible that in case of war England may adopt a waiting attitude. To this end it would be of the utmost importance for us, should it after all come to a war, that we should be able to kill the suspicion hitherto prevalent here that we had unconditionally supported the Austrian point of view, by producing some tangible—not merely formal—concession obtained from the Austrian Government through our mediation.

LICHNOWSKY.

To The Foreign Office.　　　LONDON, 31st *July*, 1914.

I have just utilized telegram 192 [1] in a talk I have had with Sir Edward Grey. The Minister in reply expressed the opinion that Russia had become somewhat sensitive with regard to war measures, as a suggestion from us on this point had been interpreted as a threat. He would, however, endeavour to use his influence as desired.

With regard to the Austro-Russian conversations, he thought that everything depended on Austria's making a concession of such a nature that Russia would put herself in the wrong were she still to decline it—then he himself would be in a position to bring pressure to bear on Paris and St. Petersburg. He also hinted that it was just this question of fairness and reasonableness that might possibly decide England's attitude, England not being bound by absolute agreements of any kind. Once France were drawn in, public opinion here would become agitated, although up to the present it had in no way taken sides against Germany ; and he must be in a position, should it prove expedient, to justify reticence on the part of England by being able to point to some palpable act of injustice on the part of Russia. He did not exactly make this last statement in so many words, but gave it clearly to be understood that it was in the event of his being able to point to some tangible concession that he would be in a position to advocate the idea of not entering the arena immediately

---

[1] The telegram in question (see [K.D. 444] and [K.D. 433]) is one from Jagow to the Ambassador at London, advising the Ambassador to try to get England to influence St. Petersburg, particularly with regard to the discontinuation of her war measures. (Tr.)

on the side of France.   He emphasized again and again the fact that
England's hands were not bound by treaties of any kind.   I assume
that he still has in mind his original suggestion of suspending military
operations in Serbia ; on my transmitting this suggestion to Your
Excellency, you authorized me to declare that you intended to use
your influence in Vienna in this sense.

I, too, am of opinion that if Count Berchtold limits himself to
the repetition of declarations and explanations with which everybody
is already familiar, the negotiations will offer little prospect of success, and that public opinion in Russia will not tolerate an invasion of
Serbia by Austrian armies, coupled, as it would be, with the destruction of towns and villages, but will force the Government to intervene,
perhaps against its will.   Judging from my personal knowledge of
conditions in Vienna, I should say that nothing short of extremely
energetic pressure exerted by Berlin will induce Vienna to make such
a concession.   The granting of such a concession might prove
decisive for the future attitude of England in the war, if war should
break out after all.

LICHNOWSKY.

[THE IMPERIAL CHANCELLOR TO THE AMBASSADOR
    AT LONDON, PRINCE LICHNOWSKY.]

BERLIN, 31st July, 1914.

On the 29th the Czar requested His Majesty by telegraph to
mediate between Russia and Austria.   His Majesty immediately
declared himself willing to do so, informed the Czar by telegraph, and
at once made a move at Vienna.   Without awaiting the result,
Russia mobilized against Austria.   His Majesty thereupon called
the attention of the Czar by telegraph to the fact that he was thereby
making the mediation action almost illusory and requested the Czar
to suspend the military preparations against Austria.   This has not
been done.   In spite of that fact, we have been continuing our
attempts at mediation in Vienna, and we have even gone, in the
extreme urgency of our proposal, to the utmost limit of what we
could venture toward a Sovereign State which is our ally.   Our
proposals at Vienna were quite along the lines of the English proposals, which we recommended to the earnest consideration of
Vienna.   They were under discussion at Vienna this morning.
During the discussion, even before it had been brought to an end,
Count Pourtalès reported officially the mobilization of the Russian

Army and Navy. This action on the part of Russia cuts off Austria's pending reply to our mediation proposal. It is directed also against us, thus against the Power from which the Czar had personally requested mediation. This action, which we cannot regard otherwise than as hostile, we have had to reply to with serious countermeasures ; unless we wanted absolutely to sacrifice the safety of our Fatherland. We cannot stand idly by as spectators and watch Russian mobilization on our borders. We have told Russia that we shall have to mobilize, unless, within twelve hours, the military preparations against Austria-Hungary and ourselves be suspended. This would mean war. We have asked France whether she would remain neutral in a German-Russian war. Please use every means to ensure this course of events being duly recognized in the English Press.

BETHMANN-HOLLWEG.

[To The Foreign Office.] LONDON, 31st *July*, 1914.

 Sir William Tyrrell informs me that local Government has so far no information concerning mobilization of entire Russian Army and Navy. He will at once get into communication with St. Petersburg.

LICHNOWSKY.

[To The Foreign Office.] LONDON, 1st *August*, 1914.

 I have just learned (2 a.m.) from the private secretary of the Prime Minister, to whose attention I had at once brought telegram No. 199 through Sir W. Tyrrell, that King George has forwarded its contents to the Czar together with some accompanying words of his own.

LICHNOWSKY.

To The Foreign Office. LONDON, 1st *August*, 1914.

 Sir Edward Grey has just sent word to me by Sir W. Tyrrell that he hopes that he will be able this afternoon, as a result of a council of Ministers that is just taking place, to make a statement to me which may prove helpful in preventing the great catastrophe. To judge by a remark of Sir W. Tyrrell's, this seems to mean that in the event of our not attacking France, England, too, would remain neutral and would guarantee France's passivity. I shall learn details this afternoon.

Sir Edward Grey has just called me up on the telephone and asked me whether I thought I could give an assurance that in the event of France remaining neutral in a war between Russia and Germany, we should not attack the French. I assured him that I could take the responsibility for such a guarantee and he will use this assurance at to-day's Cabinet meeting.[1]

Supplementary : Sir W. Tyrrell urgently begged me to use my influence to prevent our troops from violating the French frontier. Everything depended upon that. He said that in one case where German troops had already crossed the frontier, the French troops had retired.

LICHNOWSKY.

To The Foreign Office. LONDON, 1st *August*, 1914.

Inform Rome at once of this, as well as of the afternoon telegrams. As Italy will go timidly with the Triple Alliance so long as there is any fear of England's opposing her.

Sir William Tyrrell has just been to see me and told me that Sir Edward Grey wants this afternoon to make proposals for England's neutrality, even in the event of our being at war with France as well as with Russia. I shall be seeing Sir Edward Grey at 3.30 and shall report at once.

LICHNOWSKY.

[To The Foreign Office.] LONDON, 1st *August*, 1914.

According to the official report, the Prime Minister yesterday made the following declaration in the Lower House : We have just heard, not from St. Petersburg, but from Germany, that Russia has proclaimed a general mobilization of her Army and Fleet and that in consequence of this martial law was to be proclaimed in Germany. We understand this to mean that mobilization will follow in Germany if Russian mobilisation is general and is proceeded with. In the circumstances I should prefer not to answer any questions till Monday next.

GERMAN EMBASSY.

---

[1] In this passage there was a misunderstanding inasmuch as Sir Edward Grey had meant that Germany should then remain altogether neutral, even in a war between Austria and Russia. (Author's Note.)

To The Foreign Office.   London, 1st *August*, 1914.

Sir Edward Grey has just read me the following statement that was drawn up unanimously by the Cabinet :

This drivel of Grey's shows that he absolutely doesn't know what he is to do. We will now await England's decision. I have just learned that England has already cut the cable to Emden. A war measure then! While she is still negotiating.

The reply of the German Government with regard to the neutrality of Belgium is a matter of profound regret, as Belgian neutrality affects feeling in this country. If Germany could see her way to give the same positive reply as that which has been given by France, it would materially contribute to relieve anxiety and tension here, while on the other hand if there were a violation of the neutrality of Belgium by one combatant while the other respected it, it would be extremely difficult to restrain public feeling in this country.

In answer to my question whether he could give me a definite assurance concerning Great Britain's neutrality on the condition that we respected Belgian neutrality the Minister replied

Then he's a false rascal !

that that *was not possible for him*, but that this question would play an important part in connection with public opinion here. If Germany violated Belgian neutrality in a war with France, there would be a revulsion of feeling that would make it difficult for the British Government to adopt an attitude of friendly neutrality. For the

Humbug! It has not adopted it so far.
He lies! He told Lichnowsky so himself four days ago.
Unless an English equivalent is named.
So he already has my offer of yesterday afternoon, that is very plain. And then the King talks of a misunderstanding! Rot!
The rascal is crazy or an idiot. Besides that, the French have begun the war and the violation of international law with their bomb-hurling fliers.

present *there was not the slightest intention of proceeding to hostilities against us.* But it would be difficult *to draw a line beyond which we might not go* without causing them on this side to step in. He kept returning to the question of Belgian neutrality and stated that in any case this question would play an important part. He had also been wondering whether it would not be possible for us and France in the event of a Russian war to remain facing each other *without either side attacking.* I asked him whether he was in a position to give me an assurance that France would agree to a pact of that sort. Since we intended neither to destroy France nor to annex parts of her territory, I could imagine that we might enter on an agreement of that sort since it would assure us of Great Britain's neutrality.

The Minister said that he would enquire, but was not blind to the difficulties of restraining the two armies and keeping them in a state of in-activity.

My impression is that Mr. Grey is a false dog who is afraid of his own cheapness and false policy, but who will not come out into the open against us, preferring to let himself be forced by us to do it.

My general impression is that people here would like, if at all possible, to keep out of the war, but that the answer given by the Secretary of State to Sir Edward Goschen concerning Belgian neutrality has made a very unfavourable im-pression.

LICHNOWSKY.

[To The Foreign Office.]   LONDON, 1st *August*, 1914.

My to-day's telegram 205 [1] superseded by my later telegram 212.[2] As a positive proposal on the part of England is on the whole not in prospect, your telegram 204 [3] settled by that fact. Therefore I have taken no further steps.

LICHNOWSKY.

THE IMPERIAL CHANCELLOR VON BETHMANN-HOLLWEG TO THE AMBASSADOR AT LONDON, PRINCE LICHNOWSKY.

BERLIN, 1st *August*, 1914.

Paris has just reported that France mobilised this afternoon at five o'clock, that is, exactly the same time to the very minute as we did. We can naturally only keep our promise not to cross the French frontier before seven p.m. on Monday provided that France also strictly respects our frontiers.

BETHMANN-HOLLWEG.

TO THE FOREIGN OFFICE.   LONDON, 1st *August*, 1914.

The *Westminster Gazette* considers the situation to be extremely critical. England must make up her mind as to what position she intends to take up. The Prime Minister had once stated in the House (says the paper), that England in the event of a war was not compelled by treaties of any sort to participate. Thus England now had a free hand, but Germany must realize that there were in

---

[1] K.D. 562.   [2] K.D. 596.   [3] K.D. 578.

existence certain published treaties, the violation of which by Germany would place England in a difficult situation. Germany was furthermore aware that a conflict between Germany and France might have consequences that would inflame public opinion in England and induce the country to abandon its neutrality. The attempt that was being made on many sides to stir up a war fever here was altogether to be deprecated, as was also the action of those who were agitating in favour of sending an expeditionary corps to the Continent. England had to remember her responsibilities as a world empire and had especially to consider the safety of India and Egypt. England's strength lay in her sea power, and this power must serve to keep the peace for England and to keep the war between other countries within certain limits. There was, too, it was true, a certain danger in a policy of peace, but it was sincerely to be hoped that England would be able to maintain her position as a rallying ground for those who wanted peace in Europe.[1]

LICHNOWSKY.

[THE SECRETARY OF STATE FOR FOREIGN AFFAIRS
  TO THE AMBASSADOR AT LONDON.]

BERLIN, 2nd August, 1914.

In the event of England declaring war on us or of our declaring war on England, kindly inform the Government there in writing :

(1) That we shall detain merchant ships in our harbours flying their flag, but shall release them if we within forty-eight hours receive a (corresponding) promise in return.

(2) That having regard to English law, we shall suspend English claims against German subjects, unless we within twenty-four hours receive assent to the continued legal validity of German claims against English subjects.

JAGOW.

TO THE FOREIGN OFFICE.   LONDON, 2nd August, 1914.

As will be clear from my last telegrams, the matter which was again discussed in your telegram No. 206, has been completely settled and our freedom of action is not affected by it.

LICHNOWSKY.

---

[1] The Kaiser's marginal comment on this consisted of one word : ' Quatsch ' (twaddle). (Tr.)

To The Foreign Office.　　　London, *2nd August*, 1914.

Sir Edward Grey's suggestions, which were prompted by a wish to secure neutrality on the part of France for as long as possible, were made without having previously consulted France and without knowledge of the mobilization.　They have since been completely abandoned as hopeless.　Urgently request reply as to whether telegrams Nos. 212, 214 and an urgent uncoded telegram without a number have arrived.

Lichnowsky.

To The Foreign Office.　　　London, *2nd August*, 1914.

The question whether or not we violate Belgian territory in the war with France will probably decide whether England is to remain neutral or not.　My impression on this point is strengthened not only by Sir Edward Grey's remarks and by information received from the Austrian Embassy, but also by the utterances of the British Press.　Should we violate Belgian neutrality and should a war against the Belgians ensue, I do not believe that the Government will any longer be able to remain neutral in the face of the storm that is to be expected immediately public opinion here has been aroused.　Should we on the other hand respect Belgian neutrality, there is still a possibility of England's remaining neutral if we act with moderation in the event of a victory over France.　As people here now think that the violation of Belgian neutrality is an eventuality to be reckoned with, I regard it as not impossible that England will in the immediate future take sides against us.　To-day, Sunday, a Cabinet meeting is to take place [an unheard of thing] ; and I assume that this question will be dealt with.

Lichnowsky.

[To The Foreign Office.]　　　London, *2nd August*, 1914.

Ambassador has the distinct impression from conversation with Prime Minister and Minister for Foreign Affairs that England would like to remain neutral if this prove in any way possible.　In order not to make this difficult, it would be advisable that our Navy should refrain from all activities which might lead to accidents or be regarded as provocations.

In this category would belong *above all* any naval operations against the northern coast of France which has been left exposed

through France relying on England. Naval operations against
Russia are matters of no concern to England. The English will,
until further notice, not approach German waters and expect the
same consideration from us.   That is the view of the British Cabinet.
No binding agreements have been made.

MILITARY ATTACHÉ.
LICHNOWSKY.

[TO THE FOREIGN OFFICE.]   LONDON, *2nd August*, 1914.

I have succeeded so far in maintaining for us here a feeling
that is extremely friendly towards us, and I should like to utter an
urgent warning against imperilling this mood by any sort of provocative measures.   Among such I should count first an attack by the
German Fleet on the northern coast of France, as well as any encroachment of our Fleet on British waters.   I am convinced that
for the present there is not the slightest intention of declaring war
on us ; that on the contrary, they prefer first to await the course
of events.

Having learned that the decisive meeting of the Cabinet is to take
place to-day, to be followed by a statement from Mr. Asquith in the
House of Commons to-morrow, I have just called on the Prime
Minister and exhaustively discussed our point of view with him.
Tears repeatedly stood in the eyes of the old gentleman, and he said
to me ' A war between our two countries is quite unthinkable.'   I
pointed out to him the marked community of our mutual interests,
which had of late undergone so material an extension and development, and the impossibility of ever again knitting such confidential
ties once the two countries had been at war.   In order to weaken
the chief argument of the English—that of having to protect
France—I called his attention to the fact that it was really we who
most needed protection, since we had to deal with two opponents
and the French with only one.   Should Great Britain remain out
of the strife, she would be in a much stronger position to mediate
as a neutral at the rehabilitation of peace than if she took part in a
war which would then become a war of annihilation for the entire
civilization of Europe.

Asquith replied that a war between England and Germany in the
present state of public feeling would be very unpopular, but that a
neutral attitude on the part of the British Government would be
greatly hindered by two things :

(1) By the violation of the neutrality of Belgium of which England was one of the guarantors. Gladstone had said in the year 1870 that the violation of the neutrality of Belgium would be for Great Britain a cause of war. In any case there would then occur a serious reversal of public feeling.

(2) By any attack by German warships on the totally unprotected northern coast of France, which the French with a firm faith in British support, had left exposed in order to strengthen their Mediterranean Fleet. He would not say that even in such an event England would have to intervene but it would be made very difficult for the British Government to maintain the neutral attitude as at present provisionally intended here.

I have the distinct impression that England is holding back for the present, out of regard for us, but I would urgently advise bearing in mind so far as possible the state of feeling here.

I have just had another talk with Sir Edward Grey before the sitting, and once more most urgently directed his attention to the importance of not destroying for all time to come our mutual co-operation, of late so fruitful. The Minister repeated that he could give me no definite assurances. But it was plain from his words that he would prefer to refrain from any intervention. We cannot conceal from ourselves, however, that the good intentions of the Government, which undoubtedly exist, and the general friendly feeling towards Germany would, by the violation of Belgian neutrality, be put to a severe test the outcome of which, as a matter of fact, should we win brilliant victories in France or even press forward as far as Paris, would be a very doubtful one for us.

Our declaration of war on Russia has created an unfavourable impression here, since they think that the Czar was still striving to mediate further and had given his word that no soldier should pass the frontier so long as there was hope of a peaceful solution. I naturally met this reproach with a reference to the mobilization that had taken place in Russia despite the mediatory action initiated by His Majesty at the desire of the Czar.   LICHNOWSKY.

To The Foreign Office.   London, *2nd August*, 1914.

Sir Eyre Crowe stated in conversation that, according to a communication only just received here, Austria now appears to be ready to agree to discussion in principle of the points at issue between herself and Serbia by a conference of the four Powers in London. But the communication had come too late, he said, to be of any practical use.

LICHNOWSKY.

To The Foreign Office.   LONDON, *2nd August,* 1914.

Sir Eyre Crow has just informed me that a telegraphic message has been received at the Foreign Office to the effect that the German troops in the neighbourhood of Nancy have crossed the French frontier at numerous points in large numbers without any previous declaration of war in Paris. He allowed it to be seen in making this communication that the news would make a bad impression at the Cabinet meeting which is to take place in the course of the evening for further discussion of the position, and would perhaps not be without influence on the final decision. I replied to Sir Eyre Crowe that we had not received any news to this effect, and that it would appear desirable to await definite confirmation of the report from an independent source.

LICHNOWSKY.

[To The Foreign Office.]   LONDON, *2nd August,* 1914.

Booms have been placed in the naval harbours. Straits of Dover occupied by torpedo boats. According to reliable information, the first and second fleets are lying at the Forth, at Cromarty and in Scapa Flow. Patrol flotilla is patrolling the whole east coast. Flying machines are on the way by sea to a station on the east coast. Mobilization of the navy has not been proclaimed, but has been completed in the active units and on the east and south coasts.

NAVAL ATTACHÉ.
LICHNOWSKY.

To The Foreign Office.   LONDON, *2nd August,* 1914.

Mobilization of the English fleet ordered this evening. All classes of reserves under fifty-five years of age have been called to the colours and are to report at once to their ships and their land stations.

NAVAL ATTACHÉ.
LICHNOWSKY.

[To The Foreign Office.]   London, *2nd August*, 1914.

After the close of the Cabinet meeting, the Admiralty ordered the mobilization of the English naval reserves.   This measure must not be taken as the final decision of the English Government to intervene immediately in the war.   I believe that for the present the attitude will be one of waiting.

Lichnowsky.

[To The Foreign Office.]   London, *3rd August*, 1914.

Austrian military attaché has just brought information that he knows from a reliable . . . that to-day's English Cabinet meeting decided to declare war on Germany.   Nothing known so far of mobilization of expeditionary corps.

Military and Naval Attachés.
Lichnowsky.

To The Foreign Office.   London, *3rd August*, 1914.

The invasion of France without declaration of war [1] has made an ominous impression here and has severely affronted the English sense of law and justice.

I urgently beg for explanation of which I can make use.

This morning's papers condemn our action and describe us as the real disturbers of the peace.

Lichnowsky.

To The Foreign Office.   London, *3rd August*, 1914.

Papers report confiscation of British steamers in the Kiel Canal, and movement of German fleet to the west.

I urgently beg for explanation in order that I may be able to correct report.

Public opinion here has taken a decided stand since yesterday against us.

Lichnowsky.

[To The Foreign Office.]   London, *3rd August*, 1914.

The Ambassador makes the urgent request that without prejudice to any necessary precautions, the fleet avoid anything

---

[1] This report was explicitly denied by von Jagow the same day in a telegram to Lichnowsky.   (Cf. K.D. 725.)   (Tr.)

that might be regarded as a challenge to England or even as an unfriendly act. Hope that England may remain neutral has by no means disappeared.

NAVAL ATTACHÉ.
LICHNOWSKY.

TO THE FOREIGN OFFICE.   LONDON, 3rd August, 1914.

Have just made communication as instructed to Sir Edward Grey.[1] The Minister appeared to be very much put out and indicated that England would not be able to take so calmly the violation of Belgian neutrality, which she had expressly guaranteed. As for the assembling of French troops on the Belgian frontier, France had, he said, expressly stated that she would only cross the Belgian frontier if the French troops were invited by Belgium to come to her aid. Sir Edward Grey told me that he intended to make a statement this afternoon in which he would lay down the conditions on which he would remain neutral. He spoke of a ' conditional rupture.'

I urgently begged him not to put forward the neutrality of Belgium as a *sine qua non*, as this would have ominous consequences. He gave me no assurances, but I have the distinct impression *It isn't a question of ' might ' and ' would like.' It is one of honourable intention ! That is lacking !* that if it is in any way possible, he *would like to* continue to remain neutral. I bound myself to him in the terms of the following declaration :

(1) That even in the event of an armed conflict

[1] This refers to Herr von Jagow's instructions to the Ambassador at London, dated Berlin, 2nd August, 1914 (K.D. 667). Herr von Jagow's telegram to Prince Lichnowsky runs as follows : ' We have certain information that the French, in spite of their declaration, have assembled large bodies of troops along the Belgian border and are making preparations for an invasion of Belgium. In order to prevent a surprise attack, we shall presumably have to take counter-measures. In this event we will give Belgium the assurance that if she promises to observe a benevolent neutrality towards us we will, after the conclusion of the campaign, respect her integrity to the fullest extent and will accord her full compensation for requisitions and for any damage caused by us. England should see in Germany's procedure only an act of necessary self-defence against a French menace. Even in the event of a hostile encounter with Belgium, Germany will, after the conclusion of peace, guarantee that Belgium's integrity is preserved. Please communicate this information to the British Government, but not before to-morrow, Monday morning.' (Tr.)

with Belgium, we desired to maintain the inviolability of Belgian territory ;

(2) That in the event of England's remaining neutral, we did not desire to approach the Channel or the north coast of France with our fleet.

I made the latter statement after conferring with our naval attaché here. I still hope that it will be possible to reach an understanding on this basis, since it is realised here that armed conflict with us could not mean any advantage either for France or for Belgium. Whether it will be possible to avoid such a conflict depends largely upon the feeling in the Cabinet as well as upon public opinion here which may conceivably be unduly excited by our action in Belgium.

I repeat that they would like to remain neutral and are counting on our support in order to be able to do so.

A son of a German woman who lies so !
A German who writes such lies !

Sir *W. Tyrrell* has given me to *understand* that people in Austria, to judge by Sir *M. de Bunsen's* telegrams, are coming to the conclusion that as we were the aggressors and were not being attacked, the terms of the Triple Alliance *did not*

An absolute lie ! *oblige Austria to co-operate.*

LICHNOWSKY.

[To The Foreign Office.] LONDON, 3rd August, 1914.

Rumour spread here of alleged collision between British and German warships in North Sea. Please have this rumour corrected at once, and above all recommend great caution to the Navy, in order that there may be no incidents. LICHNOWSKY.

[To The Foreign Office.] LONDON, 3rd August, 1914.

I hear from well-informed financial circles that the King of the Belgians has turned here for advice. LICHNOWSKY.

[To The Foreign Office.] LONDON, 3rd August 1914.

Foreign Office informs me that the French Ambassador has officially stated on the strength of telegraphic information from

Paris that report that eighty French officers in German uniform had attempted to cross the Dutch-German frontier at Geldern in automobiles is absolutely unfounded.

LICHNOWSKY.

[TO THE FOREIGN OFFICE.]   LONDON, 3rd August, 1914.

Sir Edward Grey has just stated in the House that with relation to the European war the Government had entered upon no other agreements than those of diplomatic support. Should a foreign fleet, however, which was involved in a war which France had not sought and in which she was not the aggressor, enter the English Channel and bombard the unprotected coast of France, the act would be a *casus belli* for England, and only for such an eventuality had the latter promised her armed support to France.

He said he had stated to the French Ambassador that, in the event of the German Fleet entering the Channel or coming through the North Sea in order to proceed to hostile acts against the French coast or French shipping, England would support France by every means within her power.

LICHNOWSKY.

TO THE FOREIGN OFFICE.   LONDON, 3rd August, 1914.

Sir W. Tyrrell stated in conversation that the Belgian Minister had this afternoon communicated the text of the German ultimatum and the Belgian reply. The Cabinet was at the moment discussing them. It was probable that they would be communicated to the House of Commons. Sir W. Tyrrell added with reference to Sir E. Grey's speech of to-day that the question whether the march of German troops through Belgium would compel England to abandon her neutrality was not *for the present to be answered with either ' yes '* or *' no.'* [1] Final decisions could not be taken until the attitude of the House of the Commons was clear.

LICHNOWSKY.

[TO THE FOREIGN OFFICE.]   LONDON, 3rd August, 1914.

Although a decided depression is noticeable in Sir Edward Grey's speech of to-day and although the speech is marked by a deep distrust of our political intentions, one can nevertheless gather from it that the British Government has in all probability no

---

[1] Kaiser's marginal note : ' As always hitherto.'   (Tr.)

immediate intention of taking part in the struggle or of abandoning the attitude of neutrality hitherto observed. So far as concerns Sir Edward Grey's statement about England's undertaking the protection of the northern coast of France, this pledge, given by him to my French colleague, corresponds to the assurances[1] that I was in a position to give him.

With regard to the neutrality of Belgium, the Minister says that if facts which have so far become public are found to be correct, it would be England's duty to do her utmost to prevent the consequences of such action. This statement is not very clear, but he probably means that England would absolutely oppose any diminution of Belgian territory or sovereignty.

According to my views we can regard the speech as satisfactory and can consider it to be a great victory that England does not at once enter the fight on the side of her comrades of the Entente. I should like to repeat on this occasion that I am convinced that the British Government will strive to remain neutral. This attitude would be much easier for her to maintain if the territory of Belgium could be evacuated within a short time and without any great engagements. It is not surprising, moreover, that our policy has had an extremely irritating effect here, and that Sir Edward Grey found himself compelled to give expression to this irritation. For here in England the belief is growing more and more that we wished the war for some unknown reason, and pushed our neighbour into it, and that it would have been easy to avoid it had our intentions been of the right sort. Furthermore, the sense of justice of the English has been offended by the double breach of treaty obligations, and I believe that we should have reason to feel satisfied if the British Government were now to confine itself to a platonic protest and remain in the main content with the two conditions named : the protection of the French coast and the integrity and independence of Belgium. Whether this will prove a possibility will of course depend on the attitude of Parliament and, likewise, upon public opinion's not becoming too excited.

LICHNOWSKY.

[1] This refers to (K.D. 714), a telegram from von Jagow to Lichnowsky, dated Berlin, 3rd August, 1914 : ' We can state definitely that there will be no threatening of the northern coast of France on our part so long as England remains neutral.' (See also K.D. 784.) (Tr.)

To The Foreign Office.   London, *4th August*, 1914.

Since yesterday's statement by Sir Edward Grey in Parliament, England's permanent neutrality is no longer to be reckoned on.   Time of breaking off relations cannot yet be predicted.   In the opinion of the Ambassador, every day that England remains neutral is a day gained.   Every provocation in the shape of any activities of our fleet in opposition to England should therefore, if possible, be avoided.

Naval Attaché.
Lichnowsky.

To The Foreign Office.   London, *4th August*, 1914.

The integral text of Sir E. Grey's speech had not reached me yesterday, but only a short parliamentary report of it.   From the publication of the text in its entirety to-day I am compelled to modify the view I took yesterday is so far as I do not now believe that we can reckon much longer with the neutrality of Great Britain.

As I have frequently reported to your Excellency, the question of the violation of the Belgian neutrality has been one of the most important points influencing the British attitude of reserve.   Both Mr. Asquith and Sir E. Grey told me as much, and I was able yesterday (as reported) to convince myself before the sitting of the House that Sir E. Grey was profoundly moved by the violation of Belgian territory by our troops.

What form British intervention will take, and whether it will take place at once, is beyond my power to decide.   I do not, however, see how, after the speech in question, only extracts of which were known to me yesterday, the British Government could draw back unless we are in a position to evacuate Belgian territory in the very shortest period.   We have accordingly to reckon with the hostility of England in the near future.   The reception of Sir E. Grey's speech in the House may be taken to show that in the event of an active policy being pursued with the object of protecting France and Belgium, the Government will have the overwhelming majority of Parliament behind it with the exception of the Left Wing of its own party.

The news which arrived yesterday of the invasion of Belgium by German troops provoked a complete reversal of public opinion to our disadvantage.   The appeal of the King of the Belgians couched in agitated terms appreciably enhanced this impression.

Lichnowsky.

[THE SECRETARY OF STATE FOR FOREIGN AFFAIRS, HERR VON JAGOW, TO THE AMBASSADOR AT LONDON, PRINCE LICHNOWSKY.]

BERLIN, *4th August*, 1914.

Declarations Bethmann Reichstag to-day : [1]

We are in self-defence and needs must.   Our troops have occupied Luxemburg and perhaps have already entered Belgian territory. This is an infraction to international law.   Though the French Government have declared in Brussels to be willing to respect Belgium's neutrality as long as the adversary would respect it, we knew that France was ready for invasion.   France was able to wait, we were not.   A French aggression into our flank on the Lower Rhine would have been disastrous.   We were therefore compelled to overrule the legitimate protest of the Luxemburg and Belgian Governments.

We shall repair the wrong which we are doing as soon as our military aims have been reached.   Anybody threatened as we are and fighting for his most sacred goods must only think of pulling through.

As to the attitude of England, the statement made by Sir Edward Grey in the House of Commons has clearly laid down the point of view taken by the British Government that as long as England will keep neutral our fleet would not attack the northern coast of France and that we would not touch the territorial integrity and the independence of Belgium.   I herewith repeat this declaration publicly before the whole world and I may add that as long as England keeps neutral we would be willing, in case of reciprocity, not to undertake any hostile operations against the French commercial navigation.

JAGOW.

[TO THE FOREIGN OFFICE.]   LONDON, *4th August*, 1914.

English ships and destroyers ran out of Dover last evening.

NAVAL ATTACHÉ.
LICHNOWSKY.

[1] This telegram was drafted in ' English ' in Berlin just as it stands here. (Tr.)

To The Foreign Office.　　　London, *4th August,* 1914.

　　I have just learned that the Belgian Minister has notified the Foreign Office of advance of German troops into Belgium.

So now he is willing to believe it at last! Poor Lichnowsky. Conversation with Sir W. Tyrrell confirms my impression that after receiving news of serious German Belgian collisions, continuance of English neutrality can no longer be counted on and that a rupture of relations is imminent.

LICHNOWSKY.

[To The Foreign Office.]　　　London, *4th August,* 1914.

　　English ultimatum expires to-night at twelve o'clock. After that time the possibilities of an attack by the English fleet on our fleet must be reckoned with. I have no new information as to the whereabouts of the English battle fleet.

NAVAL ATTACHÉ.
LICHNOWSKY.

POLITICAL APHORISMS

WRITTEN SHORTLY AFTER THE GERMAN COLLAPSE IN 1918

HAD GERMANY BUT renounced the Triple Alliance and her Balkan policy, had she but refrained from threatening France and scrapped her new Navy Bills, she could have had a permanent understanding both with Russia and England.

A THOUSAND YEARS OF PEACE might have been ours had we but sided with Russia instead of Austria.

THE TRIPLE ALLIANCE was a whim of Bismarck's, conceived in a fit of spleen against Gortschakoff. Next to the Berlin Congress, it was the greatest mistake the Iron Chancellor ever made.

BISMARCK'S GRUDGE was not against Russia but against Gortschakoff.

BISMARCK'S SUCCESSORS lived on tradition, battening on the glory of a paragon whose errors were sanctified by a great name.

THE GREAT MAN is only a finger-post, says Buddha. Bismarck's successors halted beneath their finger-post. Then they bewailed their isolation.

STATES usually come to grief on the very system that had enabled them to rise to power. The means to an end becomes an end in itself and destroys what it has created.

A STATE RULED BY MILITARISM is a danger not only to its neighbours but to itself. Military considerations gradually oust all others.

OUR FOREIGN POLICY was directed alternately by pathological and oinological brains.

THE PERSISTENCE with which we identified ourselves with Austria-Hungary and Turkey and bullied all the Great Powers made the world-war a mere question of time.

430

To vex England we built a gigantic and useless fleet. To prevent the French forgetting about their *revanche*, we kept rattling our sabre and did our level best to pick a quarrel over Morocco. To drive Russia to take sides with the French, the English and the Japanese, we backed up the Austro-Magyar and the Turk and humiliated Russia both in the Bosnian and Albanian affairs.

Not a soul wanted war with us. But we made them all suspect that we wanted war with them.

The world-war was the final outcome of a policy that took the wrong turning, and went with Austria instead of with Russia.

The Triple Alliance was bound sooner or later to ' upset our apple-cart.' A clash between Russia and Austria over the Serbian question could have been postponed. It could never have been prevented.

What we needed was neither an alliance nor a war, but a treaty to ensure us against attack.

People say that the German has no talent for politics. But how can a man learn to cook if he is forbidden to enter the kitchen, and has to eat what is set before him whether he likes it or not.

An alliance, even when defensive, has a spearhead directed against the threatened encroachments of a third Power. Every alliance presupposes a common enemy. Apprehension of this enemy's intent gradually extends the original scope of the alliance, so that it finally comes to include all manner of superfluities, undreamt of in the beginning.

An alliance with Russia or England would also have been a mistake. For it would have meant friction with one or other of these two Great Powers. Both alternatives were undesirable.

Russia, relieved of anxiety on her western frontier, and assured of our non-interference in Balkan affairs, could have turned her attention towards Asia, where a clash between her interests and those of England would have been the automatic result.

Not from Petrograd, Paris or London did danger threaten us, but from Berlin and Vienna.

COMMONSENSE would have sufficed to put our relations with England and Russia on an excellent footing and made our relations with France correct. Austria-Hungary,—a little reduced in size, perhaps,—would then still be in existence.

THE FRANCO-RUSSIAN ALLIANCE was 'made in Germany,' as were also the *ententes* between Russia and Japan and between England and Russia. We achieved these feats by scaring each nation in turn.

THE ENTENTE CORDIALE, too, was forged in German workshops. It was nothing but a mutual assurance society against the danger of war.

BISMARCK consolidated the military monarchy. His work was based on success attained in the field. A military setback was bound to undo it, and help to victory the democratic forces the Great Man had sought to suppress.

FRIENDSHIP with Russia and renunciation of the policy of the 'mailed fist' and 'shining armour' would have enabled us to reduce our armaments and substitute one year's military service for three.

WHETHER WE KNEW in advance the purport of Austria's ultimatum to Serbia or not is of small import. What mainly matters is whether we knew and approved of its being deliberately drafted to provoke rejection.

THE 'STRONG MAN' POLICY was bound sooner or later to land us in the ditch. Time after time it brought us to the brink of war and finally pushed us over.

POLITICS is not sport but hard-headed business.

THE CULT OF INCOMPETENCE invites catastrophe. The inefficient are often put in office merely because they are pliable.

A MAN MAY BE a brilliant diplomat or parliamentarian without being a statesman. Statesmanship demands profound insight, independent judgment and an unfettered soul.

DESPITE THEIR MUTUAL JEALOUSY, our mandarins were always ready to adopt a united front against possible disturbers of the official dovecotes whenever the latter threatened to become inconvenient through superior talent and independence of judgment.

IN POLITICS as in war a man may be a good tactician though a poor strategist. Tactics needs only skill and experience, strategy judgment of the highest order.

ON A GOOD ROAD even a bad driver can get along without mishap. But woe betide him if the road, too, be bad.

THE PRINCIPLE of authority, though necessary for the maintenance of order, is apt to dull the critical faculty and lead to intellectual indolence.   It makes a fetish of tradition and blunts perception.

ERROR hampers progress and culminates in catastrophe.

A SYSTEM can live only so long as it continues to achieve success. Failures at once prove fatal and the system has then to make way for another—not necessarily a better one.

ALL FORMS of government are bad and open to criticism, none fulfilling what may be justifiably demanded.   But any form of organisation is better than none at all.

TRADITION is the hobby-horse of all indifferent riders.   It is an easy mount to sit, but is apt to get left behind in the race.

SO LONG AS the Slovenes and Trieste were left in her possession, Austria could have done without the Jugoslavs and without Galicia.   She would have been forced to evacuate Galicia and Bosnia, however, and in course of time would have lost them, just as she had lost Italy and Hungary.   Had we not shared her defeat when it came, we should have had a voice in matters and could have prevented her total disruption.

THE STATE IDEAL of Conservatism is dynastic and military.   The ideal of the democratic state is national and economic.

AUSTRIA RELIED essentially on the conservative state ideal. Europe's transition to the democratic principle inevitably involved Austria's disintegration.   Nor could this have been avoided unless common economic interests and geographical considerations had brought about a compromise in the Alpine and Sudetic provinces.

AUTOCRACY, incompetent statesmanship, militarism as a State within a State, the post-Bismarckian glorification of war, and, last but not least, our alliance with Austria, lay at the root of the catastrophe.   To these one may add Herr von Holstein.

ENGLAND would never have attacked us or helped others to do so, seeing that she needed us as a counterpoise to Russia and France.   But England could just as little suffer France to be defeated in a war.

ALL CIVILISATIONS, as members of one great comity, have equal rights, and therefore strive for the ideal of eternal peace. The connections existing between their ideal and their material interests and the accord of their ethical ideals forms the basis of their peaceful understanding.

THE LEAGUE OF NATIONS ought to be the outward expression of the will for eternal peace, the expression of the nations' consciousness of their common interest in these values, and of the dependence of the individual on the welfare of humanity as a whole.

THE NEW LEAGUE of Nations will be a League of States, an international organisation with measures of compulsion against the individual State. In every association there is a President, someone who takes the lead. This function will fall to the Anglo-Americans. We shall be placed under Anglo-American supervision. The Great War has made the Anglo-Saxons masters of the world. We have been side-tracked ; Russia has been made innocuous for years to come and the Latin race has been placed in a position of dependence. Who is there left to offer resistance or to enter the arena as a rival ?

ENGLAND has defeated all her rivals one after the other—the Spanish, the French, the Dutch and the Russians. And now it is our turn.

NEVER would the Vienna statesmen have adopted such a bullying tone towards Serbia had we not driven them into doing so by taunting them with their ' slackness.'

THE WAR WITH RUSSIA was a twofold error. In the first place, Czaristic Russia wanted to join hands with monarchical Germany. In the second place, the interests of the two countries nowhere clashed, seeing that Balkan politics were no affair of ours and that in the Balkans Germany's objectives were entirely economic and as such undisputed by Russia.

AFTER THE DELUGE

NOTES ON THE PERIOD AFTER THE COLLAPSE

THE BASES OF PEACE WITH RUSSIA

(Notes written on 8th January, 1918)

IN his book, *Russia as a Great Power*, published some time before the first Balkan War, Prince G. Troubetzkoy said that Russia's fundamental tasks in the Near East were, in the first place, ' to watch over the welfare of the Christian peoples,' and, in the second place, to keep an eye on the ' question of the Straits.' If Russia were not in a position to pronounce a decisive word on these points, said the Prince, her rôle as a Great Power would be at an end.

What does this mean ? Not necessarily that Russia should take possession of Constantinople but that she wanted to know for certain that the Straits were not in the hands of any Great Power of Europe or of an Ottoman Empire capable of real resistance. In addition to Russia's solicitude about the Dardanelles, she had also to bear in mind the question of the religious and national protectorate over the Balkan races of common faith and common stock and their independence. Ever since the days of Catherine these have been the leading motives of Russia's Balkan policy. They have been behind the wars waged for the possession of the coast, the enfeeblement of Turkey, the liberation of the Balkan peoples and the consolidation of the religious and political strength of Russia. The attitude of Russia in the question of the Straits was actuated by economic and military requirements. If the Straits were barred to her, her trade in the whole of the Black Sea area would be affected and the Russian Fleet would be denied access to the great seas. Associated with all these Balkan questions there were, moreover, certain imponderable factors, factors which had their roots in the theocratic character of the rule of the Tsars.

The peace concluded in 1774 between Catherine and the Porte at Kutchuk Kainardje, a village in the Dobrudja, may be regarded as having been the first step towards establishing the position of Russia in the Near East, inasmuch as it assigned to the Tsars not only free rights of navigation but also the representation of the religious interests of the Ottoman Christians.   In close connection with these successes of Russian policy in the South-West was the advance of Russia in the West against Turkey's ally, Poland.   Here, too, religious and political motives were intermingled, for the intervention of Catherine in favour of the Dissidents was the occasion for the first Partition of Poland, and this again was shortly followed, soon after the second Turkish war, by the second Partition.   The policy in the Near East and Polish policy, in close and constant association, constituted the bases of the development of Russian power.   It is not until the reign of Catherine that Russia can be regarded as a European Great Power.

Whereas in the Polish question Russia was able to come to an agreement with her two neighbours, she encountered on her road to the Balkans and the Mediterranean the opposition of several European Powers who were afraid of her influence in the Near East and in the Mediterranean—England in the first place, and thereafter France and Italy.   These Powers were joined by Austria, which had once gone hand in hand with Catherine.   Austria, however, did not actually engage in the struggle.   From the Crimean War onwards the opposition between Austria and Russia never disappears.   After the Berlin Congress, Austria-Hungary had at her back the first military Power in the world in the shape of the German Empire.   After Bismarck's retirement and against his wishes the alliance which had been concluded as a corollary of the Congress and of the cooling of Russo-German relations, was extended in such a manner that it constituted a blank cheque for the Balkan interests of the Ally.

At the Congress Bismarck, prompted rather by personal antipathies than by material considerations, gave but lukewarm support to Russia, and robbed her of the complete results of her victory. At the same time he assisted Count Andrassy to ' occupy ' Turkish territories, which were ethnographically in the main Serbian : later our attitude towards Austria's annexation of Bosnia, which destroyed Serbia's dreams of a great future, led to our further estrangement from a traditional friend, whose neutrality had made possible for us our victories of 1866 and 1870-71. The denunciation of the Re-insurance Treaty was followed by the fraternising of Russia and France, which was carried a step further after Algeciras by an understanding between Russia and Great Britain.

While a far-reaching interpretation of the alliance enabled our Austro-Magyar friends with our help to combat the Greater Serbia movement—a movement, by the way, which Russia supported— the position of prominence at which we aimed on the Bosphorus, accompanied as it was by military missions designed to strengthen the Turkish power of resistance, still further excited the disapproval of the Government of the Tsar. The German navy and Algeciras on the one hand, and the Serbian and Turkish policy on the other, created the atmosphere out of which the Entente grew.

At the London Conference of Ambassadors which followed, Albania was with our assistance pushed through in order that Serbia should be cut off from the Adriatic. Serbia was thus driven to expand towards the South and forced to occupy the Vardar line in the hope of reaching the sea at Salonica, side by side with Greece, a country with which Serbia was on friendly terms. When finally Count Berchtold, who placed his reliance on the Triple Alliance, and never really recognized the Treaty of Bucharest, proceeded to a revision of the Treaty in question, the world-war arose out of the opposition of Russia ; and the world-war has now put before Germany the task of finding new and, it is to be hoped, lasting bases for her future relations with that great country.

The path that led to war ought also to afford the best clue to the foundations of peace, the more so as there are now no direct and vital German questions at stake. Against this logical line of reasoning the following misgivings may be urged :

    1. The interests of our allies.
    2. The establishment of the Polish State.
    3. The internal condition of Russia.

To begin with the last of these three, we may bluntly ask whether the present Communist régime in Russia is likely to last, or whether it represents merely a transitional stage which by and by will develop into a democratic federative republic, after the style of the United States of America. Any restoration of the monarchy must, it seems, be regarded as out of the question, seeing that a monarchy in Russia would have no choice but to revert to the traditions of Catherine and her successors with regard to Poland and the Near East. In other words, peace and friendship with Russia could under such circumstances be permanent only on the basis of a renewal of the old Russian policy with regard to Poland and the south-western States of Europe.

Should the present mob-rule continue in Russia, it will mean that the country will return to the primitive economic system of payment in kind, a system that will take into consideration only the needs of the moment and aim only at satisfying the simple demands of the peasantry and of the workmen in the towns. The workers of Russia would then produce only what they themselves consume. Trade and industry as instruments for the formation of capital would either cease altogether or would only develop as far as they are necessary to supply the simplest needs of life ; they would, as the nihilist Bazaroff in Turgenieff's *Fathers and Sons* contemptuously puts it, suffice for the wretched ' arts of earning money and of pedicuring.' From the standpoint of the Bazaroffs of to-day the need for any position as a Great Power, the need for Imperialism and for such attributes to Imperialism as trade, army and navy, territorial expansion and spheres of influence, has vanished.

Imperialism, the assertion of the collective will expressing itself either in a nationalistic form through main force and at the cost of other civilized nations with equal rights, or in a pacifist form through civilization, culture and commerce, is inseparable from the capitalistic bourgeois form of state and society and from a strong and therefore organized collective will, from the capacity to develop power and force when occasion demands. The question as to the future of Russian Imperialism, therefore, stands or falls with her present form of government.

Even a democratic federal republic on the model of the United States, which has gradually developed from a number of primitive agrarian, colonising units into the greatest capitalistic power in the world, would be just as unable to renounce imperialistic efforts in the furtherance of its business enterprise as it would be to renounce colonisation, and commerce and the political position and power these activities demand. Has not the United States, too, in the interests of its colonists and their expansionist needs, continually added to itself new formations, and has not political influence in this case, too, followed close on the heels of economic interests ? Have not the United States acquired certain Spanish-speaking areas which we not so long ago magnanimously offered to Senor Carranza ? Has not the Union with its Monroe doctrine and the interpretation it has given to this document contrived to preclude all European interference and to secure the primacy of the Anglo-Saxon race throughout the whole of the Transatlantic Continent ?

It is perhaps not altogether impossible that Russia may develop out of its present anarchy into a similar democratic federal republic in which economic interests and the Russian language as the language spoken by the vast majority of the people will form the common bond of union. Such a development need not adopt imperialism, or necessarily imply that powerful pressure will be put on other nationalities. We shall perhaps some day have to reckon with the United States of Russia just as now we do with the United States of America, with China and Brazil or the Commonwealth of Australia.

Such a democratic and therefore pacifist federal State would, of course, be without the theocratic elements that characterized the Tsaristic régime. This being so, the question arises whether the new Russia would be likely to place itself on the modern basis of rationalism, and brush aside all considerations for the feelings of the still powerful clergy and of the orthodox country population who still stand under the influence of the Church. Will such a State be likely to prove an opponent of ecclesiastico-nationalistic pro-Slavism and leave its Orthodox kinsmen in the Balkans to their fate ? When Russia has recovered and developed into a modern constitutional State or federation of States, will she renounce all attempts to extend her influence in Asia and on the shores of the Black Sea, and will she no longer strive for access to the Mediterranean ? Such a thing is highly improbable.

Will she ever forget the pain she felt at the loss of Poland, a country that now separates her from the West, and will she continue to turn a deaf ear to the complaints of the Ruthenians, who even before the war felt Polish oppression to be a most bitter grievance. The over-hasty creation of the new Poland may form a further hindrance not only to a permanent understanding and reconciliation, but also to direct trade communication with Russia as well, a state of affairs that reminds us only too vividly of the Grand

Duchy of Warsaw. Will Poland be content to forgo access to the sea ? And what is her natural road to the sea, if not the course of the Vistula ? It is childish to think that the new Poland will halt at Alexandrovo and take off its hat and wave good-bye to the river out of sheer gratitude.

Whatever solution may be found to the problems of our foreign policy, one thing must never be lost sight of, and that is that in future we must, both politically and economically, have a good understanding with Russia. If every obstacle in the way of a reconciliation between Germany and Russia can be got rid of, a vast field of activity will be opened up, not only for German enterprise, but also for German industry and technical science in that gigantic State, a State throbbing with aspirations for a renewal of power and prosperity.

Does this mean that we should have to confront England as an enemy ? Certainly not. That is a task that we can safely leave to others.

SHOULD LARGE ESTATES BE SPLIT UP?

(Notes written on 10th and 11th December, 1918)

I

IN the next few years during the transitional period of economic reconstruction in Germany every means must be employed to increase the production of foodstuffs and raw materials. For at present trade conditions are such that it will take years to restore them to their former level, and domestic production is the only sure method of bringing the German people back to a normal economic life.

The long duration of the war has caused serious disorganization. Under these circumstances the production of foodstuffs and raw materials can be increased and restored to its pre-war level only if the conditions of ownership and management are interfered with as little as possible, at any rate during the initial or transitional period. Important as a properly conceived policy of home colonisation undoubtedly is for our future welfare, it would be folly to try to achieve this by violence. The compulsory subdivision of large agricultural estates would be absolutely certain to lead to a fatal decline in production and to ultimate famine. For, in the first place, there are at present far too few people with an adequate knowledge of agricultural production to make land settlement on a large scale feasible. In the second place, the resources available during the next few years will be insufficient to capitalise the parcelled-out estates. Finally, satisfactory results very largely depend on an exact practical knowledge of the land to be distributed, and of the climatic, marketing and other conditions of agricultural production. Such knowledge cannot be acquired overnight.

Nor, in view of the following considerations, will it be possible, even in the period following the years of transition, to proceed on principle with the division of large estates.

Large agricultural estates may be classed under three headings, according to the method of exploitation, namely :

     (i) those where the exploitation is extensive,
     (ii) those where it is intensive, and
     (iii) those where it is industrial.

To the first class belong all those estates which work with small resources of labour and capital. I need not enter into the question whether this class is justifiable on grounds of national economy. Although the methods employed on such estates may very well be technically correct for the purposes of horse and cattle breeding or of rye and potato growing, it may be admitted that such estates are nevertheless the most suitable for colonisation, because the amount of capital invested in buildings and plant is extremely small. The subdivision of these estates into small farms will therefore involve only a very small depreciation, if any, in existing values.

To the second class of large estates belong all those which work with large resources of labour and capital. In their case the amount invested in buildings and plant is very considerable, and an extensive outlay of working capital has already been made. They are therefore unsuitable for subdivision, because the value of the buildings and plant (steam ploughs, large threshing and other machines) would thereby be reduced to almost nothing. This would impose a burden on the land in question which could not possibly be shouldered by the peasant. In this class of estate, therefore, it could only be a question of detaching or dividing up those portions of land which were ill-adapted for cultivation under the existing management. The detachment of a limited acreage on these lines would in many cases be an actual advantage, for, by facilitating the concentration of sufficient labour on the remainder of the estate, it would enable this to be subjected to still more intensive cultivation.

To the third class of agricultural holding, which is characterised by industrial exploitation, belong all those which are equipped in a greater or less degree for the conversion of raw agricultural into manufactured products. These would include large fat stock farms (especially in the provinces of Saxony and Posen), beet-sugar plantations which have their own refineries, potato plantations with their own distilleries, starch and syrup factories, vegetable farms with their own drying plant, as well as richly manured pasture lands and flax-growing estates with flax mills. On such estates the capital outlay on the industrial utilisation of the raw agricultural product is often greater than the ground value, including buildings and agricultural machinery. The working capital on these industrialised estates may, indeed, on occasion be extraordinarily high.

The large industrialized estates are focussed without exception on converting their own raw produce into manufactured goods by their own resources. They are organised with this end in view at every stage, so that if they are parcelled up, or even if any part of them is compulsorily withdrawn from centralized control, this is bound to bring their existing industrial plant to a standstill, or at any rate to involve it in serious working losses. And quite apart from that, their parcelling up would mean the total depreciation of huge capital values.

Large estates with intensive and especially with industrial exploitation are of the greatest importance from the point of view of the national economy. There is no lack of incontestable evidence to prove that they produce the largest possible unit of nutritive value per unit of area. Their parcelling out would therefore substantially reduce the national production ; for small ownership is incompatible with any such degree of intensive working. An average harvest of sugar beet will produce twelve times and of potatoes eight times as many units of nutritive value as an average harvest of wheat, so that an agricultural undertaking is doing a greater or less national service according as it maintains a greater or less proportion of its total area under roots, these being the crop most prolific in nutritive values.

But since it is only the large estate that is able to place one-third and even as much as one-half of its total area under roots, a State can never afford to deprive itself of these most important sources of production, least of all in a time like the present.

The question of the State purchase of large estates for purposes of distribution and colonization is, therefore, one which must only be approached with the utmost caution and with full expert knowledge. Precipitate measures, or even a systematic scheme of expropriation which neglected the special economic conditions and other relevant problems, would lead to mistakes which would seriously endanger not only the taxable capacity of the country, but, more important still, the indispensable production of foodstuffs and raw materials. Moreover, the number of war-wounded and other would-be land colonisers with the necessary knowledge and physique, and with the requisite zeal for the toils and monotonies of an agricultural life, will certainly not be large enough to warrant compulsory measures. Besides, quite apart from State domains, plenty of estates that are now in reduced circumstances owing to the war will come into the market and provide a liberal selection for a reasoned plan of distribution. For this purpose the State might acquire the right of pre-emption, and perhaps extend it retrospectively to estates which changed hands during the war. Another question is where the money would come from to build in a short time new homesteads for hundreds of thousands of small occupiers.

Finally, the nationalisation of large agricultural estates would not bring the slightest advantage to the community, as will be evident to anyone who carries his studies of the relevant circumstances beyond mere book research. For it would involve, in the first place, the vast expense of a whole army of agricultural officials together with the necessary organs of control. Secondly, it would paralyse that free play of private initiative which was alone responsible for the prosperous development more particularly of those large estates which were given over to intensive and industrial exploitation, and would remove the stimulus to technical progress and increased productivity. The large estates *en bloc* would then have to be administered bureaucratically in accordance with some preconceived scheme.

Our own experience in connection with the 430,000 hectares of State domains in Prussia affords sufficient evidence against nationalization on these lines. The method of leasing out has here been reverted to, after direct exploitation by the State had proved unpractical and unprofitable. Yet even so the ponderous apparatus of bureaucracy is a burden to their whole development. When, for instance, a new chimney had to be built on a Royal domain, first one commission came to ascertain the facts and draw up a protocol, then a second and a third. In the end the commissions cost more than the new chimney itself. That is the sort of thing that would be happening everywhere under a system of nationalisation ! If all the industrial estates were brought into the system every third person would be a State official, and we should have a régime bureaucratised to an extent which would make the old official-ridden Prussia look like a harmless orphan in comparison.

If, on the other hand, the co-operative principle were compulsorily introduced into the large agricultural estates, such a change would of course do away with the much-lauded independence and freedom of the small man. He would be placed under State tutelage, would have his work prescribed for him in minute detail, and would not be allowed to cultivate his land according to his own lights, but would be subject to orders from above. In other words, we should have official caprice in a new form, and State interference in the most intimate affairs of private life.

The assumption that the so-called latifundia are always to be condemned as unsound from the standpoint of the national economy is contradicted by the fact that the yield of grain per acre of corn land in Germany is only exceeded in Belgium, and that with us it surpasses that of all other European countries, not excluding France, despite the system of small holdings prevalent in the latter country.

II

As far as forestry is concerned the large estate is indispensable. Forestry, that is, timber production for economic purposes, requires, no matter whether the undertaking is private or public, a long turnover period extending, with few exceptions, up to between 80 and 140 years according to the wood. These long periods, in other words the interval within which the whole of the timber in a forestry undertaking is renewed, rule out small ownership at once ; for, in the first place, the fraction of the total area annually renewable would be too small to produce successful results, and, in the second place, the owner, by reason of the insignificant returns, would have no interest in the permanence of the undertaking.

Either a regular output of timber, however, or a continual supply to the home market of the largest possible amount in the desired

varieties, implies a durable system of forestry ensured by the observance of the proper period of growth, the annual utilisation of mature
timber and a well-regulated process of renewal.   Such a system is
therefore the basic principle of every properly conducted forestry
enterprise.

Small ownership in the case of forest land is only justified when
the product supplies the requirements in timber of a proprietor
otherwise engaged in agriculture, and then only in so far as it
fulfils this purpose.   But it is not necessary, for the needs of the
agricultural population can be supplied much better by large neighbouring estates devoted to the intensive cultivation of timber.
Anyone who has had occasion to look at peasant-owned forest land
will know why ' peasants' forests ' have become a by-word.

Small ownership, for lack of scientific cultivation, will never
produce timber in anything like the same quality or quantity as
large estates, nor achieve those standards of productivity which the
community is entitled to expect.

If our forests were entrusted to society, that is, to free exploitation
by all citizens, there would soon not be a tree on the landscape, as
has happened in certain parts of Italy and the Orient.   No one will
undertake the labour of replanting unless he is doing it for his
children and grandchildren.   The nationalisation of large forest
estates in order to protect them from mismanagement is only to be
recommended where there exists no sufficient guarantee of scientific
cultivation, which, after all, is of equal service to the community
under any system.   But it is at any rate to be preferred to the
nationalisation of large agricultural estates, which are much less
susceptible to management under a fixed scientific scheme, and
whose profitableness is mainly dependent upon personal initiative
and judgment, and upon capital investments if the soil is to yield
the best results.

The parcelling out of large forest estates can therefore never be
justified, and their nationalisation only where deficient cultivation
is the cause of demonstrable loss to the community, an evil which,
for that matter, could be remedied by expert State supervision.   At
the present moment fifty per cent. of the afforested area in Prussia
and forty-six per cent. of that in the whole of Germany are in private
ownership.

If it is proposed to do away with entail (of the property so held
about one half is forest) as being out of date, or because it shows

unsatisfactory results in individual instances, especially where there is excessive resort to the method of extensive cultivation, or because it is an obstacle to colonisation, then it would be better, at least under the present laws of inheritance, to have the system of entail substitution as in England and at the same time do away with the legal portion prescribed by German law for the wife and other near relations. For every owner is naturally very much more disposed to sink money in his property (also in dwelling houses, etc.) when he feels that he is passing it on to his descendants undivided and free from the liability to alienation or partition through multiple inheritance. At all events the much maligned system of entail has hitherto in many cases afforded a secure and indispensable basis for the rational cultivation of large estates, which would otherwise have been hardly conceivable. Of the total area of the Prussian State seven per cent. is entail, or, excluding the forest lands, five per cent. Entail forest lands comprise 3·3 per cent. of the area of the State, 13·8 per cent. of the total area under forest, and 46 per cent. of the total entail.

Entail is exceptionally important in the case of forest land, seeing that the Court of Entail, in Germany, *i.e.* the Oberlandesgericht, namely, the supreme court, can prohibit any irresponsible clearance of timber, whereas the free owner has the right to fell his forests at will.

Even if large landowners voluntarily surrendered hundreds of thousands of hectares for purposes of colonisation, it would still be a work of decades to complete the process ! The returning soldier would find himself confronted at the start with a mere vacuum ! By what resources of magic could all the dwelling houses, the indispensable livestock, the farm implements be provided, even if the colonists brought with them knowledge, experience and a passion for work ? What would become of a colonisation carried out on rustic rather than economic principles if the disappointed war hero soon began saying to himself, ' I expected something quite different,' and deserted his patch ?

There is no experienced farmer who would not utter the sternest warning against attracting to the land people hitherto unaccustomed to a country life by holding out to them visions of an idyllic pastoral existence. Their inevitable disappointment would only be surpassed by the resulting injury to the economic interests of the nation. The best advice, therefore, that can be given to our soldiers is to tell them to return to their former callings. Land colonisation is a great economic and social undertaking, but it demands a great deal of time, money and understanding if it is not to end in failure and catastrophe !

Plenty of opportunities will present themselves for a fruitful policy of colonisation without resort to compulsion, whilst precipitate measures of coercion would not only fail to achieve their object but would cause a grave dislocation of the economic life of the nation.

By democracy and freedom I understand the smallest possible amount of governmental interference and legal coercion, and not the opposite procedure, no matter whether authority is adorned with the Order of the Red Eagle or not.

Let a State by all means be founded on democratic principles and inspired by ideals of social progress, but let us have no break-neck leaps into the realm of Utopia !

The levying of high direct taxes and the suppression of all indirect taxation with a view to relieving as far as possible the small man's burden (though such a measure as this would be impracticable for financial reasons and mistaken from the standpoint of national economic welfare) would render it logically all the more necessary not to kill the goose that lays the golden eggs, that is, not to prevent but to promote the formation of capital ! Without high revenues and an abundance of them high taxes cannot be collected, and high taxes are necessary in order to meet the country's vast burdens. Where are these taxes to come from if there are no more citizens capable of paying them, and if profits are forced down to so narrow a margin that there is no further stimulus to carry on business, face risks or save anything, because no man is left free to dispose of his earnings and he and his property are subject to the tutelage of ' society.'

' Socialisation ' is an ideal which we can never completely attain, though we are always approaching nearer and nearer to it. The public debt, taxation, monopolies, high wages and social legislation all tend to carry things in this direction. But complete realisation would spell the destruction both of the ideal and of ' society ' itself.

' I know,' said Confucius, ' why no true morality and justice exist. It is because the wise go too far in their intellectual pride, and the fools do not go far enough ! ' Let us hope then that our own wise men will not go too far !

People may smile and tell me I am pleading *pro domo*. I reply with Horace, ' Nam tua res agitur paries dum proximus ardet ! '

THE UNITARY STATE

(Notes written on 16th January, 1919)

THE German Empire, the creation of Bismarck, was founded on a federal-dynastic basis. Bismarck attached decisive importance to the dynastic substructure, as his *Reflections* show. The Dynasties and the three Free Cities concluded on the foundation of the Empire an ' everlasting federation,' without holding any plebiscites such as had been done in Italy. Where dynasties disappeared they did not succumb, as again in Italy, to revolution, but to the force of arms, surrendering to the strongest sovereign. The idea of solving the German question by revolutionary means was violently opposed by Bismarck himself in the Prussian National Assembly. Born in the Conservative Party, an ultra-Conservative in his youth, he never left the Conservative world of ideas, even if he later attached himself to an amenable middle-class oligarchical Liberalism. A strong sovereign power formed the foundation of the new Empire, as it had formed the foundation of the old one, though now with a national colouring and a new head. As a Conservative statesman with a dynastic policy he necessarily regarded democracy as his principal enemy, since the democratic theory of the State was incompatible with the dynastic-federalist character of his creation. It would have led to the unitary State with Parliamentary Government and have transferred the centre of power from the individual States and dynasties, or properly speaking from the leading dynastic State of Prussia, to the elected assembly of people's representatives. The oft-repeated assertion that a Parliamentary Government was incompatible with the federalist character of the Empire was in so far correct as the federalist-dynastic structure was founded on the Conservative conception of things, which magnifies the Crown (or Crowns) at the expense of the popular assembly. The dynasty is the head of such a State, the army and civil service are its bodily framework, whilst the people play the part more or less of the hands and the farmers may be called its legs. This determined Bismarck's attitude towards Social Democracy ; he could only regard it as a disturbing element in his organism, against which he must be always seeking new remedies.

The Empire, however, with its Conservative antecedents, was so powerful and underwent so brilliant a development with the aid of the capitalist bourgeoisie, which supplied new and welcome resources to the military and bureaucratic body politic, that it needed a very grave disaster to destroy it. Left to itself and favoured by a reasonable Government it might long have enjoyed exuberant health and prosperity. Its disaster was not, as in England and France, the result of financial infirmity, or, as in Russia, of a rotten administrative system ; the Germany of Bismarck was destroyed by an insane foreign policy.

In view of the certainly very distressing collapse of the firm of Hohenzollern & Co. and of the Monarchical Company Limited, the German people finds itself faced with the task of forming a new company. The principle of democracy, which had remained in discredit since the lamentable issue of the National Assembly and Revolution in 1848, has now come triumphantly to the fore, owing to the collapse in the world war of the Conservative structure, which had its foundation in the reaction of the 'fifties and in the subsequent military successes. While at that time the republican idea of unity broke down under the influence of the dynasties and the loyalty of leading circles gave way to ancient tradition, the revolution of to-day has swept away all obstacles to the realisation of democratic-national ideas of State and State unity.

As these States, with the single exception of the free cities, originated in the closest connection with the ruling families and, a century ago, were created, extended or preserved purely from the standpoint of dynastic policy, the question now arises whether with the elimination of the dynasties those creations of the dynastic régime—now known as federal States have any further justification for their continuance, or whether ancient custom, racial distinction, local patriotism and the whole gallery of such commendable virtues entitle them to the prolongation of their separate existence. Efforts may also be noted on the one hand to form new republics out of various portions of the Prussian Monarchy, and on the other to amalgamate several small States into single republics.

It cannot be denied that if the organisation on State lines of various German provinces is at all justified on historical, economic or ethnological grounds, then Silesians or Rhinelanders have the same title to separate State existence as, for instance, Bavarians or Mecklenburgers. The union of the first-named in one State is too recent to permit the obliteration of divergences in the character of the peoples or in their peculiar economic and local interests. The common bond of dynasty has disappeared even if that of the bureaucracy is still left, and it is beginning to be realised that the close connection was due in the main to a dynastic policy which has now become obsolete. And there is yet another factor : a widespread antipathy to so-called Prussianism as embodied in bureaucracy, militarism and ' Junkerdom.' It was tolerated so long as all went well and so long as it was resplendent with the successes of its past and with the integrity and vigour of its present. It was never loved, but it was held in high respect and very justly so. But with the disappearance of the ancient régime, the dynasty, militarism and the Conservative-minded bureaucracy Prussianism has lost its old glamour and is even being saddled, not, perhaps, without some modicum of justice, with a share in the responsibility for the catastrophe. ' Away from Berlin ! ' and ' Away from Prussia ! ' are becoming the watchwords : ' We want to be Germans, but we want no dictation from Prussia or Berlin ! ' The fear of Berlin mob rule, of a Berlin dictatorship from below, instead of, as before, from above, also tends to strengthen separatism and to stimulate the movement for the formation of separate republics.

Separatism, however, must be overcome no less than Communism. Both are infantile diseases of the Republic, symptoms of the sudden revolution, of the abrupt reversal of all political values !

The French Revolution obliterated all memories of the past history of France. In November 1789 the Paris National Assembly replaced the previously existing provinces by 83 departments designated according to their geographical position. ' Une et indivisible ' was the fundamental guiding principle, inspired by the idea of a powerful central authority controlling every part of the country. The great Revolution probably broke too completely with the memory of the past. With the aid of the bureaucratic prefect system centralisation has been carried out to such an extent that the destiny of France is now practically directed by Paris and the Parliament which sits there. The result has, however, been to create a homogeneous and robust organism, in which national feeling is superior to all regional and social antagonisms, and which has enabled the country to survive the most violent storms and display, as we have seen, an unexpectedly resolute power of resistance.

Italy, which, apart from the theocracy, consisted like ourselves of dynastic States, was unified by a monarchist revolution. It is divided, very like France, into 69 provinces, which are associated in 16 historical Compartimenti. Here too constitutional traditions have failed to perpetuate themselves in the guise of federalism. The principle of democracy had led to the unitary State both in France and Italy.

If North America is a federal State, that is due to the vast expanse and diversity of its territory and to the very gradual emergence of the various States, which only later joined or were incorporated in the original federation. Since it takes nearly a week to travel from one end of the country to the other the factor of distance comes into play as a hindrance to unification of the constitutional structure. But this cannot be said to apply to Germany, where a single night journey will carry you from Berlin to any frontier.

If Russia, as we may perhaps assume, emerges from the chaos of war and revolution as a federal State, this solution is favoured, as in the case of North America, Brazil and Australia, by the size of the country, also by the variety of the nations and nationalities comprising it, which were hitherto held together in a unitary system by Tsarism and its bureaucracy.

In the case of the peoples of Austria-Hungary, if they unite in a possibly smaller federation of States with or without German Austria, the basis of federalism is laid by the varieties of nationality, after the defeats of 1866 and 1918 have destroyed both unitarism and dualism. But what are the conditions in Germany which could warrant the artificial creation of new separate States or the maintenance of old ones ? Is it racial divergence or petty exclusiveness ? Is the Rhinelander more different from the Silesian than the Picardese from the Provençal or the Neapolitan from the Piedmontese ? Have not the East Prussians and Silesians hitherto lived tolerably well in the same State with the Westphalians, the Hessen-Nassauians and the Schleswig-Holsteiners ? Why should not Bavarians, Swabians and Mecklenburgers do likewise ?

The conditions for the continuance of the separate States have disappeared with the dynasties and with the social and material centres which they formed. Why should we want to go out of our way to cultivate and consolidate Rhenish or Silesian particularism, or artificially preserve a Bavarian and Saxon particularism which has lost the centres around which it crystallised ? It is as difficult to conceive of Bavarian particularism without the Wittelsbachs as of Saxon without the Wettins and their Court.

If there is to be a ' clean sweep of feudal survivals,' which, except

in the corps of aristocratic students known as the ' Borussia ' at
Bonn, in the venerable Upper Chamber called the Herrenhaus, and
in certain crack regiments, were mainly to be found among a few
sheriffs east of the Elbe and among Court dignitaries, then let a
start be made with the system of petty States whose one justification was their connection with feudal traditions.   Deprive the
petty State of its Court and there is not one valid reason left,
whether geographical, economic or administrative, for its separate
existence in a Republican régime.

It will perhaps be objected that it is not exactly a good thing for
the blood to run to the head. I quite agree.   This, however, is a
danger which is very much less likely to arise in Germany than
elsewhere, owing to the high degree of economic decentralisation and
the widespread distribution of industry over the country, not to
mention the numerous centres of art and literature.   And to protect
Parliament from mob tyranny there must, after all, be an armed
force, which no political system, not even a Republican, can do
without, unless it is to be condemned to total impotence.

In view of these considerations there are two alternative solutions
which may be recommended : either the prefect system as in France
and Italy, taking as a basis, let us say, the administrative districts
of Russia or Bavaria ; or else the amalgamation of districts
into provinces, as in Prussia, on historical and geographical lines,
but not always following necessarily the existing political boundaries.
Each province could then have its own Diet and an extension of its
administrative autonomy, and if a Senate is included in the Constitution it could be selected from the membership of the Diets.   I
would prefer the second alternative, because administrative questions
arise which override the district boundaries.   We should then have
such provinces as the following : Bavaria, Franconia, Swabia,
Thuringia, Upper Saxony, Lower Saxony, Mecklenburg, Pomerania,
Silesia, and so forth.

A German province would thus be intermediate between a French
Département and a central Parliamentary Government, an alleviated
and harmless form of the federalist idea, evading its dangers to
strength and unity.

Federalism in a democratic State is, in fact, justified only if
geographical and ethnographical conditions render a unitary system
impossible.   But Germany is almost entirely homogeneous from the
racial standpoint ; geographically she is no larger than France and

her economic life requires close co-operation between all parts of the country. The formation of federal Republics, therefore, especially after the disappearance of the paramount authority of a strongly centralised bureaucracy, might unnecessarily impair the position of the Government as a whole and cause friction which would be a source of weakness to the body politic. Financial considerations, too, plead for the unitary State.

Monarchy or Republic—which is it to be ? The issue is hardly in doubt. If, then, the German people decides for a Republic, let it pronounce resolutely for the unitary State and turn its back on that system of petty States which has for so many centuries burdened monarchical Germany.

THE RIGHT OF SELF-MUTILATION

(Notes written on 14th April, 1919)

WHEN the world war broke out there were but few persons in Germany who did not fall victims to the hypnotic influence of the outcry about ' the Fatherland invaded ' and the war that was ' forced upon a peaceful nation.' Neither people nor Parliament was consulted beforehand nor let into the secret of how it had all happened. They were suddenly confronted with accomplished facts and had willy-nilly, unless they wished to be branded as unpatriotic, to join in the general hurrahing. The nation was told that ' a world of foes ' was to be overthrown and that the war had been sprung on them by the commercial envy of Great Britain, the Imperialism of Muscovy and by Gallic lust for revenge. They were assured, too, that Germany would not cease fighting until ' guarantees ' had been obtained that would make a future war impossible, and that would secure for the German people for all time that place in the sun which no one had really forbidden them. Childish professors and obedient newspaper scribes, both fanaticized by the cult of ancestor worship in which they had been brought up, and both alike robbed of the power of free and independent thought by an idolatrous belief in authority, did their best to give foreign countries the impression that Germany, almost to the last man, welcomed the ' steel bath ' of war and endorsed a policy which neutral countries regarded as downright insanity.

Had there been a referendum taken either in the Reichstag or in the nation at large, as to whether for the sake of Serajevo or because the General Staff was afraid of Russian armaments and railways, or to rescue the honour of our ally, they were willing to embark on a war against Russia, France and England, and thus bring about the Coalition War that Bismarck had so greatly dreaded, there can be no doubt that the decision would have gone against the policy adopted by the Government.

Our victorious opponents are apparently now preparing to offer us a meal that we must gently but firmly decline to partake of, unless we wish to condemn ourselves to a slow death.   Their error consists in the fallaciousness of their premises.   The fabulous incapacity of the men who brought about the world war and the childlike simplicity of those who gave it the stamp of their approval, will, of course, have to be placed on the debit side of Germany's balance sheet.   Everywhere the German nation's will for war counts as already proven and as deserving of punishment.   As a logical corollary, France demands ' guarantees ' for the future and forgets that the only reliable guarantee is to be found in the democratic form of government now adopted by Germany, a form of government which makes it impossible for either Cabinets or military cliques to involve their country in an unwished-for war in times to come. Germany's opponents must remember that by demanding any more material guarantee they will create intolerable conditions and that such conditions cannot therefore be accepted or, if accepted, will not be accepted in good faith but with mental reservations that mean the very contrary of the disarmament and lasting peace that a peace treaty really aims at.

A dictated peace that reduced Germany to political or even financial vassalage and serfdom, that robbed her of important strips of territory, no matter whether such regions are wholly or only partly settled by Germans, determines in advance that the rule of main force shall continue, even after such a peace has been signed. Our opponents must surely see that without huge armaments a dictated and brutal peace cannot prove lasting, and that such a peace is bound to collapse directly our opponents are no longer able to force us to carry out its stipulations.   Instead of bringing about disarmament, a peace imposed on the German people against their will only forces them to arm afresh. The thought of a new world war is an abomination to every nation that took part in the war just over. But should such a peace be imposed upon us, this spectre of a new Armageddon would for all time to come continue to haunt our homes. A peace obtained by violence can only be maintained by violence and would lead to the very antithesis of that promulgated in Mr. Wilson's programme. The principles of that programme we accepted as a basis for discussion, in the expectation that they would form the foundation of all further negotiations.

During the war our annexationists clamoured for the coast of Flanders, some of the less modest of them even wanted to swallow Belgium and Northern France, while less bold spirits were ready to content themselves with Briey alone, without, however, altogether renouncing Egypt and Kurland. This was the war psychosis. Among us it has in the meantime given place to the mood of revolution, but in Paris it is still producing the most wonderful fruits. I am only astonished that the French demands halt at the Rhine instead of going right on to the Elbe. Trans-Elbian Germany could then go to Poland. Europe might thus see a restoration of the realm of Charlemagne and our frontiers would again be what they were up to the time of Otto the Great! For what can be more elastic than the term ' historical boundaries ? ' What do a few centuries more or less matter ? Did not Upper Silesia up to 1163 belong to Poland ? Do not both Poles and Germans now live there ? Was not West Prussia reconquered by the Kings of Poland in the old Battle of Tannenberg ? Was not East Prussia once a Polish fief ? Why should not all these regions now be returned to Poland ?

Where, indeed, in the whole of the German Empire is any region to be found that is ' undisputedly ' Polish ? Is not the fight for the eastern marches as old as German history itself ? But it was a fight that was finally decided in favour of the superior organisation and culture. These brought in their train prosperity and economic development to these bi-lingual ex-Polish districts. Was it not England and France themselves who at the Vienna Congress offered us Polish provinces, while Prussia preferred to content herself with the line connecting Silesia and East Prussia ? Is not this line from a geographical, strategic and economic standpoint to-day as essential for us as ever ?

Why should we not receive the same treatment as France once did ? France got back her old frontiers and her envoy, Prince

Talleyrand, was able to declare that he was the French Ministre de Sa Majesté Très-Chrétienne and that neither he nor France was responsible for the sins of the past ?   Our opponents have during the war so often declared that nobody dreamt of crushing the German people, but only the German system of autocracy and militarism, that we are doubly justified in categorically declining to accept demands that go beyond a benevolent interpretation of the Fourteen Points.

If Poland demands Danzig, the Czechs might with equal justice ask for Hamburg.   Why not ?   Both are old Hanseatic towns and Hamburg is at the mouth of the Elbe, just as Danzig is at the mouth of the Vistula.   To be independent of us, Bohemia needs Hamburg and a corridor along the Elbe.

The Polish question, as a matter of fact, defies solution, as long as the Entente insists on creating a completely independent State. Why does the Entente not embody Poland, like the Ukraine, Lithuania, Kurland and all the other component parts of the Russian Empire, in the United States of Russia, after the pattern of the North American Union ?   When Bolshevism breaks down, the moment will have come to effect this union, which is the more to be advocated when one remembers that the new Russia will, in the long run, be unable to be content with the boundaries she had in the time of Peter the Great, without a proper outlet to the sea.   The dismemberment of Germany with a zigzag frontier towards Poland would give rise to new conflicts and new wars, just as would a dismemberment of Russia, a country which, though not an ethnical unit, can at least lay claim to being a geographical and economic entity.

It should not be difficult to reach an agreement with Czechia, if we give up Northern Bohemia and Northern Moravia and meet Bohemian wishes with regard to the navigation of the Elbe and freights to Hamburg, and if at the same time we agree to support the Czech claims to East Silesia (Teschen).   Naturally the Czech State must drop all claims to territory lying within the German Reich.   Western Silesia (Troppau), which is predominantly German and from a geographical and economic standpoint belongs to Upper Silesia, ought to be joined up with Germany.

In the case of Alsace-Lorraine, we can justly demand the right of self-determination.   Should France refuse to listen to this suggestion, there will be no reason why we should permit the principle of self-determination to be applied in the east and north of Germany, unless of course our enemies intend that the peace terms are to be dictated and not reached by free discussion. Should this prove to be the case, then all the talk about a League of Nations is mere empty chatter. The League of Nations would then have to be organised on a basis of main force instead of on a basis of law and justice. A contract based upon main force can only be upheld by main force ; it would mean making the anti-German world Entente into a permanent institution—the very opposite of disarmament and the League of Nations.

In the interest of all nations, we ought to decline to listen to any proposal for a peace based on violence. No one can recommence war against us, nor dare our opponents attempt to starve us out, for fear lest the common enemy, Communist terrorism, should again reduce mankind to primeval conditions ! It is no use for the Entente to offer us the right of self-mutilation. What we want is the right of self-determination.

THE ULTIMATUM OF 1919

(Notes written on 18th June, 1919)

THE Entente has refused to listen to the German counter-proposals, although these went to the extreme limit of self-sacrifice. The German nation must, however, decline to be made responsible and suffer punishment for things for which it was not responsible. Whatever the Entente Powers may say in their Covering Note, neither the nation itself nor its present Government, but, at worst, only its former administrators and the military-bureaucratic patriarchal State are to be blamed for what is past. The Paris atmosphere with its motor excursions to the devastated areas seems to have had a disastrous effect on the British and American statesmen gathered to deliberate in the French capital. The German people is given the choice between two alternatives. It may either submit to conditions which would rob it for ever of the possibility of recuperation and prevent its taking its proper place in the peaceful rivalry of nations or, on the other hand, it may declare that it refuses to sign its own death warrant and that it must leave its opponents to apply brute force against an enemy that has been defeated and is willing to make sacrifices. By following the latter course it will rouse the conscience of the world to protest against the harshness of the terms. The last few weeks have proved that our refusal to accept the monstrous demands of the Entente has convinced many people in the enemy countries that such demands are untenable, and that some compromise is necessary. This conciliatory mood would have made still greater headway but for the action of certain politicians and publicists in our own camp. These men, by supporting the enemy standpoint, have done incalculable harm to the German cause.

Over and over again I have tried to demonstrate the importance of the eastern frontier question and to convince foreign countries that Germany cannot afford to renounce Posen, East Prussia and Upper Silesia, even though in some parts of these provinces the German population is in the minority. I have tried to show that the Polish State, which ought to revere a German statesman as its founder, is no more justified in laying any higher claim to territories in which there are Polish majorities than the German Reich would be in laying claim to all countries outside its borders that have a predominantly or purely German population. Northern Bohemia, the Sudetic Lands, German Austria, German Switzerland and especially, Alsace and Luxemburg are undoubtedly German domains. The same thing is true of the ' Moravian ' portions of the province of Silesia on the Oppa to which Bohemia is now laying claim. These districts are, it is said, to be allotted to Czechia. My own country seat and a part of my family estates lie in that region, my ancestors having belonged to the Bohemian—not to the Polish—nobility, as is proved by the ending *sky* instead of *ski*. No sane man there has, any more than I have, the slightest desire to sever his connection with Germany. In December last year the Ratibor Provincial Council unanimously passed the following resolution : ' In view of the efforts now being made both by the Czechs and the Poles to separate Upper Silesia from Prussia and the German Reich and to divide the district of Ratibor between Poland and Czechia, the Provincial Council hereby resolves to oppose any such partition and separation. The Council hereby proclaims its desire to continue to remain a part of Prussia and Germany as, quite irrespective of religion and language, it sees in such an association the only possible condition for the future prosperity of the population of Upper Silesia.

In the meantime, the powerful movement that has arisen in Upper Silesia to oppose separation has taught foreign countries that the incorporation of Upper Silesia into the dominions of foreign States would meet with the most vehement resistance from its inhabitants and would result in the creation of impossible conditions. The German Government was quite right in not proposing a plebiscite for this district, seeing that it had not belonged to Poland since 1163 and that no one can maintain that its population is predominantly Polish. In view of the systematic agitation that has been carried on among the agricultural population, and considering the bitterness felt at the undeniable hardships connected with the compulsory requisitioning system, coupled with the faulty organisation of the food distribution in the country districts, it is possible that in some parts of Upper Silesia there might be a majority in favour of Poland. The ignorant masses generally see only the evils of the moment and are only too ready to hope for improvement from any change whatever. Such people are consequently ready to lend an ear to promises that are impossible of fulfilment.

The Entente has proclaimed the right of self-determination for Upper Silesia. Much will depend on how the voting is conducted. In North Schleswig too there is to be a plebiscite. We appeal to the principles promulgated by Mr. Wilson, principles which, as Prince Max of Baden has clearly proved, have been everywhere set aside by the Allies, and we ask why the right of self-determination has not been granted to all the different areas that are to be taken from us. I have in mind Posen, West Prussia, Alsace-Lorraine and the German parts of Austria. I am convinced that this standpoint will be fully appreciated and that it will find support both in neutral countries and among pacifist associations in enemy countries. Seeing, however, that our opponents refuse to allow the right of self-determination to apply either in the case of Posen and West Prussia or in that of Alsace-Lorraine and the German parts of Austria, we have not the faintest reason to regard the granting of this right in Upper Silesia as a concession or to regard this concession as compensating for the robbery of provinces that are indispensable for Germany.

In the case of Alsace-Lorraine it must be emphatically pointed out that the so-called 'wrong' inflicted upon France in 1871 was not greater than that inflicted on the German States when these provinces were conquered by force of arms in 1674 and 1681 and that consequently the Treaty of Frankfort also meant a disannexation of a province that was more German than Posen was Polish.

The ' wrong ' inflicted on Poland in 1772, with which Entente propagandists are now so successfully stirring up harmless and ignorant minds against us, appears in quite a different light to the historian who knows the true facts. ' Even on the estates of the great nobles, the farm buildings were in a tumbledown and unusable state. Large numbers of the nobility were, too, just as unable to read and write as the peasants. The bulk of the country population lived in miserable conditions. On approaching a village, the stranger saw big huts blown askew by the wind with their thatch torn and the roof laid bare. Not a tree and not a trace of a garden was to be seen on any of these pitiful homesteads. The dirty, unkempt peasantry lived on a kind of rye meal porridge, on cabbage soup, herrings and brandy, a beverage to which men and women were alike addicted. Bread was only baked by the well-to-do, many had never in their lives seen such a dainty. Dumb and stockish, the people drank their dreadful brandy, fought each other and staggered into corners to sleep. The landed gentry were hardly to be distinguished from the peasants. They ploughed their own land and clattered about the clay floors of their huts in wooden shoes. The administration of justice languished throughout the country. Law courts were to be found in some of the bigger towns, but they were for the most part powerless to enforce their judgments. On their estates the nobles inflicted punishment with cruel arbitrariness. Villagers and peasants alike were beaten by them and flung into squalid gaols, where they were left to live or die. When these nobles quarrelled among themselves, they bribed what few courts there were that still had jurisdiction over them. In the last years before the revolution, these courts, too, had almost ceased to act, the nobles taking justice into their own hands, seeking revenge by waylaying their adversaries in ambushes and by harrying each other's lands in civil war.'

This is the account Gustav Freytag, the German novelist, gives of the conditions prevailing in West Prussia in the time of Frederick the Great. His description is based upon reports drawn up by the officials whom the Prussian king sent into that unfortunate land. As our critics will, however, be inclined to discredit such witnesses as ' boches,' two Polish authors may be cited to show that these conditions prevailed not only in West Prussia but throughout the

whole of Poland.   The Polish historian Staszic, writing at this time,
says, ' Five-sixths of the Polish population are dressed in skins and
rough cloth.   They are deformed with dirt and disease.   Their eyes
are sunken.   They are short-breathed, ill-tempered, depraved and
stockish.   They are dull of feeling and dull of mind.   Reason and
soul are hardly to be recognised in them.   They look more like
animals than human beings.'   And Archbishop Labienski of Gnesen,
Poland's foremost prelate, bears similar witness.   ' In the whole of
history, one will seek in vain to find an example of disorder like that
prevailing in Poland.   One must therefore conclude that a State
characterized by such misery will either fall a prey to its enemies or
that with time its fields will become the abode of a few nomads.'

GERMANY'S FUTURE FOREIGN POLICY

(*Written February*, 1919)

THE best guide to the principles that ought to govern Germany's
future foreign policy is obtained by clearly visualising the errors
made in the past and by examining the causes that brought about
the great catastrophe.   Although the final result of the war cannot
yet be fully estimated, we can already perceive two things, firstly,
that we must in future do almost exactly the opposite of what we
have done in the past, and second, that we shall have to carry out
our new policy under much less favourable conditions than prevailed
before the war.   At that time we were the leading military and
commercial Power on the Continent.   We were a great political
firm with which all other firms were anxious to live in peace and
harmony.   We were a State to which other States were willing in
all spheres of activity to show every courtesy, if we would but
consent to renounce our ' strong man ' policy with its frequent
humiliations of our neighbours, with its threats and provocative
acts of all kinds.   To-day we are temporarily reduced to power-
lessness and the other States no longer feel that they need take us
into consideration.   By going to war we have converted nations
that once wanted to be our friends into enemies, and others that
could never have been our friends we have made into independent
States.   Nevertheless we may assume that a nation of such cultural
and material importance as Germany, a nation of sixty, or if we

include the Austrians, of eighty million souls, although weakened and thrown back by several decades as the result of the war, will not permanently remain a negligible quantity. We may assume that international statesmanship will sooner or later again have to reckon with Germany as it will also have to reckon with Russia.

Russia's losses through the war have been even more serious than ours. It would, however, be a grave mistake at the present moment to leave Russia out of our calculations and regard her as a political and economic cipher for the years to come. As soon as Bolshevism has been overthrown, her great provinces will probably reunite on a new democratic federal basis. In spite of all the pretty theories about the right of self-determination and the League of Nations, the Russians will continue to extend their power and acquire new domains in Asia and will continue to be a semi-Asiatic Great Power. Did not the North American Union do just the same with the Indians, the French, the Spaniards, the Negroes and even with the Russians of Alaska ? Has not the Union developed out of a few primitive agrarian settlements into the foremost financial Power of the world ? Did not the Anglo-Saxon colonist press further and further west-wards and southwards over the continent carrying with him the star-spangled banner as he went ? Has not the United States within quite recent times laid hands on the Philippines, Honolulu, Cuba and Haiti ? Why should not Republican Russia proceed in exactly the same way in Persia, Central Asia and Mongolia, in lands where the Russian settler and trader, when supported by the Russian soldier, finds least resistance ?

International statesmanship will in future have to reckon with us as well as with Russia, even though we should no longer be in a position to tread the world's stage with the same energy and the same prestige as in the years lying between 1871 and 1914, and even though the possibility of carrying our flag to far-off colonies has now been taken from us. A permanent political and economic boycott is, however, improbable, seeing that such a boycott presupposes perfect unity among the other nations, and such unity is shown by experience to last only as long as the other Powers have a common enemy. Hatred and indignation alone will not in the long run suffice to hold the Entente together. Gradually other material considerations will press to the front, and the unity of our opponents, based as it was on a common danger and a common threat, will crumble and vanish. With our overthrow, the old danger that bound these nations together into a united front against us has disappeared, and though a new danger may arise for humanity in the form of Bolshevism, militarism will have ceased to be a threat. The new Holy Alliance known as the Entente will inevitably slacken with time, even though we may have to reckon with it in the form of an American honorary presidentship and an English president-ship. Neither men nor nations can live on sublime theories and beautiful maxims alone, any more than they can live on love or hate. But the League of Nations will not inaugurate any brand-new world order or state organisation any more than Social Democracy will succeed in producing a new social or economic organisation. The war will in its results merely have served to speed up the process of social development and to give this process a push towards a definite goal, the goal of the democratic ideal.

The central idea of the League of Nations is that it should be a court for compulsory arbitration in the settlement of international disputes. All States by becoming members of the League will undertake not to settle their differences by an appeal to arms, but by submitting them to an international tribunal for judgment. The League of Nations is the Entente made universal. It represents the transformation of what has hitherto been a fighting organisation into a protective organisation. And though we, too, shall perhaps be associated with this body, it will take good care that we do not seek new quarrels. For on this point no one but the political novice can be in any doubt, viz. that the League of Nations is not directed against American, English, French or Italian aggressiveness, but first and foremost against the truculence of the Teuton.

Will the United States, should the life and property of American citizens be threatened in one of the Spanish Republics or the interests of big trading companies menaced by anarchy or revolution, be likely to hand over to the League of Nations its right to settle the matter by an appeal to arms if need be ? Will England, should British interests be threatened in Persia, Afghanistan, Tibet or elsewhere, refrain from intervention and turn to the League of Nations, or will she, should there be a rising in India, Egypt or South Africa, make use of the mediation of the Court of Arbitration ? Are not Hindus, Arabs, Boers and Kaffirs human beings too, and nations with equal rights ? Will the English and Americans abolish their fleets and disarm ? They will do nothing of the sort. They regard themselves rather as the secular arm of the League of

Nations, of this universal Entente, whose historical function it is to police the world and to supply the factor of power in the organisation of peace. The world war has, as I foresaw and predicted, led to the hegemony and universal dominion of the Anglo-Saxon race. We have to reckon with this hegemony even if it appears in the form of a League of Nations. It means the pax Britannica with Rule Britannia as the pastoral ditty of the new Arcadia. If we do not obey the judgment of the Areopagus, a new world war will break out. Any other alternative is mere ideology, the chatter of pothouse orators and of political dilettantes.

England, however, needs us as a counterpoise to France and Russia. She needs us both as a market for her commodities and as a source for her supplies. Before the war we were her best customers. The chief cause of her annoyance, our fleet, which drove her into the arms of France and Russia, has been got rid of. Our Colonies are gone, our overseas trade destroyed. If immediately before the war an understanding with England had been reached in spite of our fleet, our Colonies, and in spite of our commercial rivalry, why should a similar understanding not again be possible now that we have neither fleet nor Colonies nor overseas trade. This will be possible as soon as the bitterness on the other side of the Channel has died down. But of course it will take a long time for people in England to recover their equanimity.

A *rapprochement* will, however, become the easier to reach now that it is highly improbable that either France or Belgium will again be threatened by us, and now that England has nothing more to fear at these two sensitive points. England, however, can as little tolerate an over-powerful Spain, France or Russia as she can a German hegemony on the mainland of Europe. Her whole traditional Continental policy, her wars against Philipp II., Louis XIV., Louis XV., the French Republic, Napoleon I. and Nicholas I., were all based on this principle.

The second Power with which we have to reckon is Russia. Once she has again joined together into a united State she will no longer be negligible. The Bismarckian principle of standing ' back to back ' with Russia was perfectly logical; the pity is that Bismarck, at the Berlin Congress and afterwards neglected his own maxim. Under Bismarck's successors the error grew more and more pronounced as time went on. In 1890, as is well known, the Iron Chancellor wished to wheel back into line with Russia. *Rebus sic stantibus*, as his phrase ran, he never took the Triple Alliance very seriously, the Triple Alliance being rather one of the whims of this great genius, and a bad whim at that.   For Bismarck's ill-humour was directed not against Russia but only against Gortschakoff. When the post-Bismarckian statesmen turned their backs on Russia, they made their cardinal mistake.   In the pre-war period, the era of the scatter-brained, the fantastic and of the hydrocephalous, it was this error and not our neglect of England that led to the world catastrophe.   The return to Russia is one of the main problems that our future foreign policy will have to solve.

Mutual support, but not an alliance, must be our watchword. For every alliance, even when ostensibly merely defensive, pre-supposes a common enemy, and has a spearhead directed against a third Power.   An alliance presupposes that the allies are threatened by a common danger which forms the basis of their alliance, and this original purpose, based upon a conflict of interests between the contracting parties and a third Power is gradually extended so as to include things that lie outside the original scope of the legal con-tract.   Any alliance that Germany might enter into with Russia would therefore have a spearhead directed against England.   An analogous objection might be raised against an alliance between England and Germany.   It is a not uncommon mistake for people to think that an association with Russia would necessarily involve us in a clash of interests with England, and that we have therefore to choose between England and Russia.   The very contrary is the case, for an Anglo-German understanding would be all the easier if we stood well with Russia, and relieved her of part of her burden, by leaving her a free hand in Asia and in the Near East, instead of forcing her to concentrate her attention on ourselves.   *Duobus litigantibus* . . .   The Anglo-Russian friendship was, after all, of our making ; it was a consequence of the feeling of bitterness we had aroused in both these Powers.   In the same way, the Franco-Russian alliance was a consequence of the Berlin Congress and would never have come about had we not denounced the Re-Insurance Treaty and renewed the Triple Alliance.

It will not be by any means so easy to achieve a new *rapproche-ment* with Russia as it would have been for us to have come to an understanding with Tsaristic Russia.   In the pre-war days she was so well disposed towards us that she again and again called to us across the frontier, ' *Lâchez l'Autriche et nous lâcherons les Français.*'

We have contrived to make ourselves thoroughly hated in Russia as elsewhere, and we must leave it to the Entente to take post-war bourgeois Russiandom under its wing. Charles Rivet, who for several years represented *Le Temps* at Petrograd, closes his interesting book *Le dernier Romanoff* with the hope that his work will at least give a glimpse of that Russia which has now for ever vanished, to show what Germany's adversaries have gained with the fall of the last of the Romanoffs. And when, in consequence of Liman von Sanders' foolish mission, excitement ran high in Russia and the French Press was busy trying to add fuel to flame, M. Sazonov declared to him that whatever he did, he would not succeed in stirring up dissension between Russia and Germany. M. Rivet adds that Germany herself in 1914 undertook the task that the excellent M. Sazonov so much feared.

From Russia we have nothing to fear now as we had nothing to fear then. Pan-Slavism, as it was called, and the Muscovite Imperialism were directed against Austria-Hungary, Turkey, Persia, Central Asia, China and Japan, but not against us, at least not until we placed ourselves as a shield for the Austro-Magyars and the Turks. The Polish question, on the other hand, might have formed a secure foundation for an understanding and friendship between us and Russia.

We shall have no difficulty in coming to an understanding with Japan. Since the loss of Kiaoutchaou there is no longer any outstanding difference between us and Japan, and no one will again be able to force us, as they did in 1895, to pick the chestnuts out of the fire for other people. Now that we have been politically and economically routed in Asia, the opposition of Japan to the United States and to its British ally, will redound to our advantage.

These are in brief the fundamental principles on which our future foreign policy, so far as we are able to indulge in one, will have to be based. There are no longer any differences to separate us from Russia or England, from the United States or Japan. Whatever be the conditions laid down in the Peace Treaty now under discussion, we shall in future have first and foremost to reckon with these four Powers. The differences between us and Poland, on the other hand, will not be so easily settled. Should we, however, come into the German Austrian inheritance, we shall find ourselves involved in conflict not only with the Poles but also with the Czechs, Magyars, Italians and South Slavs. The Poles and the Czechs will always find a willing support in France, the most irreconcilable of our opponents.

It is superfluous to add that Germany will never forget the pang she felt at parting with the German province of Alsace, now torn from her by France for the second time. It must, however, be confessed that the German nation has itself to blame for this, for it allowed the same party that had been preaching the doctrine of a ' fresh and frolicsome ' war for a score of years to alienate the Alsatians by denying them up to the very last the federal rights they demanded.

Peace everlasting, the *civitas Dei*, might have been ours, had we pursued that broad path of colonial expansion and unrestricted commercial development which already lay open to us without any need for war. All we had to do was to jettison our insane Triple Alliance and Balkan policy, abandon our insatiable naval programmes and cease shaking our fist at France. Then we should have had long years of peace, and gradual disarmament would have been possible. But there was no getting our so-called statesmen to listen to such simple truths as these. They insisted upon going their own mistaken way.

Shall we ever have lasting peace ? Not unless we are given our own frontiers and not unless we are spared having to accept intolerable conditions. For pressure calls forth counter-pressure and is apt to end in explosions.

Wars always have been, as they still are, justified only as a means to an end, never as an end in themselves. A statesman who enters upon a war without having a clear aim in view commits a crime not only against humanity at large, but against his own people as well.

Perhaps we are now entering upon an age in which there will be only one shepherd and one flock. Sheep we have, God wot, in plenty. But who is to be the shepherd ?

INDEX

PRINTED IN GREAT BRITAIN
BY ROBERT MACLEHOSE AND CO. LTD.
THE UNIVERSITY PRESS, GLASGOW.